D1541128

BECKY OHLSEN

SEATTLE
CITY GUIDE

INTRODUCING SEATTLE

Kayaking on Lake Union (p166)

RICHARD CU...

It's raining again, but you don't mind. This is your cue to duck inside for another latte. Maybe you'll chase it with a local microbrew, then tackle the Space Needle before rocking the Crocodile Café.

Welcome to Seattle, whose perpetually cloudy skies mean that if the sun peeks out for a second, everyone drops whatever they're doing and gears up to take their kayaks or bicycles out. They can do this because they're part-time baristas, freelance IT consultants, club bookers or chefs at all-organic small-plates restaurants. They're as likely to drink PBR as IPA, but they'd rather die than sip truck-stop coffee or down a quarter pounder with cheese. They always recycle. They've been on skid road, and they know Alki has nothing to do with the drinking habits of barflies in Pioneer Square. If you ask them, they'll tell you it really doesn't rain that much around here.

They might also tell you to watch the 'flying fish' at Pike Place Market early in the morning, visit the Olympic Sculpture Garden around sunset and take an evening ferry ride to Bainbridge Island. Most likely they'll say not to bother with the Space Needle unless the weather is brilliant. If you're game for a bar crawl, they might take you to Georgetown, the neighborhood for drinkers in the know. If you're arty, it might be an opening at an edgy Belltown gallery instead. Or you could just get hopped up on caffeine and go thrifting all day. Despite what you hear, you may be surprised at how little anyone minds the fickle weather.

SEATTLE LIFE

Seattle is the largest metro area in the Pacific Northwest, with a population of about 3.3 million (580,000 in the city proper). It's a bookish, well-educated place, but also a dynamic and inventive urban center – most of the city's recent economic growth has been fueled by tech-

'Seattle sits on the verge of major structural and demographic change'

nology: both high-tech and the old-school, engine-parts variety. The Port of Seattle is the second-largest handler of container cargo in the United States.

Two of its most successful citizens also happen to be Seattle's two largest public figures, Bill Gates and Paul Allen. And they symbolize a certain aspect of the city's contradictory attitude toward its own success. Both undeniably ambitious and indisputably successful, Gates and Allen are seen simultaneously as points of civic pride and shameless capitalists who are totally alien to the prevailing Seattle culture.

And speaking of culture, you'll be forgiven for thinking Seattle's is mostly white – at least if you hang out in hipster coffee shops or go to many indie-rock shows – but Seattle has a rich multicultural history and is home to Native American, African American, Asian American and growing Ethiopian American populations. The city ranks 23rd of the 30 largest US cities in African-American population, at 8.4% – higher than every West Coast city except Los Angeles. It also has the largest concentration of Native Americans in the Pacific Northwest. The largest group in urban Seattle is the Duwamish people, the Native Americans who originally lived on the shores of Elliott Bay.

It's been a neighborhood-centric city for most of its history, but Seattle now sits on the verge of major structural and demographic change. The area expects 40% population growth in the next two decades, and the regional transportation board has already begun reshaping the city's landscape with new mass-transit plans. It's an exciting time to visit an always exciting place.

Marching girls parade through Seattle's International District (p59)

LAWRENCE WORCESTER

HIGHLIGHTS

LAWRENCE WORC...

DOWNTOWN & FIRST HILL

Downtown Seattle is the functional business heart of the city, with a jungle of office buildings and an electric weekday buzz. It's also home to many of the city's main hotels, as well as the Seattle Art Museum. Head to First Hill to see the stately, historic Sorrento Hotel.

1 Sorrento Hotel
Dabble in decadence at the Sorrento Hotel (p51)

2 Seattle Public Library
Find peace and prose at this stylish library (p49)

3 Seattle Art Museum
Gawp at Jonathan Borofsky's 1992 sculpture *Hammering Man*, which dominates the museum entrance (p48)

RICHARD CUMMINS

RICHARD CUMM...

THE WING LUKE ASIAN MUSEUM

LAWRENCE WORCESTER

PIONEER SQUARE & INTERNATIONAL DISTRICT

Pioneer Square is the birthplace of Seattle, and its redbrick buildings and plazas give it a historical, film-set feel. It's also popular for its restaurants, bars and independent shops, which are well worth a visit. The International District is home to Seattle's Chinatown and the Wing Luke Museum of the Asian Pacific American Experience.

❶ Wing Luke Museum of the Asian Pacific American Experience
Absorb yourself in Pan-Asian history (p59)

❷ Pioneer Square Park
Step back in time to Seattle's early days (p57)

❸ Zeitgeist
Perk up on coffee in arty surrounds (p141)

ANN CECIL

CHUCK PEFLEY/ALAMY

LAWRENCE WORC

PIKE PLACE MARKET & WATERFRONT

One of Seattle's best-loved attractions, Pike Place Market is a labyrinthine fish and produce market that oozes theatricality. Find yourself entertained amid 'flying fish,' buskers, tourists and locals before stepping out along the Waterfront, where scenic views of Puget Sound and the Olympic Mountains await.

JOHN ELK III

LAWRENCE WORCEST

1 Pike Place Market
Watch the world go by at this loud, lovable market (p62)

2 Seattle Aquarium
Spy the underwater world of Puget Sound (p66)

3 Waterfront
Catch the flavour of a major seaport (p65)

BELLTOWN

The alternative scene in Belltown may have mellowed slightly, but this neighborhood can still be classed as cool. Watch a band at the Crocodile Café before taking an easy stroll to other offbeat bars in the area. Belltown is also home to the impressive Olympic Sculpture Park.

RICHARD CUMMINS

① Olympic Sculpture Park
Feel small next to Richard Serra's 2004 sculpture, *Wake* (p67)

② Ace Hotel
Be fascinated by bedtime reading at this hipster hotel (p179)

③ Shorty's
Play pinball and drink beer (p142)

LAWRENCE WORCESTER

LAWRENCE WORCESTER

RICHARD

SEATTLE CENTER & QUEEN ANNE

Seattle Center is a 1960s vision of the future, making it an endearingly retro place to visit. As well as the Space Needle, it contains numerous museums and attractions, including the Experience Music Project. Rising up on the hill above Seattle Center is the dignified Queen Anne neighborhood.

1 International Fountain
Get wet in sci-fi International Fountain (p73)

2 Queen Anne
Pose by perfectly manicured lawns (p74)

3 Experience Music Project
Be wowed by Frank Gehry's 2000 museum (p72)

4 Space Needle
Zoom to the top for incredible views (p71)

ANN CECIL

LAWRENCE WORCESTER

RICHARD CUMM

Lake Union hums with the sound of seaplanes, but you can have fun skirting the edge on a bike or boat. Nearby Capitol Hill is an artsy and diverse neighborhood, where you'll find cafes, galleries and street theater. If you need a break from kayaks and counterculture, stop at the Volunteer Park Conservatory.

1 Wall of Sound
Flip through racks of music (p114)

2 Jimi Hendrix Statue
Check out Daryl Smith's 1997 statue of the guitar legend (p80)

3 Lake Union
Paddle or cycle around this Y-shaped lake (p76)

4 Volunteer Park Conservatory
Brush past palms in Seattle's tropical corner (p80)

LAWRENCE WORCESTER

LAWRENCE WORCESTER

ANN CECIL

JOHN ELK III

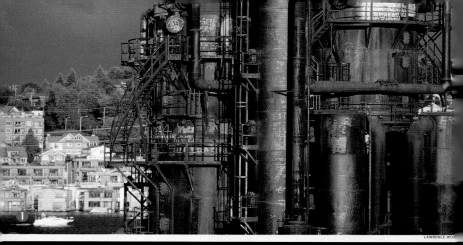

LAWRENCE WOR

FREMONT & WALLINGFORD

Fun-loving Fremont has coffee shops, pubs and some of the oddest public art that you'll ever see, making a visit to this neighborhood a must. Pleasant Wallingford, on the route of the Burke-Gilman cycle trail, is home to some noteworthy restaurants and Gas Works Park.

1 Gas Works Park
Find yourself drawn inexplicably to a strange mass of pipes (p91)

2 Fremont Troll
Quake before the 1990 statue, the Fremont Troll (p88)

3 Statue of Lenin
Consider the seven tons of Slovakian scrap that make up Emil Venkov's 1988 statue (p88)

LAWRENCE WORCESTER

LAWRENCE WORCES

BALLARD & DISCOVERY PARK

Ballard is a Scandinavian-influenced neighborhood that lies just over Ballard Bridge. It seems a world away from urban Seattle and is known for its down-to-earth bars and live-music venues, as well as the interesting Fish Ladder. Neighboring Discovery Park is 534 acres of urban wilderness.

DANITA DELIMONT/ALAMY

❶ Ballard Fish Ladder
Spot salmon on their way to spawn (p97)

❷ Nordic Heritage Museum
Learn more about Ballard's heritage (p95)

❸ Discovery Park
Walk the trails and escape the city (p98)

RON BUSKIRK/ALAMY

RICHARD CUMMINS

GREEN LAKE & PHINNEY RIDGE

If you like zoos, parks, rose gardens and low-key neighborhoods, then you'll love Green Lake and Phinney Ridge. Green Lake Park is a perfect place for sunbathing in summer or walking in fall, and Woodland Park Zoo is one of Seattle's greatest tourist attractions.

❶ Woodland Park Zoo
Strut your stuff at the zoo (p94)

❷ Seattle Rose Garden
Smell the scent of 5000 roses (p94)

LAWRENCE WORCESTER

JOHN ELK III

AROUND SEATTLE

Situated in a stunning part of the Pacific Northwest, Seattle is within easy reach of mountain ranges, the ocean, hundreds of islands and a temperate rainforest. This makes Seattle a perfect hub for getting out and exploring the natural world.

❶ Mt Rainier National Park
Climb the highest peak in the Cascades (p193)

❷ Hoh River Rain Forest
Hike in a mossy temperate rainforest (p198)

❸ San Juan Islands
Kayak around breathtaking islands (p189)

❹ Ferry across Puget Sound
Ride the waves and look back at Seattle's famous skyline (p187)

CONTENTS

Becky Ohlsen

Becky has lived in the Pacific Northwest for the past 15 years, originally drawn here from her native Colorado by the promise of great music and the ocean. Upon arrival she discovered that the area also provided excellent beer, a wide variety of pinball machines, cute skater boys and lots of rainy days in which to moodily read in coffee shops. She lives in Portland, Oregon, after surviving a brief, educational, expensive and decidedly temporary stay in New York City, where against everyone's better judgment she earned a master's degree in journalism. In addition to covering Seattle for Lonely Planet, she has worked as a copy editor and freelance writer for alternative newspapers and magazines, and occasionally reviews movies for a local independent radio station. When she's not traveling for guidebook research, Becky races vintage motorcycles very, very tentatively. She's a member of the Sang-Froid Riding Club and a veteran of the infamous '555' Ride, and much prefers two wheels to four. Her favorite bar in Seattle is Shorty's and her favorite Nirvana album is *Bleach*.

BECKY'S TOP SEATTLE DAY

When I'm in Seattle I like to wake up uncharacteristically early and go straight to Pike Place Market (p62). The scene here is fascinating any time of day, but it's best in the morning, when most of the customers are locals getting their shopping done. It's a nice place for a walking breakfast, too, with options ranging from fresh fruit to coffee and pastries to a hefty *hum bao* (steamed pork bun) big enough to power you through the whole day. After exploring the labyrinth of weird little market shops, I'll browse the progressive literature at Left Bank Books (p110) to keep myself honest and bolster hope. Afterwards, a short stroll down toward Elliott Bay gives me a panoramic view of the mountains from the new Olympic Sculpture Park (p67).

Of course I can't be in Seattle without spending some time digging around the shelves at Elliott Bay Book Company (p113), and as long as I'm this close I might as well treat myself to an artisan ice cream at Molly Moon's (p131) for lunch.

I'll spend the rest of the afternoon soaking up culture at the Seattle Art Museum (p48), abandon it for happy hour at the Nitelite Lounge (p140), then probably squander the evening and whatever's left in my pockets on pinball and beer in the back room of Shorty's (p142).

LONELY PLANET AUTHORS

Why is our travel information the best in the world? It's simple: our authors are passionate, dedicated travelers. They don't take freebies in exchange for positive coverage so you can be sure the advice you're given is impartial. They travel widely to all the popular spots, and off the beaten track. They don't research using just the internet or phone. They discover new places not included in any other guidebook. They personally visit thousands of hotels, restaurants, palaces, trails, galleries, temples and more. They speak with dozens of locals every day to make sure you get the kind of insider knowledge only a local could tell you. They take pride in getting all the details right, and in telling it how it is. Think you can do it? Find out how at **lonelyplanet.com**.

Other than finding accommodations, Seattle doesn't require a huge amount of pre-planning. Most of the can't-miss sights are clustered around downtown within easy walking distance of each other. If you bring a decent map, book accommodations in advance and have some sort of plan for transportation (whether it's a car and an idea of where you'll park overnight, or a public-transport schedule), you'll be fine. Keep in mind that the city is hillier than it looks on maps and – if you're driving – many streets in the city center are one-way only.

Once you're there, getting around is relatively easy. Driving and parking are the main annoyances – if you can avoid them, you'll be happier. Luckily this is easy to do. Buses connect to most neighborhoods of interest to visitors, although they stop running too early to be of much use for nightlife exploration. But then, that's why Mother Nature gave us taxi cabs (see the Transportation chapter, p199).

For more help with planning, visit Seattle's Convention and Visitors Bureau (Map p50; ☎ 206-461-5888, 866-732-2695; www.visitseattle.org; 701 Pike St; ☻ 9am-5pm). The website has a schedule of events, a few discount coupons and a form for ordering a visitor-information packet. Also among the bureau's services is the Citywide Concierge Center, a free service for visitors that will book you a table, a tour or transportation and answer questions about events going on while you're in town.

WHEN TO GO

Unless you're a skier or snowboarder – or *really* interested in aquatic life – Seattle in the winter makes for a pretty dreary holiday. The city receives 65% of its precipitation from November to March. But in spring the relentless downpour frequently lets up to provide gorgeous days that are well worth the wait.

April and May are best for enjoying the fruits of all that gloomy winter rain: suddenly everything is supernaturally green and covered in flowers. Summer – June, July and August – is the high season and can usually be relied upon for sunny days, warm weather and lots of people saying things like 'I thought you said it rained all the time here.' Fall, the season of Bumbershoot and Oktoberfest, is the favorite of beer lovers and music fans.

FESTIVALS
January
CHINESE NEW YEAR
☎ 206-382-1197; www.cidbia.org
Beginning toward the end of January or the start of February and lasting for two weeks, the year's first big ethnic festival takes place in the International District; you can contact the Chinatown/International District Business Improvement Association for information. The first day of the New Year festival is celebrated with parades, firecrackers, fireworks and plenty of food.

February
NORTHWEST FLOWER & GARDEN SHOW
☎ 800-229-6311; www.gardenshow.com; Washington State Convention & Trade Center
Usually held the second week of February, this popular event includes lectures and seminars, demo gardens and samples, and children's activities.

March
MOISTURE FESTIVAL
☎ 800-838-3006; www.moisturefestival.com; Hale's Palladium, 4301 Leary Way NW; tickets $5-25
With regular performances held between March 15 and April 1, the Moisture Festival has developed from a little-known quirkfest into something that locals look forward to each year. It has retained a laid-back, casual vibe and usually features random appearances by folks like Artis the Spoonman, Circus Contraption and The Bobs.

ST PATRICK'S DAY
March 17 is the day the patron saint of Ireland is honored by all those who have Irish in their blood, and by those who want to have Irish beer in their blood. Everyone wears green (otherwise you risk getting pinched). Irish bars such as Kells serve green beer, and even bars that haven't

an Irish trinket in sight get swamped with revelers. Catch the parade going from City Hall to Westlake Center along 4th Ave.

April

CHERRY BLOSSOM & JAPANESE CULTURAL FESTIVAL

☎ 206-723-2003; www.seattlecenter.com; Seattle Center

Usually held in mid-April, this celebration of Japanese heritage includes performances of music, dance and drama. It's part of the Seattle Center's series of multicultural festivals, dubbed Festál.

May

CINCO DE MAYO

May 5 commemorates the day on which the Mexicans wiped out the French Army in 1862. Now it's the day all Americans get to eat lots of Mexican food and drink margaritas. Seattle celebrates with an annual parade and exhibitions of Hispanic artwork.

OPENING DAY OF YACHT SEASON

☎ 206-325-1000; www.seattleyachtclub.org

Held the first Saturday in May at various locations on Lakes Washington and Union, this Seattle original starts with a blessing of the fleet. It features scull racing and a boat parade through the canals.

SEATTLE INTERNATIONAL CHILDREN'S FESTIVAL

☎ 206-684-7338; www.seattleinternational.org; Seattle Center

Held in mid-May, this cultural extravaganza includes a wide variety of performances and activities for kids.

NORTHWEST FOLKLIFE FESTIVAL

☎ 206-684-7300; www.nwfolklife.org; Seattle Center

This festival – the largest of its kind in North America – takes over Seattle Center during Memorial Day weekend. More than 5000 performers and artists from over 100 countries present music, dance, crafts, food and activities in celebration of the rich cultural heritage of the Pacific Northwest.

SEATTLE INTERNATIONAL FILM FESTIVAL

☎ 206-324-9996; www.seattlefilm.com

Held from late May to mid-June, this festival, the largest of its kind in the nation, brings nearly a month's worth of international film premieres to Seattle. Screenings take place at several theaters across the city, including the official SIFF Theater in Seattle Center. Check the film festival's website for a detailed schedule.

ADVANCE PLANNING

As in any large American city, planning ahead will let you spend more of your time enjoying Seattle. Things like car rental, accommodations and tours should be booked in advance. If you show up without a hotel booking in peak season, you might find yourself stranded.

Train tickets to Seattle may need to be booked in advance, as some trains do sell out. Make reservations at www .amtrak.com or by phone at ☎ 800-872-7245.

If you're hoping to see a particular performance or game, whether it's the Mariners or the opera, it's wise to buy tickets in advance. See individual listings chapters for price ranges and information on how to book (for sporting events, see p165; for theater and other performance events, see p159).

Some restaurants recommend or require booking a table in advance, and these are noted in the Eating chapter (p119). For most places in Seattle, booking a day or two ahead is enough, unless it's a holiday.

The Seattle CityPass (www.citypass.net), which offers discounts on Seattle museums and other attractions, can be ordered in advance on its website. The website www.dailycandy.com produces a 'weekend guide' to Seattle; it's worth subscribing to the mailing list before a trip.

It's useful to read up on what's happening in town via The Stranger's savvy and entertaining online blogs, Slog (for news) and LineOut (for music and nightlife) at www.thestranger.com. Rabid menu-readers will appreciate the Seattle Times' archive of restaurant reviews at www.seattletimes.com.

Seattle's Citywide Concierge Center (☎ 206-461-5888; www.visitseattle.org; 701 Pike St) can help with advance bookings of almost anything you'll need, including accommodations, tours and the CityPass.

June

FREMONT STREET FAIR

☎ 206-649-6706; www.fremontfair.com
Off-kilter Fremont is just the place you'd
want to be for a street fair. This one has live
music, food and crafts, and the overtly artsy
Solstice Parade, where human-powered
floats traipse through the neighborhood
in a lively tribute to quirkiness. It takes
place adjacent to the ship canal, usually
in mid-June.

SEATTLE PRIDE FESTIVAL

☎ 206-684-7200; www.seattlepride.org;
Seattle Center
Seattle's lesbian- and gay-pride event
usually falls on the last Sunday in June and
includes a film festival, art exhibit, parade
and the requisite food and entertainment.

July

BITE OF SEATTLE

☎ 425-283-5050; www.biteofseattle.com;
Seattle Center
This culinary celebration is usually held the
second weekend in July. Guests can sample
food from dozens of Seattle-area chefs,
including sub-$4 samples at the Just a Bite
booth, and taste local beer and wines. The
evening ends with live music.

SEAFAIR

☎ 206-728-0123; www.seafair.com
A month-long extravaganza, Seafair
is a civic celebration that began as a
hydroplane race on Lake Washington.
It's now the city's biggest festival, with
all manner of festivities extending across
Seattle. Events include a torchlight parade,
an air show, lots of music, a carnival and
even the arrival of the naval fleet. Lodging
is in short supply in Seattle on Seafair
weekends and traffic becomes hopelessly
tangled thanks to closed bridges and the
influx of visitors, so plan accordingly.

September

BUMBERSHOOT

☎ 206-281-7788; www.bumbershoot.org
Seattle's biggest arts and cultural event
takes over Seattle Center on Labor Day
weekend (the first Monday in September).
Hundreds of musicians, artists, theater

troupes and writers come from all over
the country to perform on the festival's
two dozen stages. It's hard not to find
something you like. There's also a crafts
street fair and lots of good food from
local vendors.

SEATTLE AIDS WALK

☎ 206-329-6923; www.seattleaidswalk.org
This festive and friendly event, held in late
September, grows every year. It's a 10km or
5km walk (or run). Locations vary, so check
the website for details. The walk benefits
the Lifelong AIDS Alliance.

FREMONT OKTOBERFEST

☎ 206-632-1500; www.fremontoktoberfest.org
There are versions of Oktoberfest held
all over town, but this one's a good
introduction to the concept as well as the
neighborhood. Held in late September,
it includes crafts, a car show, live
entertainment and, of course, beer tasting.

October

SEATTLE LESBIAN & GAY FILM FESTIVAL

☎ 206-323-4274; www.seattlequeerfilm.com
Held in the third week of October, this
film festival brings both mainstream
and underground queer films to various
theaters around town.

HALLOWEEN

On October 31, kids and adults dress up in
scary costumes. In the safer neighborhoods
you're likely to see children out 'trick or

top picks

OFFBEAT SEATTLE FESTIVALS

- **Bumbershoot** (left) A cultural buffet of music, theater, artwork and poetry on 25 stages.
- **Fremont Street Fair** (left) Celebrate one of Seattle's quirkiest corners.
- **Winterfest** (opposite) A celebration of all that's cold, furry and white.
- **Trolloween** (above) Just in case regular Halloween isn't weird enough for you.
- **Moisture Festival** (p16) Performances by oddball artists both local and international.

treating' door-to-door for candy. The gay and lesbian bars are especially wild places on Halloween, and Fremont has its own version, Trolloween (named after the Fremont Troll). It features a candlelit procession of costumed locals on Halloween night, followed by a public dance.

December

WINTERFEST
☎ 206-684-7200; www.seattlecenter.com
Seattle Center holds a month-long celebration of holiday traditions from around the globe, starting with Winter Worldfest, a massive concert and dance performance, and continuing with exhibits, dances, concerts and ice skating.

NEW YEAR'S EVE
☎ 206-443-2111; www.seattlecenter.com
The place to be on the 31st is Seattle Center, where festivities are focused on the Space Needle. Most people celebrate by dressing up and drinking champagne, or staying home and watching it all on TV. The following day people stay home to nurse their hangovers and watch college football.

COSTS & MONEY

As in most large cities, expenses in Seattle can vary depending on your interests and means. Accommodations will make up the bulk of your expenses. Booking in advance or planning your visit during the off-season (September–May) will generally get you better value for money.

A dorm bed in a youth hostel costs about $35 including taxes; a double room in one of Seattle's European-style hotels will go for $60 to $80, plus tax. Midrange doubles are between $100 and $200. See the Sleeping chapter (p173) for details about Seattle Super Saver hotel discount packages.

After accommodations, dining will probably be your next-largest budget item. The city offers a good range of meals, from spectacularly decadent restaurant meals to quick, budget-friendly cafe snacks. It's a foodie city that's well positioned to take advantage of fresh seafood and produce, which means that in general splurges will be rewarded with unforgettable dining experiences. Budget meals are under $15 a person; breakfast and brunch and most lunches fall in this category.

HOW MUCH?
Adult ticket up the Space Needle $18
Cover charge at the Crocodile Café $5 to $15
Gallon of gasoline $3
Late-night burrito from a taco cart $5 to $7
Liter of bottled water $2
Pint of local microbrewed beer $4.50
Room at the hip Ace Hotel $99
Souvenir T-shirt $20
Taxi from airport to Pike Place Market $35
Light-rail ticket from airport to downtown $2.50

Midrange prices hover in the $16 to $30 range, and top-end dinners start around $30, plus tax, tip and whatever you're drinking.

For discounts on sights and entertainment, consider buying a Go Seattle Card (www.goseattlecard.com) or a CityPass (www.citypass.net), both of which offer free or discounted admission to most of the city's top attractions. See the Neighborhoods chapter (p92) for details.

INTERNET RESOURCES
The following websites may be helpful in planning your travels.

Bohonus VR (www.bohonus.com/galleries) If you just can't wait until you get there, check out this site for 360-degree views of various Seattle sights, shops and hangouts.

Daily Candy (www.dailycandy.com) The Seattle edition digs up new and fun things to see, do or buy each day.

Hankblog (http://hankblog.wordpress.com) Insider art-related news and views from the folks at the Henry Art Gallery.

Lineout (http://lineout.thestranger.com) The Stranger's music blog – a great way to get plugged into the scene quickly.

Lonely Planet (www.lonelyplanet.com) Succinct summaries on traveling to most places on earth; postcards from other travelers; and the Thorn Tree bulletin board, where you can ask questions before you go or dispense advice when you get back.

Seattle DIY (www.seattlediy.com) A great source of information on underground events and house shows.

Seattle's Convention and Visitors Bureau (www.visitseattle.org) Seattle's official visitors information site.

Seattlest (www.seattlest.com) An informative (but less savvy or sassy than the Stranger) blog about various news and goings-on in and around Seattle.

Slog (slog.thestranger.com) A frequently updated blog by the staff of *The Stranger* newsweekly.

Sustainable Seattle (www.sustainableseattle.org) Though it's a bit academic, this site has thorough information on ecofriendly projects and initiatives in Seattle.

SUSTAINABLE SEATTLE

Nature is a huge part of the Seattle experience and it should come as no surprise that the city is good at being green. So what can visitors do to help?

International flights are pretty much unavoidable, so consider contributing to a carbon offset organization like www.carbonfund .org, www.terrapass.com, www.nativeenergy .com or www.driveneutral.org, where your money is transformed into support for sustainable practices. Or, if you're close enough, plan to travel on a biodiesel bus (p200) or on a train (p201).

Once you've arrived in Seattle, you can easily get by without having a car. Local bus networks are good, and biking is a great option (rentals abound). Walking and using the public transportation system are also good earth-friendly options. And if you do need a car, think about making use of www.flexcar .com, a car-sharing program. Some car-rental agencies offer hybrid vehicles, so be sure to ask around. Also, take a look at www.craigslist .com, an online bulletin board where you can find regional rideshares (look under 'community'); ie folks who are looking for people to carpool and share the cost of gas. Similarly, the adventurous can check www.couch surfing.org, where you sleep on other member's couches – exchanging cultures, saving money and using hopefully fewer resources.

In hotels, save energy by requesting that your sheets and towels not be laundered every day. Shut off lights, the TV and air-con when you're not in the room. And consider not using those inefficient little travel-sized sundries. Hostels are another option as their high-density dormitories use less space and energy. See the box, p180, for a list of hotels that are making an effort.

Sustainable Seattle, a nonprofit organization, holds an annual awards ceremony in November to recognize local businesses that meet certain sustainability criteria; visit www.sustainableseattle.org to learn more about the program.

Our GreenDex (p227) at the end of this book lists organizations and businesses that have been recognized for taking extra measures to help protect the environment, support local charities, use local products or recycled materials, or promote regional culture, among other positive practices. Here's a sample:

Chaco Canyon Café (p131) Cafe serving all vegan, 90% organic and almost half raw food; also an organic bakery.

FareStart Restaurant (p122) Profits support the FareStart program, which provides intensive job training, housing assistance and job placement for disadvantaged and homeless people.

Foster Island Wetlands Trail (p100) A waterfront trail that winds through marshlands and across to smaller islands for bird-watching, swimming, fishing and kayaking.

Fremont Sunday Market (p86) A bustling marketplace in the city's quirkiest quadrant, there's fresh produce, art and junk.

Olympic Sculpture Park (p67) An excellent use of urban space to present public art and sculpture.

Tillicum Village (p189) On Blake Island, tours include traditional Indian salmon bake, dancing and a film about Northwest Native Americans.

Tilth (p133) A certified-organic gourmet cafe in Wallingford.

Volunteer Park Conservatory (p80) A classic Victorian greenhouse with five galleries representing different world environments.

Washington Trails Association (p169) A nonprofit group that organizes hiking trips, conservation efforts and trail-building jaunts into local mountains.

Wing Luke Museum of the Asian Pacific American Experience (p59) Museum devoted to the history of Asian and Pacific culture and art in America.

HISTORY

For a major US city, Seattle's civic history begins late in the chronicle of the nation. While the rest of the country was establishing firm roots, most of today's Seattle was covered in deep forest that was perennially drenched in rain. Though native groups lived here long before, colonialist settlement didn't reach Puget Sound until 1851. The history of Seattle as a city itself only about 130 years long, but in that time it's become the cultural and economic center of the Pacific Northwest. Not that the city would ever brag about that status itself, mind you.

Despite its achievements and importance to the region, Seattle still has the mellow sense of modesty and self-deprecation that characterizes the Northwest. This dates back to its laid-back origins as 'New York Pretty Soon' (see p24). The attitude peaked in the 1950s and '60s, with the wild antiboosterism of newspaper columnist Emmett Watson (who wrote things like 'Have a nice day – somewhere else' and 'Our suicide rate is one of the highest in the nation. But we can be No 1!'). And it has colored the way the nation perceives Seattle, along with the popularization of the antiglamourous in the form of grunge, a trend whose fame still seems to mortify the city. Then there was Seattle's naive excitement at being selected to host the 1999 World Trade Organization (WTO) conference and many residents' shock at the resulting fallout. Seattle always seems to have an uncomfortable relationship with the success it has struggled to achieve.

SEATTLE FACTS

City area **83.9 sq miles**
Population **602,000 (estimated)**
King County area **2126.1 sq miles**
King County population **1.87 million**
Freshwater shoreline **147.52 miles**
Saltwater shoreline **53.38 miles**
Puget Sound **500 sq miles of water, 300 islands**

NATIVE PEOPLES OF PUGET SOUND

When the accumulated ice of the great polar glaciers of the Pleistocene Epoch lowered sea levels throughout the world, the ancestors of Native Americans migrated from Siberia to Alaska via a land bridge across the Bering Strait. By this reckoning, the present tribes of Puget Sound arrived here 11,000 or 12,000 years ago, before the glaciers receded.

Unlike the Plains Indians living further inland, who were primarily nomadic hunter-gatherers, the first inhabitants of the Pacific Northwest were intimately tied to the rivers, lakes and sea. The tribe living on the site of today's Seattle was called the Duwamish. They and other tribal groups along Puget Sound – notably the Suquamish, Coast Salish and Chinook – depended on catching salmon, cod and shellfish. On land, they hunted deer and elk, more for their protective hides than for their flesh. Though each group had its own dialect, coastal natives communicated through a language called Lushootseed, which natives today struggle to keep from extinction.

TIMELINE

9000–11,000 BC	1792	1804–06
The ancestors of the Duwamish, Suquamish, Coast Salish and Chinook tribes arrive in Puget Sound after earlier migrating from Siberia via a land bridge across the Bering Strait.	British sea captain George Vancouver sails through the Straits of Juan de Fuca and Georgia.	Meriwether Lewis and William Clark set out on their famous expedition across the Louisiana Territory, covering 8000 miles in two years, with the help of Shoshone Indian translator Sacagawea.

TODAY'S DUWAMISH PEOPLE

Seattle took its name from Chief Sealth (1786–1866), anglicized to 'Seattle', the leader of the Duwamish tribe who initially welcomed members of the Denny party when they arrived in 1851.

At the time of the Denny party's arrival, the peaceful Duwamish culture was deeply linked to the salmon that made seasonal runs on the Green and Duwamish Rivers. White settlers received permission from the Duwamish to build their first structures on the site of a summer camp that the area's native inhabitants called Duwamps – the name that the settlers applied to their little town as well. Chief Seattle urged peaceful coexistence between the people of his tribe and the whites, and he encouraged the Duwamish to work side by side with the settlers building houses, cutting trees and laying out streets.

Relations with other tribes along Puget Sound were not as good. To address growing hostilities, the US government drew up a treaty in 1854 granting area tribes $150,000 in goods and 2600 acres of reservation land in return for vacating two million acres of prime real estate in western Washington, including the present-day Seattle area. Distrust and anger soon broke out, and in 1855 warfare erupted between the natives and white settlers.

Chief Seattle persuaded the Duwamish not to become involved in the conflict, but the settlement at Duwamps was besieged by a group of hostile Indians, forcing the settlers to take shelter in the town's small stockade. A visiting navy sloop, the *Decatur*, fired its cannons into the forest above the little town to frighten the Indians away. In retaliation, the Indians burned and looted nearly all of the settlements on Puget Sound. In the end, the settlers prevailed and one of the Indian rebel leaders, Leschi, was captured, tried and hanged for murder.

So in many ways, the interactions between white settlers and the natives who lived on the land for thousands of years before they arrived have been ugly, conflicted, and rife with violence and unfairness. But if the people who settled in the Pacific Northwest have absorbed anything from the pre-existing Indian cultures, it's a sense of reverence for nature and the surrounding wilderness, even though that reverence is frequently ineffective and often comes across as hypocritical in the light of history. 'How can you buy or sell the sky, the warmth of the land?' Chief Seattle asked in his

Summer and fall were dedicated to harvesting the bounty of the sea and forest. Food was stored in massive quantities to carry the tribes through the long winter months, when the most important ancient legends and ceremonies were handed down to the younger generations. In terms of artistic, religious and cultural forms, the Northwest coastal Indians reached a pinnacle of sophistication unmatched by most Native American groups. Ornately carved cedar canoes served as transportation, and extensive trading networks evolved between the permanent settlements that stretched up and down the coast and along the river valleys.

Extended family groups lived together in cedar longhouses, which were constructed over a central pit-like living area. The social structure in these self-sustaining tribal villages was quite stratified, with an aristocratic class of chiefs holding the majority of wealth and power. Social and religious rituals were dominated by a strict clan system. Wealth was measured in goods such as blankets, salmon and fish oil. Such commodities were consumed and to some degree redistributed in ceremonial feasts in which great honor accrued to the person who gave away these valued items.

Puget Sound natives evolved complex cultural, social and economic structures, which the invasion of Euro-American settlers in the mid-1800s almost erased. Today tribes struggle for survival, respect and renewal (see the box, above).

1851	1854–55	1885
The Denny party arrives at Alki Point and settles in Puget Sound, already home to the Duwamish people. A year later, thanks to rough tides that made pier-building impossible, the settlement moves to Seattle proper.	US treaty grants 2600 acres of reservation in return for two million acres of prime real estate. Warfare erupts between tribes and white settlers. Chief Sealth delivers his masterful address.	A group of white settlers establishes the Anti-Chinese Congress, setting a deadline by which all Chinese must leave Seattle. About 500 stay, and the mob's attempt to remove them leads to riots the following year.

most famous speech, delivered at a gathering of natives and white settlers, which included territorial governor Isaac Stevens, who was attempting to purchase Puget Sound land from the area's native inhabitants. This 1855 address is considered one of the masterpieces of Native American oratory, although the standard text of the speech was penned 30 years later from notes by a literary-minded surgeon who attended the event. Oral history is vital to the Duwamish culture. Stories contain the collective wisdom of the tribe, lessons from the past about how to behave. 'Without them,' the tribe's website says, 'we are thought to be bound in a state of psychological poverty.' The website contains a list of oral histories that current tribal members have remembered and recorded.

The Duwamish were moved to the Port Madison Reservation in 1856, despite their peaceable history. In part to recognize Chief Seattle's aid and pacifist efforts, the settlers renamed their town in the chief's honor. Apparently Chief Seattle was not exactly pleased with the honor. According to Duwamish beliefs, if someone utters a dead person's name, the soul of the deceased is denied everlasting peace.

Chief Sealth's impact on the mindset of Seattle's population isn't difficult to see. The following lines from his most famous speech became a cornerstone in the New Age, environmental-preservation philosophy that is almost the default belief in the Pacific Northwest.

'The earth does not belong to human beings; human beings belong to the earth. This we know. All things are connected like the blood that unites one family. All things are connected. Whatever befalls the earth befalls the sons and daughters of the earth.'

Now, some 160 years later, the Duwamish tribe has more than 560 enrolled members and holds monthly meetings and annual gatherings. In 1983 the tribe established Duwamish Tribal Services, a nonprofit organization devoted to ensuring the social, cultural and economic survival of the Duwamish tribe. The tribe has yet to receive federal recognition, but efforts to do so are continuing (for details, visit www.duwamishtribe.org).

EARLY EXPLORATION

Puget Sound and the Pacific Northwest in general were among the last areas of the Americas to be explored by Europeans. In fact, almost 300 years passed between the arrival of white explorers in America and their 'discovery' of Puget Sound.

The first white expedition to explore the Puget Sound area came in 1792, when the British sea captain George Vancouver sailed through the inland waterways of the Straits of Juan de Fuca and Georgia. In the same year, the USA entered the competition to claim the Northwest when Captain Robert Gray reached the mouth of the Columbia River.

The major reason for European and American eagerness to claim this forested and well-watered corner of the map was its immense wealth in furs. The region's waterways were especially rich in beavers and otters, the pelts of which were a highly valued commodity in Europe and Asia and thus an important article of trade.

None of these exploration or trade expeditions led directly to a pioneer settlement or even a permanent trading post. This development came with the powerful fur-trading companies, especially the British Hudson's Bay Company (HBC). From Fort Vancouver, the HBC – and hence Britain – controlled all trade in the Pacific Northwest. The Puget Sound area was linked to the fur-trading fort by the Cowlitz River. Because of its strict code of conduct, the company had legal authority over the area's few whites, mostly French-Canadian and

1889	1897	1910
The Great Fire sweeps through the city, gutting its core and destroying the mostly wooden storefronts and log homes on stilts. This in turn leads to a new brick-and-stone city center built on regraded streets.	The Klondike Gold Rush is sparked by the arrival of the ship *Portland*. Along with general economic growth, the gold rush leads Seattle's small businesses to make quick fortunes over the next decade. The city's population doubles by 1900.	Seattle begins to grow up. Its population reaches a quarter million, making it a clear contender for the preeminent city of the Pacific Northwest.

Scottish trappers. The HBC also policed trade relationships between the whites and the region's native inhabitants.

The first US settlers straggled overland to the Pacific Northwest in the 1830s on the rough tracks that would become the Oregon Trail. The HBC chief factor, Dr John McLoughlin, sought to restrict American settlement to the region south of the Columbia River, in Oregon. In doing so, he kept the prime land along Puget Sound from settlement. McLoughlin sensed that one day the USA and Britain would divide the territory; if US settlement could be limited to the area south of the Columbia, then Britain would have a stronger claim to the land north of the river. It worked. When the settlers in Oregon voted in 1843 to become a US territory, present-day Washington remained in British hands.

American settlers continued rolling in to the Pacific Northwest. Between 1843 and 1860 some 53,000 settlers migrated across the 2000-mile-long Oregon Trail. As they pushed northward into land controlled largely by the HBC, boundary disputes between the USA and Britain became increasingly antagonistic. The popular slogan of the 1844 US presidential campaign was 'Fifty-four Forty or Fight,' which urged US citizens to occupy territory in the Northwest up to the present Alaskan border, including all of Washington state and British Columbia. Finally, in 1846 the British and the Americans agreed to the present US–Canadian border along the 49th parallel.

top picks

SEATTLE HISTORY BOOKS

- **The Good Rain (1991), Timothy Egan** The *New York Times* correspondent sheds light on the Northwest and its inhabitants, while plumbing his soul and the weather in gorgeous, lyrical prose.
- **Stepping Westward (1991), Sallie Tisdale** In this critical memoir, Tisdale casts a keen eye on the often contentious relationship between humans and nature in the Pacific Northwest.
- **Divided Destiny: A History of Japanese Americans in Seattle (1999), David A Takami** Originally created to accompany an exhibition at the Wing Luke Asian Museum, this richly illustrated book documents 100-plus years of Seattle's Japanese American community.
- **Seattle and the Demons of Ambition: A Love Story (2003), Fred Moody** A former *Seattle Weekly* editor, Moody puts a personal spin on Seattle's economic, political and cultural history.
- **Vanishing Seattle: Images of America (2006), Clark Humphrey** A collection of vintage photographs of city landmarks that have either disappeared or been radically altered.

'NEW YORK PRETTY SOON'

Arthur and David Denny were native New Yorkers who, in 1851, led a group of settlers across the Oregon Trail with the intention of settling in the Willamette Valley. On the way, they heard stories of good land and deep water ports along Puget Sound. When the Denny party arrived in Portland in the fall, they decided to keep going north. The settlers staked claims on Alki Point, in present-day West Seattle. The group named their encampment Alki-New York (the Chinookan word *Alki* means 'pretty soon' or 'by and by'). After a winter of wind and rain, the group determined that their fledgling city needed a deeper harbor and moved the settlement to the mudflats across Elliott Bay. The colony was renamed Seattle for the Duwamish chief Sealth (pronounced *see*-aalth, with a guttural 'th' being made up of a hard 't' and an 'h' that's almost a lisp off the end of the word), who was the friend of an early merchant.

1932	1942	1954
A Depression-era shantytown called 'Hooverville,' after president Herbert Hoover, forms south of Pioneer Square. Made up of lean-tos, shacks and cardboard boxes, it houses hundreds of unemployed squatters.	Japanese Americans are ordered to evacuate Seattle, sent to a 'relocation center,' or internment camp, in Puyallup, then on to another camp in Idaho, where they are detained under prison conditions for the duration of the war.	Boeing Air Transport, launched 40 years prior when William Boeing designed and produced the pontoon biplane and already a pioneer in commercial airline flight, announces production of the 707.

Traversing the Oregon Trail was an arduous and costly adventure. The Pacific Northwest was not settled by penniless wanderers, but earnest young men and women, mostly in their twenties, who had the wherewithal to make the six-month trip and were determined to establish farms, businesses and communities.

BIRTH OF THE CITY

Still, early Seattle was hardly a boomtown. The heart of the young city beat in the area now known as Pioneer Square. Although there was a small but deep harbor at this point in Elliott Bay, much of the land immediately to the south was mudflats, ideal for oysters but not much else. The land to the north and east was steep and forested. The early settlers (whose names now ring as a compendium of street names and landmarks: Denny, Yesler, Bell, Boren) quickly cleared the land and established a sawmill, schools, churches and other civic institutions. From the start, the people who settled Seattle never doubted that they were founding a great city. The original homesteads were quickly platted into city streets, and trade, not farming or lumbering, became the goal of the little settlement.

Since it was a frontier town, the majority of Seattle's male settlers were bachelors. One of the town's founders (and sole professor at the newly established university), Asa Mercer, went back to the East Coast with the express purpose of inducing young, unmarried women to venture to Seattle. Fifty-seven women made the journey and married into the frontier stock, in the process establishing a more civilized tone in the city.

Seattle's early economic growth came from shipping logs to San Francisco, a city booming with gold wealth. At the time, loggers had to go no further than the bluffs above town (now First and Capitol Hills) to find hundreds of acres of old-growth fir forest. As the sawmill was located on the waterfront, the logs had to be transported down the steep hillside. A skid road was developed on which horses and mules pulled the logs down a chute of ever-present mud. This skid road later became Yesler Way, the prototype of the term 'skid road' or 'skid row.'

THE BATTLE FOR RAILROADS

The Northwest's first rail link was the Northern Pacific Railroad, which linked Portland to Chicago in 1883. The young towns of Puget Sound – Seattle, Tacoma, Port Townsend and Bellingham – believed their dreams of becoming major trade centers depended on luring a national rail line to link them to the east. Land speculators especially profited when railroads like the Northern Pacific and the Great Northern came shopping for a Puget Sound terminus. Seattle lost out to Tacoma when the Northern Pacific built its shipyards there, but it later became the terminus for the Great Northern Railroad and the Milwaukee Rd.

ANTI-CHINESE RIOTS OF 1886

Because of the region's many railroad and mining companies, and Seattle's position on the Pacific Rim, a large number of Chinese immigrants settled in the city. The fact that Asian laborers worked at jobs that most white Americans shunned didn't prevent the perception that these 'foreign' workers were taking jobs away from 'real Americans' and then, as now, it didn't prevent episodes of ugly racism.

1959	1960	1962
While researching malaria in the Congo, University of Washington medical geneticist Dr Arno Motulsky collects a blood sample of the first documented case of HIV, the virus that causes AIDS.	The population of King County tops one million and one in 10 people work for Boeing. The '60s are a tumultuous decade in Seattle as in most of the country. Civil rights struggles shake the establishment.	The World's Fair in Seattle takes place. The headliner on opening night is singer John Raitt. His 12-year-old daughter, Bonnie, holds his sheet music.

DIGGING BENEATH THE SURFACE

Want to delve into underground Seattle – literally? Local historian Bill Speidel's Underground Tour (p206) will take you there. Leaving daily from Doc Maynard's Public House, the slightly cheesy but entertaining tour prowls the streets beneath the streets of Pioneer Square, evoking the past by digging down to the olden days.

While there's not actually much to *see* on the 90-minute tour except dirty passageways and decayed plumbing from the 1890s, the story of why there is an underground in the first place is pretty interesting. Despite its prime location on Elliott Bay, early Seattle wasn't exactly conducive to urban development. The area lacked an ideal foundation upon which to build: the land was either hilly and steep or shallow and wet. Many of the storefronts in the Pioneer Square area were built upon soggy tide flats and actually dropped below sea level at high tide. When it rained hard (and it rained hard a lot), the streets bloated into a muddy soup, sewage backed up at high tide and things got pretty messy. As you can imagine, the smell wasn't so great either.

The Great Fire of 1889 (below) gutted the city and gave city planners a chance to lift the town out of its waterlogged foundation. They decided to regrade the streets, so great piles of dirt were propped up with retaining walls, and streets were raised up to 12ft higher than they originally were. Storefronts from the old ramshackle town that were once at street level effectively became basements and, later, passageways for the Underground Tour. You can see bits of the underground by yourself in the Pioneer Square Antique Mall in the Pioneer Building and on the bottom floor of the Grand Central Arcade.

As anti-Chinese sentiment grew in outlying communities around the Pacific Northwest as more and more Chinese moved to Seattle, where the multitude of employment opportunities offered them continued security and led to a sense of community. The area south of Yesler Way was considered Chinatown, where most of the new arrivals made their homes; today it has a more varied population and is known as the International District.

The first recorded clash between the Chinese minority and white settlers came in 1885, when a Chinese immigrant was knifed to death. That year, a group called the Anti-Chinese Congress – primarily composed of radical labor unions – used fear tactics and mob assent to establish a date by which all Chinese would be forced to leave the Puget Sound area. Between 750 and 1000 Chinese workers left. But about 500 Chinese continued to live and work in Seattle. In February 1886, a mob entered Chinatown and attempted to forcibly remove the remaining Chinese, driving them onto ships. State and city officials tried to mediate, but violence erupted. Five people were shot. One white protester died from his wounds and federal troops were called in to restore order.

The Chinese population plummeted, especially in light of court rulings that barred Chinese men from sending for their wives in China. This restriction was a result of the *Chinese Exclusion Act*, which was finally repealed in 1943 when China became a US ally during WWII.

THE GREAT FIRE & THE REGRADING OF SEATTLE

Frontier Seattle was a thrown-together village of wooden storefronts, log homes and lumber mills. Tidewater lapped against present-day 1st Ave S, and many of the buildings and the streets that led to them were on stilts. No part of the original downtown was more than 4ft above the bay at high tide, and the streets were frequently a quagmire.

1973	1975	1980
Seattle's 'one percent for art' rule is established, specifying that 1% of the city's capital improvement project funds go toward the commission, purchase and installation of public artworks.	Bill Gates and Paul Allen start Microsoft, giving home-computer users everywhere an infinite supply of things to complain about and ensuring the livelihoods of antitrust lawyers for the foreseeable future.	Mt St Helens blows her top, spreading ash through five states and killing 57 people. The eruption leaves a horseshoe-shaped crater atop the mountain.

On June 6, 1889, an apprentice woodworker accidentally let a pot of boiling glue spill onto a pile of wood chips in a shop on 1st Ave and Madison St. The fire quickly spread through the young city, with boardwalks provided an unstoppable conduit for the flames. By the end of the day, 30 blocks of the city had burned, gutting the core of downtown.

What might have seemed a catastrophe was in fact a blessing, as the city was rebuilt immediately with handsome structures of brick, steel and stone. This time, however, the streets were regraded, and ravines and inlets filled in. This raised the new city about a dozen feet above the old. In some areas the regrading simply meant building on top of older ground-level buildings and streets. People had to cross deep trenches to get from one side of the street to another. Buildings were constructed around the notion that the first floor or two would eventually be buried when the city got around to filling in the trenches.

The sense of transformation inspired by the Great Fire also fueled another great rebuilding project. One of Seattle's original seven hills, Denny Hill, rose out of Elliott Bay just north of Pine St. Its very steep face limited commercial traffic, though some hotels and private homes were perched on the hilltop. City engineers determined that if Seattle's growth was to continue, Denny Hill had to go. Between 1899 and 1912, the hill was sluiced into Elliott Bay. Twenty million gallons of water were pumped daily from Lake Union and sprayed onto the rock and soil. Under great pressure, the water liquefied the clay and dislodged the rock, all of which was sluiced into flumes. Existing homes were simply undercut and then burned.

KLONDIKE GOLD RUSH

Seattle's first real boom came when the ship *Portland* docked at the waterfront in 1897 with its now-famous cargo: two tons of gold newly gleaned from northern Yukon goldfields. The news spread quickly across the USA; within weeks, thousands of fortune seekers from all over the world converged on Seattle, the last stop before heading north. That summer and fall, 74 ships left Seattle bound for Skagway, Alaska, and on to the goldfields in Dawson City, Yukon.

In all, more than 40,000 prospectors passed through Seattle. The Canadian government demanded that prospectors bring a year's worth of supplies, so they wouldn't freeze or starve to death midway. Outfitting the miners became big business in Seattle. The town became the banking center for the fortunes made in the Yukon. Bars, brothels, theaters and honky-tonks in Pioneer Square blossomed.

Many of Seattle's shopkeepers, tavern owners and restaurateurs made quick fortunes in the late 1890s – far more than most of the prospectors. Many who did make fortunes in Alaska chose to stay in the Northwest, settling in the thriving port city on Puget Sound.

Seattle grew quickly. The Klondike Gold Rush provided great wealth, and the railroads brought in a steady stream of immigrants, mostly from Eastern Europe and Scandinavia. Seattle controlled most of the shipping trade with Alaska and increasingly with nations of the Pacific Rim. Company-controlled communities like Ballard sprang up, populated almost exclusively with Scandinavians who worked in massive sawmills. A new influx of Asian immigrants, this time from Japan, began streaming into Seattle, establishing fishing fleets and vegetable farms.

At the height of the gold rush in 1900, Seattle's population reached 80,000, double the population figure from the 1890 census. By 1910, Seattle's population jumped to a quarter million. Seattle had become the preeminent city of the Pacific Northwest.

1991	1993	1996
The formerly underground style of music known as grunge goes mainstream, with Pearl Jam's *Ten* and Nirvana's *Nevermind* hitting record store shelves. Three years later, Nirvana front-man Kurt Cobain commits suicide.	Gary Locke becomes the first Asian American to be elected King County Executive. The Chinese American politician becomes governor of Washington in 1997.	The Sound Transit plan clears a second vote, opening the door to a series of much-needed upgrades to Seattle's mass transportation system and extending its coverage to outlying neighborhoods.

THE WAR YEARS

Seattle's boom continued through WWI, when Northwest lumber was in great demand. The opening of the Panama Canal brought increased trade to Pacific ports, which were free from wartime threats. Shipyards opened along Puget Sound, bringing the shipbuilding industry close to the forests of the Northwest.

One of the significant events in Seattle history occurred in 1916 when William Boeing, a pioneer aviator, designed and produced a pontoon biplane. Boeing went on to establish an airline, Boeing Air Transport (later United Airlines). But it was WWII that really started the engines at Boeing. The factory received contracts to produce the B-17 and B-29 bombers, which led in the US air war against Axis nations. Huge defense contracts began to flow into Boeing and by extension into Seattle, fueling more rapid growth and prosperity.

WWII brought other, less positive, developments to Seattle. About 7000 Japanese residents in Seattle and the nearby areas were removed forcibly from their jobs and homes. They were sent to the nearby 'relocation center,' or internment camp, in Puyallup, then on to another camp in Idaho where they were detained under prison conditions for the duration of the war. This greatly depleted the Japanese community, which up to this point had built a thriving existence farming and fishing in Puget Sound. In all, an estimated 110,000 Japanese across the country, two-thirds of whom were US citizens, were sent to internment camps. Upon their release, many declined to return to the homes they'd been forced to abandon.

Meanwhile, the boom in aircraft manufacturing and shipbuilding brought tens of thousands of new workers to the region. Because of Boeing, and the shipyards at Bremerton, Puget Sound became a highly defended area, which led to the building of several military facilities in the region. These bases also brought in thousands of new residents. By the end of the war, Seattle had grown to nearly half a million people.

BOEING & POSTWAR SEATTLE

The Boeing Airplane Company, started in 1917, was founded and named by William E Boeing and his partner, Conrad Westervelt. (Boeing tested his first plane, the *B&W*, in June 1916 by taking off from the middle of Lake Union.) For years, Boeing single-handedly ruled Seattle industry. After WWII, the manufacturer diversified its product line and began to develop civilian aircraft. In 1954 Boeing announced the 707, and the response was immediate and overwhelming. The world found itself at the beginning of an era of mass air travel, and Boeing produced the jets that led this revolution in transportation. By 1960, when the population of Seattle topped one million, one in 10 people worked for Boeing, and one in four people worked jobs directly affected by Boeing.

But the fortunes of Boeing weren't always to soar. A combination of overstretched capital (due to cost overruns in the development of the 747) and a cut in defense spending led to a severe financial crisis in the early 1970s, known as the 'Boeing Bust.' Boeing was forced to cut its work force by two-thirds; in one year, nearly 60,000 Seattleites lost their jobs. The local economy went into a tailspin for a number of years.

In the 1980s increased defense spending brought vigor back to aircraft production lines, and expanding trade relations with China and other Pacific Rim nations brought business to Boeing, too. But just a few days after Seattle was rattled by a mighty earthquake, the city received a blow that rocked it even more. Boeing head honcho Phil Condit announced in March 2001 that the world's largest airplane manufacturer, the company as synonymous with Seattle

1999	2000	2001
Seattle is rocked by the World Trade Organization riots. The same year, Microsoft is declared a monopoly and enters into lengthy negotiations over the future of its business.	In a spectacular implosion that is the result of an engineering feat, the Kingdome is collapsed, making way for the new Qwest Field, home of the Seattle Seahawks National Football League team.	On February 28, an earthquake measuring 6.8 on the Richter scale hits Seattle, toppling several historical buildings and causing more than $2 billion in damage to the city.

as rain, was blowing town. Boeing, he said, would relocate at least 50% of its headquarters staff to bigger and brighter digs in Chicago in September 2001.

At that time, the company employed 78,400 people in the Seattle area and 198,900 people worldwide. Only the headquarters was moved to Chicago; the company's major production center remains in the Seattle area. But the announcement, followed by several stages of layoffs, left Seattleites more than a little concerned about what the future would hold. As Boeing announces plans to expand its manufacturing operations beyond Seattle, those worries continue.

Boeing today employs around 150,000 people in 70 countries. Since 2003, however, the company has been second banana to European manufacturer Airbus, the current market leader. In late 2009 the company's great hope, the Boeing 787 Dreamliner – which was initially expected to be finished in 2007 – finally achieved liftoff; its success is considered critical to the company's economic health.

> ## WORD ASSOCIATIONS
>
> Seattle, like any city, has its share of clichés. It also tends to have a powerful thirst for adult beverages, be they well-crafted cocktails, regional wines or locally made microbrews.
>
> In that spirit, we present the unofficial Lonely Planet Seattle City Guide Drinking Game. It's easy to play – there's only one rule: Each time you come across one of the following words while using this guidebook, take a swig of whatever poison you've chosen. Everybody wins.
>
> Here are the words to look out for: vegan, sustainable, hipster, microbrew, flannel, rain, fishmonger, latte, Chihuly, Nirvana, *Singles*, ferry, viaduct, *Stranger*, Sonicsgate, *Frasier*, dive, monorail, Ichiro, Seahawk, Sub Pop, grunge.

THE SHAPE OF THE CITY

Seattle's population hit 565,000 in 1965 before economic realities began to draw baby boomers out of the city center and into the cheaper housing available in the suburbs. By 1970, the population of the rest of King County had passed Seattle's. It's still twice as large today.

In an attempt to win people back from the suburbs, downtown businesses dreamed up so-called 'urban renewal' projects such as razing Pioneer Square and Pike Place Market to build apartment towers and parking garages. Not many people liked this idea, of course, and the public banded together to preserve these and other historical landmarks. Around the same time, activists used new environmental-protection laws to defeat proposals for two local freeways and scale down an expansion plan for I-90. With this new interest in its preservation, downtown's vitality gradually started to return.

By 1972 voters had approved an all-bus transit system. In 1990 Metro Transit opened a bus tunnel beneath downtown. Voters gave rail transit the nod in 1996. One year later, voters also approved a new monorail system, but inadequate funding meant it never happened. Later came new stadiums for the Mariners and Seahawks, as well as voter-authorized funding for park improvements and new libraries.

The city is currently about to be reshaped yet again. Plans were approved in late 2009 to replace the Alaskan Way Viaduct – which takes Hwy 99 along the waterfront and is generally considered an eyesore, not to mention structurally unsound – with a bored-out tunnel alternative. The project also includes road improvements, expanded public transportation, the addition of a park area and the replacement of the central waterfront seawall.

2001	2003	2009
Boeing relocates its headquarters to Chicago. This removal of a financial linchpin shakes the city's confidence in its overall economy, even though Boeing keeps a substantial portion of its operations in the area.	Seattle voters say no to a proposed 10-cents-a-cup coffee tax. Starbucks Corporation purchases Seattle's Best Coffee and Torrefazione Italia, making it even more difficult to avoid the growing chain's coffee shops.	Generally dismissed as a pipe dream, the long-awaited light-rail line to the airport finally opens.

MICROSOFT

Starbucks and Boeing aside, the biggest story in Seattle's economic history is the business behemoth of Microsoft. Springing onto the scene in the mid-1970s and '80s, it was a force that would change Seattle forever. After tinkering around with a little notion called BASIC (a programming language for the world's first microcomputer), local boy Bill Gates joined up with his childhood chum Paul Allen to start Microsoft in 1975. Though the software giant, located in Redmond across Lake Washington, never achieved quite the total control over the Seattle economy that Boeing once had, it became increasingly hard to find someone who wasn't a contractor, caterer or car dealer for the Microsoft crowd. Microsoft also attracted other high-tech companies to the area.

Microsoft's heyday hit something of a capitalist brick wall in the late 1990s, when the federal government began a very long and politically hot suit against Microsoft. The Justice Department accused the company of monopolistic practices and alleged that it used – and abused – its prodigious market power to prevent any competition from getting in its way. Microsoft's long-held reputation for bullying other players on the technological playfield was deemed legally unfair.

In April 2000, Judge Thomas Penfield Jackson ruled that Microsoft had violated anti-trust laws by 'engaging in predatory tactics that discourage technological competition.' The judge ruled that Microsoft needed to divest the company. Microsoft launched a barrage of appeals, which resulted in various settlements with the federal government and several states. Then, in 2004, the European Commission found that Microsoft had violated antitrust laws, slapping it with a €497 million ($689 million) fine. The company appealed, but in September 2007 its appeal was rejected by the second-highest European court, which upheld the fine. At research time, however, Microsoft still held a substantial public-sector market lead in Europe.

ARTS

When you think of Seattle, what leaps to mind (after rain and coffee) is probably something music-related – whether it's Jimi Hendrix, Nirvana, Pearl Jam, Soundgarden, hip-hop or KEXP radio. But there are a lot of other things going on in the field of arts, as well.

A city of readers (with more bookstores per capita than any other US city), Seattle is also home to a stable of internationally recognized writers, among them Tom Robbins, Jonathan Raban and Sherman Alexie. The city's visual arts are also dynamic, as its cultural strands (from Native American and Asian to contemporary American) meet and transfuse on canvas, in glass and in sculpture. For more information on venues for the arts, see the Arts chapter (p157).

MUSIC

Indie Rock & Hip-Hop

Seattle has long had an active music scene, even if its vibrancy has tended to wax and wane. One year there will be hardly any good clubs, then two years later there are twice as many. Right now, Seattle is blessed with a decent number of live-music venues, particularly for indie rock and its subcategories. A burgeoning hip-hop scene has locals excited, particularly because Seattle seems to produce a more socially conscious brand of hip-hop than most other places. Jazz and blues, though not as epic as they were in the days when Quincy Jones was sneaking into Pioneer Square clubs, are still swinging. There are also small but thriving music scenes in Bellingham to the north (Jon Auer and Ken Stringfellow started the Posies in a Bellingham basement, and Death Cab for Cutie was formed there) and in Olympia, which is home to the riot grrrl movement (and of Sleater-Kinney, Two Ton Boa, Old Time Relijun and others).

You've almost certainly heard a few Seattle bands, whether you've realized it or not. Pioneering Northwest rock bands like the Kingsmen, the Sonics and Seattle's own legendary Jimi Hendrix helped define rock 'n' roll in the '60s. Local groups like Heart and the Steve Miller Band made it big in the '70s. Blues musician Robert Cray and saxophonist Kenny G gained notoriety during the '80s. The media represented none of these as Seattle musicians per se. Not until the city's grunge boom in the '90s did the world turn to Seattle as the origin of a unique sound.

SOUND OF SEATTLE

What most people think of as the definitive Seattle sound can be grasped pretty easily by a quick spin of these landmark grunge-era records:

- **Superfuzz Bigmuff (Sub Pop), Mudhoney** Released in 1988, the catchy debut single, 'Touch Me I'm Sick,' became an instant classic. Singer Mark Arm is allegedly the guy who came up with the term 'grunge,' although he intended it as a diss, not a marketing label destined to become pandemic.
- **Bleach (Sub Pop), Nirvana** The melodic-punk band's first album.
- **Nevermind (Geffen), Nirvana** Grunge anthem 'Smells Like Teen Spirit' became, and remains, one of the most-analyzed singles in the history of rock.
- **Ten (Epic), Pearl Jam** The first studio album by one of rock's biggest groups took a while to peak but contained three hit singles.
- **Badmotorfinger (A&M), Soundgarden** The hair-metal side of grunge.

But don't stop there. A huge variety of sounds can be found in Seattle, even if you stay within the boundaries of rock. All of the following artists – whose styles vary wildly – have their roots in Seattle, and many of them still play there frequently. Dig around online, ask questions at record stores and flip through the local papers for more.

- **Fastbacks** Pioneering NW band with an all-star cast and about 15 different drummers.
- **Foo Fighters** Nirvana drummer Dave Grohl's band.
- **Melvins** The heaviest of sludge.
- **Murder City Devils** Now-defunct band that split into the also defunct but also great Pretty Girls Make Graves and Dead Low Tide, as well as Big Business.
- **Queensryche** The band everyone forgets is from Seattle (well, Bellevue) because they're unironic prog-metal.
- **Spits** Frequently costumed garage-punk maniacs.
- **Supersuckers** Punkers turned cowpunkers led by Eddie Spaghetti.
- **The Gits** Awesome punk band that fell apart when singer Mia Zapata was brutally murdered.
- **The Trashies** Born to play basements (that's a compliment).
- **Zeke** One-minute songs about girls, drugs and cars.

Grunge, a guitar- and angst-driven derivative of punk, grew out of garage rock, where dudes with nothing else to do jammed in their garages because, before grunge, there weren't that many places to rock out in Seattle unless you were already a headlining band. These days, there's still a very active local rock scene, though it no longer has the cohesive sound that characterized most of the bands that made it big during the grunge years.

In the wake of grunge, the hipster core of Northwest music moved slightly south, to Olympia, home of riot grrrls, indie rock and renowned music scribe Greil Marcus' favorite band, Sleater-Kinney. Outlying areas also produced a number of great bands that are close enough to being Seattle bands to be thought of as such. Another big name in indie rock, Modest Mouse, formed in Issaquah, Washington. Bellingham band Death Cab for Cutie front-man Ben Gibbard went on to form The Postal Service, whose album *Give Up* became the best-selling release for Seattle's Sub Pop label since Nirvana's *Bleach*.

Seattle hip-hop in recent years has successfully crossed over and infiltrated the indie-rock universe and begun to make a serious impact. This is partly thanks to influential radio station KEXP making a habit of adding local hip-hop artists into the mix at all hours. But it's mostly due to the fact that the work coming out of the Pacific Northwest is overwhelmingly high quality and, as befits the region, generally positive and socially conscious. Seattle hip-hop artists to look for include the Blue Scholars *(Blue Scholars, The Long March)*, Specs One *(Mega, Return of the Artist)*, Silent Lambs Project *(Soul Liquor)*, Grayskul *(Deadlivers)* and the Boom Bap Project *(Reprogram)*.

See p152 for a list of live venues.

Jazz & Blues

A lot of people may not be aware that Seattle was home to a thriving jazz and blues scene back in the day. You could find raging clubs all along Jackson St in Pioneer Square in the 1930s and '40s, and the young (*too* young, legally speaking, but scrappy and talented enough to get away

lonelyplanet.com

ROCK PILGRIMAGES

The dark side of Seattle music history holds a morbid fascination for many fans. The city and its surroundings are home to several sites that might be of interest to rock 'n' roll pilgrims.

Jimi Hendrix (1942–1970) is buried in Greenwood Memorial Park in Renton, Washington. His original headstone included a drawing of a Stratocaster guitar, although it's the traditional right-handed setup, not left-handed as Hendrix played it. The guitarist's increasing popularity raised concerns that nearby graves were being disturbed by visiting fans, so in 2002 Hendrix's remains and those of his father and grandmother were moved to a separate burial site. The memorial is a large pedestal over his grave, supported by three columns, and incorporating the original gravestone. There's also a statue of Hendrix playing guitar on Broadway in Capitol Hill (p80).

Nirvana front-man Kurt Cobain (1967–1994) was born at Grays Harbor Community Hospital in Aberdeen, Washington. He spent his early childhood in a house at 1210 E 1st St, had an apartment at 404 N Michigan St, made a brief foray onto the rooftop of a building at 618 W Market St as an intoxicated teen, and in 1986 rented a dilapidated house at 1000½ E 2nd St.

Not having a whole lot else going for it, Aberdeen has embraced its lost son and the musical pilgrims who visit seeking landmarks of Cobain's youth. A sign at the entrance to the city reads 'Welcome to Aberdeen – Come as You Are' as a tribute to Cobain, and the city museum has set up a Kurt Cobain self-guided tour (www.aberdeen-museum .org/kurt.htm). The nonprofit Kurt Cobain Memorial Committee also plans to build a Kurt Cobain Memorial Park and a youth center in Aberdeen.

Cobain's body was cremated so he has no gravesite, but fans visit Viretta Park, near Cobain's former Lake Washington home, to pay tribute – particularly on the anniversary of his death.

Keeping up the mortality theme, Green River, the seminal band that included future members of Pearl Jam and Mudhoney, is named after serial killer Gary Ridgway. Known as the Green River Killer, Ridgway was still at large when the band was formed. He was arrested in 2001 in Renton and later pleaded guilty to 48 counts of aggravated murder. It is estimated that he killed at least 50 women in the Seattle–Tacoma area, most of them prostitutes or runaway teens.

Decidedly less gloomily, hair-metal grunge band Soundgarden is named after a wind-channeling pipe sculpture, the *Sound Garden*, in Seattle's Magnuson Park.

with it) Quincy Jones and his pal Ray Charles would hustle their way into all the clubs and play as much as they could. Nothing of that caliber exists in Seattle anymore, but you can still manage to hear some good jazz and blues. See p155 for a list of live venues.

Classical

Seattle offers a full array of classical music, including well-respected professional symphony and opera companies. The Seattle Symphony is regarded as a major regional orchestra, and its downtown performance hall, the Benaroya Concert Hall (p49), is as gorgeous as it is acoustically exquisite.

The Seattle Opera is another major cultural focus in Seattle. Although it's a regional company, it isn't afraid to tackle weighty or nontraditional works. Productions of Philip Glass and a summer Wagner's *Ring* cycle have given opera lovers a lot to mull over. However, the company is perhaps most noted for its unconventional staging of the traditional repertoire. The Seattle Men's Chorus, a 180-member gay chorus, delights audiences with its 30 concerts each year.

For detailed listings, see p160.

LITERATURE

The pioneers of early Seattle had city building on their minds and didn't exactly fill libraries with weighty tomes. Nonetheless, some of the city's first settlers took time to record chronicles. Arthur Denny, one of the founders of Seattle, wrote *Pioneer Days on Puget Sound* (1908). James Swan wrote *The Northwest Coast* (1869) and *Indians of Cape Flattery* (1870), while *The Canoe and the Saddle* (1863) by Theodore Winthrop recounts a young man's trip across Washington on his way to Seattle in 1853.

One of the most prolific Seattle writers in the early 20th century was Archie Binns. Of his many novels, *The Land Is Bright* (1939), the story of an Oregon Trail family, is still read today. A socio-economic chronicle of Seattle, *The Northwest Gateway* (1941) provides a good, if dated, introduction to Seattle's attitudes toward itself. Meanwhile, Murray Morgan's *Skid Road: An Informal Portrait of Seattle* (1951) enables the quirky characters of pioneer Seattle to come to life. Many of these older books, of course, are out of print, but it's worth asking at libraries and antiquarian bookstores if you're interested in tracking one down.

In the 1960s and '70s, western Washington attracted a number of counterculture writers. The most famous of these (and the best!) is Tom Robbins, whose books, including *Another Roadside Attraction* (1971) and *Even Cowgirls Get the Blues* (1976), are a perfect synthesis of the enlightened braininess, sense of mischief and reverence for beauty that add up to the typical mellow Northwest counterculture vibe.

Having, among other things, a fondness for the Blue Moon Tavern in common with Robbins, poet Theodore Roethke taught for years at the University of Washington, and along with Washington native Richard Hugo (see the box, p159) he cast a profound influence over Northwest poetry.

Raymond Carver, the short-story master whose books include *Will You Please Be Quiet, Please?* (1976) and *Where I'm Calling From* (1988), lived near Seattle on the Olympic Peninsula.

SHERMAN ALEXIE

Sherman Alexie is a 6ft 2in Spokane-Coeur d'Alene Indian with an even-larger-than-life sense of humor and an unshakeable but hard-earned confidence. He grew up on the Spokane Indian Reservation in Wellpinit, Washington. Born hydrocephalic, he wasn't expected to live; at six months of age he had brain surgery and doctors expected he would either die or be mentally handicapped.

What happened was the exact opposite. Alexie became an unstoppable reader and, in his 30s, he became a celebrated writer. He was named one of Granta's '20 Best American Novelists under the Age of 40,' and he has won masses of critical acclaim for his novels, short stories and poetry. Recently he's been writing a number of screenplays, including one for fellow Native American director Chris Eyre's fantastic *Smoke Signals,* and he wrote and directed *The Business of Fancydancing.*

Alexie's readings are the stuff of legend and no one should miss a chance to attend one. Not interested in dry recitals of static texts, Alexie memorizes whatever piece he plans to read, then performs it dramatically, much to the crowd's delight. One of the fascinating things about his public speaking appearances is that, although there's a lot of buried anger in what he says, he is also outrageously funny, which means he can, for example, throw a bunch of scathing lines about crazy, clueless white people to an audience full of white people and make them love it.

Alexie dismisses the idea that his comic presentation might distract listeners from the serious aspects of his work. 'Did Richard Pryor let people off the hook?' he asks. 'Did Lenny Bruce? I'd argue the reverse. I think the reason liberals have so little power is because we're so earnest and the reason the conservatives kick our asses is because they're funny...Give me a right-wing redneck over a vegan any time! Give me Rush Limbaugh over an Earth First-er any night of the week.'

Politics are integral to Alexie's life and work. Whether he likes it or not, he's been saddled with the role of Official Native American Spokesman. You get the idea that sometimes he likes it and sometimes he doesn't at all. 'I'm just who I am,' he says. 'I'm an individual. If anything I hope what I do gets *everybody* to question authority, to be eccentric, to get rowdy, to create art, to follow their dreams. In the end all I hope is that I've celebrated eccentricity.'

Alexie's first short-story collection, *The Lone Ranger and Tonto Fistfight in Heaven,* was published in 1993. In the decade since then, he says, the cultural milieu of Seattle has seen some changes. 'There's a lot more white-collar Indians. There's now what you would call a Native American elite. It's a very visible Indian elite. Because Seattle's so white, we stand out more.'

On the other hand, he says, day-to-day racism is seldom a problem – at least within city limits. 'In Seattle it mostly amounts to getting looked at, and not even that, necessarily. This is a liberal city. I deal with very little overt racism. Once you get outside the Seattle boundaries, that changes. In Seattle you deal with institutional racism. Outside of Seattle you deal with people who might have a gun.'

As for Seattle's literary scene, it continues to thrive: 'It's the only place in the world, I think, where writers are superstars. I get recognized every day.' When he went to the Department of Motor Vehicles to renew his driver's license, he says, they called out his name and he ended up signing autographs. 'I don't think the same thing would happen in Manhattan's DMV.'

If anything, he says, the city's literary bent has intensified. There are a lot of young people getting involved in readings and events, and there are cultural resources like the Richard Hugo House (p158). 'If you love books and want to be in a book town and want to go to a reading every night of the week,' Alexie says, 'you can.'

Carver's stark and grim vision of working-class angst has profoundly affected other young writers of his time. Carver's second wife, Tess Gallagher, also from Port Angeles and a UW alumnus, is a novelist and poet whose books include *At the Owl Woman Saloon* (1997).

Neal Stephenson, a sci-fi writer who initially rose to fame with *Snow Crash* (1992) and is perhaps best known for his three-volume historical epic 'The Baroque Cycle' (2003–04), also lives in Seattle. His original manuscripts now reside in Paul Allen's Science Fiction Museum (p72).

Ivan Doig imagines historical explorations of the Pacific Northwest in his first work of fiction, *The Sea Runners* (1982). In *Winter Brothers* (1980), Doig, who now lives in Seattle, examines the diaries of early Washington writer James Swan, who lived among the Makah Indians on the northern tip of the Olympic Peninsula. Noted travel writer Jonathan Raban, who lived in Seattle for years, then left only to return recently, has written such books as *Coasting* (1987), *Hunting Mister Heartbreak* (1990) and *Badlands* (1996). His novel *Waxwings* (2003) is a fictionalized account of two families of Seattle immigrants.

Annie Dillard, essayist and novelist, wrote about the Northwest in *The Living* (1992), while David Guterson writes about the Puget Sound area and the internment of Japanese Americans during WWII in *Snow Falling on Cedars* (1994).

Sherman Alexie (see the box, p33) is a Native American author whose short-story collection *The Lone Ranger and Tonto Fistfight in Heaven* (1993) was among the first works of popular fiction to discuss reservation life. In 1996 he published *Indian Killer*, a chilling tale of ritual murder set in Seattle, to great critical acclaim. His recent *War Dances*, a collection of poetry and stories, won the 2010 PEN/Faulkner Award for fiction.

The misty environs of western Washington seem to be a fecund habitat for mystery writers. Dashiell Hammett once lived in Seattle, while noted writers JA Jance, Earl Emerson and Frederick D Huebner currently make the Northwest home.

Local historian Bill Speidel, he of the famous Underground Tour (see the box, p26), has written a couple of enthusiastic histories dealing with Seattle's early characters, such as *Doc Maynard: The Man who Invented Seattle* (1978) and *Sons of the Profits* (1967). In *Stepping Westward* (1991), Sallie Tisdale relates her experiences of growing up in the Northwest, with insights into the culture of the region. Timothy Egan's, *The Good Rain* (1991), is an insightful and beautifully written discussion of the Northwest and its people by the local *New York Times* correspondent. Seattle preacher Robert Fulghum made it big as an inspirational writer with *All I Really Need to Know I Learned in Kindergarten* (1988). And, more recently, Fred Moody, former managing editor of the *Seattle Weekly,* synthesized the city's complex history and uncomfortable relationship with its own gradual success in his engaging history-memoir, *Seattle and the Demons of Ambition: A Love Story* (2003).

Local music critic Charles Cross caused a sensation with *Heavier than Heaven* (2001), his intimate biography of Nirvana's Kurt Cobain, and won even greater critical acclaim for his 2005 biography of Jimi Hendrix, *Room Full of Mirrors*. Fearless grunge photographer

top picks

SEATTLE FICTION

- **Black Hole (2005), Charles Burns** A graphic novel compilation of a series that began in 1995, Burns's horrifying but moving story, about a sexually transmitted 'bug' that strikes Seattle youth in the '70s, seriously gets under your skin.
- **Heavier than Heaven (2001), Charles Cross** Editor of the defunct music zine the *Rocket,* Cross uses his nearly unrestricted access to paint a moving portrait of Nirvana's Kurt Cobain.
- **Come as You Are: The Story of Nirvana (1993), Michael Azerrad** A local journalist interviewed the band for this rock bio, recording something like 25 hours of audiotape.
- **Indian Killer (1996), Sherman Alexie** In Alexie's most controversial book, a series of scalping murders of white men threatens to destroy the Indian community.
- **Waxwings (2003), Jonathan Raban** Elegant travel writer Raban illuminates Seattle's recent high-tech boom in a novel that tells the parallel stories of two immigrants.
- **The Terrible Girls (1992), Rebecca Brown** One of Seattle's most prominent contemporary writers dissects the complicated hearts of women in this experimental collection of short stories about lesbian relationships.
- **Another Roadside Attraction (1971), Tom Robbins** A mainstay of the Pacific Northwest counterculture, Robbins' wacky word carnival imagines Jesus alongside a flea circus at a pit stop.

Charles Peterson, with cooperation from musicians including Mudhoney's Steve Turner and Pearl Jam's Eddie Vedder, has published a great book of photos from the heydays of grunge, named after the Mudhoney song *Touch Me I'm Sick* (2003). Greg Prato's oral history *Grunge Is Dead* (2009) lets the musicians and record producers who lived it tell the story of Seattle's music scene in their own words.

One peculiar phenomenon is the relatively large number of cartoonists who live in the Seattle area. Lynda Barry (*Ernie Pook's Comeek, Cruddy*) and Matt Groening (creator of *The Simpsons*) were students together at Olympia's Evergreen State College. Gary Larson, whose *Far Side* animal antics have netted international fame and great fortune, lives in Seattle. A good number of underground comic book artists live here, too, among them the legendary Peter Bagge (*Hate*), Jim Woodring (*The Frank Book*), Charles Burns (*Black Hole*), and Roberta Gregory (*Naughty Bits*). It could well have something to do with the fact that Fantagraphics, a major and influential publisher of underground comics and graphic novels, is based here.

top picks

SEATTLE ART GALLERIES

- **Roq la Rue** (p69) Devoted to showing counterculture art, this Belltown gallery is anything but stodgy.
- **Center on Contemporary Art** (p98) A major force in the Seattle art scene, this artist-run collective makes a point of putting on high-energy, envelope-pushing shows.
- **Greg Kucera Gallery** (Map p56; ☎ 206-624-0770; 212 3rd Ave S) Kucera has been around for 20-plus years and frequently hosts big names – cult filmmaker John Waters, for example – as well as supporting unknown artists in his large gallery.
- **Lawrimore Project** (Map p56; ☎ 206-501-1231; www.lawrimoreproject.com; 831 Airport Way S) A no-holds-barred modern art space, the Lawrimore Project is a big, pliable warehouse-like gallery that consistently has some of the most inventive exhibitions you'll see in Seattle.

VISUAL ARTS

Museums and galleries in Seattle offer a visual-arts experience as varied as the rest of the city's culture. The newly expanded Seattle Art Museum (p48) has a substantial European art collection, a range of modern art that's well suited to its new exhibition spaces, and an impressive collection of native artifacts and folk art, especially carved wooden masks. There's also several exhibition spaces around the city devoted to contemporary Native American carvings and paintings. A considerable Asian art collection is located at the Seattle Asian Art Museum (p80) in Volunteer Park. More experimental and conceptual art is displayed at the University of Washington's Henry Art Gallery (p82) and at the Frye Art Museum (p51).

A specialty of the Puget Sound area is glassblowing, led by a group of inventive and influential artisans known as the Pilchuck School. The most famous of these is Dale Chihuly, whose flamboyant, colorful and unmistakable work is on display at the Benaroya Concert Hall and in a number of galleries.

Pushing the envelope of contemporary art is the specialty of several younger galleries around town, notably Belltown's Roq la Rue (p69) and the Center on Contemporary Art (p98), which also now has a new Belltown gallery space (at 2721 1st Ave). These unconventional spaces display provocative, boundary-distorting artwork of all kinds, usually by unknown or underground artists. They also regularly host rock shows, theatrical performances and film screenings. Check the local weeklies for listings.

The artist-enclave neighborhood of Georgetown (p105) hosts a monthly Art Attack, an art walk through various stops on the hip main drag. It's the second Saturday of the month; for details and a map, visit www.georgetownartattack.com.

Public Art

Seattle is also known for its interesting and plentiful public art. A King County ordinance, established in 1973, stipulates that 1% of all municipal capital-improvement project funds be set aside for public art. The 'one percent for art' clause, which other cities across the nation have

TOTEM POLES OF THE NORTHWEST COAST

Though Puget Sound tribes did not typically carve them, totem poles are found along the Northwest Pacific Coast, roughly between northern Washington state and Alaska. Carved from a single cedar log by the Haida, Tlingit, Tsimshian and Kwakiutl tribes, totem poles identify a household's lineage in the same way a family crest might identify a group or clan in Europe, although the totem pole is more of a historical pictograph depicting the entire ancestry. Like a family crest, totem poles imply a sense of prestige and prosperity.

Totems serve a variety of functions: freestanding poles welcome visitors to a waterfront or village; a memorial pole is often erected outside a deceased chief's home; and mortuary poles are implanted with a box of the honored individual's decomposed remains. Incorporated into the design of a house, totem poles also appear as house posts and front doors. Shame poles, carved with upside-down figures denoting social or ritual transgressions, were temporary fixtures and are found only in museums today. Traditional poles vary greatly in height, though rarely exceed 60ft. Modern poles can be much taller. The world's tallest totem pole at Alert Bay in British Columbia is 173ft.

Despite the saying 'low man on the totem pole,' the most important figures are usually at eye level; figures at the bottom usually have an integral, grounding function that supports the rest of the pole. Figures can represent individuals, spirits, births, deaths, catastrophes or legends.

Unless you're an expert, it's not so easy to identify what's what on a totem. Here are a few rules of thumb. Birds are always identified with a pronounced beak: ravens have a straight, mid-sized beak; eagles have a short, sharp, down-turned beak; hawks have a short, down-turned beak that curls inward. Bears usually have large, square teeth, while beavers have sharp incisors and a cross-stitched tail. A few animals appear as if viewed from overhead. For example, killer whales' fins protrude outward from the poles as if their heads face downward. Long-snouted wolves also face downward, as do frogs. Pointy-headed sharks (or dogfish), with grimacing mouths full of sharp teeth, face upward, as do humpback whales.

Though totem symbols are usually interconnected and complex, these animals possess certain undeniable characteristics:

- beaver – industriousness, wisdom and determined independence
- black bear – a protector, guardian and spiritual link between humans and animals
- eagle – intelligence and power
- frog – adaptability; ability to live in both natural and supernatural worlds
- hummingbird – love, beauty and unity with nature
- killer whale – dignity and strength; often a reincarnated spirit of a great chief
- raven – mischief and cunning; the perennial trickster
- salmon – dependable sustenance, longevity and perseverance; a powerful symbol
- shark – ominous, fierce and solitary
- thunderbird – strong, supernatural; the wisdom of proud ancestors

since adopted, has given Seattle an extensive collection of artworks ranging from monumental sculpture and landscape design to individualized sewer hole covers.

Fremont is a good place to start looking for examples of off-beat and often inspired public art in Seattle. Fremont boasts, among other things, the *Waiting for the Interurban* sculpture (p88), a community centerpiece often decorated with politically pointed costumes and trappings.

All of the county's public artwork is commissioned through a public process. A panel of artists and project and city planners gets together to choose an artist out of thousands of applicants. Keep your eyes open and your art radar on high. You'll find public art throughout Seattle, in the metro bus tunnels, in public parks, on building walls and embedded in the sidewalks.

CINEMA & TELEVISION

Seattle has come a long way as a movie mecca since the days when Elvis starred in the 1963 film *It Happened at the World's Fair,* a chestnut of civic boosterism. Films with Seattle as their backdrop include *Tugboat Annie* (1933); *Cinderella Liberty* (1974), a steamy romance with James Caan and Marsha Mason; and *The Parallax View* (1974) with Warren Beatty. Jessica Lange's movie *Frances,* about the horrible fate of outspoken local actor Frances Farmer (she was jailed on questionable pretenses, then institutionalized for years and eventually lobotomized), was shot here in 1981. Debra Winger's hit *Black Widow* (1986) shows many scenes shot at the University of Washington.

John Cusack starred in *Say Anything* (1989), Michelle Pfeiffer and Jeff Bridges did it up in *The Fabulous Baker Boys* (1989), and Sly Stallone and Antonio Banderas flopped in *Assassins* (1995), all partly filmed in and around Seattle. Horror hit *The Ring* and JLo vehicle *Enough* both had a few scenes shot in Seattle and on local ferries.

The two most famous (until recently) Seattle movies happened when the city was at the peak of its cultural cachet in the '90s: *Singles* (1992), with Campbell Scott, Kyra Sedgwick, Matt Dillon and Bridget Fonda, captured the city's youthful-slacker vibe. (Incidentally, both *Singles* and *Say Anything* were directed by Cameron Crowe, who is married to Seattle rock band Heart's Nancy Wilson.) And then there was *Sleepless in Seattle*, the 1993 blockbuster starring Tom Hanks, Meg Ryan and, perhaps more importantly, Seattle's Lake Union houseboats. As a Seattle-based film phenomenon, however, nothing tops the tween-vampire soap opera *Twilight* and its sequels, set in the town of Forks (p198). See the box, p38, for more on this phenomenon.

Sherman Alexie, having brought mainstream national attention to the city as a literary center, has expanded into the realm of filmmaking as well. *Smoke Signals* (1998), which Alexie wrote based on one of his short stories, starred Adam Beach and was directed by Chris Eyre. An entirely Native American effort, it was a huge success. For his follow-up, *The Business of Fancydancing* (2002), Alexie both wrote the screenplay and directed the film.

Some interesting documentaries have also been produced here. *Dragon: The Bruce Lee Story* follows the career of the one-time Seattle resident. *Hype!* (1996) is a documentary about the explosion of underground music in the Northwest and the resulting fallout, with lots of interviews and great live-music footage. On the other end of the spectrum is the always controversial English rabble-rouser Nick Broomfield's 1998 film *Kurt & Courtney*, which delves without restraint into the troubled lives of Seattle's one-time king and queen of rock.

The locally filmed *Zoo* (2007) is a documentary co-written by *Stranger* columnist Charles Mudede about a community of, ahem, extreme animal lovers that was inspired by news reports of a man's death after an unusually close encounter with a horse. The excellent and critically acclaimed documentary *Iraq in Fragments*, shown at Sundance, was filmed in Iraq and directed by Seattle filmmaker James Longley. In late 2007 came *Battle in Seattle*, a locally filmed feature about the WTO riots starring Charlize Theron, Woody Harrelson, Ray Liotta and Michelle Rodriguez. The scrappy *Sonicsgate: Requiem for a Team* (2009) looks at how Seattle lost its NBA team through some underhanded dealings.

TV's *Northern Exposure*, filmed in nearby Roslyn, Washington, and *Frasier* both did a lot to boost Seattle's reputation as a hip and youthful place to live. The creepy, darker side of the Northwest was captured in the moody *Twin Peaks: Fire Walk with Me*. And let's not forget, of course, MTV's *The Real World: Seattle*.

THEATER

Seattle has one of the most dynamic theater scenes in the country. There are reportedly more equity theaters in Seattle than anywhere in the US, except New York City. This abundance of venues provides the city with a range of classical and modern dramatic theater. Check out the Arts chapter (p159) for detailed listings.

In addition to quality professional theater, the city also offers a wide array of amateur and special-interest troupes, including both gay and lesbian theater groups, puppet theaters, children's theater troupes, cabarets and plenty of alternative theaters staging fringe plays by

top picks

SEATTLE FILMS

- The Twilight Saga: Eclipse (2010) Vampires roam Seattle in this third installment in the tween saga, though it was actually filmed in Vancouver, BC.
- Sleepless in Seattle (1993) Meg Ryan and Tom Hanks are irresistibly adorable in this riff on *An Affair to Remember*.
- Singles (1992) Attractive slackers deal with apartment life and love. Look for cameos by Pearl Jam's Eddie Vedder, Soundgarden's Chris Cornell and other local celebrities.
- Twin Peaks: Fire Walk with Me (1992) David Lynch rolls his warped eye toward the dark underbelly of the Northwest.
- Say Anything (1989) John Cusack instantly became everyone's dream boyfriend with his boom-box serenade.
- Hype! (1996) An excellent time capsule of the grunge years.

TWI-HARDS WITH A VENGEANCE

If you or someone close to you is female and between the ages of, oh, say 12 and 65, you've probably heard about the *Twilight* phenomenon. Stephenie Meyer's series of young-adult vampire-romance books – and, even more so, the movies based on them – are a pop-culture powerhouse that has drawn nationwide attention to a very unlikely, mossy, rainy little corner of the world and reshaped the economy of an entire small town.

Though the movies were actually filmed mostly in Vancouver, BC, they're set in the town of Forks, on the Olympic Peninsula (p197). Until recently, people visited Forks on their way to somewhere else – a hike through the Hoh Rain Forest or along the rugged beaches of the Northwest Coast. But these days, the most prominent feature on the Forks visitor center website (www.forkswa.com) is the one that says 'Home of Twilight.' In the wake of the books and films, Forks is no longer a means to an end; it's a destination in its own right. According to the Chamber of Commerce, the number of visitors who came through town increased 400% between 2008 and 2009.

This much of an upswing in traffic, naturally, has had a profound effect on the small town. Before *Twilight*, Forks was a sleepy, one-stoplight lumber town struggling to get through the economic recession. Now it feels like a buzzy tourist mecca, and the energy is palpable. Aside from the occasional grumble, locals have embraced the *Twilight* phenomenon and the jolt it's given their economy. Restaurants and coffee shops have *Twilight*-themed items on the menu, hotels offer *Twilight* suites, there's an annual 'Bella's Birthday' party in town, the visitors center gives *Twilight* tours, and locals have enthusiastically signposted key sites from the series, including Bella's house, the Cullens' house and the hospital where Dr Cullen works.

If a fondness for vampires and werewolves brings you out here, make the most of your visit: check out the nearby Hoh Rain Forest and the beaches of La Push, and ask about hikes or scenic drives in the area. After all, it was the natural beauty of the Olympic Peninsula that inspired the series in the first place.

local playwrights. The arts and culture sections of local papers will have the most up-to-date listings and recommendations.

DANCE

Seattle is home to the nationally noted and famously well-attended Pacific Northwest Ballet, considered one of the nation's five best ballet companies. It's justifiably renowned for its performance of *The Nutcracker*, which it has been doing since 1983.

Seattle is a springboard for dancers. The modern dance pioneer Merce Cunningham was born and raised in nearby Centralia and was trained at Cornish College in Seattle. Choreographer Mark Morris, known for his fusion of classical and modern dance, is native to Seattle and has worked everywhere from small opera houses to Broadway and now works mostly in Europe. New York-based avant-garde dancer Trisha Brown is originally from Aberdeen, Washington, and classical ballet choreographer Robert Joffrey hails from Seattle.

Keep an eye out for UW's annual World Series (☎ 206-543-4880, 800-859-5342; www.uwworldseries.org) of music, performance and dance from all over the world. Smaller dance groups, such as On the Boards (www.ontheboards.org), which performs at the Behnke Center for Contemporary Performance (Map p75; ☎ 206-217-9888; 100 W Roy St), bring an exciting, experimental edge to the city's dance scene.

ARCHITECTURE

Architecturally, Seattle is as notable for what is missing as for what remains. The Great Fire of 1889 ravaged the old wooden storefronts of downtown, which were replaced by the stone and brick structures around the city's old center in Pioneer Square. Architect Elmer Fisher is responsible for more than 50 buildings erected immediately after the fire. Any Victorian places that escaped the Great Fire did not escape the Denny Regrade (1899–1912), which flattened a steep residential hill in order to make room for more downtown commercial properties.

Seattle's next big building phase came in the early decades of the 20th century. The beaux arts and art-deco hospitals that fill the skyline on First and Beacon Hills are good examples of the civic buildings of that era. Smith Tower (p57), near Pioneer Square, was built in 1914, and with 42 stories it was for many years the tallest building in the world outside of New York City. The campanile-like tower of white terra-cotta brick is still one of the city's beauties. Also during this ime, Capitol and Queen Anne hills were filled with homes of the popular Georgian, Federal, English, and Arts and Crafts styles.

More recent additions to the downtown skyline include the West Coast's tallest building, the Columbia Center (formerly Columbia Seafirst Center, then the Bank of America Building; see p49), a monolith with no other distinction than its 76-story shadow. Six others rise higher than 50 stories. Only the Washington Mutual Building, with its plaid-like facade and turquoise glass, makes a pleasant impression.

As the architectural icon of Seattle, no other modern structure comes close to the Space Needle (p71). Built for the 1962 World's Fair, its sleek but whimsical design has aged amazingly well. Perhaps the most controversial addition to Seattle architecture is the Frank Gehry–designed Experience Music Project (p72), which has a curvy metallic design that caused quite a commotion. The city's sparkliest architectural jewel at the moment, though, is the almost universally admired Seattle Public Library building (p49).

ENVIRONMENT & PLANNING

Environmental issues in many ways dominate life in the Pacific Northwest. Seattle was founded on resource-extracting industries. The city's first major employer was a sawmill, and the ability to export the area's wealth in timber was key in the city's development. Fishing Puget Sound and the area's rivers for salmon was also a major source of employment, especially for immigrant workers from Japan and Scandinavia. Today, endangered fish runs, especially of seagoing salmon, top the list of environmental concerns. While jet manufacturing and software dominate Seattle's present economy, the older resource-based industries continue to be an active feature of the city's economic and political landscape.

Seattle sits right alongside the Cascadia Subduction Zone, one of the earth's most active seismic regions. Beneath the Strait of Juan de Fuca, two tectonic plates – the North American Plate and the Juan de Fuca Plate – struggle against each other, grinding away as the North American Plate slides underneath, causing pressure to build and the earth to rumble. The most recent of these rumblings happened on February 28, 2001, when an earthquake measuring 6.8 on the Richter scale rocked the Seattle area. The quake caused one death, rang up more than $2 billion in damages and caused some dramatic geological change. The earthquake narrowed the Duwamish River by a few inches, shifted Seattle about a fifth of an inch to the south-southwest and pushed the Eastside about a third of an inch further east.

A snapshot of this area taken 60 million years ago would show a vista of jumbled offshore islands, low coastal mountains and marine marshlands invaded by the shallow Pacific. Plants and animals thrived in the tropical climate, which extended inland unobstructed by mountains. Coastal sediments and offshore islands started wedging together, forming today's Olympic Range and setting the stage for three intense periods of volcanic activity, which would utterly change the face of the region. The line of volcanoes that shot up as the Cascade Range caused enormous explosions of lava, ash and mud. The region's most recent volcanic activity drew worldwide attention in 1980 when Mt St Helens, just 150 miles south of Seattle, blew her top, killing 57 people and spreading ash through five states and three Canadian provinces. Volcanic activity continues in the region.

The land on which Seattle now stands was once dense forest, and the waters of Puget Sound and the freshwater lakes that surround the city once teemed with wildlife. While metropolitan Seattle hardly accounts for a natural ecosystem, you don't have to go far from the center of the city to find vestiges of the wild Pacific Northwest.

GREEN SEATTLE

In keeping with its 'green' reputation, Seattle has one of the most comprehensive curbside recycling programs in the USA. Depending on where Seattleites live, their recycling is picked up either weekly or monthly. The cost is included in the price of regular garbage collection. Recycling here is easy. As such, you won't find anyone chucking a tin can or ditching a plastic bottle. Coffee drinkers basically boycott Styrofoam, and don't be surprised if somebody scolds you for littering.

Even if you're just visiting and don't have access to curbside recycling, it's easy to find a place to recycle the cans, bottles and papers that accumulate as you travel. Most public areas and food courts will have separate recycling bins for various kinds of products. See the Getting Started chapter (p20) for more on how you can contribute to the city's ecofriendliness.

Other contentious environmental issues that get locals' ire up include the history and continued practice of logging in old-growth forests, the fate of endangered salmon and the much-publicized protection of the endangered spotted owl and its natural habitat.

URBAN PLANNING & DEVELOPMENT

Seattle's spectacular economic and population growth during the '90s altered the city's political landscape in ways that still cause problems. Partly due to the explosive growth of Microsoft – and the sudden young millionaires its stock options created – Seattle faced outrageous real estate bidding wars and a glut of traffic.

Transportation is still one of the city's thorniest issues. With the Puget Sound area's population growing fast, the transportation infrastructure simply isn't holding up. Traffic jams are often horrendous, due partly to topography but also to the lack of effective planning for public transportation. Voters continually swing back and forth in support of funding light-rail commuter trains, but inevitably a glitch keeps the construction at bay. However, things are looking up. In May 2007, the Sound Transit board gave final approval to a set of long-range plans that will add some 50 miles of light-rail extensions around the city.

The skyrocketing cost of housing in Seattle is also a major political and social concern. Seattle is playing catch-up with urban growth and land-use planning. The city's rapid growth, especially on the Eastside, has turned thousands of acres of farmland into anonymous tract developments, and the suburbs are rolling up to the foothills of the Cascades. In the Bellevue suburb of Medina, where Bill Gates built his 48,000-sq-ft mansion, a limit is now enforced on how many 'mega houses' are allowed. For an example of creative and artistic land use, check out the Olympic Sculpture Park (p67) tucked between high-rises and a highway at the edge of Belltown.

GOVERNMENT & POLITICS

Seattle is governed by a mayor and a nine-person city council. All city council members are elected to four-year terms on an at-large basis, meaning they are not assigned to a specific council district. Although city posts are nonpartisan, political ideology in Seattle dependably veers to the left-leaning side of the Democratic Party.

Greg Nickels was elected mayor in 2001 and won a second term in 2005. During his time in office he strengthened the role of the mayor and made transportation a top priority. Mike McGinn succeeded Nickels in January 2010, having campaigned on a platform that focused on the tunnel plan to replace the Alaskan Way Viaduct.

MEDIA

Seattle's daily print newspaper is the *Seattle Times*. For several years it ran under a joint-operating agreement with the city's other daily, the *Seattle Post-Intelligencer*, meaning that all advertising, production, marketing and circulation operations, as well as most business functions for both papers, were shared (and managed by the Seattle Times Company, part of Heart Corp), while the news and editorial operations of the two newspapers were separate and competitive. The joint operating agreement was a source of constant friction between the two papers, but it continued until the *Post-Intelligencer* ended print publication in March 2009. (It still runs an active website.)

The city also has a lively alternative publishing scene, led by one of the best alt-weeklies in the nation, the *Stranger* (www.seattleweekly.com). Started by Tim Keck (once of the *Onion*), it's a valuable source for an irreverent take on politics, underground culture, film and music information, and is also a great guide to the clubs. It's edited by 'Savage Love' columnist Dan Savage.

The *Seattle Gay News*, referred to mostly as *SGN*, covers the gay and lesbian scene. The *Seattle Weekly* is the baby-boom generation's alternative news. It has full listings of arts and entertainment and investigative pieces exposing city hall's bad guys.

The arts scene receives thorough coverage from *CityArts* magazine, a glossy monthly available free in all the usual places. It contains refreshingly long feature stories about everything arts-related in the area, from galleries to music, as well as events listings and snippets of arts news. The magazine sponsors a monthly First Thursday Art Walk Awards program, held in a different gallery or venue each month, and an occasional live-music question-and-answer show; check its website (www.cityartsonline.com) for the latest events.

It would be unseemly to mention Seattle radio without a shout-out to KEXP (90.3 FM), one of the best radio stations in the country. It used to be the UW station, but has taken off and become internationally known online, particularly for its promotion of world music.

The University of Washington's news-oriented National Public Radio (NPR) affiliate is heard on KUOW at 94.9 FM (which also carries the BBC World Service). See the Directory chapter (p207) for a list of Seattle's favorite commercial radio stations.

FASHION

Once upon a time, Seattle ruled the freak-fashion world. Even as recently as the early '90s, youth culture was marked by bizarre, usually homemade, always parent-upsetting fashion creations that expressed…*something,* whether it was angst, sexuality, gloom or simple frustration. Then came grunge, the fashion that ate itself. It's odd to imagine that an aesthetic so absent of effort would be so easily and instantly co-opted by the mainstream, but it was. Very soon after Nirvana hit it big, major fashion designers were dressing catwalk models in ripped clothes, long johns and unwashed hair. It's almost no wonder much of Seattle has opted for more of a Banana Republic-Nordstrom brand of chic over anything new that might call attention to itself.

The default Pacific Northwest outfit, of course, consists of outdoorsy, rain-friendly REI practicality. People wear yoga pants, Teva sandals and polar fleece to dinner. But it's still easy to find pierced, dyed and tattooed specimens here, mostly in Capitol Hill, Georgetown and the U District. The young and hip will dress to the nines to go out on the town: whether that means satin and heels, plaid zippered bondage pants or a perfectly aged, faded-black vintage Aerosmith T-shirt. And there are a number of young, hip fashion designers selling their wares at chic boutiques around town. Go to the Shopping chapter (p107) for more.

LANGUAGE

English is spoken by the overwhelming majority in Seattle, but there are a number of Asian languages spoken, particularly in the International District, where signs on shop fronts frequently don't include an English translation. Several Native American languages are also spoken and taught here, such as the Duwamish dialect Lushootseed, a branch of the Salishan language family. Many tribes in the region have devoted themselves to the preservation and growth of these endangered languages.

NEIGHBORHOODS

top picks

- **Seattle Art Museum** (p48)
  SAM is settling into its expanded space, with exciting, up-to-the-minute exhibits complementing a strong permanent collection.
- **Pike Place Market** (p62)
  One of those mandatory sights — everybody does it, but there's a good reason for that.
- **Woodland Park Zoo** (p94)
  A classic family outing and one of the nicest zoos in the country.
- **Seattle Asian Art Museum** (p80)
  An extensive collection in an interesting space.
- **Henry Art Gallery** (p82)
  Small but impeccably curated university gallery.

What's your recommendation? www.lonelyplanet.com/seattle

In Seattle, neighborhood is everything. Though the city is actually very compact, each area has its own distinct feel, and the different parts of town can seem worlds apart. This is most likely because of the disconnected terrain: before bridges and ferries made it easy to navigate the canal and lakes, most people just stayed close to home, resulting in the outlying neighborhoods being pretty isolated. That's why Ballard still feels like a Scandinavian fishing village, Chinatown feels like Chinatown and Capitol Hill could be its very own artsy, freewheeling universe. Today, though, it's easy to get around

'Ballard still feels like a Scandinavian fishing village, Chinatown feels like Chinatown and Capitol Hill its own artsy, freewheeling universe.'

the city, and it's fun to compare and contrast the various neighborhoods beyond the downtown core. The primary hassle will be finding a parking place, so it's highly recommended that visitors use public transportation to reach sights within the city center. See the Transportation chapter (p199) for details about how to get around the city using public transportation.

Of course, that's not to say visitors should neglect downtown itself. Downtown Seattle sits on a long isthmus between Lake Washington and Elliott Bay. Short-term visitors will probably spend most of their time here. North of Seattle's downtown area is another freshwater body, Lake Union. The lakes are linked to Puget Sound by the canals and locks of the Lake Washington Ship Canal. Although Seattle is a major Pacific port, the ocean is 125 miles away, which can be a little confusing because there's water everywhere. It's a good idea to look at a map to see how all the bodies of water connect, and trace the long route that ships must sail from Seattle to the open seas.

The downtown area butts up against Elliott Bay and encompasses the financial and shopping areas, First Hill, Pioneer Square, Pike Place Market, the Waterfront and Belltown. Seattle Center, with many of Seattle's cultural and sports facilities and attractions, including the Space Needle, is just to the north. West of Seattle Center is funky Lower Queen Anne, which is connected to Upper Queen Anne by Seattle's steepest hill. East of Seattle Center is gritty Capitol Hill, the city's gay quarter and hub of youthful urban culture. The Central District, Madison Valley, Madison Park and Madrona are residential neighborhoods on the east side of the Seattle peninsula.

Lake Union and the Lake Washington Ship Canal divide the city into northern and southern halves. The northern neighborhoods include the U District (named for the University of Washington campus), Wallingford, Fremont and Ballard. Each of these areas has a lively commercial center filled with restaurants, shops and bars. Just north of Fremont and Wallingford is Green Lake, the focal point of a large park area that also contains the city zoo.

To the west of Seattle, across Elliott Bay, is another peninsula, appropriately named West Seattle. This is where the original pioneer settlers founded Seattle.

It's worth noting that four bridges (besides the freeway bridges) cross the ship canal. The University and Montlake Bridges connect neighborhoods south of the canal with the U District. West of Lake Union, the Fremont Bridge crosses from Queen Anne to Fremont. The westernmost, Ballard Bridge, links the neighborhood of Magnolia, west of Queen Anne, with Ballard.

ITINERARY BUILDER

The table below allows you to plan a day's worth of activities in any area of the city. Simply select which area you wish to explore, and then mix and match from the corresponding listings to build your day. The first item in each cell represents a well-known highlight of the area, while the other items are more off-the-beaten-track gems.

AREA ACTIVITIES	Sights	Eating	Shopping
Downtown & First Hill	Seattle Art Museum (p48) Seattle Public Library (p49) Frye Art Museum (p51)	Wild Ginger (p122) FareStart Restaurant (p122) Georgian (p122)	Macy's (p108) Nordstrom (p108) Niketown (p108)
Pioneer Square	Klondike Gold Rush Historical Park (p55) Pioneer Square Park (p57) Smith Tower (p57)	Salumi (p123) Zaina (p123) Bakeman's (p123)	Foster/White Gallery (p109) North Face (p110) Pioneer Square Antique Mall (p109)
International District	Wing Luke Museum of the Asian Pacific American Experience (p59) Hau Hau Market (p61) Hing Hay Park (p61)	House of Hong (p124) Pho Bac (p125) Tamarind Tree (p124)	Kinokuniya (p110) Uwajimaya (p110) Pacific Herb & Grocery (p61)
Pike Place Market & Waterfront	Pike Place Market (p62) Seattle Aquarium (p66) Victor Steinbrueck Park (p66)	Café Campagne (p126) Steelhead Diner (p126) Chez Shea (p126)	Left Bank Books (p110) Made in Washington (p111) Metsker Maps (p111)
Belltown	Olympic Sculpture Park (p67) Roq la Rue (p69) Crocodile Café (p69)	Dahlia Lounge (p127) Black Bottle (p128) Shiro's Sushi Restaurant (p127)	Patagonia (p112) Singles Going Steady (p112) Elliott Bay Bicycles (p112)
Seattle Center & Queen Anne	Space Needle (p71) Experience Music Project (p72) Pacific Science Center (p73)	Canlis (p129) Paragon Bar & Grill (p129) 5 Spot (p129)	Channel 9 Store (p112) Once Upon a Time (p112) Queen Anne Books (p112)
Capitol Hill & Volunteer Park	Seattle Asian Art Museum (p80) Jimi Hendrix Statue (p80)	Sitka & Spruce (p130) Coastal Kitchen (p130) Café Presse (p130)	Babeland (p113) Sonic Boom (p114) Wall of Sound (p114)
U District	Henry Art Gallery (p82) Burke Museum (p82) Suzzallo Library (p84)	Cedars Restaurant (p131) Flowers (p131) Agua Verde Café (p131)	Bulldog News & Espresso (p115) Hardwick's Hardware Store (p115) Recycled Cycles (p114)

GREATER SEATTLE

Carkeek Park

Underwater Sports

NE Northgate Way

Lake City

522

5

North Beach

Holman Rd NW

Lake City Way NE

Sand Point Way NE

Magnuson Park

Golden Gardens Park

99

N 80th St

N 80th St

NE 75th St

15

Shilshole Bay

7

NE 65th St

24th Ave NW

8th Ave NW

Phinney Ridge

Winona Ave N

NE 55th St

Discovery Park

Ballard

NW 65th St

Green Lake

Woodland Park Zoo

Green Lake

Laurelhurst Playfield

Fort Lawton Military Reservation

NW 54th St

N 50th St

NE 45th St

15th Ave NE

Roosevelt Way NE

12th Ave NE

25th Ave NE

Discovery Park

Gilman Ave W

Thorndyke Ave W

15th Ave W

W Nickerson St

6

Fremont

Fremont Ave N

Aurora Ave N

Stone Way N

10

Wallingford

U District

University of Washington

Foster Island

520

4

Salmon Bay

W Emerson St

Broadmoor Golf Club

Foster Island

34th Ave W

Magnolia Blvd W

Queen Anne

Lake Union

Eastlake Ave E

Harvard Ave E

3

Broadmoor Golf Club

Puget Sound

W Galer St

14

4th Ave N

Westlake Ave N

Capitol Hill

15th Ave E

10th Ave E

E Madison St

23rd Ave E

Madrona

Lake Washington

Mercer St

13

Belltown

Madison Park

Lake Washington Blvd

2

Ferries to Bainbridge Island

11

5

Downtown

Madison Park

E Cherry St

17

Ferries to Bremerton

12

90

Ferries to Vashon Island

Elliott Bay

S Holgate St

Mercer Island

Alki Beach

Alki Ave SW

Harbor Ave SW

West Waterway

Harbor Island

Alaskan Way S

1st Ave S

4th Ave S

Airport Way S

Rainier Ave S

23rd Ave S

Lake Washington Blvd S

Lake Park Dr S

Beach Dr SW

West Seattle

West Seattle Fwy

99

West Marginal Way SW

S Spokane St

Mount Baker Park

California Ave SW

Delridge Way SW

Georgetown

8

Jefferson Park Golf Course

Beacon Ave S

Columbia

Martin Luther King Jr Way S

S Orcas St

Seward Park

Lincoln Park

35th Ave SW

S Lucile St

15th Ave S

Rainier Valley

S Michigan St

South Seattle Community College

5

Museum of Flight

Rainier Ave S

Lake Washington

Boeing Field/King Co International Airport

Duwamish River

To Sea-Tac Airport (15mi)

Lake Washington

DOWNTOWN & FIRST HILL

Shopping p108, Eating p121, Drinking p140, Sleeping p174

Downtown Seattle is a bit of an anomaly. Instead of being the beating heart of the city, it's a fairly quiet, functional business district adjacent to Seattle's twin hearts: Pike Place Market and Pioneer Square. What most people mean by 'downtown' is the collection of office buildings, hotels and retail shops between 2nd and 7th Aves. It's best to visit on a weekday, when throngs of people are working and shopping in the area. At night and on weekends, this part of town feels rather desolate.

Flanked to the south by Pioneer Square and to the north by Belltown (also referred to sometimes as the Denny Regrade), today's city center is bordered to the east by First Hill, where Seattle's pioneer elite built elaborate mansions with views of downtown and Elliott Bay. The jungle of high-rises teetering on Seattle's steep streets makes downtown look very imposing when viewed from a distance. The city seems especially daunting on the incoming ferry ride from Puget Sound or when you first glimpse it from the I-5. The actual core, however, is quite compact. No part of downtown is more than a brisk 20-minute walk from another, and the multiple transit options make it easy to get around. Be warned that abrupt uphill or one-way streets and expensive and limited parking make driving downtown a little hectic. Parking around here is pure hell; instead of driving, take one of a dozen or more buses that serve downtown, stopping at 3rd Ave and Union St and several other stops. Any bus that says 'downtown' on the front will get you here.

Downtown is home to much of the city's important charming architecture – it's worth following the 'Downtown Architecture' walking tour (p52) for a closer look. Seattle's retail heaven extends from the corner of 5th Ave and Pike St two or three blocks in all directions. A block north, on 5th Ave at Pine St, is the flagship store of Nordstrom, the national clothing retailer that got its start in Seattle. Just to the west of Nordstrom is Westlake Center.

Across Pine St, the pedestrian plaza at Westlake Center is a popular people-watching haven and a great place to plop down on a bench and eat lunch or sip coffee on sunny days. Skateboarders and bike messengers careen through crowds of trench-coat-clad professionals and shoppers teetering under the weight of their bags. Buskers pipe out songs, entrepreneurs hawk T-shirts, and preachers bellow fire and brimstone. Don't miss artist Robert Maki's water sculpture, which you can walk through without getting wet.

First Hill, with its commanding position directly to the east and above downtown, became the foremost status neighborhood for early Seattleites. Throughout the area you'll still find traces of the early glory, including a few magnificent old mansions and some excellent examples of early Seattle architecture. But most mansions of the once mighty have long since been torn down and replaced by hospitals. Now nicknamed 'Pill Hill,' First Hill is home to three major hospitals. With the accompanying research and support facilities, it can seem that practically everything up here is related to the medical industry. But there's also a good museum and a historical hotel worth visiting.

To reach First Hill, catch bus 2 on the west side of 3rd Ave downtown and get off at the Swedish Medical Center. First Hill is out of the Ride Free Area, however, so be prepared to pay up if you take the bus from here. On foot, First Hill is a short walk uphill from downtown. From Westlake Center, head over to University St and walk uphill through Freeway Park or, if you're in the business district, walk straight up Madison St to Terry Ave, and you will be at the Sorrento Hotel.

DOWNTOWN

SEATTLE ART MUSEUM Map p50

SAM; ☎ 206-654-3100; www.seattleartmuseum.org; 1300 1st Ave; adult/senior/student/child $15/12/9/ free, admission free 1st Thu of month; � 10am-5pm Wed & Sat-Sun, 10am-9pm Thu & Fri

Since its 2007 expansion, the Seattle Art Museum has twice as much gallery space

and a lot of new art to show off – to the tune of about $1 billion worth of gifts and 1000 new acquisitions. The original Robert Venturi–designed building of limestone and ornamented terra-cotta (with Jonathan Borofsky's enormous moving sculpture, *Hammering Man,* at its front door) contains 150,000 sq ft of space. Architect Brad Cloepfil's design expanded the museum

NEIGHBORHOODS DOWNTOWN & FIRST HILL

into the adjoining Washington Mutual building, adding 118,000 sq ft, including a number of new spaces that are free to the public.

The sense of excitement is palpable from the museum's entrance up to the main floors. Above the ticket counter hangs Chinese artist Cai Guo-Qiang's *Inopportune: Stage One* – a series of white cars exploding with neon. Between the two museum entrances is the 'art ladder,' a free space with various art installations cascading down a wide-stepped hallway.

Moving up into the galleries, two of the first things that you will see are Andy Warhol's painting of Elvis and an enormous sculpture by Korean artist Do-Ho Suh, *Some/One*, a cloak made of thousands of dog tags. Nearby is a room that's dedicated to the work of Harlem Renaissance painter Jacob Lawrence, who spent his last 30 years in Seattle, and to Gwendolyn Knight, his wife and fellow painter. There are also now dedicated spaces for the museum's impressive collections of masks, canoes and totems from Northwest coastal Indian tribes, as well as collections of Australian Aboriginal art and American and Native American textiles. There's a huge glass and porcelain showroom, and, on the top floor, the Italian Room – an entire reassembled room of carved wood and leaded glass from Chiavenna, northern Italy, originally built around 1600. And, of course, there's also a chic museum restaurant.

If you're thinking of multiple visits, consider a museum membership (adult/senior/student $65/35/30), which includes unlimited free admission to SAM, the Seattle Asian Art Museum and the Olympic Sculpture Park; travelers from 60 or more miles outside Seattle get a $10 discount.

SEATTLE PUBLIC LIBRARY Map p50
☎ 206-386-4636; www.spl.org; 1000 4th Ave; admission free; ☼ 10am-8pm Mon-Thu, 10am-6pm Fri & Sat, noon-6pm Sun

There's not much chance you'll miss glimpsing the Seattle Public Library, but it's worth going inside for a closer look. Designed by Rem Koolhaas and LMN Architects, the $165.5 million sculpture of glass and steel was designed to serve as a community gathering space, a tech center, a reading room and, of course, a whole bunch of book storage. The main room, on Level 3, has especially high ceilings, a teen

center, small gift shop and coffee stand. There's an underground level for parking ($9 Mon-Fri, $6 Sat-Sun). Near the top is the Seattle Room, a 12,000-sq-ft reading room with 40ft glass ceilings. It has amazing light, nice views of downtown and seating for up to 400 people.

But the importance of the building's function certainly hasn't cost it anything in the form department. In short, it looks awesome, as striking as any other building in the city including the Space Needle. The overall style of the place is as far from stodgy as you can possibly get – sort of like when that sexy librarian finally takes off her spectacles. Lemon-yellow escalators, hot pink chairs and zippy wi-fi connections make for a modern, tech-friendly experience. There are also 132 research computers available in the Mixing Chamber, where librarians in teams help with in-depth research. And the Book Spiral, spanning several floors, holds most of the library's nonfiction books organized by the Dewey decimal system with numbers marked on small mats on the floor. Guests can take free one-hour group tours (for a schedule, see the website) or a self-guided podcast tour.

BENAROYA CONCERT HALL Map p50
☎ 206-215-9494; 200 University St

With a hefty bill of almost $120 million in construction costs, it's no wonder the Benaroya Concert Hall, Seattle Symphony's primary venue, oozes luxury. From the minute you step into the glass-enclosed lobby of the performance hall you're overwhelmed with views of Elliott Bay; on clear days you might be lucky enough to see the snowy peaks of the Olympic Range far in the distance. Even if you're not attending the symphony, you can walk through the foyer and marvel at the 20ft-long chandeliers, specially created by Tacoma glassmaker Dale Chihuly.

COLUMBIA CENTER Map p50
☎ 206-386-5151; 701 5th Ave; observation deck $5; ☼ 8:30am-4:30pm Mon-Fri

Formerly the Columbia Seafirst Center, then the Bank of America Tower, this striking structure is also known as the 'Darth Vader' building. Catch a breathtaking view from the observation deck on the 73rd of its 76 floors.

DOWNTOWN & FIRST HILL

SEATTLE TOWER Map above
1218 3rd Ave
Formerly the Northern Life Tower, this 26-story art-deco skyscraper, built in 1928, was designed to reflect the mountains of the Pacific Northwest. The brickwork on the exterior blends from dark at the bottom to light on top, the same way mountains appear to do. Check out the 18-karat-gold relief map in the lobby.

1001 FOURTH AVE PLAZA Map above
Built in 1969, this was one of the city's first real skyscrapers. At the time, 1001 Fourth Ave Plaza was a darling of the architectural world, though nowadays the 50-story bronze block looks dated. Locals nicknamed it 'the box that the Space

Needle came in.' In the plaza outside is the Three Piece Sculpture: Vertebrae, a sculpture by Henry Moore – a result of Seattle's 'one percent for art' clause.

ARCTIC BUILDING Map above
700 3rd Ave at Cherry St
The Arctic Building, completed in 1917, is unique for its intricate terra-cotta ornamentation and 25 walrus heads peeking off the building's exterior. Though the walruses' tusks were originally authentic ivory, an earthquake in the 1940s managed to shake a few of them loose to the ground. To protect passersby from the unusual urban hazard of being skewered by falling tusks, the ivory was replaced with epoxy.

DOWNTOWN & FIRST HILL

TIMES SQUARE BUILDING Map opposite
Olive Way & Stewart St
This terra-cotta and granite structure, guarded by eagles perched on the roof, was designed by the Paris-trained architect Carl Gould (who also did the Seattle Asian Art Museum and the UW's Suzzallo Library). It housed the *Seattle Times* from 1916 to 1931.

WASHINGTON STATE CONVENTION & TRADE CENTER Map opposite
206-447-5000; 7th Ave & Pike St (main entrance)
It's hard to miss this gigantic complex decked out with ballrooms, meeting rooms, space for exhibitions and the Seattle Convention and Visitors Bureau (206-461-5840; www.visitseattle.org; 9am-5pm). An arched-glass bridge spans Pike St between 7th and 8th Aves, with what looks like a giant eye in the middle of it. Strewn across the various decks and patios, Freeway Park provides a leafy, fountain-laden downtown oasis.

WESTLAKE CENTER Map opposite
4th Ave & Pine St
Scorned by locals, this cheeseball shopping mall is useful these days primarily as a landmark. The courtyard-like area outside has become a favorite place for activist gatherings and political protests, and it offers rich if sobering opportunities for people-watching. (Keep tabs on your wallet.) This is also where the monorail (p201) stops and starts on its 1.2-mile trip to and from Seattle Center.

FIRST HILL

FRYE ART MUSEUM Map opposite
206-622-9250; http://fryemuseum.org; 704 Terry Ave; admission free; 10am-5pm Tue-Sat, 10am-8pm Thu, noon-5pm Sun; 64, 303, 941, 942 & others;
This small museum on First Hill preserves the collection of Charles and Emma Frye. The Fryes collected more than 1000 paintings, mostly 19th- and early-20th-century European and American pieces, and a few Alaskan and Russian artworks. If this inspires a stifled yawn, think again. Since its 1997 expansion, the Frye has gained a hipness that it once lacked; fresh ways of presenting its artwork, music performances, poetry readings and interesting rotating exhibits from traveling painters to local printmakers make the museum a worthwhile stop.

SORRENTO HOTEL Map opposite
900 Madison St; 64, 303, 941, 942 & others
This grand working hotel located on First Hill is a fine example of Italian Renaissance

STREETWISE

Seattle street addresses are confusing, and few visitors will have time to figure out how the system works. It's easier to use neighborhoods to indicate where things are found: '10th Ave in Queen Anne' indicates which 10th Ave is being referred to; likewise '1st Ave in Wallingford' as opposed to 1st Ave downtown. So it's important to get a working knowledge of Seattle's neighborhoods. With so many different numbering systems, it's the only easy way to make sense of the city.

Downtown is in the middle of the hourglass part of Seattle; Pioneer Square is to the south of it. Capitol Hill lies to the northeast, and the Central District is to the east. The U District is north of Capitol Hill, across Lake Washington. Belltown, Seattle Center and Queen Anne are slightly northwest of downtown. Fremont, Wallingford and Green Lake are north, across Lake Union, and Ballard is off to the northwest. Georgetown is south, and West Seattle – well, that's easy.

Generally speaking, avenues run north and south, and streets run east and west. Yesler Way near Pioneer Square is the zero street for numbering addresses on downtown avenues; Western Ave is the zero street for addresses on streets. Usually Seattle's avenues have a directional suffix (6th Ave S), while its streets have directional prefixes (S Charles St); however, downtown streets and avenues have neither.

architecture. Built in 1909 by a Seattle clothing merchant, the Sorrento was one of the first hotels designed to absorb the crowds of prospectors journeying through town on their way to Alaska in search of gold; see p175 for more information on the hotel. Don't miss a chance to peek inside – the lobby, bars and dining areas are all simply gorgeous.

STIMSON-GREEN MANSION Map p50
☎ 206-624-0474; www.stimsongreen.com; 1204 Minor Ave; tours $10, registration required; 🕙 1-2:30pm 2nd Tue each month; 🚌 64, 303, 941, 942 & others

One of the first homes on First Hill, the baronial Stimson-Green Mansion is an English Tudor-style mansion completed in 1901 by lumber and real-estate developer CD

Stimson. Built from brick, stucco and wood, this stately home is now owned by Stimson's granddaughter and used for private catered events such as weddings and themed dinners. The interior rooms are decorated to reflect the different design styles popular at the turn of the 20th century. To register for a tour, call the Washington Trust for Historic Preservation (☎ 206-624-9449).

DOWNTOWN ARCHITECTURE
Walking Tour
1 Arctic Building
Start this walk on the south end of downtown at the Arctic Building (p50). Crane your neck to get a look at the walrus heads on the building's exterior. Then walk up Cherry St and take a left onto 4th Ave.

2 Columbia Center
The Columbia Center (p49), formerly the Bank of America Tower and the Columbia Seafirst Center, takes up the block between 4th and 5th Aves and Columbia and Cherry Sts. This is the tallest building on the West Coast. If you have time, check out the observation deck on the 73rd floor.

3 1001 Fourth Ave Plaza
Follow 4th Ave to Madison St, to the 1001 Fourth Ave Plaza (p50), one of the city's first real skyscrapers, built in 1969.

4 Seattle Public Library
Just across 4th Ave, hop into the library (p49) and take a quick ride up the lime-green escalators

top picks

IT'S FREE!

- Frye Art Museum (p51) First Hill's small but well-stocked art museum.
- Olympic Sculpture Park (p67) Alfresco artwork overlooking the Olympic Mountains and Elliott Bay.
- Volunteer Park Conservatory (p80) This Victorian greenhouse is Volunteer Park's crowning jewel.
- Fremont Sunday Market (p86) You don't have to spend a dime to enjoy this bustling marketplace in the city's quirkiest quadrant.
- Ballard Fish Ladder (p97) Betcha didn't know fish could climb ladders.

DOWNTOWN ARCHITECTURE WALKING TOUR

WALK FACTS

Start Arctic Building
End Westlake Center
Distance 2 miles
Duration One hour
Fuel stops Georgian

enter off 3rd Ave to explore the building's stunning interior.

7 Benaroya Concert Hall

Cross University St to Benaroya Concert Hall (p49). Walk into the glass-enclosed lobby of the performance hall, where you can take in excellent views of Elliott Bay. Check out the 20ft-long chandeliers.

8 Seattle Art Museum

Since you're this close, continue along University to get an eyeful of the new Seattle Art Museum (p48). It may not be one of the seven wonders of the architecture world, especially from the outside, but it is a clever solution to the problem of finding more and better gallery space in a downtown area without much available real estate.

9 Cobb Building

Walk back up University St, across 3rd Ave to the corner of 4th Ave. Look up at the 1910 Cobb Building and see remnants of an older Seattle. Peering out from the building is the dour terra-cotta head of a Native American chief.

10 Rainier Tower & Fairmont Olympic Hotel

Continue on University St across 4th Ave to Rainier Tower. Taking up an entire block between 4th and 5th Aves and University and Union Sts is Rainier Square, a shopping center connected to the top-heavy tower. Cross University St and gaze in wonder at the Fairmont Olympic Hotel (p174), undoubtedly one of the classiest remnants of Seattle's early-20th-century heyday. The block-square building looks sober and unrevealing on the outside, but journey through the revolving doors to discover a sumptuous lobby dominated by chandeliers, marble walls and exotic carpets. Take a peek into the Georgian Room to see a dining room right out of a stylish 1930s film.

to see how good architecture can combine practicality and beauty. There are good views from the top levels.

5 Seattle Tower

Continue north on 4th Ave to University St and take a left, walk half a block and look up. Formerly the Northern Life Tower, the Seattle Tower (p50), an art-deco skyscraper built in 1928, was designed to reflect the mountains of the Pacific Northwest.

6 Washington Mutual Tower

Continue down University St across 3rd Ave. The beauty of the Seattle skyline is the blue-and-cream Washington Mutual Tower at 3rd Ave at Seneca St, which changes colors with the clouds and sunsets. Don't be shy;

11 Freeway Park

Continue northeast on University St past 6th Ave; look ahead to Freeway Park. Meander through it, then follow signs to the Washington State Convention & Trade Center (p51) and the visitors center inside. Leave the convention center through its front doors on Pike St. Follow Pike (you'll see Pike Place Market at the end of the street) to 5th Ave.

12 Coliseum Theater

You won't be able to miss the imposing Banana Republic store at the corner of 5th Ave and Pike St. It is located in the wonderful old terra-cotta-faced Coliseum Theater, a film palace dating back to 1916. In its heyday, the theater filled its 1700 seats with eager moviegoers. The building suffered from neglect over the years until it was saved by Banana Republic's multimillion-dollar rehabilitation project, completed in 1985.

13 Westlake Center

Take a right on 5th Ave to Pine St; turn left, toward the specter of Westlake Center (p51). Stop for a latte and park yourself in front of the entrance for some entertaining amateur street theater.

From here you can go to the top of the mall and catch the monorail to Seattle Center, or head back south along 4th Ave to Cherry St.

PIONEER SQUARE

Browsing the Pioneer Square Historic District is rather like visiting a movie set of early-20th-century Seattle, except that the food and the shopping are better. This is the birthplace of Seattle, and the redbrick district of historical buildings and totem-lined plazas is still a real crossroads of the modern city.

Seattle's first town-site at Pioneer Square is an enclave of handsome old buildings and shaded squares. The area is also full of restaurants and cafes and some of the best non-chain store shopping in the city, with great bookstores, antique markets, art galleries and gift shops. Even die-hard antishoppers should stop at a couple of the old storefronts. The Grand Central Arcade (p57) has a good bakery-cafe, plenty of tables, a cozy fire and staircases leading to the underground shopping arcade. You can walk straight through here to Occidental Park (p57). At night, Pioneer Square pubs and clubs kick up an energetic party scene that offers quantity, if not quality (p140).

In the early days of Seattle, Pioneer Square was a haphazard settlement of wooden storefronts, log homes and lumber mills. The Great Fire of 1889 leveled 30 blocks – the original town – but the city rapidly rebounded: almost all of the buildings that now stand in the Pioneer Square area were constructed between 1890 and 1905. As many as 50 of these structures were designed by one architect: Elmer Fisher. As part of this massive rebuilding project, city planners took the dramatic step of regrading Denny Hill, one of Seattle's original seven steep hills that rose sharply out of Elliott Bay. This raised the new city about a dozen feet above the original settlement. Back in the good old days, the underground tunnels that remained were used as opium dens and speakeasies (see Organized Tours, p206).

Many post-fire buildings were built in the grand Romanesque Revival style already popular in Boston and Chicago, which displayed wealth and prosperity to the pioneers. Plus, no one wanted to see the town go up in flames again – brick, stone and steel are a lot less likely to burn.

Pioneer Square fell on hard times for years – amazingly, there were plans to level the area in the late 1960s to make room for parking lots and office buildings. But alert citizens banded together to rescue the city's atmospheric core. Eventually, bank loans, cheap rents and Historic Register status brought in businesses, art galleries, antique shops and interior-design stores. These days, many Pioneer Square restaurants play up the frontier image while serving notably good food. Pioneer Square is also a major center for live music and nightlife.

Perhaps mirroring its early days when this was a rough-and-tumble frontier town, Pioneer Square still sees some rowdiness; there's often a juxtaposition of drunken tourists and Seattle's homeless hanging around the bar scene. Though the ruckus may be a little unnerving, especially at night, there's not much to worry about beyond drunken frat-boy brawls and some pan-handling.

This is the oldest part of town, full of historical buildings and fun just to wander around in. It's also likely to be the first part of town you see if you arrive in Seattle by train. As you meander through the neighborhood, be on the lookout for informative signs on statues and plaques on historical buildings.

Pioneer Square is a few short blocks from the heart of downtown, meaning that any of the city buses that stop in downtown will get you pretty close.

KLONDIKE GOLD RUSH HISTORICAL PARK Map p56

☎ 206-220-4240; www.nps.gov/klse; 319 2nd Ave S; admission free; ⏰ 9am-5pm

In an early example of Seattle civic boosters clamoring to put the city 'on the map,' the Seattle *Post-Intelligencer* trumpeted the news that a ship full of gold had arrived in town on July 17, 1897. Masses of gold-fevered unfortunates swarmed the city on their way to the Klondike River area in the Yukon Territory, and local merchants made a killing. Seattle's seminal position as the outfitting and transportation hub for the Alaskan and Yukon Gold Rush is recognized at Klondike Gold Rush National Park, one of the USA's few indoor national historical parks. It's easy to miss, but worth seeking out. Exhibits, photos and news clippings document the era and give an idea of how much gear, food and true grit were necessary to stake a claim in the Klondike.

lonelyplanet.com

PIONEER SQUARE

| | 0 | 250 m |
| | 0 | 0.1 miles |

NIGHTLIFE (p151)
Contour 30 C2
Fuel 31 C3
J&M Café 32 C3
Last Supper Club 33 C3
Owl & Thistle 34 B2
Tiki Bob's Cantina 35 C3

THE ARTS (p157)
Comedy Underground 36 C3
Greg Kucera Gallery 37 C3
Lawrimore Project 38 D4
WaMu Theater .... (see 8)

SPORTS & ACTIVITIES (p163)
Seattle Mariners .... (see 9)
Seattle Seahawks .... (see 8)
Seattle Sounders .... (see 8)

SLEEPING (p173)
Alexis Hotel 39 B2
Best Western Pioneer
   Square Hotel 40 B2
Hotel 1000 .... (see 17)
Silver Cloud Hotel 41 C5

INFORMATION
Bill Speidel's Underground Tour 1 C2
King County Metro Transit 2 C3

SIGHTS (p55)
Glasshouse Studio .... (see 14)
Grand Central Arcade 3 C3
Klondike Gold Rush Historical Park ... 4 C3
Occidental Park 5 C3
Pioneer Building 6 C2
Pioneer Square Park 7 C3
Qwest Field (Seahawks Stadium) ... 8 C4
Safeco Field 9 C5
Smith Tower 10 C2
Waterfall Park 11 C3

SHOPPING (p107)
Elliott Bay Antiques 12 C3
Foster/White Gallery 13 C3
Glasshouse Studio 14 C3
Jackson Street Gallery 15 C3
Jean Williams Antiques 16 C3
Legacy Ltd Gallery 17 B1
North Face 18 B1
Pioneer Square Antique Mall 19 C2
Seattle Mystery Bookshop 20 C2

EATING (p119)
Bakeman's 21 C2
Cherry Street Coffee House .... (see 20)
FX McRory's Steak, Chop & Oyster
   House 22 C3
Grand Central Baking Co .... (see 3)
New Orleans Creole Restaurant 23 C2
Salumi 24 C3
Zaina 25 C2

DRINKING (p139)
Central Saloon 26 C3
Marcus' Martini Heaven 27 C2
Pyramid Ale House 28 C5
Zeitgeist 29 C3

Gold panning is demonstrated by park rangers, and you can sit down and view a slide presentation about the gold rush.

KING STREET STATION Map above

303 S Jackson St

The old Great Northern Railroad depot is now in use as an Amtrak station. This one-time jewel of a train station – built in 1906 by Reed & Stem, who also designed New York City's Grand Central Station – has been blighted since the 1960s by a horrible ceiling-lowering revamp, but the fabulous old Italianate plasterwork and detailing are still there. The old depot's stately brick tower has long been an integral (though now dwarfed) piece of the downtown skyline. Continuing renovations to the building are under way to restore and

NEIGHBORHOODS PIONEER SQUARE

reveal its original architecture, as well as to improve its practical functions.

OCCIDENTAL PARK Map opposite
btwn S Washington & S Main Sts, just off 1st Ave S
Notable in this cobblestone plaza are the totem poles carved by Duane Pasco, a nationally respected Chinookan carver and artist from Poulsbo on the Kitsap Peninsula. The totems depict the welcoming spirit of Kwakiutl, a totem bear, the tall Sun and Raven, and a man riding on the tail of a whale. For more on the art and purpose of totem poles, see p36.

Also eye-catching is the Firefighters' Memorial, featuring life-size bronze sculptures of fire-fighters in action. Engraved on the granite slabs surrounding the sculpture are the names of Seattle firefighters who have been killed in the line of duty since the depart-ment's inception after the Great Fire. The artist is Hai Ying Wu, a University of Washington graduate.

OCCIDENTAL SQUARE Map opposite
btwn S Main & S Jackson Sts
Occidental Square, with its cobblestone plaza flanked by unusually handsome Victorian buildings, is one of the nicest places in this area. Visit Glasshouse Studio (Map p109) to see local artists' impressive works of blown, cast and lamp-worked glass. If you need a shot of caffeine or a chance to catch your breath, make the pilgrimage to Zeitgeist (Map opposite). This coffeehouse is a local haunt of artists and architects. Along S Jackson St you'll find an excellent concentration of antique stores and some of the city's most prestigious galleries.

PIONEER BUILDING Map opposite
606 1st Ave S
Built in 1891, this magnificent structure facing Pioneer Square Park is one of the finest Victorian buildings left in Seattle; many mining companies had offices here during the Klondike Gold Rush years. It was designed by Elmer Fisher, whose fingerprints are all over Pioneer Square. Resting on the site of Henry Yesler's original home, the building now houses, in part, Doc Maynard's Public House, a handsome old bar and restaurant that serves as the ticket office for Bill Speidel's Underground Tour (p206). Be sure to peek in at the Italian marble in the lobby.

PIONEER SQUARE PARK Map opposite
cnr Cherry St & 1st Ave S
The original Pioneer Square is a cobblestone triangular plaza where Henry Yesler's sawmill cut the giant trees that marked Seattle's first industry. Known officially as Pioneer Square Park, the plaza features a bust of Chief Seattle (Sealth, in the original language), an ornate pergola and a totem pole. Some wayward early Seattleites, so the story goes, stole the totem from the Tlingit natives in southeastern Alaska in 1890. An arsonist lit the pole aflame in 1938, burning it to the ground. When asked if they could carve a replacement pole, the Tlingit took the money offered, thanking the city for payment of the first totem, and said it would cost $5000 to carve another one. The city coughed up the money and the Tlingit obliged with the pole you see today.

The decorative pergola was built in the early 1900s to serve as an entryway to an underground lavatory and to shelter those waiting for the cable car that went up and down Yesler Way. The reportedly elaborate restroom eventually closed due to serious plumbing problems at high tide. In January 2001, the pergola was leveled by a way-ward truck, but it was restored and put back where it belonged the following year, looking as good as new.

GRAND CENTRAL ARCADE Map opposite
☎ 206-623-7417; 214 1st Ave S
This lovely meeting point was originally Squire's Opera House, erected in 1879 by Watson Squire, who became one of Washington's first senators after it achieved statehood. When the Opera House burned down, it was rebuilt as the Squire-Latimer Building and later became the Grand Central Hotel. The hotel died during the Depression, but it underwent a major restoration in the 1970s and now contains two floors of shops, including the excellent Grand Central Baking Co (p123).

SMITH TOWER Map opposite
☎ 206-622-4004; 506 2nd Ave S at Yesler Way; observation deck adult/senior & student/child $7.50/6/5; ☉ 10am-dusk May-Sep, 10am-5pm Apr & Oct, 10am-4pm Sat & Sun Nov-Mar
You can't miss Seattle's first skyscraper. For half a century after its construction in 1914, the 42-story Smith Tower was

well known as the tallest building west of Chicago. The distinctive tower was erected by LC Smith, a man who built his fortune on typewriters (Smith-Corona) and guns (Smith & Wesson). Smith died during the building's construction, so he never got to see the beauty that still bears his name. Walk into the onyx- and marble-paneled lobby, step aboard one of the brass-and-copper manually operated elevators and let it whisk you up to the 35th-floor observation deck for a great view of Seattle's Waterfront. The ride up is as exciting as the view.

WATERFALL PARK Map 56
cnr S Main St & 2nd Ave S
This unusual park is an urban oasis commemorating workers of the United Parcel Service (UPS), which grew out of a messenger service that began in a basement at this location in 1907. The artificial 22ft waterfall that flows in this tiny open-air courtyard is flanked by tables and flowering plants. This is a perfect spot to eat a brown-bag lunch or to rest weary feet.

YESLER WAY Map p56
Seattle claims its Yesler Way was the coining ground for the term 'skid road' – logs would 'skid' down the steeply sloped road linking a logging area above town to Henry Yesler's mill. With the decline of the area, the street became a haven for homeless people. Soon the nickname 'skid road' or 'skid row' was being used for equally destitute areas around the country, sort of the opposite to 'easy street.'

As for Arthur Yesler himself, local historians paint him as an ambitious business zealot who clashed frequently with the wild-and-woolly Doc Maynard. These two men, who by all accounts were equally stubborn, both owned part of the land that would eventually become Pioneer

Square. This resulted in a highly symbolic grid clash, in which Yesler's section of the square had streets running parallel to the river, while Maynard's came crashing in at a north–south angle. Yesler maintained, not unreasonably, that Doc was drunk when he submitted his portion of the plans.

SAFECO FIELD Map p56
☎ general information 206-346-4241, ticket information 206-622-4487; 1250 1st Ave S; adult/child $9/7; ✆ 1hr tours 10:30am, 12:30pm & 2:30pm on nongame days Apr-Oct; 12:30 & 2:30pm Tue-Sun Nov-Mar
The Mariners' $517 million ballpark, Safeco Field, opened in July 1999. The stadium, with its retractable roof, 47,000 seats and real grass, was funded in part by taxpayers and tourists; more than half the money came from taxes on food sold in King County restaurants and bars, and from taxes on rental cars. Money also came from profits on scratch-lottery tickets. The Mariners coughed up most of the difference. The stadium's unique design means it commands fantastic views of the surrounding mountains, downtown and Puget Sound. There's no 2:30pm tour on game days and no tours if the game is before 6pm.

QWEST FIELD (SEAHAWKS STADIUM) Map p56
800 Occidental Ave S
The late, mostly unlamented Kingdome, long Seattle's biggest eyesore, was once the sports stadium that served as home field for the city's professional baseball and football franchises. Then it was imploded spectacularly in 2000 and replaced by the 72,000-seat Qwest Field, or Seahawks Stadium. Seattle's soccer team, the Sounders, also play here; the Mariners now play at Safeco Field.

Shopping p110, Eating p124, Drinking p141

Not far from Pioneer Square, but feeling worlds away, is the International District – Seattle's Chinatown, where Asian groceries and restaurants line the streets. The updated moniker reflects both Seattle's tendency to be politically correct and the gradual diversification of the area. The Chinese were among the first settlers in Seattle in the late 1800s (the original Chinatown was around 2nd Ave and Washington St), followed by Japanese, Filipinos, Vietnamese, Laotians and others. Later immigrants settled just to the east of present-day Chinatown, in an area known as Little Saigon.

Although 'International District' seems a pretty useful term for this mix of races and cultures, it is in fact a relatively recent and controversial moniker, fashioned in the early 1970s. The Chinese grew resentful of the term when the renaming seemingly left 'Chinatown' as a dirty word, but other Asian groups welcomed the representation. Scuffles about who the neighborhood belongs to continue, as they have throughout the area's history. Many Seattleites still refer to the area as Chinatown or simply 'the ID.'

Asian immigrants had an important presence in Seattle pretty much from the beginning. The muscle behind this early Asian settlement was the Wa Chong Company, labor contractors who brought in Chinese workers for timber, mining and railroad jobs in the 1860s and 1870s. After the anti-Chinese riots of 1886 (p25), the population of Chinatown dropped from an estimated 1500 to about 500; large numbers of Chinese immigrants didn't start coming back to the area until after the Great Fire of 1889. At that point, Chinatown shifted to where it is now, around the King St and Jackson St area.

Immigrants from Japan settled the area in the later 1800s and remained the largest minority group until WWII. 'Japantown' was just to the north of Chinatown, and the Japanese population at one point was about 6000. From the 1920s to '40s, this was a bustling place, thriving with Asian markets and other businesses that were built and patronized by the country's highest concentration of Japanese and Chinese Americans. African Americans and Filipinos also moved in, but the area remained a veritable Japantown, with Japanese newspapers, schools, banks and restaurants.

The neighborhood took another massive hit during WWII, when all inhabitants of Japanese descent were forcibly moved out and interned at labor camps in the US interior. The once-bustling shops were boarded up. When released, few of those who had been in the internment camps chose to return here to their old homes, but those who did return – including the Moriguchis who founded the Uwajimaya store – made quite an impact on the future development of the neighborhood.

When the I-5 pushed through the heart of the district, destroying many blocks of housing, the area became even more blighted and its identity even more divided. The arrival of Vietnamese immigrants in the 1970s and '80s, and a more recent influx of immigrants from Hong Kong and mainland China, have breathed new life into the city's Asian community. District activists strive to keep the area vital by stressing anti-crime measures and maintaining a strong community voice in housing and commercial development.

The 'ID' has all of the trappings of a multiethnic neighborhood, from bustling markets and fun import shops to amazing places to eat. There's also a lot of history here, as explained most thoroughly in the Wing Luke Museum. As you explore the nooks and crannies of the neighborhood, keep your eyes peeled for hidden treasures, like that sketchy pet shop straight out of *Gremlins* tucked away in a back alley.

Metro bus 7 runs here frequently from 3rd Ave downtown.

WING LUKE MUSEUM OF THE ASIAN PACIFIC AMERICAN EXPERIENCE

Map p60

☎ 206-623-5124; www.wingluke.org; 719 S King St; adult/student/child $12.95/9.95/8.95, under 5 free; ☷ 10am-5pm Tue-Sun, 10am-8pm first Thu & third Sun each month, closed Mon; 🚌 7, 14, 36

This pan-Asian museum is devoted to Asian and Pacific American culture, history and art. Named after the first Asian elected official in the continental US, it examines the often difficult and violent meeting of Asian and Western cultures in Seattle. Particularly fascinating are the photos and

INTERNATIONAL DISTRICT

lonelyplanet.com

displays on Chinese settlement in the 1880s and the retelling of Japanese American internment during WWII. The museum's new home, in the historical East Kong Yick Building, housed many immigrant workers from China, Japan and the Philippines; a typical first apartment is re-created here.

The intimate 2nd-floor Community Portrait Galleries tell the stories of the various Asian-American communities in the Seattle area, and the George Tsutakawa Art Gallery houses exciting contemporary work by Asian artists from around the country. Opt for a guided tour (included with admission) if possible. The museum also coordinates guided tours of the rest of the ID (adult/child $17.95/10.95), based on various themes – call to make arrangements, or ask at the ticket counter.

DANNY WOO INTERNATIONAL DISTRICT COMMUNITY GARDENS
Map above
S Main St
The Danny Woo International District Community Gardens is a 1.5-acre plot reserved for about 120 older and low-income International District residents, who grow

a profusion of vegetables and fruit trees. Visitors can wander along the gravel paths and admire both the tidy gardens and the Seattle skyline, as well as good views of Elliott Bay. Unfortunately, while you take in the view you'll have about 17 lanes of I-5 traffic right at your back.

UWAJIMAYA Map above
☎ 206-624-6248; 600 5th Ave S; ⏱ 9am-10pm
Founded by Fujimatsu Moriguchi, one of the few Japanese to return here from the WWII internment camps, this large department and grocery store – a cornerstone of Seattle's Asian community – has everything from fresh fish and exotic fruits and vegetables to cooking utensils, and you'll come face-to-face with those dim sum ingredients you've always wondered about. The current location is a self-styled 'community' that includes living quarters and occupies a whole block. There's a food court in addition to the grocery store. It's a great place to browse. Sharing the same building as Uwajimaya, Kinokuniya (p110) bookstore has an excellent collection of books about Asia and by Asian

NEIGHBORHOODS INTERNATIONAL DISTRICT

writers in several Asian languages and English, as well as imported CDs and DVDs.

HAU HAU MARKET Map opposite
☎ 206-329-1688; 412 12th Ave S
Hau Hau is a modern and bustling Chinese and Vietnamese food market where you can get cheap produce, specialty meats such as pork ears and chicken feet, fireworks, and Asian gifts and knickknacks.

HING HAY PARK Map opposite
cnr Maynard Ave S & S King St
If you need a tranquil spot to rest while wandering the ID, Hing Hay Park lends a little green to the otherwise austere district. The traditional Chinese pavilion was a gift from the people of Taipei. On Saturdays in August you can catch a free outdoor movie here beginning at sunset, sponsored by the Seattle Chinatown-International District, which also runs the summer Night Market here; for a full schedule, go to www.cidbia.org.

INTERNATIONAL CHILDREN'S PARK
Map opposite
cnr S Lane St & 7th Ave S
If the kids aren't up for exploring the Asian markets or sitting still for a dim sum brunch, bring them here to work off some energy by playing on the bronze dragon sculpture, designed by George Tsutakawa,

a Seattle native who spent much of his childhood in Japan, then returned to become an internationally renowned sculptor and painter and a professor at the University of Washington.

PACIFIC HERB & GROCERY Map opposite
☎ 206-340-6411; 610 S Weller St, btwn 6th Ave & Maynard Ave S
A good place to get a sense of Chinatown is along S Weller St. Apart from the many restaurants, there's Pacific Herb & Grocery, where the herbal-medicine specialists can tell you all about the uses of different roots, bones, flowers and teas. The shop next door is a great place to buy tofu at low prices – you can even watch them make it on the premises.

UNION STATION Map opposite
401 S Jackson St
Another landmark that benefited from restoration fever is Union Station, the old Union Pacific Railroad depot (1911) that was unoccupied between 1971 and 1999. The restoration project included the preservation of the original tile floors, clocks and windows. More than 90 years of build-up was hand-scrubbed off the exterior brick. The Great Hall, half the size of a football field, remains an impressive space.

PIKE PLACE MARKET & WATERFRONT

Shopping p110, Eating p125, Drinking p141, Sleeping p177

These two neighborhoods are perhaps Seattle's most visited areas. They're divided by the Alaskan Way Viaduct, but linked by several corridors and stairways, and it's easy to thoroughly explore both in the same day. The best bet is to hit the market early in the morning, relax in a waterfront park at midday, then stroll the shops along the boardwalk in the afternoon and watch the sun set over Elliott Bay while you munch a seafood dinner.

This area of town rewards early birds. It's particularly important to get to the market early if you want to avoid that cattle-truck feeling: weekdays and before 10am on weekends are best. The waterfront is more weather dependent; a sunny weekend afternoon finds it swarming, while on a misty weekday morning you'll have the place pretty much to yourself.

Sound Transit light rail from Seattle-Tacoma Airport stops at Westlake Station, which is four blocks from the market entrance. Several Metro bus routes stop near the market on 1st Ave.

PIKE PLACE MARKET

One of the best ways to fall in love with Seattle is to wake up early and head down to Pike Place Market, stroll around and watch people do what they do. A girl walking a puppy passes by a despondent-looking man on the corner selling *RealChange* newspapers. An Indian with long braids goes by on one crutch. A hipster couple with matching turquoise hair walks by, intertwined. Tourists line up to photograph the singing fish throwers; one joker throws a stuffed plush-toy fish right into the crowd, provoking giggles. An ancient black busker sings 'Mamas, Don't Let Your Babies Grow Up to Be Cowboys.'

The market is one of Seattle's most popular tourist attractions, as much for its exuberant theatricality as for its fish and produce stands. The lively, always bustling buildings that make up the market fill daily with the bounty of local farms, rivers and the sea. Add in arts and crafts, loads of restaurants and cafes, and buskers and other performers, and you'll discover why this mazelike market is Seattle at its irrepressible best. It sees about 40,000 visitors a day, and a good portion of them are locals out shopping for groceries.

DIY SEATTLE

Carrying a map around the Pike Place Market will only make you dizzy, so here's our advice: ditch the map, put this guidebook down and go exploring on your own. The market labyrinth holds surprises around every corner; even if you end up walking in circles, you're likely to see something new with each lap. So start at one corner, browse without an agenda or a timeline, stop wherever you feel like it, and see what happens.

The market features some of the most boisterous fishmongers in the world, whose daredevil antics with salmon merge gymnastics, theater and cuisine. Despite the tourist-tickling showiness, the market maintains a down-home authenticity; real people work and buy here. A tip: don't eat before you go. This is one of the hotbeds of Seattle snacking and dining. You can get everything from a freshly grown Washington apple to a pot sticker, or even a seven-course French meal. Some of Seattle's favorite watering holes are also tucked into unlikely corners of the market buildings – for more details, see the Eating (p125) and Drinking (p141) chapters.

Pike Place Market is the oldest continuously operating market in the nation. It was established in 1907 to give local farmers a place to sell their fruit and vegetables and bypass the middleman. Soon, the greengrocers made room for fishmongers, bakers, ethnic groceries, butchers, cheese sellers and purveyors of the rest of the Northwest's agricultural bounty. The market wasn't exactly architecturally robust – it's always been a thrown-together warren of sheds and stalls, haphazardly designed for utility – and was by no means an intentional tourist attraction. That came later.

An enthusiastic agricultural community spawned the market's heyday in the 1930s. Many of the first farmers were immigrants, a fact the market celebrates with annual themes acknowledging the contributions of various ethnic groups; past years have featured Japanese Americans, Italian Americans and Sephardic Jewish Americans.

By the 1960s, sales at the market were suffering from suburbanization, the growth of supermarkets and the move away from local, small-scale market gardening. Vast

PIKE PLACE MARKET & WATERFRONT

0 ————— 500 m
0 ————— 0.25 miles

INFORMATION
Argosy Cruises..1 D4
Market Information Booth....................2 D3

SIGHTS (p62)
Corner Market Building..........................3 D3
Down Under...(see 5)
Economy Market Building......................4 D3
Main Arcade..5 C3
North Arcade...6 C3
Sanitary Market Building.......................7 D3
South Arcade...9 D3
Seattle Aquarium....................................8 C4
Triangle Building..................................10 C3
Victor Steinbrueck Park......................11 C3

SHOPPING (p107)
Beecher's Handmade Cheese.........(see 16)
DeLaurenti's..(see 4)
Golden Age Collectibles.....................(see 5)
Great Wind Up......................................(see 6)
Left Bank Books....................................(see 3)
Made in Washington............................(see 5)
Metsker Maps..12 D3
Nordstrom Rack.....................................13 D3
Peter Miller Architecture &
   Design Books....................................14 C3
Pike & Western Wine Shop...............(see 15)
Pure Food Fish......................................(see 7)
Souk...15 C3
Sur La Table..16 C3
Tenzing Momo......................................(see 4)
Ye Olde Curiosity Shop.......................17 D4

EATING (p119)
Café Campagne...................................(see 18)
Campagne..18 C3
Chez Shea...(see 3)
Etta's Seafood.......................................19 C3
Ivar's Acres of Clams...........................20 D5
Le Panier...(see 10)
Le Pichet..21 C3
Lowell's Restaurant..............................(see 5)
Matt's in the Market............................(see 5)
Mee Sum Pastries................................(see 10)
Pink Door Ristorante...........................22 C3
Procopio Gelati.....................................23 C3
Steelhead Diner....................................24 C3

DRINKING (p139)
Alibi Room..(see 4)
Athenian Inn...(see 5)
Pike Pub & Brewery.............................(see 9)
Virginia Inn Tavern...............................25 C3
White Horse Trading Co.....................(see 27)
Zig Zag Café..26 C3

NIGHTLIFE (p151)
Kells..27 C3
Showbox..28 D3

THE ARTS (p157)
Market Theater......................................(see 4)

SLEEPING (p173)
Edgewater..29 B2
Green Tortoise Hostel..........................30 D3
Inn at the Market.................................(see 18)
Pensione Nichols...................................31 C3

TRANSPORT
Tillicum Village Tours Ferry................(see 1)
Victoria Clipper (Ferry to San
   Juan Islands & Victoria, BC)..........32 A2
Washington State Ferries (To
   Bainbridge Island).............................33 D5

NEIGHBORHOODS PIKE PLACE MARKET & WATERFRONT

tracts of agricultural land were disappearing, replaced by such ventures as the Northgate Mall and the Sea-Tac airport. The internment of Japanese American farmers during WWII had also taken its toll. The entire area became a bowery for the destitute and a center for prostitution and peep shows.

In the wake of the 1962 World's Fair, plans were drawn up to bulldoze the market and build high-rise office and apartment buildings on this piece of prime downtown real estate. Fortunately, public outcry prompted a voter's initiative to save the market. Subsequently, the space was cleaned up and restructured, and it has become once again the undeniable heart and soul of downtown; some 10 million people mill through the market each year. Thanks to the unique management of the market, social services programs and low-income housing mix with market commerce, and the market has maintained its gritty edge. These initiatives have prevented the area from ever sliding too far upscale. A market law prohibits chain stores or franchises from setting up shop and ensures all businesses are locally owned. The one exception is, of course, Starbucks, which gets away with its market location because it marks the coffee giant's first outlet (it opened in 1971).

Pike Place is made up of several buildings, covering about eight labyrinthine blocks at the top of the bluff overlooking the Waterfront. It's easy to get lost here – in fact, experiencing a slight sense of mayhem and dislocation is part of the charm of your initial acquaintance with the market. Don't let the sometimes seedy nature of the neighborhood bother you; while the streets around the market are still dotted with sex shops and off-putting vagrancy, there's very little real danger in the area.

If you're coming from downtown, simply walk down Pike St toward the Waterfront; you can't miss the huge Public Market sign etched against the horizon. Incidentally, the sign and clock, installed in 1927, constituted one of the first pieces of outdoor neon on the West Coast. From the top of Pike St and 1st Ave, stop and survey the bustle and vitality of the market. Walk down the cobblestone street, past perpetually gridlocked cars (don't even think of driving down to Pike Place) and, before walking into the market, stop and shake the bronze snout of Rachel the Market Pig, the de facto mascot and presiding spirit of the market. This life-size piggy bank, carved by Whidbey Island artist Georgia Gerber and named after a real pig, collects about $6000 each year. The funds are pumped back into market social services. Nearby is the market information booth (☎ 206-682-7453; Pike St & 1st Ave), which has maps of the market and information about Seattle in general. It also serves as a Ticket/Ticket booth, selling discount tickets to various shows throughout the city.

Pike Place Market is on the western edge of downtown, off 1st Ave. Buses 15, 18, 21, 22 and 56 run up and down 1st Ave from Pioneer Square. You can also take any bus along 3rd Ave and get off at the University Street Station, then walk west, toward the water. Along the Waterfront Streetcar route, Pike St Station is the stop for Pike Place Market; from there you need to climb the hill to the market itself. On foot, the market is just minutes from most downtown hotels. Walk down Pike, Pine or Stewart Sts toward the Waterfront and you're there.

CORNER & SANITARY MARKET BUILDINGS Map p63
Pike Pl & Pike St
Across Pike Place from the Main Arcade are the 1912 Corner Market Building and the Sanitary Market Building, so named because they were the first of the market buildings in which live animals were prohibited. It's now a maze of ethnic groceries and great little eateries, including the Three Girls Bakery, which has a sit-down area (it's always packed) and a take-out window with some of the best breads and sandwiches around. This is also the home of Left Bank Books (p110), an excellent source for all your radical reading needs.

DOWN UNDER Map p63
As if the levels of the market that are above ground weren't labyrinthine enough, below the Main Arcade are three lower levels called the Down Under. Here you'll find a fabulously eclectic mix of pocket-size shops, from Indian spice stalls to magicians' supply shops and military-button booths.

ECONOMY MARKET BUILDING Map p63
cnr 1st Ave & Pike St
Once a stable for merchants' horses, the Economy Market Building on the south side of the market entrance has a wonderful Italian grocery store, DeLaurenti's (p111) – a great place for any aficionado of Italian foods to browse and sample. There's also Tenzing Momo (p110), one of the oldest apothecaries on the West Coast, where you can pick up herbal remedies, incense, oils and books. Tarot readings are available here on occasion. Look down at the Economy Market floor and you'll see some of the 46,000 tiles that line the floor. The tiles were sold to the public in the 1980s for $35 apiece. If you bought a tile, you'd get your name on it and be proud that you helped save the market floor. Famous tile owners include Cat in the Hat creator Dr Seuss and former US president Ronald Reagan.

MAIN & NORTH ARCADES Map p63
Western Ave
Rachel the Market Pig marks the main entrance to the Main and North Arcades, thin shed-like structures that run along the edge of the hill; these are the busiest of the market buildings. With banks of fresh produce carefully arranged in artful

displays, and fresh fish, crab and other shellfish piled high on ice, this is the real heart of the market. Here you'll see fishmongers tossing salmon back and forth like basketballs (many of these vendors will pack fish for overnight delivery). You'll also find cheese shops, butchers, tiny grocery stalls and almost everything else you need to put together a meal. The end of the North Arcade is dedicated to local artisans and craftspeople – products must be handmade to be sold here. The Main Arcade was built in 1907, the first of Frank Goodwin's market buildings.

POST ALLEY Map p63

Between the Corner Market and the Triangle Building, tiny Post Alley is lined with more shops and restaurants. Extending north across Stewart St, this street offers two of the area's best places for a drink: the Pink Door Ristorante (p126), an Italian hideaway with a cool patio, and Kells (p154), an Irish pub. In Lower Post Alley beside the market sign is the LaSalle Hotel, which was the first bordello north of Yesler Way. Originally the Outlook Hotel, it was taken over in 1942 by the notorious Nellie Curtis, a woman with 13 aliases and a knack for running suspiciously profitable hotels with thousands of lonely sailors lined up nightly outside the door. (She's the inspiration for the Pike Place Pub & Brewery's equally tempting Naughty Nellie's Ale.) The building, rehabbed in 1977, now houses commercial and residential space.

SOUTH ARCADE Map p63
1411 1st Ave
If you continue past DeLaurenti's, you'll come into the South Arcade, the market's newest wing, home to upscale shops and the lively Pike Pub & Brewery (p141).

TRIANGLE BUILDING Map p63
Pike Pl & Post Alley
All in a row in the Triangle Building are Mr D's Greek Deli, Mee Sum Pastries (p127; try the steamed pork bun), a juice bar and Cinnamon Works – all great choices for a quick snack.

WATERFRONT

This area faces dramatic change in the next few years, thanks to the city's newly approved plan to replace the decrepit Alaskan Way Viaduct with a tunnel. The viaduct, completed on April 4, 1953, is an elevated section of Washington State Route 99 that parallels the waterfront. It was damaged in the 2001 earthquake, and is old and ugly besides, so state and city planners had to figure out whether to repair, replace or remove it. After seemingly endless debate and a couple of public-opinion votes to test the waters, planners finally acknowledged in mid-2007 that Seattleites, understandably, don't want a gigantic highway dividing their downtown from their playground. In 2009 the state legislature approved a $3.1 billion project that will replace the viaduct with a tunnel, as well as improving public transportation around the area and replacing the Elliott Bay seawall. Construction had already begun in 2010, with the new roadway expected to be completed by 2015 and the viaduct removed the following year. The project has been a long time coming, and it'll be exciting to see what it does to this visitor-friendly neighborhood.

The waterfront is indelibly tied to Seattle's beginnings. Thousands of Klondike fortune hunters left from here on ships for Alaska in 1897 to seek gold, many returning with the wealth that served to boom the town into one of the foremost cities along the Pacific Rim. Seattle's waterfront is still a busy place, although today tourist facilities far outnumber actual port activities. Most of Seattle's considerable traffic in containers and imports is handled at the port area south of the historical waterfront.

Visitors can catch the flavor of a major seaport by walking along the Seattle Waterfront, something that's sure to be infinitely more pleasant after the viaduct replacement – it's hard to ignore the huge, pulsing artery of traffic racing along uncomfortably close to the boardwalk. Getting down to the waterfront should also be easier at that point; currently it can be a little tricky to figure out just where you find the series of zigzagging stairs that take you to the water, let alone tromping up and down them. But it's worth doing at least once on a visit. This is a fun, if tacky, place to eat seafood and shop for souvenirs. Most of the piers are now enclosed with endless tourist shops and clam-chowder venues. If you're looking for that 'I Heart Seattle' T-shirt, a souvenir coffee mug or a mass-produced trinket, this is the place.

The Port of Seattle has redeveloped much of the Waterfront area to the north of Seattle Aquarium. Pier 66, also known as the Bell Street Pier, is now home to the Bell Harbor International Conference Center as well as some of the city's better seafood restaurants.

Take a break from the carnival atmosphere of the Waterfront by walking north on Alaskan Way, past Pier 71, to Myrtle Edwards Park, a fringe of lawn and trees along Elliott Bay, and the adjacent Olympic Sculpture Park (p67). The path is a favorite of joggers and power-walkers pursuing lunchtime fitness. In warm weather, the linked parks, with stupendous views over the Sound to the Olympic Mountains, make a good place for a picnic.

Along the length of the Waterfront – amid the horse-drawn carriages, pedicabs and cotton-candy vendors – are a number of companies that offer harbor tours and boat excursions – see the Directory chapter (p206) for details.

The Waterfront is relatively cut off from the rest of downtown Seattle, although the nicely landscaped Hillclimb Corridor (at the end of Pike St) serves as a handy people-funnel between the Waterfront and Pike Place Market. Still, the steep hillsides make access problematic for some; it can be as much as an eight-story descent down open stairways from 1st Ave to Alaskan Way. And until something actually happens to the Alaskan Way Viaduct, it remains a psychological barrier that's hard to ignore. While it in no way infringes upon getting from one place to the other, Alaskan Way is incredibly noisy and the parking areas under the freeway can be scary at night. Be sure not to leave anything valuable in your car if you park here.

The main tourist areas of the Waterfront are between Piers 52 and 59. Waterfront Park is the name given to Pier 57; it's just a boardwalk on the pier, but at least you can get out onto the Sound and get a feeling for the area. It's also the best place to tote your corn dogs and fish and chips from the adjacent piers, then take a seat on a waterside bench. Keep your eyes on your fries, however, as Waterfront seagulls can resemble a pack of hungry bears. Piers 54, 55 and 56 are devoted to shops and restaurants, including novelty venues such as the 100-year-old Ye Olde Curiosity Shop (p111), a bizarre cross between a cornball old-time museum and a souvenir shop.

The Waterfront Streetcar runs along Alaskan Way, the Waterfront's main thoroughfare. The trolleys are more for show than for transport, although they do go from near Seattle Center (from the base of Broad St), along the Waterfront (including near Pike Place Market) and on to Pioneer Square and the International District. Still, if you're anywhere downtown, it's just as easy to walk to the Waterfront.

Washington State Ferries operates transportation to Bainbridge and Blake Islands from the piers, while privately owned ferries travel to the San Juan Islands and Victoria, BC. For more information on ferry operators and routes, see the box, p187.

SEATTLE AQUARIUM Map p63

☎ 206-386-4300; 1483 Alaskan Way at Pier 59; adult/child $17/11, with Argosy harbor cruise $30/19.25, free with CityPass; ⏲ 9:30am-5pm
Probably the most interesting site in the Waterfront area, this well-designed aquarium offers a view into the underwater world of Puget Sound and the Pacific Northwest coast. In 2007 the pilings that support the building were found to be rotten, so they were replaced and the aquarium added a cafe, gift shop and two new exhibits. 'Window on Washington Waters' is a look at the sea floor of the Neah Bay area, where rockfish, salmon, sea anemones and more than 100 other fish and invertebrate species live. 'Crashing Waves' uses a wave tank to show how marine plants and animals cope with the forceful tides near shore.

Other exhibits include re-creations of ecosystems in Elliott Bay, Puget Sound and the Pacific Ocean, including tide pools, eelgrass beds, coral reefs and the sea floor. The centerpiece of the aquarium is a glass-domed room where sharks, octopi and other deepwater denizens lurk in the shadowy depths. The passages eventually lead outdoors to a salmon ladder and a pool where playful sea otters and northern fur and harbor seals await your attention. Combination tickets with Argosy Tours are available at each site in different combinations. If you're tired of lugging all your Waterfront purchases around, you can rent a locker at the aquarium for 50 cents.

VICTOR STEINBRUECK PARK Map p63
Western Ave & Virginia St
When you've had enough of the market and its crowds, wander out the end of the North Arcade and cross Western Ave to Victor Steinbrueck Park, a grassy area designed in 1982 by Steinbrueck and Richard Haag. You'll find benches, a couple of totem poles designed by Quinault tribe member Marvin Oliver, a few shuffling vagrants and great views over the Waterfront and Elliott Bay. Rallies and political demonstrations are often held here.

BELLTOWN

Shopping p112, Eating p127, Drinking p142, Sleeping p178

Belltown is a textbook illustration of the progress of the urban ecosystem. A featureless area of warehouses and low-slung office buildings, this formerly scruffy and edgy-in-a-bad-way neighborhood was dismissed by many in the 1970s. But one of city planning's greatest mysteries is the way seedy, low-rent neighborhoods tend to be spawning grounds for raw musical and artistic talent – and so become cool, then gradually more expensive, and then 'ruined' by the influx of the cashed-up crowd. Eventually, the cachet wears off and the neighborhood settles into a comfortable balance between the funky, artsy people who made it cool in the first place and the new crowd of condo-buying salary earners who keep the chic restaurants and boutiques in business, thereby drawing visitors. This is the stage Belltown seems to have settled into.

The area is also sometimes referred to as the Denny Regrade, for the massive sluicing project that reduced what was Denny Hill to a more convenient flat grade, intended to open up Belltown for a business explosion and rapid economic growth. It didn't exactly work, and the area languished for years. Yet this allowed underground musicians and artists to move in and become part of an explosion of creative ferment that catapulted Seattle to international noteworthiness in the early 1990s: the grit and grime of Belltown were crucial ingredients in grunge music.

After that, the area went seriously upscale, making Belltown one of the hottest neighborhoods for new clubs and restaurants, and a couple of chic hotels. These days, that vibe has calmed down somewhat, and the string of bars along Belltown's main drag has instead been discovered by Seattle's young mainstream: the post-college, ex-fratboy party crowd. One or two grubby punk dives still dot the neighborhood though, as well as grunge-era landmarks like the Crocodile Café (p153). Many locals thought this neighborhood was 'over' a few years back. But the tenacity of places such as Shorty's (p142), Singles Going Steady (p112) and the Crocodile – plus the air of excitement among the people crowding the streets, restaurants and clubs every night – indicate that reports of Belltown's death have been exaggerated.

Belltown is long on entertainment but relatively short on tourist attractions – at least until recently. The neighborhood is now home to the Seattle Art Museum's ambitious new Olympic Sculpture Park, an outdoor sculpture and botanical garden that anchors the neighborhood and should serve as a major draw for visitors.

Most Metro buses going along 3rd Ave from downtown will take you to the heart of Belltown.

OLYMPIC SCULPTURE PARK Map p68

☎ 206-654-3100; www.seattleartmuseum.org/visit/osp; 2901 Western Ave; admission free; ☼ 30min before sunrise–30min after sunset

Hovering over train tracks, in an unlikely oasis between the water and busy Elliott Ave, is the 8.5-acre, $85-million Olympic Sculpture Park. Worth a visit just for its views of the Olympic Mountains over Elliott Bay, the park has begun to grow into its long-range plan. Among the highlights is the *Eagle,* Alexander Calder's 39ft-tall red steel creation from 1971, which crouches along the horizon of the park. The thing probably weighs about a ton, but from where it's positioned, it looks like it's about to launch itself off the top of the hill and into the distant mountains.

The sculpture park is an excellent lesson in how to make the most out of limited urban space. Its Z-shaped path slinks back and forth between Belltown, busy Elliott Ave, and the edge of the bay, rescuing three parcels of land and filling them with art and plant life.

Starting from the bottom, Tony Smith's *Wandering Rocks* zigzags up the hill in the Ketcham Families Grove, described on signs as 'a deciduous forest of quaking aspen' – well, eventually. It's just beginning to sprout now, but it's still pretty. More than 20 large pieces of sculpture dot the landscape, including Claes Oldenburg and Coosje van Bruggen's *Typewriter Eraser, Scale X,* with its weird blue sprouts bristling over Elliott Ave.

The glass building at the top of the park contains a small cafe, restrooms, a gift shop and visitor information.

DENNY PARK Map p68

Seattle's oldest park was originally designated as a cemetery – but that status ended up being rather temporary, and the

BELLTOWN

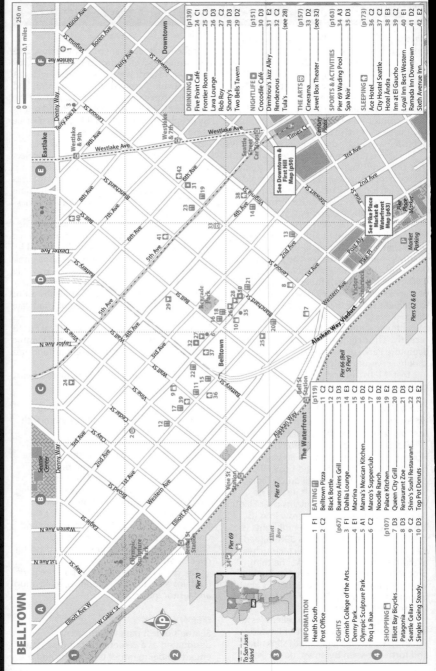

0		250 m
0		0.1 miles

INFORMATION
Health South..................................1 F1
Post Office....................................2 C2

SIGHTS (p67)
Cornish College of the Arts..............3 F1
Denny Park....................................4 E1
Olympic Sculpture Park....................5 A1
Roq La Rue....................................6 C2

SHOPPING (p107)
Elliott Bay Bicycles........................7 D3
Patagonia.....................................8 D3
Seattle Cellars...............................9 C2
Singles Going Steady.....................10 D3

EATING (p119)
Belltown Pizza..............................11 C2
Black Bottle.................................12 C2
Buenos Aires Grill.........................13 D3
Dahlia Lounge..............................14 E3
Macrina......................................15 C2
Mama's Mexican Kitchen................16 D2
Marco's Supperclub.......................17 C2
Noodle Ranch..............................18 D2
Palace Kitchen..............................19 E2
Queen City Grill............................20 D3
Restaurant Zoe.............................21 D3
Shiro's Sushi Restaurant.................22 C2
Top Pot Donuts............................23 E2

DRINKING (p139)
Five Point Café.............................24 C1
Frontier Room..............................25 C3
Lava Lounge................................26 D3
Rob Roy.....................................27 C2
Shorty's.....................................28 D3
Two Bells Tavern...........................29 D2

NIGHTLIFE (p151)
Crocodile Café.............................30 D3
Dimitriou's Jazz Alley....................31 E2
Rendezvous.................................32 C2
Tula's..(see 28)

THE ARTS (p157)
Cinerama....................................33 D2
Jewel Box Theater.........................(see 32)

SPORTS & ACTIVITIES (p163)
Pier 69 Wading Pool......................34 A3
Spa Noir.....................................35 D3

SLEEPING (p173)
Ace Hotel....................................36 C2
City Hostel Seattle.........................37 D2
Hotel Ändra.................................38 E3
Inn at El Gaucho...........................39 C2
Loyal Inn Best Western..................40 E1
Ramada Inn Downtown..................41 D2
Sixth Avenue Inn..........................42 E2

The Waterfront

land was rededicated as parkland. The park was later flattened in the Denny Regrade of 1910, over protests by preservationists.

ROQ LA RUE Map opposite

☎ 206-374-8977; 2312 2nd Ave; ☻ 1-6pm Wed-Sat
This Belltown gallery has secured its reputation by taking risks: the work on view here skates along the edge of urban pop-culture. Since opening in 1998, the gallery, which is owned and curated by Kirsten Anderson, has been a significant force in the pop surrealism field, and is frequently featured in *Juxtapoz* magazine. It also has an entertaining blog about the undercurrents of Northwest art (http://roqlaruenews.blogspot.com).

CORNISH COLLEGE OF THE ARTS
Map opposite

☎ 800-726-2787; 1000 Lenora St
The south campus of the ornamental Cornish College of the Arts, built in 1921, has survived many bouts of debt and is now a top-notch school for music, art, dance and drama.

THE BELLTOWN HUSTLE
Walking Tour

1 Two Bells Tavern

Start the tour by fueling up with an enormous Swiss-mushroom burger at the Two Bells Tavern (p142) on 4th Ave between Bell and Battery Sts. If the weather's nice, have your burger and a beer in the garden out back; otherwise, enjoy the conviviality of the main room, full of people who all seem to know and like each other.

2 Crocodile Café

Wander down 4th Ave toward Blanchard St. Take a right on Blanchard and walk down to 2nd Ave. On the corner of 2nd Ave at Blanchard St, you'll see the snakeskin-green sign of the Crocodile Café (p153), one of the best rock clubs in the country and a key venue in the rise of the grunge movement. Many an up-and-coming band has rocked the crowd here. During the day it's a decent greasy-spoon cafe. Check its windows for upcoming shows.

3 Shorty's

Next to the Crocodile is Tula's (p155), a great local jazz venue. If that sounds good, stop in

THE BELLTOWN HUSTLE WALKING TOUR

WALK FACTS

Start Two Bells Tavern
End Cyclops
Distance 1 mile
Duration One hour to whole evening
Fuel stops Noodle Ranch and Mama's Mexican Kitchen

and hear some of Seattle's best-kept secrets. If you're after more active pursuits and you're thirsty, keep walking. Right in the middle of the block, you'll find Shorty's (p142), otherwise known as pinball heaven. Grab a cheap beer or a slushy blue cocktail and head straight to the back room to test your reflexes.

4 Lava Lounge

When the pinball wears you out or simply beats you into submission, hop next door to the Lava Lounge (p142), another groovy nightspot. Its comfy wooden booths and tiki decor will soothe your battered ego.

5 Singles Going Steady

On your way out, peek across the street at Singles Going Steady (p112), an excellent punk-rock record store.

6 Rendezvous

Continue on past legendary nosh spots the Noodle Ranch and Mama's Mexican Kitchen. In the next block is Rendezvous (p153), a classy place with a curvilinear bar and an adorable,

lonelyplanet.com

recently gussied-up Jewel Box Theater in the back. Head back a block, then up Bell St toward 3rd Ave to Regrade Park.

7 Frontier Room

Walk back down Bell St to 1st Ave: look left and halfway down the block you'll see the flashing neon sign of the Frontier Room (p142), a perfect symbol of Belltown's evolution – formerly a no-frills whiskey joint where you stood at the bar and didn't ask too many questions, it shifted into a frat-boy hangout and is now a barbecue joint.

8 Cyclops

Head toward the corner of 1st Ave and Wall St, where you'll find Cyclops (2421 1st Ave; www .cyclopsseattle.com; ☺ 5pm-2am daily, plus 9am-2pm Sat-Sun), half restaurant, half bar and a prime location for observing the street's late-night dramas. If you're lucky enough to be staying at the Ace Hotel (p179), you can chill at the Cyclops until your eyes match the bleary, bloodshot one hanging over the door, then stumble upstairs and fall into bed. End of tour.

SEATTLE CENTER

Shopping p112, Drinking p143, Sleeping p179

In the early 1960s, Seattle was confident and ready for company. And the 1962 World's Fair gave the city the perfect opportunity to display its self-assured, high-tech vision of itself and of the future. The fair, also known as 'Century 21 Exposition,' was a summer-long exhibition that brought in nearly 10 million visitors from around the world. A 74-acre warehouse area north of downtown was leveled, and a futuristic international enclave of exhibition halls, arenas and public spaces sprang up.

Today, that 74-acre site has been set aside as the Seattle Center, a mecca for museums, entertainment and cultural venues. Varnished by time, the place now evokes a distinctly 1960s notion of tomorrow's world; like relics from World's Fair expos everywhere, the buildings here still seem 'futuristic,' but in a nostalgic, *Jetsons*-esque way. There's no better example of this than the Space Needle (p71), the 520ft-high observation tower and restaurant that has become emblematic of Seattle. If you think it looks otherworldly now, spiking out of the skyline, try picturing it in its original color of bright orange.

The monorail, a 1.5-mile experiment in mass transit, was another signature piece of the 1962 fair. Like it, a number of the exhibition halls have been adapted for civic use, such as the Opera House (renovated and reopened in 2003 as the Marion Oliver McCaw Hall, home of the Seattle Opera and Pacific Northwest Ballet) and the Bagley Wright, Intiman and Seattle Children's Theaters. Two sports complexes were also created, including the Key Arena, a concert venue and now home to the Seattle Storm (a WNBA basketball team). Other public buildings include the Pacific Science Center and the Seattle Children's Museum. Various other museums and art spaces are also remnants of the World's Fair. The Fun Forest Amusement Park, near the monorail stop, is replete with carnival rides.

top picks

YOU KNOW: FOR KIDS!

Children will enjoy accompanying their parents on many of the activities described in this book, but a few places are keyed specifically to the short-pants set. Here are some of the best:

- **Experience Music Project** (p72) Has the Sound Lab where kids can lay down some tracks.
- **Seattle Aquarium** (p66) Sharks, octopi, otters, harbor seals and more.
- **Burke Museum** (p82) Dinosaur skeletons, cedar canoes and totem poles.
- **Children's Museum** (p73) An old-school learning center with an attached theater.
- **International Children's Park** (p61) Features George Tsutakawa's bronze dragon sculpture that doubles as play equipment.
- **Pacific Science Center** (p73) An interactive museum with virtual-reality exhibits, butterfly house, laser shows, holograms and an Imax theater.
- **Alki Beach Park** (p104) Fun in the sun on this 2-mile stretch of beach.

Additions to Seattle Center include a skateboard park, a public basketball court and the Experience Music Project. The Seattle Center also hosts many of the city's major annual events, including the popular Bumbershoot (p18) music festival, the Northwest Folklife Festival (p17) and the Seattle International Children's Festival (p17). On a nice day, Seattle Center is a pleasant place to wander around, and no matter what season you're here, there's always a lot going on. If you're a kid or are traveling with any, this area is ground zero for good times.

The most entertaining way to get back and forth to Seattle Center is by monorail (automatically fun). This service provides frequent transportation between downtown's Westlake Center, at Pine St and 4th Ave, and Seattle Center; it runs about every 10 minutes. Smart visitors will pack a lunch or snacks, as the food available here can be of the overpriced carnival type.

SPACE NEEDLE Map p72

☎ 206-905-2100; www.spaceneedle.com; adult/senior/child $17/15/9; ☼ 9am-midnight

Seattle's signature monument, the Space Needle (originally called 'The Space Cage') was designed by Victor Steinbrueck and John Graham Jr, reportedly based on the napkin scribblings of World's Fair organizer Eddie Carlson. The part that's visible above ground weighs an astounding 3700 tons. The tower takes advantage of its 520ft-high observation deck – offering 360-degree views of Seattle and surrounding areas – to bombard visitors with historical information and interpretive displays. On clear days, zip to the top on the elevators (43 seconds) for excellent views of downtown, Lake Union, Mt Rainier and the Olympic Range mountains way across Puget Sound; don't bother spending the cash on cloudy days. If you're coming up to take aerial photos, be forewarned that there's fencing around the observation deck's perimeter, making clear shots impossible. Its revolving restaurant, Sky City, is way overpriced for the quality, but reservations in the dining room do give you a free ride up the elevator.

EXPERIENCE MUSIC PROJECT Map above

☎ 206-367-5483; www.empsfm.org; 325 5th Ave N; admission incl Science Fiction Museum adult/child $15/12; ☯ 10am-7pm Jun–mid-Sep, 10am-5pm mid-Sep–May

The Experience Music Project (EMP) is worth a look for the architecture alone. The shimmering, abstract building – designed by Frank Gehry – was inspired by Microsoft cofounder Paul Allen's passion for Jimi Hendrix's music and was initially intended

as a tribute to Hendrix alone. It now houses 80,000 music artifacts, including handwritten lyrics by Nirvana's Kurt Cobain and a Fender Stratocaster that Hendrix demolished. There's also Janis Joplin's pink feather boa, the world's first steel guitar and Hendrix's signed contract to play at Woodstock.

Appropriately, the best exhibits are the Hendrix Gallery, a major tribute to Jimi; the Northwest Passage, displaying everything from Ray Charles' debut album (recorded in Seattle) to Heart's stage apparel; and a long hallway that details the evolution of grunge. Upstairs is the Sound Lab, a futuristic studio that lets you lay down vocal tracks and play guitars, drums and keyboards. Kids will love it, as will anyone obsessed with Northwest music, but others may find themselves yawning. If you're on the fence about paying, the Sky Church theater and Revolution bar are accessible free of charge.

SCIENCE FICTION MUSEUM Map left

☎ 206-724-3428; www.empsfm.org; 325 5th Ave N; admission incl Experience Music Project adult/

child $15/12; ⏱ 10am-7pm Jun–mid-Sep, 10am-5pm mid-Sep–May

Barnacled onto the hull of the EMP is this nerd paradise: a collection of costumes, props and models from various sci-fi movies and TV shows. Highlights include the actual alien queen from the movie *Aliens* (1986) – never fear, she's behind Plexiglas in the cargo bay – and the only 3D model of the Death Star made for *Star Wars: A New Hope* (ie the original movie). Lowlights include a bedraggled Twiki costume from the *Buck Rogers* TV series. Rare books and manuscripts – including Neal Stephenson's handwritten *Baroque Cycle,* stacked as tall as the ET figure next to it – lend the display credibility. But mostly it just makes you want to go and rent *Blade Runner* again.

CHILDREN'S MUSEUM Map opposite

☎ 206-441-1768; www.thechildrensmuseum .org; 305 Harrison St; adult & child/grandparent $7.50/6.50; ⏱ 10am-5pm Mon-Fri, 10am-6pm Sat & Sun

In the basement of Center House near the monorail stop, the Children's Museum is an anachronistic learning center that offers activities and displays seemingly imported from an earlier time; it's a museum that might itself belong in a museum. But it's all very charming, if lacking in modern-day bells and whistles.

The play area includes a child-size neighborhood and an area dedicated to blowing soap bubbles. Also nearby is the Seattle Children's Theater (Map opposite; ☎ 206-441-3322; www.sct.org, tickets $10), a separate entity with summer performances in the Charlotte Martin and Eve Alvord Theaters.

PACIFIC SCIENCE CENTER Map opposite

☎ 206-443-2001; www.pacsci.org; 200 2nd Ave N; adult/child 6-12/child 3-5 $14/9/7, incl Imax Theater & laserium $18/13/11; ⏱ 10am-6pm

This interactive museum of science and industry once housed the science pavilion of the World's Fair. Today, the center features virtual-reality exhibits, a tropical butterfly house, laser shows, holograms and other wonders of science, many with hands-on demonstrations. Also on the premises is the vaulted-screen Imax Theater (☎ 206-443-4629; adult/child 6-12/child 3-5 incl laserium $9/7/6), a laserium and a planetarium.

INTERNATIONAL FOUNTAIN Map opposite

☎ light-show schedule 206-684-7200

This is the place to be on sunny days. With 287 jets of water (recycled, of course) pumping in time to a computer-driven music system, the International Fountain at the heart of the Seattle Center is a great place to rest your feet or eat lunch on a warm day. On summer nights, there's a free light-and-music show.

QUEEN ANNE

Shopping p112, Eating p129, Drinking p143, Sleeping p179

Rising above Seattle Center, Queen Anne is an old neighborhood of majestic redbrick houses and apartment buildings, sweeping lawns manicured to perfection, and gorgeous views of the city and Elliott Bay. It has some of the most prestigious addresses in Seattle and a generally quiet, dignified atmosphere – not quite stodgy, but not exactly Capitol Hill either.

Named for the prominent Queen Anne–style houses first built on the neighborhood's lower slopes, Queen Anne Hill was one of the original seven hills of Seattle. At 456ft, it's also the steepest and highest, rising precipitously above Elliott Bay and Lake Union. Spend a little time here and it will become clear that the Queen Anne neighborhood has two distinct sides – roughly speaking, the bluebloods live up top and the young urbanites down below. Funky Lower Queen Anne (or as it's more evocatively known, the Bottom of Queen Anne) flanks Seattle Center to the west and butts up against Belltown on the other side of Denny Way. This area has a pleasant, old-fashioned and lived-in quality despite its busy urban locale. Because of their proximity to Seattle Center, the bars and restaurants in Lower Queen Anne get quite a workout before and after home games at Key Arena or when there's a performance at the Opera House.

Upper Queen Anne, on top of the hill, has lots of pretty gingerbread houses, excellent views of the city and some great restaurants, especially for upscale Asian and Spanish food. This part of the neighborhood has a grown-up vibe and sense of the establishment and old money. Public ordinances decree that no one should sit or lie down on public sidewalks, so if you're thinking about it, make sure there's a bench between you and the curb.

Other than to eat or shop, the main reason to visit Upper Queen Anne is to check out the old mansions and spectacular views. Top to bottom, the whole neighborhood has a quaint feel, thanks to its well-preserved architecture and mostly small businesses.

Metro bus 2 runs frequently to Queen Anne from downtown and Seattle Center, as do several others – any bus saying East or West Queen Anne will get you up the hill.

GABLE HOUSE Map opposite
1 W Highland Dr at Queen Anne Ave N
This 14-gabled house was built in 1905 by Harry Whitney Treat, a friend of William F 'Buffalo Bill' Cody. Treat also built the Golden Gardens Park (p98). It's long since become an office building, but both the building and the hillside setting are worth a look.

KERRY PARK Map opposite
211 W Highland Dr
This is where to go if you want to get postcard-perfect photos of the Seattle skyline, Mt Rainier and the Space Needle. Kerry Park, along the stroll-friendly and prestigious Highland Dr, has one of the three best views in town (the others are from Gas Works Park near Wallingford and Duwamish Head in West Seattle). It's a magical vista, especially at night or sunset. Going a little further along W Highland Dr will take you to the lesser-known Betty Bowen Park, an excellent spot for views across Puget Sound to the Olympic Mountains. Across the way, check out Parsons Garden, a public garden that's especially popular for summer weddings.

QUEEN ANNE COUNTERBALANCE
Map opposite
Queen Anne Ave N, north of W Roy St
The streetcar that chugged up and down the steep grade along Queen Anne Ave started operating on overhead-wire electricity in 1900, but it still needed some help to manage the hill. So engineers designed a system of counterweights – a 16-ton train that ran in a tunnel beneath the street would go up when the cable car went down and vice versa. The cable cars were retired in 1943, but the underground tunnels are still there.

TURRET HOUSE Map opposite
W Halladay St & 6th Ave W
This adorable castle-like building, with gables and (appropriately enough) turrets galore, was once the home of the Love Israel Family, an ex-hippie commune turned religious cult. Love Family members were famous for huffing noxious gasses, refusing to cut their hair and believing they were each part of the body of Jesus Christ. The Turret House has since been converted to apartments.

INFORMATION		
Post Office	1	C5

SIGHTS		(p74)
Betty Bowen Park	2	B4
Gable House	3	C4
Kerry Park	4	C4
Parsons Garden	5	B4
Queen Anne Counterbalance	6	C5
Turret House	7	B2

SHOPPING		(p107)
Easy Street Records	8	C5
Once Upon a Time	9	C4
Queen Anne Books	10	C4

EATING		(p119)
5 Spot	11	C4
Canlis	12	D2
Paragon Bar & Grill	(see 13)	
Queen Anne Café	13	C3

DRINKING		(p139)
Hilltop Ale House	14	C3
Mecca Café	15	C5
Uptown Espresso Bar	16	C5

THE ARTS		(p157)
Behnke Center for Contemporary Performance	17	C5
Uptown Cinemas	18	C5

SPORTS & ACTIVITIES		(p163)
Queen Anne Pool	19	C3
Sierra Club	20	C1

SLEEPING		(p173)
Hampton Inn	21	D5
Inn at Queen Anne	22	C5
MarQueen Hotel	23	C5

See Fremont Map (p87)

See Seattle Center Map (p72)

NEIGHBORHOODS QUEEN ANNE

LAKE UNION

Shopping p113, Eating p129, Sleeping p180

Lake Union isn't quite the neat-and-tidy neighborhood that's typical of the rest of Seattle. For one thing, it's mostly afloat: Lake Union is known for having the largest houseboat population in the US. The Y-shaped lake's waters lap up against the shores of many traditional neighborhoods, including Fremont, southern Wallingford, Eastlake and the eastern slopes of Queen Anne. What ties this area together is the number of restaurants, lodgings and recreational facilities clustered around the lake. Lake Union is also a transportation hub for flights by seaplane to the San Juan Islands (p189) or Victoria, BC (p196).

South Lake Union is perennially in the news, as its relatively undefined nature makes it deeply attractive to developers. It was mostly left to its own devices – kind of a backyard neighborhood full of unglamorous storefronts and low-income housing – but then came efforts to raze many of the area's small businesses and transform 61 acres of land into a Seattle Commons park. The neighborhood (aka the people whose houses would've been squashed to make room for the park) voted down the plan in 1995 and '96, but the park initiative led to some interesting results. Microsoft co-founder Paul Allen wound up owning 11 acres here, and Allen's company, Vulcan, spent about $200 million buying up land bit by bit over the intervening years. Allen's vision, to be completed over the next dozen years, has already started taking shape. The plan calls for much of the land to be developed as a biotech research center and residential community, with 10 million sq ft of offices, apartments, condos, hotels, restaurants and shops. The 12-acre Lake Union Park opened along the waterfront in 2008. The South Lake Union Trolley, or SLUT, started running in 2007, and connects Westlake Center downtown to the south end of Lake Union.

A couple of resources for being active and outdoorsy in Seattle can be found in Lake Union. The area is on the verge of undergoing radical change, with thousands of new jobs (mainly in biotech) coming in to the neighborhood. Stay alert!

CENTER FOR WOODEN BOATS
Map opposite

☎ 206-382-2628; www.cwb.org; 1010 Valley St; sailboat rental per hr weekday/weekend $25/30, rowboat $20/25; beginner sailing course $375; ⏱ 12:30pm-dusk Sat & Sun & by appointment Oct-Apr; 12:30pm-dusk Tue-Sun May-Sep

If you have an interest in the history and craft of wooden boats, then you'll definitely want to visit the Center for Wooden Boats. This museum and enthusiast's center features vintage and replica boats, and offers sailing lessons, including an excellent beginner course that gives you as many lessons as it offers in a four-month period (usually eight to 12 lessons). Seasoned sailors who are a little rusty can take a one-on-one lesson for around $50 per hour, and there are also classes on sail repair and boat building. You can rent sailboats and rowboats, but one person in your party has to know how to sail and must do a checkout ($10 fee) before you'll be permitted to rent. It's pretty straightforward: you need to demonstrate tacking, jibing and docking. The center also offers free boat rides every Sunday afternoon.

REI Map opposite

☎ 206-323-8333; 222 Yale Ave N; ⏱ 9am-9pm Mon-Sat, 10am-7pm Sun

As much an adventure as a shopping experience, this giant state-of-the-art megastore has its own climbing wall – a 65ft rock pinnacle to the side of the store's entryway. The wall is open for scrambling at various times daily, except Tuesday when it's reserved for private groups. (You can climb free of charge, but be prepared to wait your turn.) You can also check out the rain-proofing of various brands of gear by entering a special rainstorm shower; or road-test hiking boots on a simulated mountain trail. REI also rents various ski packages, climbing gear and camping equipment – call for daily and weekly rates.

SEATTLE BY BOAT

Seeing Seattle from the water is one of the best ways to fall in love with the city. A number of places rent kayaks and canoes (see p167), or you can arrange a guided tour through the Northwest Outdoor Center, the University of Washington's Waterfront Activities Center or the Moss Bay Rowing Club (see p166 for details of these operations). The Center for Wooden Boats (above) offers sailing lessons in addition to sailboat rentals.

SIGHTS (p76)
Center for Wooden Boats...............1 B5
REI...2 C6

SHOPPING 🛍 (p107)
Feathered Friends..........................3 C6
Patrick's Fly Shop..........................4 C2

EATING 🍴 (p119)
Chandler's Crabhouse &
 Fresh Fish Market.......................5 C5
Cicchetti..................................(see 6)
Serafina...6 C3

NIGHTLIFE ★ (p151)
El Corazon......................................7 C6

SPORTS & ACTIVITIES (p163)
Forest Service/National
 Park Service...........................(see 2)
Moss Bay Rowing & Kayak
 Center..8 C4
Northwest Outdoor Center.........9 B3
Sailing in Seattle.........................10 B3
Spa Blix...11 C6

SLEEPING 🛏 (p173)
Courtyard Marriott......................12 B5
Marriott Residence Inn...............13 C5
Silver Cloud Inn Lake Union 14 C4

TRANSPORT
Sailing in Seattle.....................(see 10)

CAPITOL HILL & VOLUNTEER PARK

Shopping p113, Eating p130, Drinking p143, Sleeping p180

Northeast of downtown, Capitol Hill is probably Seattle's most diverse and lively neighborhood because of its distinctly edgy personality. Long a counterculture oasis, Capitol Hill probably boasts more nose rings, tattoos and poetry readings than anywhere else in the Pacific Northwest. Trendy young students and urban homeless street kids share the sidewalks and cafe tables, although most people might not be able to spot the difference immediately.

Strictly speaking, the Pike–Pine Corridor (roughly from Minor Ave to 15th Ave) isn't part of what Seattleites usually consider Capitol Hill, but we're including it here for ease of navigation; it's a great strip for rowdy nightlife. East of Broadway, on 15th Ave E, is where some of the city's wealthiest residents live in the grand old mansions along the tree-lined streets; this is also where some of the best B&Bs are. Add to these demographics Capitol Hill's thriving gay and lesbian community, and you have a very lively and colorful mix of residents.

When Capitol Hill was still thick forest, Seattle pioneer Arthur Denny claimed land here in the hope that the area would become the Washington state capital. Though his hope was never realized (that honor went to Olympia, south of Seattle), Henry Yesler had already set to work logging the area and soon people were building elaborate mansions on the slope that overlooks the east side of Lake Union. A streetcar route was installed up Broadway from Yesler Way to City Park, later renamed Volunteer Park, and the area grew quickly. Some fantastic vestiges of the early architecture are well worth exploring.

This neighborhood boasts three major commercial areas, each of which attracts a different kind of crowd. The main commercial street is Broadway. It is lined with coffeehouses, restaurants, bars, trendy boutiques, bookstores and well-concealed supermarkets. Dilettante Chocolates (p113), decked out in pink with umbrellas, is well known for confection truffles and 'adult' milkshakes. All along Broadway are good, inexpensive ethnic restaurants, many of which cater to a student or long-haul traveler's budget. This is where the crowds are thickest and the vitality most engaging. Running perpendicular to Broadway is the Pike–Pine Corridor, a stretch of aging brick warehouses and former 1950s car dealerships. With most of the city's gay and lesbian bars, dance and live-music clubs, coffeehouses, record stores and fashionable restaurants, this is nightlife central for Seattle. East of Broadway, the quieter business district along 15th Ave E has well-established restaurants, book and record stores, and a couple of comfortable pubs and coffee shops.

The 'Corridor' doesn't look like much in the daylight, but after dark the area becomes party central. This was once a predominantly gay- and lesbian-oriented area and it's still the location of most of the good queer clubs, but sexual orientation has taken a back seat lately to catwalk fashions and sleek concept bars. At any rate, being straight here certainly won't make you feel unwelcome.

There seem to be a few bars on every block, but there's more to do here than just drink and dance. Late-night coffeehouses feature live music, poetry readings or pool tables. Here and there are antique stores and more unusual shops, including Babeland (p113) and the new home of the awesome Elliott Bay Book Company (p113). This area is also the center of the city's tattoo culture.

As you wander, look for brass inlaid dance-step diagrams set into the sidewalk along Broadway. Inventively called *The Broadway Dance Steps,* they're a public artwork designed by Jack Mackie. If you decide to attempt a tango on a street corner, you assuredly won't be the most unusual sight on Broadway.

Along 15th Ave E, the crowds aren't as thick as on Broadway. Instead, with an organic grocery store and a couple of mellow bars as its anchors, 15th Ave feels like an ex-hippie enclave and a settled-in community. One of Seattle's favorite places for brunch and lunch, Coastal Kitchen (p130), is here.

It should come as no surprise that most of the things to see and do on Capitol Hill are arts related, whether they're galleries, museums, literary hangouts or music venues. This is also just a great neighborhood for wandering around and people-watching. And the street theater can't be beaten.

Several Metro buses, including bus 49 and bus 10, go to Capitol Hill from downtown.

CAPITOL HILL & VOLUNTEER PARK

SEATTLE ASIAN ART MUSEUM Map p79
☎ 206-654-3100; www.seattleartmuseum.org; 1400 E Prospect St, Volunteer Park; adult/student & senior/child $7/5/free; ☻ 10am-5pm Wed-Sun, 10am-9pm Thu

For almost 60 years the Seattle Art Museum occupied a prestigious Carl Gould–designed space in Volunteer Park. When it moved downtown in the early 1990s, the Seattle Asian Art Museum moved in. The museum now houses the extensive Asian art collection of Dr Richard Fuller, who donated this severe art moderne–style gallery to the city in 1932. Admission is free on the first Thursday (and from 5pm to 9pm on the second Thursday) of each month.

VOLUNTEER PARK CONSERVATORY Map p79
☎ 206-684-4743; 1400 E Galer St; admission free; ☻ 10am-4pm Tue-Sun

The conservatory is a classic Victorian greenhouse built in 1912. Filled with palms, cacti and tropical plants, it features five galleries representing different world environments. Check out the creepy corpse flower.

JIMI HENDRIX STATUE Map p79
1600 Broadway
Guitar genius of the last century and Seattle's favorite son, Jimi Hendrix rocks out eternally in this bronze sculpture by local artist Daryl Smith, created in 1997. Hendrix fans have been known to leave flowers, candles and notes at the base of the kneeling statue.

ST MARK'S CATHEDRAL Map p79
☎ 206-323-0300; 1245 10th Ave E; ☻ performances 9:30pm Sun

Go north on Broadway (as the chaos turns to well-maintained houses with manicured lawns) until it turns into 10th Ave E and you're within a block of Volunteer Park. At the neo-Byzantine St Mark's Cathedral, various choirs perform on Sundays, accompanied by a 3944-pipe Flentrop organ. The performances are free and open to the public. There's also a concert series held in the cathedral, for which tickets can be purchased at the cathedral shop or by phone at ☎ 206-323-1040.

LAKEVIEW CEMETERY Map p79
One of Seattle's oldest cemeteries and the final resting place of many early settlers, Lakeview Cemetery borders Volunteer Park to the north. Arthur Denny and his family, Doc and Catherine Maynard, Thomas Mercer and Henry Yesler are all interred here. This is also the gravesite of Princess Angeline, the daughter of Duwamish Chief Sealth, after whom Seattle was named.

Most people, however, stop by to see the graves of martial arts film legends Bruce and Brandon Lee. Flowers from fans are usually scattered around Brandon's red and Bruce's black tombstones, which stand side by side in a tiny part of the cemetery. The graves are not easy to find: enter the cemetery at 15th Ave E and E Garfield St; follow the road in and turn left at the Terrace Hill Mausoleum. At the crest of the hill you'll see the large Denny family plot on your left. Look a little further along the road, and you'll find the Lees. Even if you're not usually into graveyards, you'll at least enjoy the beautiful views at this one.

LOUISA BOREN LOOKOUT Map p79
15th Ave E at Garfield St
Outside the Volunteer Park boundaries, the Louisa Boren Lookout provides one of the best views over the university and Union Bay. The small park is named after the longest-surviving member of the party that founded Seattle in 1851.

WATER TOWER OBSERVATION DECK
Map p79
1400 E Prospect St
Keen seekers of views can climb 107 steep steps to the top of Volunteer Park's 75ft water tower. Built in 1907, it provides wonderful vistas of the Space Needle and over Elliott Bay.

SEATTLE MUSEUM OF THE MYSTERIES Map p79
☎ 206-328-6499; 954 E Union St; adult/child $3/2; ☯ noon-8:30pm Mon-Fri, noon-10pm Sat, 1:30-5:30pm Sun
Now in its new location at 10th and Union, the Museum of the Mysteries is more a cache of obscure and alternative knowledge than a museum in the traditional sense. Odd but fascinating, this den in Capitol Hill has a number of treasures that reveal themselves to those with the patience to explore. It's kitschy, but it's fun. There's also an oxygen bar ($5 for a five-minute treatment) and tarot readings.

U DISTRICT

The U District, named for the 'U Dub' (what locals call the University of Washington), feels like its own little college town. The streets are full of tiny cheap eateries, thrift stores, record stores, second-hand bookstores, tattoo parlors and a couple of bars. Everyone on the sidewalks around here seems to be between the ages of 18 and 24. There used to be a thriving drug trade along the main drag (University Way NE, called 'the Ave'), which could make nighttime strolling unpleasant, but the city has cracked down and the number of down-and-outers has decreased dramatically.

The number of cheap places to eat, especially Indian and Asian, make the Ave the best place to find an inexpensive meal. Coffeehouses grow like weeds in this area and owners are used to students buying one coffee and sitting around for three hours. The absolutely cavernous University Bookstore (p115) takes up an entire city block. It has an excellent selection of general books and more scholarly tomes, along with a giant section of yellow and purple Huskies clothing.

At University Way and NE 50th St, the Grand Illusion Cinema (p160), an excellent though tiny theater, shows interestingly chosen programs of foreign and art films. The coffee shop next door is a popular place to have a latte and settle into a novel. At 25th Ave NE you'll find the University Village, an upscale, semi-outdoor mall geared more toward the parents of the UW students than the students themselves, with highbrow chains such as Anthropologie, Eddie Bauer and Pottery Barn. Along NE 45th St, east of the Ave, are some of UW's sorority and frat houses.

The University of Washington campus, sitting at the edge of this busy commercial area, is beautiful and lends itself to leisurely, tranquil walks. A great way to explore the campus is on a bicycle: the Burke-Gilman Trail follows the south side of campus, providing an excellent arterial for getting to and from the university. The campus also has a couple of excellent buildings worth checking out, as well as one of the city's finest galleries and a great museum. The student population lends the area a youthful, unpretentious feeling.

Several Metro buses, including buses 70, 73 and 74, run frequently to the U District from downtown Seattle.

HENRY ART GALLERY Map opposite

☎ 206-543-2280; cnr 15th Ave NE & NE 41st St; adult/senior/student $10/6/free, Thu free; ☽ 11am-4pm Wed, Sat & Sun, 11am-9pm Thu-Fri

The university's sleek fine-art gallery mounts some of the most intelligent exhibits and installations in Seattle and serves as a touchstone for the arts community. There are dedicated spaces for video and digital art, and a small permanent collection, as well as rotating shows (35 a year). Part of the permanent collection is Skyspace, by James Turrell, an artist whose medium is light. Turrell's installation over the sculpture garden will alter the way you look at the ever-changing Seattle sky. If you pay $1 extra for a ticket here, you get free entry to the Burke Museum on the same day.

BURKE MUSEUM Map opposite

☎ 206-543-5590; cnr 16th Ave NE & NE 45th St; adult/senior/student $9.50/7.50/6, 1st Thu of month free; ☽ 10am-5pm, 1st Thu of month 10am-8pm

This museum of natural history and anthropology is located on the University of Washington's campus. There's a good collection of dinosaur skeletons, but the real treasures here are the North Coast Indian artifacts, especially the collection of cedar canoes and totem poles. On the ground level of the museum is the pleasant Museum Café (☎ 206-543-9854), a high-ceilinged, atmospheric place with warm pine paneling and wooden tables. The Burke/Henry dollar deal applies (see Henry Art Gallery, left).

UNIVERSITY OF WASHINGTON
Map opposite

☎ visitors center 206-543-9198; 4014 University Way; ☽ 9am-5pm

Established in 1861, the University of Washington was first built downtown on the site of the present Fairmont Olympic Hotel. The university moved to its present location along Lake Washington's Union Bay in 1895. Much of the 639-acre site constituted the grounds of the 1909 Alaska-Yukon-Pacific Exposition. Dozens of new buildings were constructed for this gathering, which was similar to a World's Fair.

Today, the university is the largest in the Northwest, with around 35,000 students, 211 buildings and 4000 faculty members. Noted programs include law and medicine; it's also highly regarded for computer science and liberal arts. More than half of its students are in graduate programs. The university publishes its own paper, aptly named the *Daily*. In it you'll find out about whatever's currently causing the angst around campus, details about campus events and U District classifieds.

The collective name given to all the U Dub sports teams is the Huskies (p165). They compete in 25 intercollegiate sports, most notably basketball and football. Most teams play at Husky Stadium and the Edmundson Pavilion, both on the east side of campus. To find out about athletic events and tickets, call ☎ 206-543-2200.

U DISTRICT

The university's main arts venue is the 1200-seat Meany Hall. Live dance, theater and musical performances also take place at U Dub's other three theaters – the Penthouse, Playhouse and the Studio. For information and tickets, call or stop by the UW Arts Ticket Office (Map p83; ☎ 206-543-4880; cnr University Way NE & NE 40th St).

The university is a lovely, lively place; it is definitely worth touring, especially in spring when bulbs and azaleas paint the verdant campus with brilliant colors. Maps are available from the UW Visitors Information Center (Map p83; ☎ 206-543-9198; 4014 University Way NE). The center also offers free 90-minute campus tours that start at its offices at 10:30am weekdays.

SUZZALLO LIBRARY Map p83

Those architecturally minded will be interested in the University of Washington's Suzzallo Library. Designed by Carl Gould around 1926, this bibliophile's dream was inspired by Henry Suzzallo, UW's president at the time. Suzzallo wanted it to look like a cathedral, because 'the library is the soul of the university.' Unfortunately for him, his bosses disagreed; on reviewing the building, they deemed it too expensive and fired Suzzallo for his extravagance. Gould was the founder of the university's architecture program; he created the plans for 18 campus buildings.

CENTRAL PLAZA (RED SQUARE) Map p83

The center of campus is more commonly referred to as Red Square because of its base of red brick. It's not the coziest, but it fills up with students cheerfully sunning themselves on nice days and it looks impressive at night. *Broken Obelisk,* the 26ft-high stainless-steel sculpture in the square, was made by noted color-field painter Barnett Newman. Just below Red Square is a wide promenade leading to lovely Rainier Vista, with spectacular views across Lake Washington to Mt Rainier.

DRUMHELLER FOUNTAIN Map p83

Drumheller Fountain sits inside of what was originally known as Geyser Basin (now 'Frosh Pond'), one of the few remaining pieces leftover from the 1909 expo that beefed up the university.

QUAD Map p83

The Quad is home to many of the original campus buildings. When the ivy turns red in the fall, the effect is more reminiscent of New England than the Northwest.

RAVENNA PARK Map p83

Just north of the U District is Ravenna, a residential neighborhood that's home to a lot of professors and university staff. At its heart is Ravenna Park, a lush and wild park with two playgrounds on either side of the mystery-drenched ravine carved by Ravenna Creek.

U DISTRICT
Walking Tour

1 Burke Museum
Start this tour at the Burke Museum (p82), which you may choose to visit now (this will add at least an hour to the tour time) or simply note to check out later. Its collection of Northwest native art is definitely not to be missed. From here, walk along NE 45th St to Memorial Way – take a right and amble into campus through the university's north gate.

2 Central Plaza (Red Square)
Stroll along Stevens Way to Pierce Lane, which leads to the center of campus, Red Square (opposite).

3 Suzzallo Library
From Red Square you'll see the gorgeous, cathedral-like Suzzallo Library (opposite). Admire it from the inside and out, then take a sharp left when you exit the library.

4 Drumheller Fountain
Descend the stairs and walk straight ahead toward Drumheller Fountain (opposite), which spews out of the circular pool known as 'Frosh Pond.' On the way, along the pathway leading to the fountain, you'll be stunned (if it's a clear day) by the views from what is appropriately named Rainier Vista.

5 Henry Art Gallery
Head back toward Red Square, and bear left at the library. This will lead you to the Henry Art Gallery (p82), one of the best galleries in Seat-

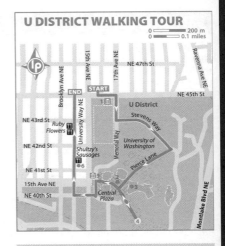

U DISTRICT WALKING TOUR

WALK FACTS
Start Burke Museum
End Henry Art Gallery or the Ave
Distance 2 miles
Duration One hour
Fuel stops Ruby, Flowers and Schultzy's Sausages

tle. The cafe downstairs is a good place for coffee and a panini. Or press on to 'The Ave,' bustling University Way NE, where there's a string of affordable coffee-shops and ethnic restaurants to kick back in (see the Eating chapter, p131).

6 The Ave
Wander up the Ave, peeking in shops and cafes along the way. The tour concludes when you reach the busy intersection with NE 45th St; this is the core of the U District.

lonelyplanet.com

FREMONT

Shopping p115, Eating p133, Drinking p146

Historically the most fun-loving of the northern neighborhoods, Fremont is known for its unorthodox public sculpture, junk stores, summer outdoor film festivals and general high spirits. In the evenings, the pubs, restaurants and coffeehouses fill with a lively mix of old hippies, young professionals and gregarious students. Except for the odd glitch, chain stores stay away from Fremont. Unlike the flashy urban disenfranchisement that gives Capitol Hill its spirit, life in Fremont is conducted with humor and a sense of community well-being. Fremont's motto, *De Libertas Quirkas*, gives it the 'Freedom to be Peculiar,' and its residents happily live up to that proclamation. Though some of its quirks have been smoothed over recently by an influx of deep-pocketed real-estate investors, this district is still one of the more entertaining to visit.

However, Fremont wasn't always cool and, like a child who lacks natural talent, had to work hard to get where it is. The completion of the high-flying Aurora Bridge (officially known as the George Washington Memorial Bridge, a fact unknown even to most Seattleites) in the 1930s meant people didn't need to come through Fremont anymore, which sent its commercial district into a sharp decline. Through the 1950s and '60s, Fremont experienced a tragic architectural blight, when many of the old mill-workers' houses were converted into cookie-cutter duplexes and cheaply built apartment buildings. Through the 1960s, Fremont had more vacant stores than occupied ones and it lacked even neighborhood necessities like a grocery store or pharmacy. The low-rent buildings attracted a rather dowdy and rowdy bunch who didn't have much energy for making Fremont a better place.

In the 1970s things started to change. The first Fremont Street Fair danced its way along the neighborhood streets in 1972. The Fremont Public Association, today the envy of every neighborhood association, was created in 1974 to provide shelter, food and help to disadvantaged residents. The association did (and still does) wonders for Fremont, although it has changed its name to Solid Ground (www.solid-ground.org). Its formation spawned a number of other thriving community associations, including the Fremont Arts Council (www.fremontartscouncil.org).

Public art, often wacky and unconventional, famously decorates neighborhood streets, and blatant eccentricity is encouraged. In 1994 Fremont citizens declared that they had seceded from Seattle, and the neighborhood was thenceforward the 'Republic of Fremont, Center of the Known Universe.'

Today, Fremont thrives economically, but it has other problems. Like a teenager who suddenly becomes popular, everyone wants to hang out with it. Rents have skyrocketed here, stores and restaurants are pricier, and prime real estate is being sold to people who can afford it – generally not Fremont locals. The U-Park lot behind the former Redhook Brewery long held the infamous Fremont Almost-Free Outdoor Cinema, where movies played on a building wall and filmgoers brought couches from home, sat back in the parking lot and watched movies. That lot was bulldozed in 2001. The ever-expanding Lake Union Center, which houses software giant Adobe among others, brought more than 500,000 sq ft of office space to the formerly building-free Fremont waterfront.

One great Fremont must-do is the Fremont Street Fair (p18), a colorful, musical and beer-filled event that takes place on the weekend nearest the summer solstice in June. Another annual event, Trolloween (p18), features a candlelight procession of costumed locals on Halloween night (October 31), followed by a dance. Throw a costume on and join the fun. But be warned: don't even think about parking in Fremont during either of these events.

Fremont's changed a lot over the years, but it hasn't stopped thinking of itself as the center of the universe. And despite the influx of normality lately, the funky little corner of Seattle still has plenty going for it. Where else can you see dinosaurs, tour a chocolate factory, walk underneath a rocket and get your photo taken with Lenin, all in the space of a couple of blocks?

Several Metro buses, including bus 5, run frequently from downtown Seattle to Fremont.

FREMONT SUNDAY MARKET
Map opposite

☎ 206-781-6776; www.fremontmarket.com; Phinney Ave N; ☽ 10am-5pm Sun Jun-Aug, to 4pm Dec-Feb

Fremont is an especially great place to be during the Sunday Market, which features fresh fruits and vegetables and an incredible variety of artists and people selling junk. In summer the market is held

NEIGHBORHOODS FREMONT

SIGHTS	(p86)
Apatosaurs	1 C3
Fremont Bridge	2 D4
Fremont Rocket	3 D3
Fremont Sunday Market	4 C3
Fremont Troll	5 D3
History House	6 D4
Statue of Lenin	7 D3
Theo Chocolate Factory	8 C3
Waiting for the Interurban	9 D4

SHOPPING	(p107)
Deluxe Junk	10 D3
Evo	11 B3
Fremont Place Book Co	12 D3

EATING	(p119)
Baguette Box	13 D4
Paseo	14 D1

See Queen Anne Map (p75)	

DRINKING	(p139)
Brouwer's	15 C3
Dad Watson's Restaurant & Brewery	16 D3
Hale's Brewery & Pub	17 A1

NIGHTLIFE	(p151)
Nectar	18 C3

SPORTS & ACTIVITIES	(p163)
Sound Mind & Body	19 C3
Yoga Tree	20 D1

outdoors in the parking lot; in winter, it moves inside. Fremont's market has joined forces with its sister market in Ballard, which also runs every Sunday but is more a traditional farmers market.

FREMONT BRIDGE Map above

Look across Fremont Ave N and you'll see the Fremont Bridge, which is not exactly a spectacular structure or piece of art, but interesting nonetheless. The bridge was built in 1916 when construction of the Washington Ship Canal sliced a gully between Fremont and the northern reaches of Queen Anne. The bridge went up, providing a vital link across the canal. It was painted industrial green – after all, this was long before Fremont became so

colorful. When the revitalization of the neighborhood began in 1972, the bridge was to be repainted with the same shade of green. In the process, a coat of orange primer was painted on the bridge and a few people thought, 'Hey, that orange isn't bad!' Of course just as many people thought the orange was awful, but it won out and the bridge stayed orange until the mid-1980s, when it needed yet another repainting. The orange-haters were still adamant and the decision about what color to repaint the bridge was put to a vote. Orange wasn't even on the ballot, and an acceptable shade of blue won. But the orange-lovers were not to be deterred and a group of Fremont rebels went out in the middle of the night and painted orange accents on the blue bridge. This orange-and-blue combination stuck and is now the official color scheme every time the bridge gets repainted.

FREMONT ROCKET Map p87
Evanston Ave N off N 36th St

Fremont has adopted this phallic and zany-looking rocket as its community totem. Constructed in the 1950s for use in the Cold War, the rocket was plagued with difficulties and never actually went anywhere, leaving the engineering team with the unfortunate problem of 'not being able to get it up.' Before coming to Fremont, the rocket was affixed to an army surplus store in Belltown. When the store went out of business, the Fremont Business Association snapped it up. Beneath the rocket you'll find a coin box affixed to the building. Drop in 50 cents and the rocket will 'launch' by blowing a bunch of steam, but true to its under-performing nature, it won't go anywhere.

STATUE OF LENIN Map p87
cnr N 36th St & Fremont Pl N

This is the latest and most controversial addition to Fremont's collection of public art. This bronze, 16ft statue of former communist leader Vladimir Lenin weighs 7 tons. It was brought to the USA from Slovakia by an American, Lewis Carpenter, who found the statue in a scrap pile after the 1989 revolution. Carpenter spent a fortune to bring it over, sure that some crazy American would want to buy it. No one did, so here it stands biding its time in Fremont, allegedly still on sale for $250,000.

WAITING FOR THE INTERURBAN
Map p87
N 34th St & Fremont Ave N

Seattle's most popular piece of public art, this lively sculpture in recycled aluminum depicts people waiting for a train that never comes. The train that once passed through Fremont stopped running in the 1930s, and the people of Seattle have been waiting for a new train – the Interurban – ever since. Finally, in 2001, Sound Transit trains started once again to connect Seattle with Everett, much like the original train did. The sculpture is prone to regular 'art attacks,' where locals lovingly decorate the people in outfits corresponding to a special event, the weather, someone's birthday, a Mariners win – whatever. Rarely do you see the sculpture 'undressed.' Take a look at the human-faced dog peeking out between the legs of the people. That face belongs to Armen Stepanian, one of the founders of today's Fremont and its excellent recycling system. Sculptor Richard Beyer and Stepanian had a disagreement about the design of the piece, which resulted in Beyer's spiteful yet humorous design of the dog's face.

THEO CHOCOLATE FACTORY Map p87
☎ 206-632-5100; www.theochocolate.com; 3400 Phinney Ave N; tour $5; ☽ 10am-6pm, tours 1 & 3pm daily plus 11am Sat

What, perhaps you wonder, could possibly take the place of the free beer that came at the end of a Redhook Brewery tour? How about free chocolate? That's right – the old Redhood Brewery (empty for years since the company moved operations to Woodinville) has reopened as a chocolate factory, and it does tours. Enough said.

ROCKETS, RUSSIANS & TROLLS, OH MY!

There's a good chance that one of the first things you'll hear about from any Seattle resident is the Fremont Troll. People get a little weird about the troll. Understandably, of course – it's an unlikely attraction to find in a city, or rather, it *would* be unlikely anywhere but in Fremont. But keep in mind, this is the corner of Seattle that's also home to topiary dinosaurs (opposite), an inoperative rocket sticking out of a building (above), a statue of Lenin brought over from Slovakia and still available for purchase (above), and a statue of people waiting for a train that's never passed the spot (above). In that context, the Fremont Troll makes perfect sense.

The troll is easy enough to find: it lurks beneath the north end of the Aurora Bridge (not the Fremont Bridge) at N 36th St. It's an 18ft-high cement figure, made of 2 tons of ferro-concrete, and it's in the process of consuming a whole Volkswagen Beetle. The troll's creators – artists Steve Badanes, Will Martin, Donna Walter and Ross Whitehead – won a competition sponsored by the Fremont Arts Council in 1990. The team took seven weeks to complete the troll, whose menacing chrome eye keeps watch over Fremont.

APATOSAURS Map p87

Along the banks of the ship canal, Fremont Canal Park extends west following the extension of the Burke-Gilman Trail. Right at the start of the park, at the bottom of Phinney Ave N, you'll see two giant, life-sized 'apatosaurs.' These are the world's largest known topiaries, given to Fremont by the Pacific Science Center.

HISTORY HOUSE Map p87

☎ 206-675-8875; 790 N 34th St; admission $1; ☉ noon-5pm Wed-Sun

The History House contains rotating exhibits focused on the history of Seattle neighborhoods. It's a good place to see photos of early Seattle. The building's colorful metal fence is another piece of public art, built by blacksmith and welder Christopher Pauley. The fence features brightly colored houses with open doors, a reflection of Fremont's welcoming attitude.

CENTER OF THE UNIVERSE
Walking Tour

1 Fremont Rocket

Exploring Fremont can take as much or as little time and energy as you want. Start the walk on Evanston Ave N between N 35th and N 36th Sts at the rather conspicuous Fremont Rocket (opposite), Fremont's community totem.

2 Vladimir Lenin

Walk north (away from the water) up Evanston Ave N to N 36th St. Take a right onto Fremont Place N. On N 36th St at Fremont Place N, you'll see a controversial addition to Fremont's collection of public art. It's a bronze, 16ft statue of former communist leader Vladimir Lenin (opposite) weighing 7 tons. Brought to the USA from Slovakia, it's for sale and still awaiting a buyer.

3 Deluxe Junk

Walk half a block east along Fremont Place N. Stop at one of Seattle's most kitschy second-hand shops, Deluxe Junk (p115), located in a former funeral parlor. Continue east along Fremont Place N, cross Fremont Ave N and go east on N 35th St, which you'll follow to Aurora Ave N. You should now be underneath the Aurora Bridge. Turn left and head for the dark, shadowy space where the bridge meets the ground.

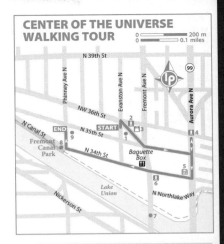

CENTER OF THE UNIVERSE WALKING TOUR

NEIGHBORHOODS FREMONT

WALK FACTS

Start Fremont Rocket
End Theo Chocolate Factory
Distance 0.75 miles
Duration One hour
Fuel stop Baguette Box

4 Fremont Troll

Watch out! It's the Fremont Troll (opposite). This incredible piece of public art is a must-see for anyone interested in the peculiar things in life. He's an 18ft cement figure busily munching on a VW bug, a reference to the children's story, 'The Three Billy Goats Gruff.' Back away slowly, then head back down Aurora Ave N to N 34th St. Turn right.

5 History House

On your right, you'll see the colorful metal fence of the History House (left). The fence features colored houses with open doors. Inside are exhibits about the history of Seattle neighborhoods.

6 Waiting for the Interurban

Follow N 34th St west, toward the Fremont Bridge. Here you'll find Seattle's most popular piece of public art, Waiting for the Interurban (opposite), showing people waiting for a train that never comes. Their clothes change regularly, as locals like to decorate them.

7 Fremont Bridge

Continue west and look left down Fremont Ave N, and you'll see the Fremont Bridge (p87), with an orange-and-blue color scheme that seems to fit perfectly in this slightly wacky neighborhood.

8 Apatosaurs

From the bridge, go west along N 34th St for two blocks until you get to Phinney Ave N. Along the banks of the ship canal, Fremont Canal Park extends west following the extension of the Burke-Gilman Trail. Right at the start of the park, at the bottom of Phinney Ave N, you'll see two giant, life-sized apatosaurs (p89),

giant topiaries given to Fremont by the Pacific Science Center.

9 Theo Chocolate Factory

Near the corner of Phinney Ave N and N 35th St is the building that used to house the Redhook Brewery and the Trolleyman Pub. The brewery has moved, and been replaced by the only thing that could possibly be better: a chocolate factory (p88). Which means it's time for you to get your sugar fix – and officially end our tour.

WALLINGFORD

Shopping p115, Eating p133, Drinking p146

Wallingford has blossomed from an old working-class neighborhood into a pleasant district of interesting shops, bookstores and inexpensive eateries, all just across the I-5 freeway from the University of Washington. The best thing about Wallingford is that it's not built upon a gimmick or tourist draw: this is as real as a neighborhood gets. The people who hang out here live here; you can still find an old-fashioned hardware store and a locals' pub among the espresso shops. Some excellent ethnic restaurants line N 45th St, along with some fun local bars and cool shops you don't want to miss.

Teahouse Kuan Yin (p147) is a great place to stop for a pot of exotic tea and a wireless internet session. Seattle's best travel bookstore is Wide World Books (p116). Another bookstore worth noting is Open Books (p115), which is devoted entirely to poetry; call to ask about readings and events. If you're not up for shopping, the Guild 45th St Theater (☎ 206-781-5755; www.landmarktheatres.com; 2115 N 45th St) shows mainstream movies as well as artsy flicks.

Wallingford is a quiet, mostly residential area that is nice for a wander, even though it doesn't have too many tourist attractions. The Burke-Gilman Trail comes through here near Gas Works Park, which itself is a great spot to hang out, watch kayakers go by and admire the Seattle skyline.

Several Metro buses, including 74, 71 and 26, run frequently from downtown to Wallingford.

GAS WORKS PARK off Map below
Meridian Ave at N Northlake Way

Urban reclamation has no greater monument in Seattle than Gas Works Park. The former power station here produced gas for heating and lighting from 1906 to 1956. The gas works was thereafter understandably considered an eyesore and an environmental menace. But the beautiful location of the park – with stellar views of downtown over Lake Union, and sailboats and yachts sliding to and from the shipping canal – induced the city government to convert the former industrial site into a public park in 1975. Rather than tear down the factory, landscape architects preserved much of the old plant. Painted black and now highlighted with rather joyful graffiti, it looks like some odd remnant from a former civilization. It also makes a great location for shooting rock album covers and music videos.

The soil and groundwater beneath the park still contain chemical contamination. Though this apparently poses no health risks to humans, state government and environmental agencies occasionally close the park to complete various cleanup and research projects, primarily to avoid further contamination of Lake Union.

NEIGHBORHOODS WALLINGFORD

DISCOUNT PASSES

If you're going to be in Seattle for a while and plan on seeing its premier attractions, consider buying a CityPass (adult/child aged 3-12 $59/39). Good for nine days, the pass gets you entry into the Space Needle, Experience Music Project, Pacific Science Center, Seattle Aquarium, Argosy Cruises' Seattle Harbor Tour, the Museum of Flight and the Woodland Park Zoo. You wind up saving about 50% on admission costs and you never have to stand in line. You can buy one at any of the venues or online at www.citypass.com /city/seattle.html.

Another option is the Go Seattle Card (www.go seattlecard.com; adult $45-134, child $28-89), which offers free or discounted admission to a long list of sights and entertainment. Available in one-, two-, three-, five- and seven-day versions, the cards get you in free to a number of the city's top attractions.

Despite its toxic history, this is still one of Seattle's best-loved parks. People come here to fly kites, picnic near the lake or simply to take in the view. And it *is* like nothing else you've ever seen. Be sure

to climb the small hill in order to see the sundial at the top. This is famous as one of the best places from which to photograph Seattle's skyline, especially at sunset when you can see the sun glistening in the windows of downtown buildings.

Before the trail was extended to Fremont and Ballard, the Burke-Gilman Trail (see Bicycling, p167) started in Gas Works Park. This is still a great spot to pick up the trail that you can then follow east to the University of Washington.

WALLINGFORD CENTER Map p91
Wallingford Ave N & N 45th St
This boutique and restaurant mall, inhabiting the nearly condemned, refurbished old Wallingford grade school, is the hub of the area. Out front, the *Wallingford Animal Storm* sculpture, created by artist Ronald Petty, depicts wildlife found in and around the neighborhood. It's not a destination, particularly, but it makes a good landmark or a handy place to park yourself on a bench and relax for a moment.

GREEN LAKE & PHINNEY RIDGE

Shopping p116, Eating p134, Drinking p147

Just north of Fremont and Wallingford – and closely tied to both – is Green Lake, a small natural lake that's the hub of a large park complex and a pleasant low-key neighborhood. The lake is packed with crowds in summer, but it's even better in fall, when the leaves are changing, or on a rare rain-free day in winter. Any time of the year, it's a great spot for a walk or a run or to sit back on a bench and watch the rowers on the water. People circling the lake seem pretty serious about getting their exercise – if you just show up for a stroll in your street clothes, you might get some funny looks.

If you want to get away from the lakefront crowds, the small but serviceable business district, just to the east along NE Ravenna Blvd, offers the requisite coffee shops and restaurants.

Below Green Lake, the Woodland Park Zoo is absolutely a must-see. And don't neglect to head further up to Phinney Ridge, the hilltop neighborhood north of the zoo along Phinney Ave N, as it also has some good pubs (p147) and restaurants (p134).

This is a tree-heavy, outdoorsy part of town, with its centerpiece, Green Lake Park, being the obvious favorite among local bodies of water that are circumnavigated by soccer moms, rollerbladers, joggers and babysitters.

Several Metro buses, including bus 26, run frequently from downtown to Green Lake and Phinney Ridge.

GREEN LAKE PARK Map below

One of the most popular spots in the city for recreationalists and sunbathers, scenic Green Lake Park surrounds Green Lake, a small natural lake created by a glacier during the last ice age. In the early 1900s, city planners lowered the lake's water level by 7ft, increasing the shoreline to preserve parkland around the lake. After the lowering, however, Ravenna Creek, which fed the lake, no longer flowed through. Green Lake became stagnant and filled

GREEN LAKE & PHINNEY RIDGE

GREEN LAKE & PHINNEY RIDGE

with stinky green algae. Massive dredging efforts to keep Green Lake a lake (instead of a marshy wetland) continue. The lake is prone to algae blooms, which can cause an unpleasant condition called 'swimmer's itch' to anyone venturing into the water. Warning signs are usually posted on the beach if this is a risk.

Two paths wind around the lake, but these aren't enough to fill the needs of the hundreds of joggers, power-walkers, cyclists and in-line skaters who throng here daily. In fact, competition for space on the trails has led to altercations between speeding athletes; the city government now regulates traffic on the paths. With this in mind, beware the synchronized roller-skating couples holding hands; they're not dangerous, but they may induce nausea.

Green Lake also has a soccer field, bowling green, baseball diamond, basketball and tennis courts, plus boat, bike and in-line skate rentals. Two sandy swimming beaches line the north end of the lake, but on sunny days the entire shoreline is massed with gleaming pale bodies.

BATHHOUSE THEATER Map p93
The Bathhouse Theater, on the west side of the lake, is a 1928 bathing pavilion that was converted to a live-performance venue in 1970.

WOODLAND PARK ZOO Map p93
☎ 206-684-4800; www.zoo.org; 5500 Phinney Ave N; adult/child $11/8 Oct-Apr, $16.50/11 May-Sep; ☽ 9:30am-4pm Oct-Apr, 9:30am-6pm May-Sep
In Woodland Park, up the hill from Green Lake Park, the Woodland Park Zoo is one of Seattle's greatest tourist attractions, consistently rated as one of the top 10 zoos in the country. It was one of the first in the nation to free animals from their restrictive cages in favor of ecosystem enclosures, where animals from similar environments share large spaces designed to replicate their natural surroundings. Feature exhibits include a tropical rain forest, two gorilla exhibits, an African savanna and an Asian elephant forest.

SEATTLE ROSE GARDEN Map p93
admission free; ☽ 7am-dusk
The 2.5-acre Seattle Rose Garden, near the entrance road to the zoo off N 50th St, was started in 1924 and contains 5000 plants, including heirloom roses and a test garden for All-America Rose selections.

BALLARD & DISCOVERY PARK

Shopping p117, Eating p135, Drinking p147

Settled by Scandinavian fishermen in the early 20th century, at first Ballard feels like your average lutefisk-flavored blue-collar neighborhood. Once a seedy district where people spilled out of bars at 6am only to puke on the sidewalk and go back in, Ballard has learned how to hold its own. Unlike other former lowbrow-turned-fashionable neighborhoods, such as Belltown or Fremont, Ballard still attracts folks looking for no-nonsense venues, where they can eat a greasy breakfast, drink $3 beers and listen to good down-home folk or rock and roll. How long historical Ballard's well-guarded seediness lasts in the face of the current hipster invasion is anyone's guess.

Though just a bridge away, Ballard seems distant from urban Seattle. Settled principally by Swedes, Norwegians and Danes (incorporated in 1890 and annexed by Seattle in 1907), this area has long been a Scandinavian enclave. Early Nordic settlers came to work at sawmills and to fish. These seafaring immigrants were instrumental in establishing greater Seattle's fishing fleet. Today, boats no longer leave Ballard to fish the high seas; instead they depart from Fishermen's Terminal, just across the shipping canal.

Ballard still maintains a decidedly Nordic air, though only about a third of today's population is of Nordic descent, and some of the key Scandinavian landmark shops have disappeared. Still, most of the names on local businesses' signs are of Scandinavian origin, and many of the older folks on the streets and in the shops still speak with distinct accents, even if they're not actually speaking their mother tongue.

The heart of old Ballard stretches along Ballard Ave NW, which seems to have hardly changed, at least architecturally, since the 1890s. This is where you'll find Ballard's notable concentration of live-music venues. Seven blocks here have been named a Historic Landmark District, but fortunately the buildings have not been thoughtlessly glamorized: the structures in this district are old, not 'olde.' Pick up a copy of the *Historic Ballard Ave Walking Tour* pamphlet for background on the buildings. The Ballard Historical Society (www.ballardhistory.org) also gives occasional tours.

The 'Historic' designation helps protect Ballard from overcommercialization or other undesirable growth. Any proposed development has to be approved by a board of locals, and the locals are pretty picky about who they let in. Ballard is fun and casual; here you can let your proverbial hair down, do shots with a fisherman, eat cheap food, get a tattoo or sit in a bar and get drunk all day – in Ballard, you won't be the only one.

Discovery Park is 534 acres of urban wilderness northwest of downtown Seattle and just southwest of the mouth of Chittenden Locks. Locals love to come here to escape the ever-present manicure of city gardens and get windswept along the park's many trails. Though it's easy to reach, it feels utterly remote. There are good walking trails, long beaches, picnic areas and a helpful visitors center.

Metro buses 18 and 24 run frequently from downtown to Ballard.

BALLARD

NORDIC HERITAGE MUSEUM Map p96

☎ 206-789-5707; www.nordicmuseum.org; 3014 NW 67th St; adult/senior/child $6/5/4; ⏰ 10am-4pm Tue-Sat, noon-4pm Sun; 🚌 17 from downtown at 4th Ave & Union St

This museum preserves the history of the northern Europeans who settled in Ballard and the Pacific Northwest, as well as bringing in special exhibits of new work by contemporary Scandinavian artists. It's the only museum in the USA that commemorates the history of settlers from all five Scandinavian countries. A permanent exhibit, with one room for each country, features costumes, photographs and maritime equipment, while a second gallery is devoted to changing exhibitions. The museum also offers Scandinavian language instruction, lectures and films.

To get here, take bus 17 from downtown at 4th Ave and Union St, get off at 32nd Ave NW and walk one block east on NW 67th St.

HIRAM M CHITTENDEN LOCKS
Map p96

☎ visitors center 206-783-7059; 3015 NW 54th St; ⏰ 24hr; 🚌 17 from downtown at 4th Ave & Union St

BALLARD & DISCOVERY PARK

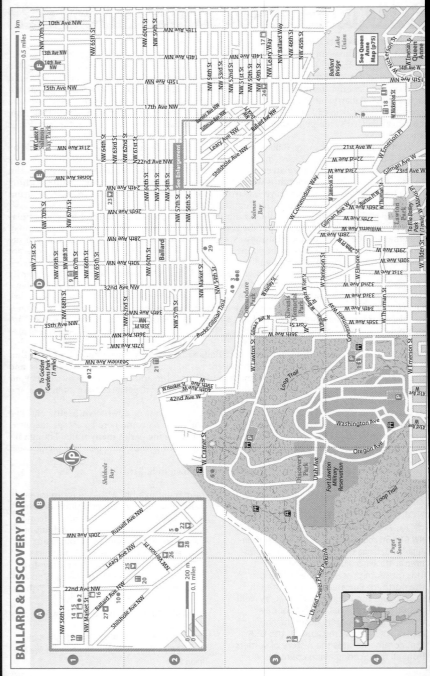

BALLARD & DISCOVERY PARK

These locks, also known as the Ballard Locks, are about a half mile west of Ballard off NW Market St. Watching boats cross the two locks on the Lake Washington Ship Canal holds a strange attraction for locals and tourists alike. The process takes between 10 and 30 minutes, depending on tides and lake levels and on whether the large or the small lock is used. Walkways along the locks allow an intimate look at the workings of these water elevators and a chance to see the vessels coming and going from Puget Sound to Lakes Union and Washington.

BALLARD FISH LADDER Map opposite

☎ visitors center 206-783-7059; 3015 NW 54th St; ☼ ladder & gardens 7am-9pm, visitors center 10am-6pm May-Sep, 10am-4pm Thu-Mon Oct-Apr
On the southern side of the Hiram M Chittenden Locks, the fish ladder was built in 1976 to allow salmon to fight their way to spawning grounds in the Cascade headwaters of the Sammamish River, which feeds Lake Washington. Visitors can watch the fish from underwater glass-sided tanks or from above (there are nets to keep salmon from over-leaping and stranding themselves on the pavement). Sea lions munch on the salmon while the fish attempt to negotiate the ladder. Just what to do about the sea lions has stymied environmentalists, anglers and the local Fish & Wildlife Department. The best time to visit is during spawning season, from mid-June to September.

On the northern entrance to the lock area is the Carl English Jr Botanical Gardens, a charming arboretum and specimen garden. Trails wind through gardens filled with flowers and mature trees, each labeled. Flanking the gardens is a small museum and visitors center documenting the history of the locks. Free tours are offered at 1pm and 3pm daily from March to November; call ahead to arrange a time.

FISHERMEN'S TERMINAL Map opposite

19th Ave & W Nickerson St; 🚌 15, 17 or 18
Seattle's fishing fleet resides at Fishermen's Terminal, in a wide recess in the ship canal called Salmon Bay on the south side of the Ballard Bridge. Fishermen's Terminal is a popular moorage spot because the facility is in freshwater, above the Chittenden Locks. Freshwater is much less corrosive to boats than saltwater.

It's great fun to wander the piers, watching crews unload their catch, clean their boats and repair nets. Many of these fishing boats journey to Alaska in summer and return to dry dock while they wait out the winter. Outdoor interpretive displays explain the history of Seattle's fishing fleet, starting with the native inhabitants who first fished these waters in canoes, to the Slavs and Greeks, who dominated salmon fishing in the early 1900s. A statue, the bronze Seattle Fishermen's Memorial at the base of the piers, commemorates Seattle fishers lost at sea. This memorial is also the site of the ceremonial blessing of the fleet, held annually on the first Sunday in May.

In the two terminal buildings are some good restaurants specializing in the freshest seafood in Seattle, a tobacconist, a ship chandler and a charts and nautical gifts store. Stop at the Wild Salmon Seafood Market (p117) to buy the freshest pick of the day's catch.

CENTER ON CONTEMPORARY ART
Map p96

COCA; ☎ 206-728-1980; www.cocaseattle.org;
6413 Seaview Ave NW; admission free; ☯ 10am-
5pm Mon-Fri, to midnight Thu

This gallery has been a force in Seattle's
contemporary art scene for two decades.
After moving around a lot, it has opened
a new branch in Belltown (2721 1st Ave) as well
as this primary space in the Shilshole Bay
Beach Club.

GOLDEN GARDENS PARK off Map p96
8498 Seaview Pl NW

Golden Gardens Park, established in 1904
by Harry W Treat, is a lovely 95-acre beach
park with sandy beaches north of Shilshole
Bay Marina. There are picnic facilities,
restrooms, basketball hoops, volleyball
nets, gangs of Canadian geese, lots of
parking and plenty of space to get away
from all the activity. Rising above Golden
Gardens is Sunset Hill Park (NW 77th St & 34th Ave),
a prime perch for dramatic sunsets and
long views.

SHILSHOLE BAY MARINA Map p96
Seaview Ave NW

The Shilshole Bay Marina, about 2 miles
northwest of the locks along Seaview Ave,
offers nice views across Puget Sound and,
as Seattle's primary sailboat moorage,
a glittery collection of boats. Inside the
marina, you can rent sailboats or take
classes at Windworks (☎ 206-784-9386; 7001
Seaview Ave NW).

DISCOVERY PARK

This park was originally Fort Lawton, an army
base established in 1897 to protect Seattle
from unnamed enemies. Fort Lawton didn't
see much activity until WWII, when it was
used as barracks for troops bound for the
Pacific. Over the course of the war it held up
to 1400 German and Italian prisoners. When
the fort was declared surplus property in the
1960s, the City of Seattle decided to turn it
into a park (although significant areas of the
park are still used for military housing). The
fort was finally proclaimed public parkland
in 1972.

For a map of the park's trail and road system,
stop by the visitors center (☎ 206-386-4236; 3801
W Government Way; ☯ 8:30am-5:30pm) near the
Government Way entrance. The park runs

educational programs including Saturday
nature walks, day camps for children and
bird-watching tours.

DAYBREAK STAR INDIAN CULTURAL
CENTER Map p96

☎ visitors center 206-386-4236; www.unitedindians
.org/daybreak.html; W Cramer St; ☯ 8:30am-5pm
Tue-Sun

In 1977 Native American groups laid claim
to the land in this area, and 17 acres of
parkland were decreed Native American
land on which now stands the Daybreak
Star Indian Cultural Center, a community
center for Seattle-area Native Americans.
Discovery Park has over 7 miles of hiking
trails, several of which lead to the Daybreak
Star Center. Except for a small art gallery,
there are few facilities for outside visitors.
The vista point in front of the center affords
beautiful views of the Sound, and several
steep trails lead down through the forest to
narrow, sandy beaches.

WEST POINT LIGHTHOUSE Map p96
About a mile off from the 3-mile paved
loop that circles the park, a trail skirts
the water's edge all the way to the still-
functioning West Point Lighthouse. It's
a great spot for panoramic views of the
Sound and mountains to the west.

OLD BALLARD
Walking Tour
1 Portland Building
A great example of the decorative brickwork
that graces many of the buildings along
Ballard Ave, the Portland Building (5403-5407 Ballard
Ave NW) has housed all kinds of businesses since
its construction, including taverns and dry-
goods stores. It was renovated in 1985.

2 GS Sanborn Building
Continue along Ballard Ave, noting the cute
wood-frame buildings at 5341 Ballard Ave –
this particular building was rescued and
brought here from the International District
(rumor says it was once a bordello), but it's
in the same style as most of this street's early
buildings. The GS Sanborn Building (5323 Ballard Ave)
is Ballard's only example of Romanesque
architecture, a style that was popular on the
East Coast in the 1880s. It has a sandstone
face and a third-story arch, and housed some

OLD BALLARD WALKING TOUR

NW Market St

8

END

7

Russell Ave NW

START

1

Leary Ave NW

22nd Ave NW

Ballard Ave NW

20th Ave NW

2

4

3

NW Vernon Pl

King's
Hardware

6

5

0   200 m
0   0.1 miles

WALK FACTS

Start Portland Building
End Ballard Building
Distance half mile
Duration 30 min to one hour
Fuel stops Conor Byrne and King's Hardware

of Ballard's key businesses in the early 1900s, including a department store.

3 Ballard Savings & Loan Building

At 5301 Ballard Ave is the adorable little Ballard Savings & Loan Building, with the helpful motto 'thrift' carved into the roofline. This neoclassical building housed the local Savings & Loan, which was notable for doing comparatively well during the Great Depression.

4 Scandinavian American Bank Building

Across the road is the second-empire-baroque-style Scandinavian American Bank Building (5300 Ballard Ave), a nice example of the early-1900s tendency to flatter by imitation: its concrete surface is treated to look like stone. You can still see the 'Bank Building' sign embedded in the top corner of this building. It became the Starlight Hotel and now holds the headquarters of the Ballard Farmers Market (10am-3pm Sun year-round).

5 Conor Byrne

Continue past the intersection of 20th Ave NW. On your left is one of Seattle's oldest still-operating taverns; its first liquor license was granted in 1902, when it was called the Owl. Now called Conor Byrne (p148), it still has the original mahogany bar.

6 Cors & Wegener Building

Retrace your steps to the intersection and turn right. On your right is the Cors & Wegener Building (5000-5004 20th Ave NW). Once the offices of the early local broadsheet, *Ballard News*, it's still one of the most impressive in the area. One of the first in the area to be revitalized, it's now mostly shops, apartments and office space.

7 Bell Tower

Continue to Leary Ave NW, turn left and head to NW Market St. On the corner of it and Ballard Ave is a commemorative Bell Tower. This corner is the original location of the Ballard City Hall, sometimes called 'Hose Hall,' which also contained the jail and the fire department hose company (hence the nickname). Weakened by a series of earthquakes, the building was demolished in 1965, but the columns and bell were saved and made into this little landmark.

8 Ballard Building

Back on Market St, you'll see the Ballard Building (2208 NW Market St). Ballard's only major terracotta structure, it was built in the 1920s by the Fraternal Order of Eagles. It once held a community hospital and now houses the *Ballard News-Tribune*.

CENTRAL DISTRICT, MADRONA & MADISON PARK

Eating p135

Running down the east slope of First Hill to the upscale neighborhoods that flank Lake Washington, the Central District – sometimes called 'the CD' – represents the heart of Seattle's African American community. Few blacks lived in Seattle until WWII, when they moved to the area in large numbers to work in the shipyards and contribute to the war effort. Today the CD is overrun with empty storefronts, which is ironic considering the high price of real estate in nearby Capitol and First Hills. Despite the lack of a business buzz, the CD is a friendly place where you can find some great soul food and barbecue joints (p135).

Madrona is one of Seattle's more ethnically diverse neighborhoods, blending elements of the CD's African American community to the west with the predominantly white neighborhoods that ring Lake Washington proper. Once a relatively unheard-of neighborhood, Madrona has been gentrified recently and now draws crowds from around the city, notably at one of the most popular brunch places in Seattle, the Hi Spot Café (p136).

If you follow Madison St from downtown (or take bus 11), you're following the old trolley line that once served the eastern side of Capitol Hill and the amusement park and beach at Madison Park. Today these tranquil neighborhoods are quietly upscale, home to little commercial hubs lined with understated shops and good restaurants. When it gets hot in the summer, locals make the pilgrimage to Lake Washington to sprawl out on the small sandy-grassy beaches.

The first neighborhood you come to is Madison Valley, where the biggest attractions are two notable restaurants: Rover's, considered one of the best restaurants in Seattle, and Café Flora, a vegetarian's dream. Continue toward Lake Washington to reach Madison Park, another cute little neighborhood with the usual hub of trendy restaurants and cafes butting up against the water's edge.

In the 1890s Madison Park comprised an amusement park, bathhouse, ballpark and racetrack. Ferries left from here to cross Lake Washington to Bellevue. Nowadays, Madison Park is a much quieter place and very genteel. The park proper is the most northerly of the public parks and beaches along Lake Washington's western shore. In summer, the popular beach sees a sizable gay male contingent mixed in with local families. The beach here is one of the more pleasant places to swim and sunbathe.

Though it's soon to be gentrified – or, in the case of Madison Park, already has been for years – this area still has a comfortable, unfancy neighborhood vibe. There are community churches and family parks, as well as a fairly high-profile museum and the park that serves as a pilgrimage site for fans of Nirvana's Kurt Cobain.

WASHINGTON PARK ARBORETUM
Map opposite

This wild and lovely park offers a wide variety of gardens, a wetlands nature trail and 200 acres of mature forest threaded by paths. More than 5500 plant species grow within the arboretum's boundaries. In the spring Azalea Way, a jogger-free trail that winds through the arboretum, is lined with a giddy array of pink- and orange-flowered azaleas and rhododendrons. Trail guides to the plant collections are available at the Graham Visitors Center (2300 Arboretum Dr E; ☺ 10am-4pm). Free guided tours of the grounds take place at 1pm on Saturday and Sunday from January to November.

FOSTER ISLAND WETLANDS TRAIL Map opposite

The northern edge of Washington Park Arboretum includes this wonderful woodchip-paved trail around Foster Island in Lake Washington's Union Bay, a picnic spot that once was a burial ground for Union Bay Indians. The waterfront trail winds through marshlands and over a series of floating bridges to smaller islands and reedy shoals. Bird-watching is popular here, as are swimming, fishing and kayaking (for kayak rentals, see p167). It's just too bad that the busy, elevated Hwy 520 roars above the island. The nature trail is best accessed from the Mohai parking lot (see p102).

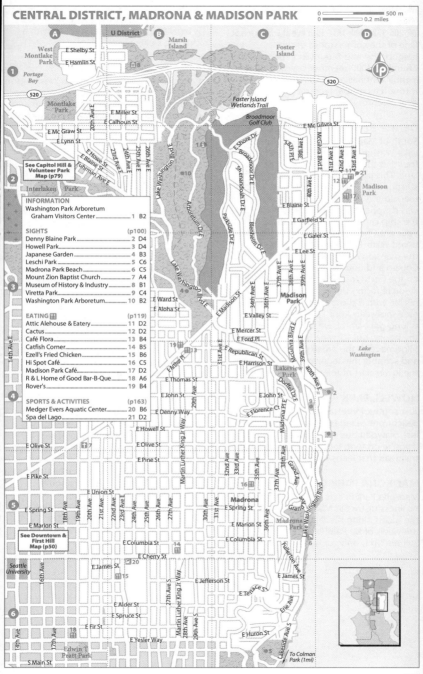

0   500 m
0   0.2 miles

**See Capitol Hill &
Volunteer Park
Map (p79)**

INFORMATION
Washington Park Arboretum
   Graham Visitors Center 1 B2

SIGHTS   (p100)
Denny Blaine Park 2 D4
Howell Park 3 D4
Japanese Garden 4 B3
Leschi Park 5 C6
Madrona Park Beach 6 C5
Mount Zion Baptist Church 7 A4
Museum of History & Industry 8 B1
Viretta Park 9 C4
Washington Park Arboretum 10 B2

EATING   (p119)
Attic Alehouse & Eatery 11 D2
Cactus 12 D2
Café Flora 13 B4
Catfish Corner 14 B5
Ezell's Fried Chicken 15 B6
Hi Spot Café 16 C5
Madison Park Café 17 D2
R & L Home of Good Bar-B-Que 18 A6
Rover's 19 B4

SPORTS & ACTIVITIES   (p163)
Medger Evers Aquatic Center 20 B6
Spa del Lago 21 D2

**See Downtown &
First Hill
Map (p50)**

To Colman
Park (1mi)

MOUNT ZION BAPTIST CHURCH
Map p101

☎ 206-322-6500; 1634 19th Ave at E Madison St

One of the cornerstones of this neighborhood is Mount Zion Baptist Church, a 2000-member congregation with a choir that has reached national acclaim through its gospel recordings. The church is over a century old.

DENNY BLAINE PARK Map p101

South of Madison Park toward the tail of Lake Washington Blvd is Denny Blaine Park, found at the end of a looping tree-lined lane. This predominantly lesbian beach is surrounded by an old stone wall, which marked the shoreline before the lake level was dropped 9ft during construction of the ship canal. Just a little further south on your right-hand side, you'll find the two-tiered Viretta Park, from which you can see the mansion once owned by Nirvana's Kurt Cobain and Courtney Love – it's the house on the north (or left) side of the benches if you're facing the water. Cobain took his life with a shotgun in the mansion's greenhouse in April 1994. The greenhouse is long gone and Love no longer owns the house, but Nirvana fans still make the pilgrimage to this small park to pay tribute and scribble messages on the benches in the lower part of the park.

HOWELL PARK Map p101

Just south of Viretta Park is a small beachfront called Howell Park. It is usually less crowded due to the lack of parking. If you're on foot, look for a small sign and trailhead that leads to the beach.

MADRONA PARK BEACH Map p101

Madrona Park Beach, down from the business district in Madrona Park, is one of the nicest along the lake. In clear weather the views of Mt Rainier are fantastic. Swimming is only for hardy souls, however, as the water's icy cold, even in summer. Further south, past the yacht moorage, is Leschi Park, a grassy green space with a children's play area.

COLMAN PARK off Map p101

Continue south along the Lake Washington Blvd E through the very upscale Madrona Park neighborhood and you'll end up at Colman Park. The entire lakefront stretch between here and Seward Park is parkland. This is an especially good area for bike riding. On the weekends the boulevard is closed to cars.

MUSEUM OF HISTORY & INDUSTRY
Map p101

Mohai; ☎ 206-324-1126; www.seattlehistory.org; 2700 24th Ave E; adult/senior & student $8/7; ☾ 10am-5pm, 10am-8pm first Thu of month

Generally near the top on any list of the city's best attractions, this museum at the northwest corner of Washington Park Arboretum documents the history of Seattle and the Puget Sound in regard to its lumber, fishing and shipping industries. There's also a big Boeing presence, including a 1920s mail plane. Usually called by its acronym, Mohai has an entertaining collection of historical photos, old planes, memorabilia from the Great Fire, and artifacts and lore from Seattle's great seafaring era.

JAPANESE GARDEN Map p101

☎ 206-684-4725; adult/senior & student $5/3; ☾ 10am-7pm or 8pm Apr-Sep, 10am-dusk Oct-Mar

At the southern edge of Washington Park Arboretum, this 3.5-acre formal garden has koi pools, waterfalls, a teahouse and manicured plantings. Granite for the garden's sculptures was laboriously dragged in from the Cascades. Tea ceremony demonstrations are frequently available. Call for a schedule.

WEST SEATTLE

Shopping p117, Eating p137, Drinking p148

West Seattle is the nose of land across Elliott Bay to the west of downtown Seattle, beyond the Port of Seattle and Harbor Island. West Seattle hasn't yet succumbed to gentrification and still feels working class, and although access to downtown is good, it seems removed from the rest of the city. From here the views can be stellar, both of the city center and of the islands to the west.

Alki Point, the westernmost point of the peninsula, initially attracted the Denny party, which landed in the schooner *Exact* on November 13, 1851, establishing the first non-native settlement on Elliott Bay – the village that would grow to become Seattle. Although the settlers only spent one winter before moving across the bay to what is now Seattle proper, there's a monument to the pioneers on the beach.

The main reason to visit West Seattle, especially in good weather, is to go to Alki Beach Park. The sober and purposeful settlers who landed here wouldn't recognize the place today. This 2-mile stretch of sandy beach is a madhouse in summer. As if in imitation of southern California, the volleyball nets go up, sunbathing occupies the strand and teens in souped-up cars prowl the streets. It's Seattle's only real beach scene and the views of Seattle from Duwamish Head, at the northern end of the beach, are spectacular. The claustrophobic might want to avoid Alki on summer weekends, but good beachside cafes, quaint fish-and-chips joints, the miniature replica of the Statue of Liberty on the beach and the Alki Point Lighthouse make this area a nice getaway most other times.

The main commercial strip on West Seattle is along California Ave SW, centering at the junction of SW Alaska St. There's nothing particularly compelling about the shops here, except that they seem at least a generation and 200 miles removed from the rest of Seattle. Old five-and-dime stores slumber next to old diners, neither looking like they have changed much since the 1950s.

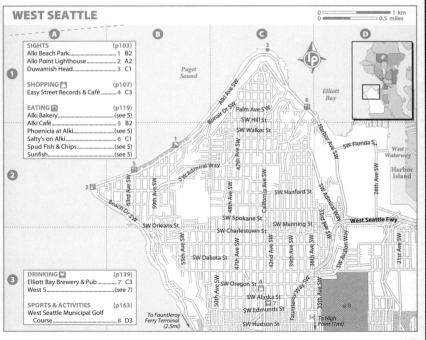

WEST SEATTLE

If you're interested in a ferry ride, follow Fauntleroy Way SW down through West Seattle to Fauntleroy Ferry Terminal at Henderson St SW, south of Lincoln Park. Here you can take a half-hour ferry ride to Vashon Island (p188), a semirural island that also serves as a bedroom community to Seattle.

Metro buses 5 and 55 run frequently from downtown to West Seattle.

DUWAMISH HEAD Map p103

Popular for its views of Elliott Bay and downtown, this is the former site of Luna Park. In its days as an over-the-top amusement center, the park covered more than 10 acres and boasted the 'longest bar on the bay.' This grand assertion unfortunately led to claims of debauchery and carousing, and the park was eventually closed in 1913 by the conservative powers-that-were.

ALKI BEACH PARK Map p103

Alki Beach has an entirely different feel from the rest of Seattle: this 2-mile stretch of sandy beach could almost fool you into thinking it's California, at least on a sunny day. There's a bike path, volleyball courts on the sand, and rings for beach fires. Look for the miniature Statue of Liberty, donated by the Boy Scouts (currently removed for repair and replaced by a copy). There's also a pylon marking Arthur Denny's landing party's first stop in 1851, which for some reason has a chip of Massachusetts' Plymouth Rock embedded in its base.

ALKI POINT LIGHTHOUSE Map p103

☎ 206-217-6123; btwn Beach Dr & Point Pl, Alki Beach

The US Coast Guard maintains this lighthouse. It has limited public hours and you can't just walk up to it, but tours are available by appointment. Call for a current schedule and more information.

FAUNTLEROY FERRY TERMINAL
off Map p103

☎ 206-464-6400; Fauntleroy Way SW & Henderson St

Washington State Ferries to Vashon Island leave daily from this dock.

HIGH POINT off Map p103

SW Myrtle St & 35th Ave

This intersection marks the highest point in Seattle, 518ft above sea level.

GEORGETOWN

Shopping p117, Drinking p149

About 3 miles south of Seattle proper, Georgetown is an old neighborhood that's recently been deemed cool. Annexed in 1910, it's basically a residential core surrounded by restored warehouses full of hip bars, shops and restaurants. Roughly speaking, it lies between I-5 to the east, the Duwamish river to the west, Boeing Field to the south and the train tracks to the north. Although the Denny party's arrival at Alki Point gets credit for being the start of Seattle proper, in 1851 an explorer named Luther Collins (1813–60) claimed a plot of land right here about a week before Denny landed.

Perhaps more importantly, Georgetown is the birthplace of Rainier Beer. Noticing how nicely hops thrived in the valley, John Clausen and Edward Sweeny decided in 1883 to build a brewery, which would become the Seattle Brewing & Malting Co and, eventually, Rainier. It was staffed mostly by Germans and Belgians, a fact not particularly evident in the Rainier Beer we drink today. (The brewery closed in 1999 and the building now holds mixed-use studios and businesses.)

Before Seattle annexed it, Georgetown had become an incorporated city in 1904 to skirt a law prohibiting sales and manufacture of liquor within a mile of any city – at that time it contained not only the brewery but also seven saloons. Its reputation as Seattle's watering hole quickly grew, and to some extent that's still the way people think of it now. It has a bunch of excellent places for slaking one's thirst (p149), whether you're after microbrewed beer in a saloon or a fabulous latte in an industrial-chic designer coffee house.

But what really drives this neighborhood is its independent, scrappy, artistic sensibility. Since the initial influx of lowbrow artists in the 1980s, the area's old warehouses have largely been revamped as studios and funky little shops, and the arts scene here is thriving. (See the Background chapter, p35, for more about the monthly Georgetown Art Attack.) The neighborhood feels like a small, tightly knit, extremely cool community.

Metro bus 26 runs frequently from downtown to Georgetown.

OXBOW PARK Map p106
6400 S Corson Ave
This public park in a quiet residential part of Georgetown contains a community pea patch and is home to the giant, carefully restored, bright orange and blue Hat 'n' Boots, a beloved pair of relics from a quirky roadside service station. This attention-grabbing landmark was built in 1955 and moved here in 2003 – you paid for your gas under the hat, and peed in the boots. Photo opportunity!

GEORGETOWN ART CENTER Map p106
☎ 206-851-1538; 5511 Airport Way S;
🕙 11am-5pm Mon, 10am-4pm Tue & by appointment
A former dance studio, the community friendly art center hosts rotating exhibits as well as studio space, classes and workshops. It's one of several key stops along the route of the Art Attack, Georgetown's monthly art walk. Stop by on a Wednesday night from 6pm to 9pm for its open life-drawing class ($12).

GEORGETOWN POWER PLANT MUSEUM Map p106
☎ 206-763-2542; 6605 13th Ave S; admission free;
🕙 by appointment, open house 10am-2pm 2nd Sat each month
The Georgetown Steam Plant, built in 1906, has one of the last working examples of the large-scale steam turbines that doubled the efficiency of electricity production and shifted the public's view of electricity from a luxury to a standard part of modern living. The plant ceased operations in 1972 and in 1980 was declared a Historic American Engineering Record site. It's now an education-oriented museum, with exhibits as well as classes in steam engineering. Hours are limited; call ahead for access. Exhibits include miniature steam locomotives, a Calliaphone (steam-powered organ) and vintage fire engines.

FANTAGRAPHICS BOOKSTORE & GALLERY Map p106
☎ 206-658-0110; www.fantagraphics.com/bookstore; 1201 S Vale St; 🕙 11:30am-8pm Mon-Sat, 11:30am-5pm Sun; 🚌 131

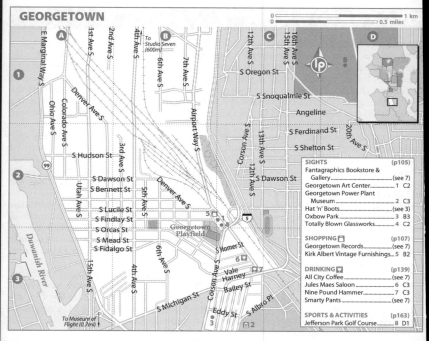

GEORGETOWN

One of the coolest comic book publishers around, Fantagraphics is based here in Georgetown, and it's worth making a pilgrimage if you have even a passing interest. Don't miss the Damaged Room, with out of print and steeply discounted books. The store holds readings and events several times a month; check online for a schedule. There's also an exhibition space with new shows each month.

TOTALLY BLOWN GLASSWORKS
Map above

☎ 206-768-8944; 5607 Corson Ave S; ⏰ 10:30am-5pm Mon-Fri, 10:30am-3:30pm Sat

This glassworks studio and shop makes all its work in-house; if you've never seen a glassblowing demonstration, it's worth checking out. The studio welcomes spectators any Monday, Tuesday, Thursday or Friday from 8am to 4pm. This is another popular stop on the monthly Art Attack art walk.

MUSEUM OF FLIGHT off Map above

☎ 206-764-5720; 9404 E Marginal Way S, Boeing Field; adult/senior/youth/child $15/13/8/free, free

5-9pm 1st Thu each month; ⏰ 10am-5pm Fri-Wed, 10am-9pm 1st Thu each month; 🚌 174 from downtown

Aviation buffs wholeheartedly enjoy the Museum of Flight, while others traipse through suppressing yawns, so be choosy about who you bring.

The museum presents the entire history of flight, from da Vinci to the Wright Brothers to the NASA space program. More than 50 historical aircraft are displayed, including a recently acquired British Airways Concorde. The restored 1909 Red Barn, where Boeing had its beginnings, contains exhibits and displays. The six-story glass Great Gallery has 20 airplanes suspended from its ceiling. Vintage fliers reside on the grounds outside the buildings. There's also a hands-on area where visitors get to work the controls and sit in the driver's seat.

Films about flight and aircraft history are shown in the small theater, and there's a gift shop and cafe.

To get here by car, take I-5 south from downtown to exit 158, turn west and follow East Marginal Way north.

top picks

- **Elliott Bay Book Company** (p113)
- **Uwajimaya** (p110)
- **DeLaurenti's** (p111)
- **Metsker Maps** (p111)
- **Babeland** (p113)

SHOPPING

When it comes to shopping, Seattle has the best of both worlds: you can power-shop at the big-nam stores in the malls – Barney's and Tiffany & Co in Pacific Place – and you can also seek out the quirk one-of-a-kind shops hidden away in some back alley with a spray-painted sign on the door.

The city also has some of the greatest bookstores in the country, and a lot of them. Give Seattle's rich music culture, record stores are also a good bet, although the owners tend to kno what they have and charge accordingly.

Naturally, any shopping excursion in Seattle must include Pike Place Market, where yo can find anything from stacks of crabs to used books to spiced teas to goth toys. And browsin this historical labyrinth is just as much fun as buying. Downtown dominates Seattle's reta scene with big-name shopping malls. But take a look in the corners of Pioneer Square for a and antique shops, make the Waterfront your stop for obligatory souvenirs, and for fashion c novelties, browse on Capitol Hill.

DOWNTOWN & FIRST HILL

The main shopping area in Seattle is downtown between 3rd and 6th Aves and between University and Stewart Sts. If you're anywhere nearby, you can't miss it.

CAMERAS WEST Map p50 · Cameras
☎ 206-622-0066; 1908 4th Ave
The foremost selection of film and photographic supplies (including cameras, batteries, storage cards, tripods and so on) in Seattle is Cameras West, right in downtown.

BROOKS BROTHERS Map p50 · Clothing
☎ 206-624-4400; 1330 5th Ave
This is the undisputed destination for classy men's clothing in the area. The salespeople are total pros – they greet you at the door, take your measurements and avoid all signs of being pushy.

MACY'S Map p50 · Clothing
☎ 206-344-2121; 1601 3rd Ave
Seattle's oldest and largest department store, this hard-to-miss classic – formerly Bon-Marché, but renamed Bon-Macy's

TAXES & REFUNDS
A 9.5% sales tax is added to all purchases except food to be prepared for consumption (ie groceries). Unlike the European VAT or Canadian GST, the sales tax is not refundable to tourists.

in August 2003 when it was bought by Macy's, then shortened for convenience – is a mainstay of clothing and housewares shopping.

NIKETOWN Map p50 · Clothin
☎ 206-447-6453; 1500 6th Ave
The huge Niketown has its roots in the Northwest – it was founded by Phil Knight in Eugene, Oregon. The store sells all kinds of Nike clothing, shoes and accessories, anc acts as a sort of museum for the company's marketing campaign, with posters and quotations from some of its endorsement stars covering the walls.

NORDSTROM Map p50 · Clothing
☎ 206-628-2111; Pine St btwn 5th & 6th Aves
Born and raised in Seattle, this chain department store occupies a giant space in the former Frederick and Nelson Building. Closer to Pike Place Market, Nordstrom Rack (Map p63; ☎ 206-448-8522; 1601 2nd Ave) offers closeouts and returns from the parent store.

SWAY AND CAKE Map p50 · Clothing
☎ 206-624-2699; 1631 6th Ave
This cute little upscale boutique has cute little designer dresses and jeans from hot names like Rag & Bone, Diane von Furstenberg and Helmut Lang. Sales staff are friendly, even if you're dressed down.

PACIFIC PLACE Map p50 · Mall
☎ 206-405-2655; 600 Pine St
Seattle's best-quality boutique mall feels a bit like the lobby of an upscale hotel – it's

cylindrical, and the total lack of that hectic shopping-mall vibe makes it very pleasant to walk around. Clothiers include J Crew (☎ 206-652-9788), Club Monaco (☎ 206-264-8001) and BCBG (☎ 206-447-3400). The large stores of Restoration Hardware (☎ 206-652-4545) and Williams-Sonoma (☎ 206-621-7405) are fun to look around in. Take a moment to gape in the window at Tiffany & Co (☎ 206-264-1400) or saunter inside for a special gift. The mall's top level features a movie theater, a pub and a couple of restaurants. This is also where you'll find the nicest public restrooms in downtown Seattle.

WESTLAKE CENTER Map p50　　Mall
☎ 206-467-3044; 4th Ave & Pine St

This 'boutique mall' – also the starting point for the Monorail – has turned into a landmark, partly because of its location and the fact that its concrete patio and steps make a nice gathering point. It's somehow heartening to see ragtag groups of antiwar protesters (and an inordinate number of cops) rallying in front of such a monument to the big American dollar. Inside you'll find shops like Fossil watches (☎ 206-652-2332), LUSH (☎ 206-624-5874) and Made in Washington (☎ 206-623-9753). Local stores include an outlet of Fireworks (☎ 206-682-6462), which offers inexpensive arty products by regional craftspeople – they make great gifts.

PIONEER SQUARE

Not surprisingly, given its historical importance to the city, Pioneer Square is where to shop for antiques. It's also a good place to find reasonably priced artwork and crafts by local artists, particularly blown glass and traditional art by coastal Native American artists.

ELLIOTT BAY ANTIQUES Map p56　Antiques
☎ 340-0770; 165 S Jackson St

Since opening in 1995, this shop has been devoted to early 20th-century Chinese furniture, as well as stone carvings, Japanese prints, screens and other furnishings; the owner is particularly interested in the Chinese roots of art deco.

JEAN WILLIAMS ANTIQUES
Map p56　　　　　　　　　　　Antiques
☎ 622-1110; 115 S Jackson St

If you're looking for a Louis XVI chest of drawers or an English mahogany desk, this

top picks

SHOPPING STRIPS

- Pike Place Market (p110) Everything under the sun.
- Downtown (opposite) Big-name stores and designer boutiques.
- Broadway (p113) New and vintage clothes, bookstores and record shops.
- Pioneer Square (below) Art and antique shops.
- The Ave in the U District (p114) Cheap eats and lots of bookstores.

is the place – Jean Williams specializes in English and French period antiques, and will also search out rare, hard-to-find items if there's something in particular you're after.

PIONEER SQUARE ANTIQUE MALL
Map p56　　　　　　　　　　　Antiques
☎ 206-624-1164; 602 1st Ave

The Antique Mall is a warren of little shops across from the Pioneer Square pergola; it's actually part of the Seattle 'underground' and can be somewhat claustrophobic, but if you're a patient gem hunter, you'll definitely score. There's lots of vintage clothing, jewelry, photos, cameras, china and knickknacks.

FOSTER/WHITE GALLERY Map p56　Art
☎ 206-622-2833; 220 3rd Ave S

The famed Foster/White Gallery, which opened in 1968, features glassworks, paintings and sculpture by mainstream Northwest artists in a beautifully renovated 7,000-square-foot space.

GLASSHOUSE STUDIO Map p56　　Art
☎ 206-682-9939; 311 Occidental Ave S;
demonstrations 10am & 1-5pm Mon-Sat

The Seattle area is known for its Pilchuck School of glassblowing art, and this is the city's oldest glassblowing studio. Stop by to watch the artists in action and pick up a memento right at the source.

JACKSON STREET GALLERY Map p56　Art
☎ 206-447-1012; 322 1st Ave S

This longstanding gallery has a focus on Native American artwork and photography.

LEGACY LTD GALLERY
Map p56   Arts & Crafts
☎ 206-624-6350; 1003 1st Ave
Legacy Ltd is an internationally known and widely respected source of Northwest Coast Indian and Inuit art and artifacts, including baskets and jewelry. It's good for a browse even if you don't happen to be a museum curator or a millionaire.

SEATTLE MYSTERY BOOKSHOP
Map p56   Books
☎ 206-587-5737; 117 Cherry St
The name gives it away – Seattle Mystery Bookshop is a specialty store for page-turners and whodunits.

NORTH FACE Map p56   Outdoors
☎ 206-622-4111; 1023 1st Ave
For hardcore camping, climbing and hiking clothing and equipment, go to the North Face, downtown toward the Waterfront.

INTERNATIONAL DISTRICT

In addition to the behemoth Uwajimaya, it's worth exploring nooks and crannies in this neighborhood for odd shopfronts and imported wares.

KINOKUNIYA Map p60   Books
☎ 206-587-2477; 525 S Weller St; ☽ 10am-9pm Mon-Sat, 10am-8pm Sun
A great source for hard-to-find imported books and magazines in Asian languages (and in English about Asian culture), this bookstore inside Uwajimaya Village is also one of the few shops in the country where you can buy the lesser-known films of Kinji Fukasaku and other masters of Asian cinema on DVD. It has a fabulous supply of wrapping paper, cards and notebooks, not to mention imported comics and toys. Hello, Kitty!

UWAJIMAYA Map p60   Groceries & Gifts
☎ 206-624-6248; 600 5th Ave S; ☽ 9am-10pm Mon-Sat, 9am-9pm Sun
Dried squid? Check. Sheets of seaweed? Check. Dumpling steamers, teapots, chopsticks? Check, check, check. The enormous Asian grocery and supply store Uwajimaya, anchoring an eponymous shopping center, has everything needed to prepare Thai, Japanese, Chinese and just about any other type of Asian specialties. You'll find fresh and frozen meat and fish, canned and dried produce, and intriguingly labeled treats of all kinds, as well as cooking tools, small appliances, spices, cookbooks, toiletries and gift items. It also has a deli and bakery, and a number of hole-in-the-wall restaurants edge the building.

PIKE PLACE MARKET & WATERFRONT

For the compulsive browser, amateur chef, hungry traveler on a budget or student of the human condition, Seattle has no greater attraction than Pike Place Market. This is shopping central in Seattle: dozens of market food stalls hawk everything from geoduck clams to fennel root to harissa. (For suggestions on where to eat in the market, see p125.) We list a few shops here, but do explore on your own.

For the full gamut of souvenirs, simply stroll up and down the boardwalk along the Waterfront.

TENZING MOMO Map p63   Apothecary
☎ 206-623-9837; Economy Market Bldg, Pike Place Market
One of the coolest shops in Pike Place Market, Tenzing Momo, in the Economy Market Building, is an old-school natural apothecary, with shelves of mysterious glass bottles filled with herbs and tinctures to treat any ailment.

LEFT BANK BOOKS Map p63   Books
☎ 206-622-0195; Pike Place Market, cnr 1st & Pike Pl
This legendary bookstore and distributor is small but fierce, with an essential collection of political theory, off-center fiction and surrealist literature. A sign in the anarchist section humbly requests that, if you're going to steal books, you do it from a corporate chain store, not a workers-run collective.

PETER MILLER ARCHITECTURE & DESIGN BOOKS Map p63   Books
☎ 206-441-4114; 1930 1st Ave
This store, whose window arrangements can make a bibliophile or a design fiend drool, specializes in luxurious architecture books. It also sells gorgeous stationery and

writing instruments, sketchbooks and some art supplies.

BEECHER'S HANDMADE CHEESE

Map p63   Cheese

☎ 206-956-1964; 1600 Pike Pl

This shop has specialty cheeses of all kinds, with different samples to taste each day, plus a mean mac and cheese, which you can get in a little (or big) to-go container for a picnic.

SUR LA TABLE Map p63   Cookware

☎ 206-448-2244; 84 Pine St

It's hard to miss this gigantic cookware store. It's a chain, but a good one, and it started here in Seattle. The rich supply of cookware, books, gear and gadgets are bound to entice any foodie, gourmand or gourmet.

DELAURENTI'S Map p63   Food

☎ 206-622-0141; SW cnr 1st & Pike Pl

DeLaurenti's is a mandatory market stop for the Italian chef or continental food enthusiast. Not only is there a stunning selection of cheese, sausages, hams and pasta, but there's also the largest selection of capers, olive oil and anchovies that you're likely to find this side of Genoa. The wine selection is also quite broad.

PURE FOOD FISH Map p63   Food

☎ 206-622-5765; 1511 Pike Pl

Perhaps the gift that says 'I heart Seattle' the most is a whole salmon or other fresh seafood from the fish markets. All the markets will prepare fish for transportation on the plane ride home, or you can just call and have them take care of the overnight shipping; Pure Food Fish has the best reputation locally for quality and value.

METSKER MAPS Map p63   Maps

☎ 206-623-8747; 1511 1st Ave

In its high-profile location on 1st Ave, this legendary map shop sells all kinds of useful things for the traveler, from maps to guidebooks to various accessories. It also has a good selection of armchair-travel lit and pretty spinning globes for the dreamers.

MADE IN WASHINGTON

Map p63   Souvenirs

☎ 206-467-0788; 1530 Post Alley

If you're looking for something more authentically Northwest than most souvenir shops offer, head to Made in Washington. One of several locations around the city, it stocks arts and crafts, T-shirts, coffee and chocolate, smoked salmon, regional wines, books and handy creations like the 'Bite of Washington' gourmet-food gift basket.

YE OLDE CURIOSITY SHOP

Map p63   Souvenirs

☎ 206-682-5844; Pier 54; ⏰ 9am-9pm

This landmark shop, on Pier 54, now has a lesser sibling, Ye Olde Curiosity Shoppe Too – but never mind that. The original shop is where you'll find cabinets of shrunken heads, piglets in jars and dried puffer fish – not for sale, of course, just for atmosphere. Also not for sale are the famous black diamond, Chief Seattle's hat, a variety of stalagmites and 'tites, and some pretty cool fortune-telling machines. The funniest souvenir available for purchase is a Mt St Helens 'snowglobe' – instead of snow, it

CLOTHING SIZES

Women's clothing

Aus/UK	8	10	12	14	16	18
Europe	36	38	40	42	44	46
Japan	5	7	9	11	13	15
USA	6	8	10	12	14	16

Women's shoes

Aus/USA	5	6	7	8	9	10
Europe	35	36	37	38	39	40
France only	35	36	38	39	40	42
Japan	22	23	24	25	26	27
UK	3½	4½	5½	6½	7½	8½

Men's clothing

Aus	92	96	100	104	108	112
Europe	46	48	50	52	54	56
Japan	S		M	M		L
UK/USA	35	36	37	38	39	40

Men's shirts (collar sizes)

Aus/Japan	38	39	40	41	42	43
Europe	38	39	40	41	42	43
UK/USA	15	15½	16	16½	17	17½

Men's shoes

Aus/UK	7	8	9	10	11	12
Europe	41	42	43	44½	46	47
Japan	26	27	27½	28	29	30
USA	7½	8½	9½	10½	11½	12½

Measurements approximate only; try before you buy

has little gray particles meant to look like ash from the volcano's eruption.

SOUK Map p63 Spices
☎ 206-441-1666; 1916 Pike Pl
Supplies here include Middle Eastern and North African spices and foods. Named after the Arabic word for marketplace, the shop sells everything you'll need to get from cookbook to curry – including cookbooks and curries.

GOLDEN AGE COLLECTABLES
Map p63 Toys
☎ 206-622-9799; downstairs, 1501 Pike Place Market
A haven for geeks, kids and, especially, geeky kids, this shop has comics and comic-book-inspired toys, novelty items (hopping nuns etc), costumes and loads of goth-friendly knickknacks.

GREAT WIND UP Map p63 Toys
☎ 206-621-9370; North Arcade, Pike Place Market
This kids' heaven in the market has every wind-up toy and gizmo known to humankind, and then some.

PIKE & WESTERN WINE SHOP
Map p63 Wine
☎ 206-441-1307; 1934 Pike Pl
A good selection of regional wine and friendly service make this shop at the northern end of Pike Place Market a great place to get introduced to the wines of the Northwest. In-store wine tastings are open to the public from 4pm to 6pm Wednesdays ($5) and 3pm to 6pm Fridays (free).

BELLTOWN

Belltown's shopping runs the gamut from a punk-rock record store to the polar-fleece-happy Patagonia. Be prepared for anything, and you'll probably find something.

ELLIOTT BAY BICYCLES Map p68 Bicycles
☎ 206-441-8144; 2116 Western Ave
This place aims itself toward pro or hardcore cyclists who are prepared to slap down big bucks for top-end road bikes. Custom-built Davidson cycles, renowned for their beauty and inventiveness, are assembled out the back. The shop also does repairs.

SINGLES GOING STEADY Map p68 Music
☎ 206-441-7396; 2219 2nd Ave; ☷ 11am-7pm Mon-Sat, noon-6pm Sun
Singles Going Steady specializes in punk, hip-hop and ska, mostly in the form of 7-inch vinyl singles, as well as posters, patches and other accessories. There's a good little magazine selection, too.

PATAGONIA Map p68 Outdoor
☎ 206-622-9700; 2100 1st Ave
The fashionable outdoor clothing at Patagonia may seem to be only for the very adventurous, but experience a sodden winter in Seattle and you'll understand why this is where the locals shop for rain gear and outdoor apparel.

SEATTLE CELLARS Map p68 Wine
☎ 206-256-0850; 2505 2nd Ave
A good source for regional wines, Seattle Cellars can help you find gifts to take back home. Ask about open tastings on Thursday nights and some Saturday afternoons.

SEATTLE CENTER & QUEEN ANNE

QUEEN ANNE BOOKS Map p75 Books
☎ 206-283-5624; 1811 Queen Anne Ave N
This quiet little nook is a charming neighborhood bookstore, with frequent special events and a nice selection of children's materials. The adjoining El Diablo coffee shop, a Cuban cafe, has a lovely little patio where you can sip a coffee and pore over your latest book purchase.

ONCE UPON A TIME Map p75 Children's
☎ 206-284-7260; 1622 Queen Anne Ave N; ☷ 10am-6pm
This children's store stocks top international brands like Baby Bjorn for savvy parents who like to dress their renaissance tots in labels from around the world. You'll find everything from the practical to the simply adorable: strollers, knit toys, train sets, books, games, little socks and hats, and more.

CHANNEL 9 STORE Map p72 Toys
☎ 206-615-5448, 800-937-5387; 401 Mercer St; ☷ 10am-6pm Mon-Fri

n the lobby of KCTS TV, this cool shop is filled with educational videos and games that educate as much as they entertain. It also benefits public broadcasting.

LAKE UNION

With its own climbing wall, artificial rain-storms and a simulated mountain trail, the state-of-the-art REI megastore has become a tourist destination in its own right – see p76 for details.

FEATHERED FRIENDS Map p77   Outdoors
☎ 206-292-2210; 119 Yale Ave N
Near REI, Feathered Friends stocks high-end climbing equipment, made-to-order sleeping bags and backcountry ski gear. Products made with down are the specialty.

PATRICK'S FLY SHOP Map p77   Outdoors
☎ 206-325-8988; 2237 Eastlake Ave E
Located near Lake Union, this shop has been around as long as anyone can re-member. It offers workshops on fly-fishing, sells equipment and gives advice.

CAPITOL HILL & VOLUNTEER PARK

Shopping on Capitol Hill makes you instantly hipper; even just window shopping is an edu-cation in cutting-edge popular culture. This is the place to find great record stores, unusual bookstores, vintage clothing shops and risqué toy stores.

BABELAND Map p79   Adult
☎ 206-328-2914; 707 E Pike St; ◷ 11am-10pm Mon-Sat, noon-7pm Sun
Opened in 1993 as Toys in Babeland, this sex-positive toy store – inspired by the riot-grrrl aesthetic and staffed by possibly the friendliest and least judgmental people on earth – has since abbreviated its name and expanded its business to include shops in New York and Los Angeles.

CRYPT Map p79   Adult
☎ 206-325-3882; 1516 11th Ave E
Now in a bigger space after moving from its cavernlike original location, the Crypt sells clubwear and leather clothing (mostly but not entirely for guys), DVDs, sex toys and novelties.

VELO BIKE SHOP Map p79   Bicycles
☎ 206-325-4526; 1535 11th Ave
Velo has a good selection of road and mountain bikes, along with helpful staff. They do last-second repairs, and there's an air-compressor hose out front for use free of charge if you just need a quick refill.

ELLIOTT BAY BOOK COMPANY
Map p79   Books
☎ 206-624-6600; 1521 10th Ave
In its new home on Capitol Hill, the venerable Elliott Bay Book Company has gone from creaky and labyrinthine to vast and soaring-ceilinged. At first everyone worried about the relocation, but the new space has an open, energetic vibe – maybe even better than the original (sacrilege!). Still the best bookstore in town, and one of the best in the North-west, Elliott Bay is also the local leader in author appearances, with writers appearing at a reading or signing almost nightly (think Tom Robbins, Sherman Alexie and David James Duncan). Readings are held in a dedicated room downstairs. They are usually free and generally start at 7pm. Pick up a schedule near the store entrance.

TWICE SOLD TALES Map p79   Books
☎ 206-324-2421; 1833 Harvard Ave; ◷ 10am-9pm, to 10pm Fri & Sat
Twice Sold Tales' Capitol Hill location has moved, but it's still a cozy den full of used books at excellent prices, stacked haphazardly along narrow aisles. A book 'happy hour' discount kicks in after 6pm. A bunch of aloof cats roam the shop, actively ignoring everybody.

DILETTANTE CHOCOLATES
Map p79   Chocolate
☎ 206-329-6463; 416 Broadway E
If you have a sweet tooth to satisfy, try the confection truffles here. There's a great selection of desserts, too. You can taste chocolates in the shop, along with good coffee and other snacks, or pick up a box to take home. The European-style chocolates are made in-house.

APRIE Map p79 — Clothing
☎ 206-324-1255; 310 Broadway E
A small boutique with a well-curated selection of trendy tops, dresses and skinny jeans from brands too hip to list here (I mean, if you don't know, I'm not gonna tell you). Aprie is a miniparadise for fashionistas.

CROSSROADS TRADING CO
Map p79 — Clothing
☎ 206-328-5867; 325 Broadway E
This used-clothing store is less expensive than Red Light but also generally less hipster-chic, which is nice if you just want to shop for basics without having some too-cool clerk stare down her nose at your khaki slacks. There's another branch in the U District (Map p83; ☎ 206-632-3111; 4300 University Way NE).

RED LIGHT Map p79 — Clothing
☎ 206-329-2200; 312 Broadway E
Red Light carries stylish, painstakingly selected vintage clothing, organized by decade or sometimes by color. It's a cool shop…maybe too cool. Rest assured, you will be judged by your purchases. There's also a branch in the U District (Map p83; ☎ 206-545-4044; 4560 University Way NE).

URBAN OUTFITTERS Map p79 — Clothing
☎ 206-322-1800; 401 Broadway E
Urban Outfitters in the Broadway Market sells clothing geared toward young folks looking to score points on the hip scale without having to think too hard about putting together a look.

top picks
SEATTLE BOOKSTORES

- Elliott Bay Book Company (p113) Drenched in atmosphere.
- Seattle Mystery Bookshop (p110) All the suspense that's fit to print.
- Magus Books (right) Used treasures in the U District.
- Twice Sold Tales (p113) Don't be insulted when the cats ignore you.
- Left Bank Books (p110) A light in the darkness.

SONIC BOOM Map p79 — Music
☎ 206-568-2666; www.sonicboomrecords.com; 1525 Melrose Ave; ⏲ 10am-10pm Mon-Sat, 10am-7pm Sun
A local institution, Sonic Boom has moved from 15th Ave to this arguably handy spot, and also has a location in Ballard (Map p96; 2209 NW Market St). This awesome indie record store has a great selection of new and used CDs and vinyl, and staff will order you something if they don't have it in stock. Ask about in-store performances by bands coming through town.

WALL OF SOUND Map p79 — Music
☎ 206-441-9880; 315 E Pine St; ⏲ 11am-7pm Mon-Sat, noon-6pm Sun
One of the coolest record stores in town, this smart shop stocks music you've never heard of, from obscure noise artists to gypsy folksongs, but nothing the owners and staff wouldn't listen to at home. The wall of magazines, comics and small-press books is top-notch, too.

U DISTRICT

Bookstores and record stores are the main thing here, although everyone should make time to explore the bins at Hardwick's Hardware Store (p115). University Way NE, called 'the Ave,' is the main drag in the U District, lined with shops and a wild variety of cheap eateries.

RECYCLED CYCLES Map p83 — Bicycles
☎ 206-547-4491; 1007 NE Boat St
Recycled Cycles, at the bottom of the U District along Lake Union, sells used and consignment bikes. It also has a wide selection of parts including cranks, forks, pedals, tires and tubes. Staff members are candid with their advice and know what they're talking about.

ALL FOR KIDS Map p83 — Books
☎ 206-526-2768; 2900 NE Blakely St
Near the University District, All For Kids has one of the largest selections of children's books in town and also stocks a lot of children's music.

MAGUS BOOKS Map p83 — Books
☎ 206-633-1800; 1408 NE 42nd St
Magus is a great used-book store, the kind of place where you can literally spend

hours getting lost in the crooked, narrow aisles on the hunt for that obscure title you're not sure you can even remember anymore.

UNIVERSITY BOOKSTORE Map p83 Books
☎ 206-634-3400; 4326 University Way NE; ◷ 9am-9pm Mon-Fri, 10am-7pm Sat, noon-5pm Sun

University Bookstore is vast and all-purpose, though lacking the time-worn charm of many of Seattle's other, quirkier bookstores. It does have absolutely everything, though, including textbooks and highlighter-abused secondhand books.

BUFFALO EXCHANGE Map p83 Clothing
☎ 206-545-0175; 4530 University Way NE
Somewhere between Crossroads and Red Light in terms of quality and hipster quotient, this secondhand clothing store is comfortable to browse in, but can be hit-and-miss in terms of good finds. Some of its merchandise is on the square side – which doesn't, ironically, make it any easier to sell your old clothes here: staff are notoriously picky.

PITAYA Map p83 Clothing
☎ 206-548-1001; 4520 University Way NE
This is a cute little clothing boutique with carefully selected dresses, hipster jeans and cool accessories.

HARDWICK'S HARDWARE STORE
Map p83 Cool Junk
☎ 206-632-1203; 4214 Roosevelt Way NE; ◷ 8am-6pm Mon-Fri, 9am-6pm Sat, later hours in summer

Locals in the know come to Hardwick's to explore the rows and rows of buckets filled with bizarre little gadgets and gizmos. Some people probably know what these objects are for, but most shoppers are looking for things to use in their art projects. It's a hive of a place that's fun just to explore.

BULLDOG NEWS & ESPRESSO
Map p83 Newsstand
☎ 206-632-6397; 4208 University Way NE
The newsstand of choice at the university, this place has pretty much every magazine or newspaper you might want, from imports and big glossies to stapled-together zines. Good coffee, too.

FREMONT

Once a warren of junk shops and craft-supply stores frequented by granola crunchers, Fremont has become a bit more of a soccer-mom neighborhood. Still, it's a fun place to browse regardless of whether you're in the mood to spend money.

FREMONT PLACE BOOK CO
Map p87 Books
☎ 206-547-5970; 621 N 35th St
This is a friendly little place with a relatively small but interesting collection of new fiction and nonfiction. Ask about in-store author readings and monthly discussion groups.

DELUXE JUNK Map p87 Cool Junk
☎ 206-634-2733; 3518 Fremont Pl N
A local landmark, Deluxe Junk is one of Seattle's most kitschy secondhand shops. Located in a former funeral parlor, it carries a deeply weird assortment of, well, junk. But some of it is pretty nice junk, retro and glitzy and sometimes fabulous – from retro sundresses and fluffy feather boas to home wares and furniture from the 1950s.

EVO Map p87 Outdoors
☎ 206-973-4470; 122 NW 36th St; ◷ 10am-8pm Mon-Sat, 11am-7pm Sun
Skateboards, skis and snowboards, funky gear and a tuning service are all to be found at this huge new space, which also includes a small art gallery.

WALLINGFORD

Some of the city's most interesting bookstores are in this area – don't miss Wide World Books & Maps for travelers, Alphabet Soup for kids and Open Books for anyone interested in poetry.

ALPHABET SOUP Map p91 Books
☎ 206-547-4555; 1406 N 45th St; ◷ 10am-6pm Thu-Sun, closed Mon-Wed
Alphabet Soup is a darling little cottage dedicated entirely to children's books, with both new and used, reasonable prices and helpful staff.

OPEN BOOKS Map p91 Books
☎ 206-633-0811; 2414 N 45th St; ◷ noon-6pm Tue-Sun

Open Books in Wallingford is devoted totally to poetry; call to ask about readings and events.

WIDE WORLD BOOKS & MAPS
Map p91   Books & Maps

☎ 206-634-3453; 4411 Wallingford Ave N; ☺ 10am-9pm Mon-Sat, 11am-6pm Sun
Travelers will want to make a pilgrimage to Wide World Books & Maps. In addition to a great selection of travel guides, this pleasant store offers a full array of travel accessories and a staff of seasoned globe-trotters. Ask for a calendar of events such as slideshows and author readings.

COMICS DUNGEON Map p91   Comic Books
☎ 206-545-8373; 250 NE 45th St
Nestled right between the U District and Wallingford, Comics Dungeon stocks a good selection of comics and graphic novels plus the usual accompaniments of gothy dolls, toys and action figures.

ARCHIE MCPHEE Map p91   Novelty
☎ 206-297-0240; 1300 N 45th St; ☺ 9am-8pm Mon-Sat, 11am-6pm Sun
No longer in Ballard, but still crammed to the gills with all manner of wacky goodies you probably didn't even know you needed, Archie McPhee is a Seattle tradition and a lot of fun, whether you're buying or just marveling at the selection. Inflatable meatloaf, anyone? Maybe some Cthulhu mints?

EROTIC BAKERY Map p91   Novelty
☎ 206-545-6969; 2323 N 45th St
Kind of worn-out and vaguely icky in a not-all-that-hilarious way, the Erotic Bakery nevertheless clings to its 'local landmark' status with boob cookies, penis cakes and other baked goods shaped like body parts. Send one anonymously to your boss on his or her birthday.

NOT A NUMBER Map p91   Novelty
☎ 206-784-0965; 1905 N 45th St; ☺ 11am-7pm Mon-Fri, 11am-8pm Sat, noon-6pm Sun
Slightly less wacky than Archie McPhee is this card and gift shop in Wallingford, selling smarty-pants books, cards and knickknacks, plus some enviro-friendly toys and gadgets. The signs in the shop's front window give you a pretty good idea

of what you'll find here, in terms of both product and attitude.

FAST GIRL SKATES Map p91   Skates
☎ 206-633-0811; 252 N 45th St; ☺ noon-6pm Tue-Sun
A one-stop supply shop for the roller-derby crowd, this rad little place sells skates plus skate-friendly clothing, helmets, safety gear and accessories, including adorable, crazy-patterned knee socks and short shorts.

CITY CELLARS Map p91   Wine
☎ 206-632-7238; 1710 N 45th St
There's no snobbery at City Cellars, but there are lots of great wines and reasonable prices. In the adjoining storefront, check out Bottleworks Inc (☎ 206-633-2437; Suite 3, 1710 N 45th St), which sells mostly imported bottled beer.

GREEN LAKE & PHINNEY RIDGE

GREGG'S CYCLES Map p93   Bicycles
☎ 206-523-1822; 7007 Woodlawn Ave NE
This is Seattle's largest bicycle dealer. Near Green Lake, it has a huge stock of all kinds of bikes and accessories and a very helpful staff.

RISING STARS Map p93   Children's
☎ 206-781-0138; 7321 Greenwood Ave N; ☺ 10am-6pm Mon-Sat, 10am-5pm Sun
This children's store carries adorable tiny rain-slickers, toys, books and carefully selected clothing. It shares a building with Metropolis (below).

FROCK SHOP Map p93   Clothing
☎ 206-297-1638; www.shopfrockshop.com; 6500 Phinney Ave N
Look for the sign advertising the 'Phinney Ave Beauty Salon' – that's what this building used to be, and it maintains the original atmosphere. Get gorgeous in style with flirty little dresses you can try on in front of movie-star mirrors.

METROPOLIS Map p93   Novelty
☎ 206-782-7002; 7321 Greenwood Ave N; ☺ 10am-7pm Mon-Fri, 10am-6pm Sat, 11am-5pm Sun
In the same building as Rising Stars is this hodgepodge of a novelty shop, selling small gifts, cards, wacky stickers, magnets and various objets d'kitsch.

top picks

SEATTLE RECORD STORES

- **Easy Street Records & Café** (right) A fun place to hang out and browse.
- **Georgetown Records** (right) And you thought they didn't make 'em like this anymore.
- **Wall of Sound** (p114) Obscurities, as well as great publications.
- **Sonic Boom** (p114) Alt-rock and indie rock essentials.
- **Singles Going Steady** (p112) Totally punk rock.

BALLARD & DISCOVERY PARK

Ballard is a fun place to browse, especially right along the core of Market Street, where there's a little cluster of interesting shops, including a branch of indie record store Sonic Boom (see p114).

WILD AT HEART Map p96   Adult
☎ 206-782-5538; 1111 NW Leary Way
This women-owned shop sells sex toys, fetish-wear, clubwear, lingerie and DVDs.

SECRET GARDEN BOOKSHOP
Map p96   Books
☎ 206-789-5006; 2214 NW Market St
The children's collection, especially the fiction selection, is excellent at this bookstore, and the staff will order you anything they don't have.

BUFFALO EXCHANGE Map p96   Clothing
☎ 206-297-5920; 2232 NW Market St
Usually rewarding for the patient browser, this used clothing store has an unpretentious selection and non-intrusive salespeople.

WILD SALMON SEAFOOD MARKET
Map p96   Seafood
☎ 206-283-3366, 888-222-3474; 1900 W Nickerson St

At Wild Salmon Seafood Market – in the Fishermen's Terminal on the south side of the Ballard Bridge, which is technically Magnolia, but still – you can buy fresh salmon and shellfish directly from the fishermen who caught it. The market will also ship fresh fish at reasonable prices.

WEST SEATTLE

EASY STREET RECORDS & CAFÉ
Map p103   Music
☎ 206-938-3279; 4559 California Ave SW
This place has everything: rock-and-roll, coffee, beer, food…and an open, airy place to hang out while enjoying all of the above. Any place where you can shop for new import records, have a beer and then kick back on the couch for a while is bound to attract attention, and you might have to elbow some hipsters out of your way to grab that coveted album – just try not to spill. Also at Queen Anne (☎ 206-691-3279; 20 Mercer St; ☷ 9am-midnight Mon, 9am-11pm Tue-Sat, 9am-9pm Sun).

GEORGETOWN

KIRK ALBERT VINTAGE FURNISHINGS
Map p106   Furnishings
☎ 206-931-6208; 5517 Airport Way S
Not so much stocked as curated, this funky, beautiful store represents the obsessions and tastes of its owner, a designer with a strongly original aesthetic. Come to browse and leave inspired by the stunningly brilliant combinations of one-of-a-kind, oddball treasures.

GEORGETOWN RECORDS
Map p106   Records
☎ 206-762-5638; 1201 S Vale St
This awesome record store has cool customers (Jeff Ament and Ben Shepherd, anyone?) and an even cooler vibe, not to mention a great selection of new and used CDs and vinyl. It also hosts in-store performances and is part of the Georgetown art walk.

EATING

top picks

- Dahlia Lounge (p127)
- Steelhead Diner (p126)
- Coastal Kitchen (p130)
- Tilth (p133)
- Salumi (p123)
- Cicchetti (p129)
- Pho Bac (p125)

What's your recommendation? www.lonelyplanet.com/seattle

EATING

It's easy to become food obsessed in Seattle. The city's focus on locally produced, fresh, organic ingredients, whether from nearby farms or the bounteous sea, means dinner is never just dinner – it's a sociopolitical act. Guilt-free indulgence is the rule: upscale restaurants that *don't* emphasize sustainable fishing and farming are the exception. The biggest boast a Seattle restaurant can make these days is that the chef helped reel in the day's catch, or that they're lifelong pals with the farmer who grew your salad, or that they can name the chicken who laid the egg that's now beside your toast.

'Northwest cuisine' is a fairly inclusive term in the sense that it can mean anything from surf-and-turf and pasta to sushi and pad Thai; what defines it is an insistence on showing off the best of what the region produces: seafood so fresh it squirms, fat berries freshly plucked, mushrooms dug out of the rich soil and cornucopias of fruits and vegetables.

Going hand in hand with the regional emphasis on sustainable, organic, unfussy food is the prevalence of vegan and vegetarian restaurants here. This is the kind of city where it's automatically understood that vegan cupcakes are sexier than the regular kind. The city has won attention and praise in the national press for its combination of healthy gourmet restaurant options, sustainable farming and cooking practices, inventive use of ingredients and overall quality of life. Of course, Seattle also loves a good steak – especially one that's led a happy, grass-fed life on a farm just outside of town.

The restaurant world is an ever-shifting one, and the metaphorical kitchen-of-the-moment award is definitely a traveling trophy. Check the dining sections of the local papers for new developments, and ask around – practically everyone in town is a food expert and most will be quite happy to recommend their favorite spot.

Food-related internet forums such as eGullet (www.egullet.org, click on the Pacific Northwest Dining division) or Chowhound (www.chowhound.com/boards/4) can be helpful in tracking down the latest news about which restaurants are hot, which have fallen off their game, and which places local foodies are hoping to keep all to themselves.

PRACTICALITIES

Opening Hours

Specific opening hours are listed in reviews if they differ from the norm; otherwise we simply note which meals each restaurant serves. Breakfast is typically served from 7am to 11am; brunch from 7am to 3pm; lunch from 11:30am to 2:30pm; and dinner from 5:30pm to 10pm.

How Much?

The range of eateries in Seattle means it's possible to find dining options that suit most budgets, whether that's a $2 taco from a parking-lot stand, a $5 bowl of noodles in the U District or a $30 wedge of hazelnut-encrusted line-caught wild salmon with organic field greens served in a chic converted warehouse. Typically, breakfast and lunch fall in the $8 to $10 range per person, and dinner can be anywhere from $16 to $60 or more.

Booking Tables

Most Seattle restaurants don't require advance bookings, but the hot new places fill up quickly, so it's best to call ahead if you want to be sure to avoid disappointment. Many restaurants also have a bar section where you can wait for a table to open up if you don't have reservations. In the listings below, where reservations are recommended or mandatory it's noted in the review.

Tipping

Tips are not figured into the check at a restaurant. In general, 15% is the baseline tip, but

PRICE GUIDE	
$$$	over $30
$$	$15-30
$	under $15

These guides reflect the cost of an average meal, whether that's a main dish or a number of small plates, per person, not including drinks or a tip.

20% is usually more appropriate, and 25% if you enjoyed the service. If you're just ordering coffee at a counter, tip with change, but if someone makes you a specialty drink, leave 10% to 20%. There's also a 9.3% tax on food and beverages purchased in restaurants and bars (included in prices listed here).

DOWNTOWN & FIRST HILL

You'll have to dig deep to fill your belly in the central downtown area, but this is the place to find classic Northwest food in old-fashioned oyster bars and cavernous steakhouses, as well as a couple of celebrity chef Tom Douglas's flagship restaurants (see the box, p125) and the posh dining rooms of some of the city's finest hotels.

METROPOLITAN GRILL

Map p50   Steak & Seafood $$$

☎ 206-624-3287; 820 2nd Ave; starters $10-19, steaks $38-47; ⊙ lunch Mon-Fri, dinner daily
This handsome and atmospheric business favorite fills up with stock analysts and bankers who pour out of nearby office towers. Though you can get seafood, 'grilled portobello mignon' or even Beluga caviar, beef is the big thing here – steaks are custom-aged and grilled over mesquite charcoal. Locals usually name the Met as the top chophouse in the city.

WHAT IS NORTHWEST CUISINE?

A lot of Seattle's gourmet restaurants describe their style of cuisine as 'Northwest.' But what does that actually mean? Besides the high quality of the raw materials found naturally in this region, the thing that distinguishes Northwest cuisine from standard US food is the influence of Asian cooking traditions. Pan-Asian cooking, often referred to as Pacific Rim cuisine or fusion food, is the blending of American or European standards with ingredients from Asia. It results in some unusual combinations – don't be surprised if you get wasabi on your French fries.

Not surprisingly, seafood is a cornerstone of Northwest cuisine. Crab, often Dungeness fresh from the boat, is available almost everywhere – you'll see stacks and stacks of crabs at Pike Place Market. In restaurants, crab is usually served in salad or with garlic butter, but you can also get crab cakes, crab bisque or even crab burgers. The better seafood restaurants print a new list of what's freshly caught each day; you might love seared *ahi* (tuna), but during the (very limited) season for native coho salmon, for example, you'd be silly not to choose that instead, and a good restaurant will tell you so.

Locally caught fish include red snapper, flounder, sole, tuna, halibut and cod. Shrimp is another major catch. For most of the year, salmon, which is still a menu staple, is as likely to be from Alaska as from the Northwest. Local trout is also found in fish markets and on menus: try the vibrantly yellow golden trout.

The chilly waters of the Pacific produce sweet-tasting, delicately tangy oysters, sourced from oyster farms all along the coast. In the best places, discerning diners can choose which Northwestern bay their oysters on the half-shell hail from. Clams, usually steamed in broth or seawater, and mussels, which cover practically every rock along the Pacific Coast, are common as appetizers, frequently in combination. The elongated, delicately flavored razor clam, in particular, gets nobility status on the West Coast.

The Northwest offers an incredibly rich diversity of fruit, which the best chefs sprinkle like jewels all over their creations, or whip into decadent sauces to drizzle over meat and fish. Blueberries thrive in the acidic soil, and they appear in pies, breads, muffins and scones. The mild climate is also good for strawberries and raspberries. Washington is the nation's largest producer of apples, and other notable orchard crops include pears, cherries and peaches. Blackberry brambles, which snag clothing and grab at the legs of hikers, are a great annoyance until late summer and early fall, when they produce a heady abundance of purple-black fruit. A favorite of black bears, wild huckleberries are found high up in mountain meadows. Washington state is also a major producer of tart, bright-red cranberries, which appear frequently in local dishes.

Rainy Washington is also a mushroom lover's paradise. The best chefs use wild mushrooms gathered in the forest that morning. Don't miss a chance at the saffron-colored chanterelles, whose brief season, intense hue and unique flavor make them a sought-after commodity. Other mushrooms that grow in Northwest forests include the oyster, morel, porcini and shiitake, which are shipped worldwide.

No discussion of food from the Northwest would be complete without mentioning nuts. Filberts (hazelnuts) grow profusely here, as do walnuts. For that special Northwest touch, look for hazelnut gift packs (some jazzed up in smokehouse or jalapeno style) or hazelnuts served in baked goods or with meat.

GEORGIAN Map p50 — Continental $$$

☎ 206-621-7889; 411 University St; express lunch $15, mains $20-35; ☽ breakfast & lunch daily, dinner Tue-Sat

A treat above treats, the Georgian at the Fairmont Olympic Hotel is one of the most imposing restaurants in the city – the ornate high ceilings and dripping chandeliers, shiny silver and gilt details will have you swooning. The food is equally eye-catching and inspired by regional ingredients, such as scallops with truffles or roasted sea bass. Service is tops, and it's one of the few places where Seattleites tend to be sharply dressed; jackets aren't required but they're certainly not discouraged. Reservations are recommended. Bargain-hunters or those short of time should try the express lunch, which includes soup, salad, sandwich and dessert delivered all at once.

MCCORMICK'S FISH HOUSE & BAR
Map p50 — Steak & Seafood $$

☎ 206-682-3900; 722 4th Ave; starters $6-10, dinner mains $17-36; ☽ lunch & dinner Mon-Fri, dinner 4-10pm Sat & Sun

A mainstay of traditional Seattle dining and the flagship of a small Northwest chain, this classy, wood-lined place is a network of cubbyholes that looks like an old-boys' club (it was built as a hotel in 1827). The food is consistently good, with daily fresh fish specials (mostly grilled with zesty sauces) and a fine selection of local oysters, chops and steak. Try the crab cakes or the seared *ahi* (tuna), or just ask your server what's fresh. The bar menu is awesome, with a number of substantial snacks for less than $2.

HUNT CLUB Map p50 — Northwest $$$

☎ 206-343-6156; Sorrento Hotel, 900 Madison St; starters $8-16, mains $19-30, afternoon tea $35; ☽ breakfast, brunch & dinner daily, lunch Mon-Fri, afternoon tea 11am-4pm Sat by reservation

The Hunt Club ought to be on the shortlist if you're looking for a special-occasion, top-end restaurant. The setting is ultra posh and absolutely beautiful: an intimate mahogany-paneled dining room shimmering with candles and decked with flowers. The food is equally stellar, featuring local lamb, fish and steaks from sustainable farms, accentuated by inventive sauces and regional produce. Reservations are recommended.

WILD GINGER Map p50 — Asian $$

☎ 206-623-4450; 1401 3rd Ave; satay $3-6, lunch $8-16, dinner mains $14-28; ☽ lunch Mon-Sat, dinner to 11pm Sun-Thu, to midnight Fri & Sat

Seattle was more or less introduced to the satay bar by this popular Indonesian fusion restaurant, where throngs of diners sit and sample bite-size, skewered bits of fiery grilled chicken, vegetables or scallops, plus luscious soups and daily specials. More substantial dishes include Burmese curry crab and cinnamon-and-anise-spiced duck. The bar is a happening place, and there's a live music venue, the Triple Door, downstairs.

FARESTART RESTAURANT
Map p50 — Northwest $$

☎ 206-443-1233; www.farestart.org; 700 Virginia St; soups & salads $2.50-9.50, lunch mains $8-12, 3-course dinner $25; ☽ 11am-2pm Mon-Fri, dinner Thu

FareStart serves substantial meals that benefit the community. The constantly changing lunch menu is pretty darn gourmet for the price – try the veggie reuben, or a flatiron steak in blue-cheese sauce. All proceeds from lunch and the popular Thursday-night Guest Chef dinners – when FareStart students work with a famous local chef to produce outstanding meals – go to support the FareStart program, which provides intensive job training, housing assistance and job placement for disadvantaged and homeless people. Reservations are strongly recommended for dinner.

CYBER-DOGS Map p50 — Vegetarian $

☎ 206-405-3647; 909 Pike St; dogs $2-5; ☽ 10am-midnight; ♿ Ⓥ

One of those all-things-to-some-people places, Cyber-Dogs is an all-veggie hot-dog stand, espresso bar, internet café (internet free for first 20 minutes, then $6 per hour) and youngster hangout/pick-up joint. Its advertising campaign is based on miniature hand-scribbled-and-stapled chapbooks with cute indie-rock-style cartoons. But the best thing about the place is trying out the weird, insanely imaginative non-meat 'not-dogs' with tastes-better-than-it-sounds toppings (eggplant, potatoes, hummus).

PIONEER SQUARE

Pioneer Square is the ideal place to be if you're looking for a meal in an old-school steak and seafood restaurant with loads of atmosphere and traditional service. It also has a good range of budget-friendly options that are inexpensive without lacking character.

FX MCRORY'S STEAK, CHOP & OYSTER HOUSE Map p56   Steak & Seafood $$
☎ 206-623-4800; 419 Occidental Ave S; oyster sampler $14, starters $6-10, dinner mains $12-35; ⊗ lunch & dinner Mon-Sat, longer hours on stadium event days

This vast Pioneer Square landmark across from the sports stadiums is a weird blend of class and ass – it's a majestic old space with a bar on one side, a fancy dining room on the other and an oyster bar in between, but the ball-cap/jock quotient gets high on days when the Seahawks or Mariners play. McRory's claims to have the largest selection of bourbon in the world – believable when you ogle the pyramid of booze behind the bar. Tuck into classic fare like prime rib or Dungeness crab, or share a seafood platter of oysters on the half-shell, smoked salmon, prawns, crab, Penn Cove mussels and scallops.

SALUMI Map p56   Sandwiches $
☎ 206-621-8772; 309 3rd Ave S; sandwiches $8-12, plates $12-15; ⊗ 11am-4pm Tue-Fri

Sure, you'll have to wait in line. This is Mario Batali's dad's place, after all. But the line to get a Salumi sandwich is like its own little community. People chat, compare notes, talk about sandwiches they've had and loved…it's nice. When you finally get in the door of this long, skinny shopfront, you're further teased by display cases of hanging meats and cheeses. Sandwiches come with any of a dozen types of cured meat and a handful of fresh cheese on a hunk of bread – you can't go wrong. There's only a couple of seats, so be prepared to picnic. On Tuesdays, family members hand-roll gnocchi in the window.

NEW ORLEANS CREOLE RESTAURANT Map p56   Southern $$
☎ 206-622-2563; 114 1st Ave S; lunch $6-8, gumbo $7-9.50, mains $7-13; ⊗ lunch Mon-Fri, dinner Mon-Sat; ⊛

Enjoy some live Dixieland jazz with your homemade gumbo or jambalaya in one of the coolest spaces in Pioneer Square. This bourbon-heavy institution serves unpretentious food in an attractive space (warm lighting and exposed brick walls decorated with portraits of jazz greats) that's kid-friendly until 10pm. There's live music most nights, including blues and zydeco.

ZAINA Map p56   Middle Eastern $
☎ 206-624-5687; 108 Cherry St; gyros $8-11; ⊗ 10am-9pm Mon-Fri, 11am-9pm Sat

This friendly cafe, bejeweled with a mish-mash of sparkly decorations and pulsing with Middle Eastern pop, dishes out juicy falafel sandwiches stuffed to overflowing, as well as shawarma, tabbouleh, hummus, great baklava and freshly squeezed lemonade. On weekend nights the vibe goes clubbish, with hookahs and belly dancers in the house.

GRAND CENTRAL BAKING CO
Map p56   Soup & Sandwiches $
☎ 206-622-3644; Grand Central Arcade, 214 1st Ave S; sandwiches $4-10; ⊗ 7am-5pm Mon-Fri, 8am-4pm Sat

This artisan bakery in the Grand Central Arcade builds sandwiches on its own peasant-style loaves and baguettes, with soups, salads, pastries and other treats. Breakfast sandwiches are made with cage-free eggs, while Beecher's artisan cheese is also a great deal.

BAKEMAN'S Map p56   Diner $
☎ 206-622-3375; 122 Cherry St; sandwiches $4-7; ⊗ 10am-3pm Mon-Fri

top picks

WORTH THE WAIT

Some of the most popular restaurants in Seattle are not only worth the wait, but also actually make it fun to hang out and kill time before your meal.

- **Salumi** (left) Chat with hungry fellow meat-seekers in Seattle's friendliest and possibly longest line. Why aren't these people crankier? Because they know what awaits them at the end of that line.
- **Steelhead Diner** (p126) Stake out a spot at the bar and score an awesome view of the bay.
- **La Carta de Oaxaca** (p135) The fun bar here, stocked with premium tequilas, makes the inevitable wait for a table pass quickly.
- **Thai Tom** (p132) Cram into the storefront of this tiny place with everybody else, and watch the spicy, steamy cooking action.

Legendary for its theatrical counter service and its roasted-fresh-daily turkey-and-cranberry sandwich, this subterranean diner demands that you know what you want and aren't afraid to ask for it.

INTERNATIONAL DISTRICT

The International District (ID) is a great neighborhood for to grab cheap eats or go all-out on a sumptuous eight-course dinner banquet. It's also a good place to seek out decent food after the bars close. The many Vietnamese, Thai and Chinese restaurants that line S Jackson St between 6th and 12th Aves give you plenty of options. East of 8th Ave S and I-5, Little Saigon takes over and the flavor becomes decidedly Vietnamese.

Locals argue fiercely over which place does the best *pho* and, especially, the best dim sum, so ask around and try a bunch.

HOUSE OF HONG Map p60   Chinese $

☎ 206-622-7997; 408 8th Ave S; dim sum $2-3 per item, mains $12-15; 9am-11pm; ♿
This huge mainstay of the neighborhood serves dim sum from 10am until 4:30pm every day – handy if your craving hits in the middle of the day.

SHANGHAI GARDEN Map p60   Chinese $

☎ 206-625-1688; 524 6th Ave S; lunch specials $8, dinner mains $10-16; lunch & dinner
Hand-shaved barley noodles are the specialty of Shanghai Garden, and they frankly trounce all expectations you might ordinarily have of a noodle. They're wide and chewy, almost meaty, and just barely dressed with perky spinach and nicely integrated globs of chicken, tofu, beef or shrimp. It might seem odd to get all rapturous about a plate of noodles, but these deserve it. The sugar-pea vines are also a favorite, and if neither of those options tempts you, there are about 75 other choices.

TAMARIND TREE Map p60   Vietnamese $

☎ 206-860-1414; 1036 S Jackson St; starters $6-8.50, pho $5-9, mains $10-16; 10am-10pm Sun-Thu, 10am-midnight Fri & Sat
Serving upscale food at lowbrow prices in a beautiful dining room, this elegant place has a *huge* menu, including

everything from satays and salad rolls to big bowls of *pho* and a tasty version of the traditional scallop-prawn-pork-mushroom fried crepe. It also donates some of its profits to the Vietnam Scholarship Foundation. Reservations are recommended on weekends.

PURPLE DOT CAFÉ Map p60   Chinese $

☎ 206-622-0288; 515 Maynard Ave S; mains $7-14; breakfast, lunch & dinner, open to 3:30am Fri & Sat
The Purple Dot looks like the inside of an '80s videogame (it is actually purple) and draws a late-night drunken-disco crowd on weekends, but most of the time it's a calm, quiet place to get dim sum and Macaostyle specialties (meaning you can feast on baked spaghetti and French toast along with your Hong Kong favorites).

CHINA GATE Map p60   Chinese $

☎ 206-624-1730; 516 7th Ave S; starters $4-12, mains $8-15; 10am-2am; ♿
Like House of Hong, the China Gate now has all-day dim sum. The Hong Kong–style menu offers a couple of hundred choices, and the building is interesting in its own right – it was built in 1924 as a Peking Opera house.

JADE GARDEN Map p60   Chinese $

☎ 206-622-8181; 424 7th Ave S; dim sum items $2-3, mains $8-12; 10am-10pm
Usually mentioned near the top of the list of best places for dim sum in the ID, Jade Garden offers a good range of the delicacies, with everything from standard, newbie-friendly shrimp dumplings and steamed pork buns to the more exotic plates, like black cylinders of sesame-paste gel and, of course, chicken feet. The more things you try, the more fun you'll have. The Jade Garden's hot pots are also recommended.

GREEN LEAF Map p60   Vietnamese $

☎ 206-340-1388; 418 8th Ave S; starters $5-9, pho $7.95, specials $11.95; lunch & dinner
A tiny nook with shiny black tables, this cozy joint is known for inexpensive noodle dishes packed with flavor, as well as huge bowls of traditional or vegetarian *pho* and a swoon-inducing version of *bahn xeo* – sort of a cross between a pancake and an omelet.

TOM DOUGLAS

A fixture in the Seattle foodie scene, chef Tom Douglas helped define what people mean when they talk about Northwest cuisine. He opened his first restaurant, Dahlia, in 1989; it was followed by Etta's Seafood, Palace Kitchen, and, more recently, Lola and Serious Pie. Douglas won the 1994 James Beard Award for Best Northwest Chef, and the James Beard Foundation named *Tom Douglas' Seattle Kitchen* the Best American Cookbook in 2001. Douglas also battled Masaharu Morimoto in an episode of *Iron Chef America* – and won.

Clearly, the guy knows his way around a dinner plate. So when we asked him to describe his perfect Seattle afternoon, naturally there was food on the menu – including dessert.

Douglas starts his trek at his favorite local landmark, Pike Place Market. 'I would stop for lunch first at the Pink Door (p126), out on their deck, which overlooks Elliott Bay there and the market itself,' Douglas says. 'There's something about being outdoors in the market. When it's nice out and you can sit outdoors and eat, there's nothing quite like it. So I love sitting up there.

'When I'm at the Pink Door I'll have the lasagne verde, which is just this perfect little lasagne that my wife and I had there for our wedding reception 24 years ago, and they still have it. That's our date food. And we have a little pink prosecco to go with it, to "put you in the mood." Then we kinda stroll through and head down the Pike Place Hillclimb, and by the time you're down the Hillclimb, I'm ready for dessert. I go down to that little Procopio (p127) and have a little cantaloupe or coconut sorbet or gelato.

'And then we stroll over to the ferry, and if you've never been on one of the Washington State Ferries here, it's the best way to see Seattle. I think it's even better than the Space Needle because of the water and the movement and the sea life. It's just so grand on the top deck of the ferries. We pack refreshments in a brown paper bag and just go to and from the city. If you have time you can stop in Bainbridge, but I like just riding the ferry back and forth. It's just an hour and 10-minute ride – cheap.

'And then my favorite thing to do from there is walk over to the stadium and get an early baseball game. You can get the Ichi-roll in center field: there's a good little sushi bar. Safeco Field (p58) is awesome.'

There you have it.

PHO BAC Map p60   Vietnamese $
☎ 206-568-0882; 1240 Jackson St; pho from $6.50; ☺ 7am-9pm
You can get three sizes of *pho* at this well-established restaurant, with its huge windows gazing onto Little Saigon, as well as excellent salad rolls wrapped in fresh herbs and other classic Vietnamese dishes. Bonus: iconic Seattle chef Tom Douglas (see the box, above) famously loves the place.

PIKE PLACE MARKET & WATERFRONT

For a wide selection of fresh produce, bakery products, deli items and takeout ethnic foods, head to Pike Place Market. Explore the market on an empty stomach and commit to a few hours of snacking; you'll be full by the time you leave, and it doesn't have to cost you much. And if you're looking for serious dining, you can find that here, too; some of Seattle's favorite restaurants are tucked in mysterious corners in the market district.

For a full directory and map of everything in the market, be sure to pick up a copy of the pamphlet *Welcome to the Pike Place Market* from the market information booth on 1st Ave at Pike St, in front of the main entrance.

CAMPAGNE Map p63   French $$$
☎ 206-728-2800; 86 Pine St; small plates $8-19, bar menu $9-14, mains $26-48; ☺ dinner Tue-Sun, bar until midnight
You have to love a place that cut off part of its building to save the one tree in the market, as the bar at Campagne did. Nestled in the courtyard of the Inn at the market, this is a favorite among Seattle's traditional French restaurants. Try the mussels with pommes frites or the crispy pork shoulder with fingerling potatoes. The Campagne burger costs $33, but it's dressed with foie gras and truffles. Reservations are recommended.

MATT'S IN THE MARKET
Map p63   Northwest $$$
☎ 206-467-7909; www.mattsinthemarket.com; 94 Pike St, ste 32; lunch $7-23, small plates $13-18, dinner mains $27-39; ☺ lunch & dinner Mon-Sat
A beloved spot that's been dramatically renovated, Matt's is deep in the heart of the market and draws from its surroundings. A pulled-pork sandwich is made with

Stumptown coffee barbecue sauce; several dishes use locally grown potatoes and organic meats. The menu leans heavily toward seafood, and fresh fruit abounds, but you certainly won't be forced to endure a meal without pork belly.

CHEZ SHEA Map p63 Mediterranean $$$
☎ 206-467-9990; 94 Pike St, ste 34; starters $7-15, mains $18-36, lounge menu $9.50-11.50; ☽ dinner Tue-Sun

Another treasure hidden in one of the market's many corners (upstairs in the Corner Market Building), Chez Shea has great views over Puget Sound that combine with spectacular multicourse meals to make this one of the city's most romantic restaurants. The chef's tasting menu (seven courses, $75) makes the rounds of basically every edible thing to be found in the Pacific Northwest, depending on season. There's also a seasonal menu and the more modest Shea's Lounge menu.

CAFÉ CAMPAGNE Map p63 French $$
☎ 206-728-2233; 1600 Post Alley; breakfast menu $9-18, lunch menu $19, French 101 dinner menu $29; ☽ breakfast & lunch Mon-Fri, brunch 8am-4pm Sat & Sun, dinner daily

At this casual younger sibling of the upscale Campagne (p125), the quality of the French-style cooking is what you'd expect from such a talented kitchen, Plus the prices are more manageable, and you don't have to dress up for dinner. The weekend brunch is a treat.

STEELHEAD DINER
Map p63 Southern, Diner $$
☎ 206-625-0129; http://steelheaddiner.com; 95 Pine St; starters $9-14, sandwiches $12-13, mains $15-28; ☽ 11am-10pm

'Highbrow diner' sounds like an oxymoron, but the Steelhead does it right – hearty, homey favorites like fish and chips, buffalo meatloaf or pork rib chops become fine cuisine because they're made with the best of what Pike Place Market has to offer and paired with cleverly chosen sides. 'Sequimbled Eggs' (named after Sequim Bay, known for its crab and oysters) come poached over Dungeness crab on toast; a fried-chicken sandwich is fall-apart moist and lemony; and the crab cakes make local foodies swoon. The place is all windows, which is great considering it's perched right

over the market and Elliott Bay, and decorations include tied flies in glass. Reservations are recommended.

PINK DOOR RISTORANTE
Map p63 Italian $$
☎ 206-443-3241; 1919 Post Alley; mains $16-24; ☽ 11:30am-10pm Mon-Thu, 11:30am-11pm Fri & Sat, 4-10pm Sun

Beloved for its atmosphere at least as much as its food, the Pink Door is an old-school favorite – on a nice evening, stopping for dinner and drinks on the deck overlooking the market is hard to beat. The menu is traditional Italian, and the vegetarian lasagne comes highly recommended.

LE PICHET Map p63 French $$
☎ 206-256-1499; 1933 1st Ave; snacks $4-12, lunch $4-10, dinner mains $8-34; ☽ 8am-midnight

This tiny French café, bistro and wine bar is elegant and tasteful, and yet it's casual enough to quickly become a favorite haunt. The menu features traditional French cuisine without the aorta-clogging heaviness that this often implies. Breakfast is simple and delicious, and small snack plates of olives, almonds or various rillettes (potted meats) are available all day. For a treat, order the roasted chicken with celery and potatoes ($34); it's made only on request and takes an hour, but is worth the wait.

ETTA'S SEAFOOD Map p63 Seafood $$
☎ 206-443-6000; 2020 Western Ave; brunch $8-15, mains $12-25, happy hour oysters $1; ☽ brunch 9am-3pm Sat & Sun, lunch & dinner daily

Famous for its gourmet seafood brunch, which includes such mouth-waterers as poached eggs with Dungeness crab and chipotle hollandaise, Etta's is a reliable and classy place with a fish-focused dinner menu –you can never go wrong with the king salmon.

IVAR'S ACRES OF CLAMS
Map p63 Seafood $
☎ 206-624-6852; Pier 54, 1001 Alaskan Way; fish & chips $8-9; ☽ lunch & dinner; ♿

Ivar Haglund was a beloved local character famous for silly promotional slogans ('Keep clam!'), but he sure knew how to fry up fish and chips. Ivar's is a Seattle institution that started in 1938. Forgo the dining room for the outdoor lunch counter; the chaotic ordering system involves a lot of yelling, but it seems to work, and then you can enjoy your clam strips or fish and chips outdoors on the pier.

LOWELL'S RESTAURANT Map p63 Diner $
☎ 206-622-2036; 1519 Pike Pl; mains $6-9; ☺ breakfast, lunch & dinner
If you want a sit-down meal but nothing fancy, head to Lowell's, which is well loved by shoppers, businesspeople and fellow market operators for its classic, eye-opening breakfasts and cheap-and-cheerful lunches. Order up eggs Benedict, salmon omelets or fish and chips from the chalkboard menu, then take it over to a window seat and enjoy the view.

LE PANIER Map p63 Bakery $
☎ 206-441-3669; 1902 Pike Pl; pastries $2-5; ☺ breakfast, lunch & dinner
A great place to grab a coffee and croissant and watch the market action, Le Panier calls itself a 'very French bakery' and tends to live up to the name.

PROCOPIO GELATI Map p63 Gelato $
☎ 206-622-4280; 1501 Western Ave; gelato $2-5; ☺ 9am-6pm
If the Pike Place Hillclimb wears you out – or even if it doesn't – stop for an authentic Italian-style gelato. The owner learned his trade from a Milanese gelato maker, and he uses only super-fresh ingredients for completely undiluted flavors.

MEE SUM PASTRIES Map p63 Asian $
☎ 206-682-6780; 1526 Pike Pl; bao $2.95; ☺ breakfast, lunch & dinner
This little storefront window is famed for its giant *hum bao* – eminently portable meat- or vegetable-filled steamed buns that make a great snack or small meal. The steamed pork *bao* is tops. Next-door is a smoothie stand, where you can round out your tidy little meat bomb with some fresh fruits and vegetables.

BELLTOWN
Formerly scruffy but now condo-clean, Belltown makes it easy to spend either a little or a lot and still get a fabulous meal. Peppering its rows of bars and cocktail lounges is a great variety of cafes, delis, top-of-the-line restaurants and low-budget noodle huts frequented by arty musicians and starving students. The other advantage of Belltown is that you're more likely to be able to find late-night dining, thanks to an active cocktail scene that encourages many restaurants to serve at least a bar menu until 2am.

BUENOS AIRES GRILL
Map p68 Steakhouse $$$
☎ 206-441-7076; 2000 2nd Ave; starters $8.50-14, steaks $29-42; ☺ dinner daily, until midnight Fri & Sat
Tucked into a Belltown side street, this Argentinean steakhouse serves minty-fresh cocktails, unusual salads (like hearts of palm) and huge portions of well-prepared steak. The cooking aromas will lure you in; the fun vibe and the staff's tendency to tango on request will make you linger.

DAHLIA LOUNGE Map p68 Northwest $$$
☎ 206-682-4142; 2001 4th Ave; lunch $10-22, dinner starters $9-15, mains $22-38; ☺ lunch & dinner Mon-Fri, dinner until 11pm Sat & Sun
Owner Tom Douglas started fusing flavors at this Seattle institution in the late 1980s and single-handedly made Seattleites more sophisticated; his empire has grown a lot since then, but the flagship restaurant remains a local favorite. There's a bakery next door where you can pick up one of the Dahlia's fabulous desserts to go. Reservations are recommended.

SHIRO'S SUSHI RESTAURANT
Map p68 Japanese $$
☎ 206-443-9844; 2401 2nd Ave; starters $5-8, mains $8-15, sushi dinner $26.75; ☺ dinner daily
Kyoto-born sushi master Shiro Kashiba ran Seattle's first sushi restaurant, Nikko, for 20 years. He spends a lot of time shopping for the freshest ingredients, hence his reputation as the go-to guy for raw fish in Seattle. He's a cheerful-looking fellow, but takes his sushi very seriously – get a seat at the bar if you can, and watch him work.

RESTAURANT ZOE Map p68 Northwest $$
☎ 206-256-2060; 2137 2nd Ave; salads $9-16, small plates $10-22, mains $19-36; ☺ dinner daily
Chef-owner Scott Staples' sleek, attractive restaurant still has people lining up for dinner. The menu depends on the freshness of the ingredients; there's a lot of barely seared fish and seasonal vegetables. What's

on offer will change with the season, but small plates have included braised morel gnocchi, green beans with figs and Stilton, and a lamb heart confit, while the mains – wild boar, pork with apricots, halibut with summer squash – reveal a knack for doing interesting things to meat. Reservations are recommended.

MARCO'S SUPPERCLUB

Map p68   International $$

☎ 206-441-7801; 2510 1st Ave; starters $8-13, mains $18-23; ☽ lunch & dinner Tue-Sat, brunch Sun

Marco's Supperclub travels the globe with its short but ever-shifting, multi-ethnic menu, including such items as Jamaican jerk chicken and potato-and-goat-cheese pierogi (dumplings). Charismatic owner Marco himself is often found circulating the dining room, distributing tidbits of cheese and telling jokes.

PALACE KITCHEN Map p68   Northwest $$

☎ 206-448-2001; 2030 5th Ave; starters $9-15, mains $15-26; ☽ dinner to 1am

Owned by the Dahlia's Tom Douglas, the Palace is a see-and-be-seen hotspot that really picks up for the late-night cocktail scene. Daily dinner specials present such wonders as spaetzle-stuffed pumpkin or traditional pork loin. Snack on appetizers – including a smoked-salmon-and-blue-cheese terrine or a sampler plate of regional cheeses – or go for the whole shebang with grilled trout, leg of lamb or roasted chicken with blackberries and nectarines. There's a late-night happy hour starting at 11pm that includes barbecued short ribs and other awesome deals ($4 to $5), plus drink specials.

QUEEN CITY GRILL Map p68   Seafood $$

☎ 206-443-0975; 2201 1st Ave; starters $8-17, salads $5-12, mains $12-33; ☽ dinner daily, to midnight Fri & Sat

This longtime Belltown favorite specializes in grilled seafood from its daily menu and a solid selection of meats and chicken from its seasonal menu. The goat-cheese appetizer, crab cakes, and rib eye are all highly rated, and the warm lighting makes the room feel cozy yet sophisticated. Reservations are recommended.

BELLTOWN PIZZA Map p68   Pizza $

☎ 206-441-2653; 2422 1st Ave; starters $6-8, sandwiches $10, pizzas $12-17; ☽ dinner

Pizza and beer is great, but pizza and hard liquor works quicker. Started as a tiny bar serving New York-style pizza, Belltown Pizza has expanded a lot since then but maintains its original mission of good food and good fun at grown-up hours (the bar's open until 2am). A large pie is enough to feed four hungry people. You can also get salads, pasta and sandwiches.

NOODLE RANCH Map p68   Asian $

☎ 206-728-0463; 2228 2nd Ave; mains $9-10; ☽ lunch & dinner Mon-Sat; Ⓥ

In the same block as Mama's, this old standby looks like a modernized greasy diner, but serves pan-Asian noodle dishes, many of them vegetarian. The tofu spring rolls, green curries and pad Thai are worth trying if you need some cheap, effective stomach-padding before (or after) your bar crawl.

MAMA'S MEXICAN KITCHEN

Map p68   Mexican $

☎ 206-728-6262; 2234 2nd Ave; starters $4-10, burritos $7-9; ☽ lunch & dinner

Wildly popular, California-style Mama's Mexican Kitchen is always packed. But that's no surprise for a place that serves scrumptious burritos, huge combination plates and killer margaritas (cheapest during happy hour from 4pm to 6pm Monday to Saturday). It's in a great location for people-watching, but the kitsch Mexican artifacts plastering the walls are equally absorbing. Velvet Elvises!

BLACK BOTTLE Map p68   Northwest $

☎ 206-441-1500; http://blackbottleseattle.com; 2600 1st Ave; mains $5-12, flatbreads $9; ☽ 4pm-2am

The huge crowd congregating outside the front door of this new Belltown restaurant is your first clue that something interesting is happening inside. The menu has a lot more clues: octopus carpaccio, lemon-caper-squid salad, saffron risotto cakes, eggplant-mozzarella flatbread. It's a spartanly decorated but warm-looking space, with friendly service and a chic atmosphere. Reservations are accepted, and might be a good idea if you want to avoid a wait.

MACRINA Map p68   Bakery $

☎ 206-448-4032; 2408 1st Ave; pastries $2-3.75; ☽ 7am-7pm

You might have to wait in line, especially if you want to sit at a table, but as soon as you bite into your breakfast roll or lemon lavender coffeecake, you won't care. Macrina makes some of the city's best artisan bread and decadent snacks.

TOP POT DONUTS
Map p68   Coffee & Doughnuts $
☎ 206-728-1966; 2124 5th Ave; doughnuts $1-3; ⏲ breakfast, lunch & dinner

At Top Pot it's all about the doughnuts – and no, it is not wrong to eat them three meals a day. The doughnuts here are hand-forged as quickly as the little Seattleites can gobble them up, and this huge store gives you plenty of room to enjoy them. They're also available at various coffee shops around town, but it's best to go to the source. Krispy what?

QUEEN ANNE

Many of the dining options in Lower Queen Anne, just west of Seattle Center, are geared toward the pre- or post-game crowd attending games at Key Arena. Instead, head up the hill to Upper Queen Anne, where restaurants have more of the neighborhood's quiet, grown-up, family-friendly atmosphere.

CANLIS Map p75   Northwest, American $$$
☎ 206-283-3313; 2576 Aurora Ave N; starters $18-28, mains $36-96; ⏲ dinner Mon-Sat, also Sun in Dec

This place is old-school enough for either prom night or your grandma's birthday dinner. The traditional, classic food and service are both top-notch, and you can rest assured that none of the style is affected. Canlis has been around since 1950 and its authenticity shows. The view is lovely, too. Reservations are recommended, especially for weekends.

PARAGON BAR & GRILL
Map p75   American $$
☎ 206-283-4548; 2125 Queen Anne Ave N; brunch $5-14, small plates $8-14, dinner mains $12-22; ⏲ brunch Sun, lunch Mon-Sat, dinner daily

The Paragon is a bastion of American regional cooking, specializing in grilled fish and updated classics. Try the baby back ribs or a plate of fried green tomatoes. There's an open fireplace and a lively bar scene (the bar's open until 2am). Most

nights there's live music or DJs playing everything from indie rock and hip-hop to funk and soul.

5 SPOT Map p75   Northwest $
☎ 206-285-7768; 1502 Queen Anne Ave N; breakfast scrambles $9-10, lunch $8-12, dinner mains $10-16; ⏲ breakfast, lunch & dinner until midnight, closed 3-5pm Sat & Sun; ♿

In Upper Queen Anne, everyone's favorite breakfast and hangover diner is the 5 Spot. Good strong coffee keeps the staff ultraperky. Try a local legend, like the red flannel hash ($9.50), or get crazy with the wild-salmon cakes. On weekends, go early to avoid the lines snaking out the door – or go for lunch or dinner; this is an excellent place for a quiet meal featuring good American cooking.

QUEEN ANNE CAFÉ Map p75   Northwest $
☎ 206-285-2060; 2121 Queen Anne Ave N; breakfast $8-10; ⏲ breakfast, lunch & dinner Mon-Fri, brunch Sat & Sun

Locals flock to this trendy neighborhood spot for traditional comfort food, including broiled pork chops and various sandwiches, but the place really shines at breakfast. Expect a bit of a wait for weekend brunch.

LAKE UNION

The area around Lake Union might not benefit from the kind of hype that surrounds other more traditionally foodie-friendly neighborhoods, but it does have a couple of eateries that are well worth your time seeking out.

CHANDLER'S CRABHOUSE & FRESH FISH MARKET Map p77   Seafood $$$
☎ 206-223-2722; 901 Fairview Ave N; starters $12-17, salads $7-13, mains $20-60; ⏲ brunch Sat & Sun, lunch Mon-Fri, dinner daily

With great views of Lake Union, Chandler's may feel a bit like a chain restaurant (because it is), but it's the reliable place to go if you want to sit near the water and dine on ocean-fresh seafood. You can also buy fish or crab to ship home.

CICCHETTI Map p77   Mediterranean $$
☎ 206-859-4155; www.serafinaseattle.com /cicchetti; 121 E Boston St; small plates $4-15, cocktails $8; ⏲ 5pm-midnight Tue-Thu, 5pm-1am Fri & Sat

The sister restaurant to Serafina (below), and right round the corner, Cicchetti has a small kitchen built around a wood-fired brick oven and a menu of Mediterranean-influenced snack plates that, in combination, add up to an immensely satisfying meal. Try the Turkish fried-eggplant sandwich with feta and tomato sauce ($7), the perfectly roasted asparagus (if it's in season; $6), and anything with lamb – a recent dish of Moroccan-spiced shredded lamb with lentils and harissa yogurt ($15) blew us away. The cocktail list is stellar, too – never did Bitter Tears taste so sweet.

SERAFINA Map p77 — Italian $$
☎ 206-323-0807; www.serafinaseattle.com; 2043 Eastlake Ave E; starters $5-12, pastas $12-18, mains $19-28, prix fixe lunch $14.95; ⏲ brunch Sun, lunch Mon-Fri, dinner to midnight daily
This lovely neighborhood restaurant in Eastlake specializes in Tuscan-style cooking, with simply prepared meat and fish as well as pastas that can be ordered as a first or a main course. A gorgeous, leafy deck area behind the restaurant now doubles as the entryway to Cicchetti (p129), Serafina's new sibling. Reservations are recommended.

CAPITOL HILL & VOLUNTEER PARK

The scene on Capitol Hill is almost as much about style as food: it's no use enjoying a fabulous dinner if no one can see how chic you look while you're eating it. Then again, great ambience hardly detracts from a fine-dining experience, so who's complaining? The restaurants along Broadway and 15th Ave and the Pike–Pine Corridor offer the full range of Seattle dining options.

SITKA & SPRUCE Map p79 — Northwest $$
☎ 206-324-0662; www.sitkaandspruce.com; 1531 Melrose Ave E; small plates $8-24; ⏲ breakfast & lunch daily, dinner Tue-Sat
Now in a new location in the Capitol Hill 'hood, this small-plates fine-diner has won acclaim for its casual vibe, constantly changing menu, good wine selection and involved chef-owner (he'll be the guy who brings bread to your table). All the ingredients are obtained from local producers, and the idea is to assemble a meal out of a bunch of different taster-size dishes. Only a few

reservations are accepted each night, and the wait can be long, so grab yourself a beer and spend some time studying the chalkboard menu until it's your turn.

KINGFISH CAFÉ Map p79 — Southern $$
☎ 206-320-8757; 602 19th Ave E; breakfast $5-10, sandwiches $7-12, dinner mains $12-18; ⏲ brunch Sat & Sun, lunch Wed-Sun, dinner Mon-Sat
The Coaston sisters' cafe, opened in 1997, turns out fried chicken that has locals lined up for miles – not to mention a catfish po'boy, succotash and other soul food standbys. The space is cool, too – high ceilings and big windows in a brick building, with wrought-iron flourishes, wooden tables and an open kitchen. Don't forget to save room for dessert: the sweet-potato pie and Red Velvet Cake are the stuff of legend.

COASTAL KITCHEN Map p79 — Northwest $$
☎ 206-322-1145; 429 15th Ave E; lunch mains $7-12, starters $6-8, dinner mains $9-19; ⏲ breakfast 8am-3pm, lunch & dinner to 11pm
This longtime favorite turns out some of the best food in the neighborhood – it has an eclectic mix of Cajun, Mayan and Mexican inspirations, and an Italian-language instruction tape running in the bathroom, if that gives a clue about influences. Menus rotate by theme, but constant favorites include roasted chicken, pork chops and all-day breakfast. Fish dishes are startlingly fresh and always interesting. Pasta lunch specials are also highly recommended.

CAFÉ PRESSE Map p79 — French $
☎ 206-709-7674; 1117 12th Ave; croque monsieur $6, half chicken $14; ⏲ 7am-2am
This dreamy new cafe, opened by the owners of the cute French bistro Le Pichet (p126), specializes in unfussy dishes the likes of which you'd find once upon a time in a terrace cafe around Saint-Germain-des-Prés. The croque monsieur and madame are huge slabs of creamy goodness, steak frites are perfectly cooked and filling, and the vegetables are fresh and crispy. There's a handful of outdoor tables outside the beautiful cafe-bar; a long list of aperitifs and digestifs adds to the classy Euro feel. The cafe's adorable servers seem to have been hired based on their resemblance to Jean Seberg in Breathless.

BIMBO'S CANTINA Map p79   Mexican $

☎ 206-329-9978; 1013 E Pike St; tacos $2.95, burritos $5.50-7.50; ☽ lunch & dinner daily, to 2am Fri & Sat

It's moved, but not so far that you'll get lost trying to find it when you need it. Bimbo's slings fat tacos, giant burritos and juicy quesadillas until late. The space is less crammed now, but still has its kitschy knickknacks, including velvet matador portraits, oil paintings with neon elements and a hut-style thatched awning. The best feature of the restaurant is still the attached bar, the Cha-Cha Lounge.

HONEYHOLE Map p79   Sandwiches $

☎ 206-709-1399; 703 E Pike St; sandwiches $5-12; ☽ 10am-2am

Cozy by day, irresistible at night, the Honeyhole has a lot to recommend it: big stuffed sandwiches with cute names (Luke Duke, the Texas Tease), greasy fries, a full bar, DJs and a cool cubbyhole atmosphere at night.

MOLLY MOON'S Map p79   Ice cream $

☎ 206-708-7947; 917 E Pine St; ice cream $3-5; ☽ noon-11pm

The lines out the door start to make sense once you get your first taste of Molly Moon's salted caramel ice cream. The boutique creamery gets its ingredients locally, including hormone-free dairy from Washington cows, and specializes in improbably brilliant flavors like garlic, cardamom and strawberry balsamic, as well as old reliables like chocolate and vanilla. The original location is in Wallingford (Map p91; ☎ 206-547-5105; 1622 N 45th St).

U DISTRICT

This is one of the best districts in Seattle for cheap and authentic ethnic food, and it's also easy to find vegan and vegetarian options. When you're browsing for lunch or dinner, don't be put off by unappetizing-looking storefronts; some of the most interesting food comes from places that have the outward appearance of rundown five-and-dime stores. The adventurous will be rewarded.

CEDARS RESTAURANT

Map p83   Indian & Middle Eastern $$

☎ 206-527-5247; 4759 Brooklyn Ave NE; starters $6-8, lunch mains $7-12, dinner mains $8-15; ☽ 11:30am-10pm Mon-Sat, 1-9pm Sun; Ⓥ

Cedars serves enormous curries and vindaloos so smooth and creamy you want to dive into them. Eat here just once and you will dream about it later. There's also a great selection of Mediterranean specialties like shish kebabs, falafel and gyros, much of which is vegetarian. The covered wooden patio is a cool hangout in nice weather.

AGUA VERDE CAFÉ Map p83   Mexican $

☎ 206-545-8570; 1303 NE Boat St; starters $2-6, 3 tacos from $9.75; ☽ 11am-9pm Mon-Sat, 9am-8pm Sun, takeout window 7:30am-2:30pm Mon-Fri

On the shores of Portage Bay at the southern base of University Avenue, Agua Verde Café is a little gem that overlooks the bay and serves fat tacos full of lemony cod, shellfish or portabella mushrooms, plus other Mexican favorites. There's usually a wait for a table, but you can have a drink and wait on the deck, or order from the walkup window. You can rent kayaks (p167) in the same building, in case you want to work off your dinner.

ARAYA'S VEGETARIAN PLACE

Map p83   Vegan Thai $

☎ 206-524-4332; 1121 NE 45th St; mains $7-8, lunch buffet $8; ☽ lunch & dinner Mon-Sat; Ⓥ

The vegan lunch buffet here may come as a relief to diners accustomed to worrying about the animal-derived ingredients of various sauces in their favorite Thai dishes. Arrive early for the best selection and most freshly prepared examples of pad Thai and veggie curry. On the regular menu, the avocado curry also earns rave reviews.

FLOWERS Map p83   Eclectic $

☎ 206-633-1903; 4247 University Way NE; lunch buffet $8, mains $7-15; ☽ lunch & dinner to 2am; Ⓥ

One of the most stylish places in the U District, Flowers has a vegetarian buffet served until 5pm, and dinners include meat choices. The lunch menu includes 20 sandwiches, each around $5. After hours, it becomes an inviting place to sip a cocktail, munch on an appetizer and 'do homework' with a promising study partner.

CHACO CANYON CAFÉ Map p83   Vegan $

☎ 206-522-6966; 4757 12th Ave NE; juices $3-5, sandwiches $7-12; ☽ 7am-9pm Mon-Fri, 9am-9pm Sat, 10am-4pm Sun; Ⓥ

Now in a new location, this super-Northwest cafe has a menu that's all vegan, 90% organic and almost half raw food. If you're a newbie to the raw-food movement (it's pretty much what it sounds like), try the spicy Thai grinder or the gluten-free kiwi lime tart. There's also a long list of vegan sandwiches, smoothies and juices, coffee and tea, and a little window by the entrance where you can pick up vegan, gluten-free, wheat-free baked treats from the Flying Apron organic bakery on your way in or out.

THAI TOM Map p83   Thai $
☎ 206-548-9548; 4543 University Way NE; mains $7-10; lunch & dinner
First you notice the delicious aroma wafting down the street. Then you see the crowd of hungry people crammed into the doorway of this teeny storefront. It's an open-kitchen lunch counter in a long narrow nook decorated with elephant heads on dark brown walls. There's minimal seating, and the menus are written in gold on wooden blocks. Cash only.

HILLSIDE QUICKIE VEGAN SANDWICH SHOP Map p83   Vegan $
☎ 206-632-3037; 4106 Brooklyn Ave NE; sandwiches $7-9, breakfast $10; 11am-9pm Mon-Sat; V
This organic vegan Jamaican sandwich shop has annoyingly erratic hours (it's supposed to be open until 9pm but seems to close early a lot), but also has indisputably delicious vegan sandwiches and wraps. The Hillside Quickie educates U-Dub students about the glories of tofu, tempeh and seitan. There's usually only one person working, but guilt-free indulgences like the fake steak or the spicy tofu wrap are worth the wait.

SCHULTZY'S SAUSAGES Map p83   Meat $
☎ 206-548-9461; 4142 University Way NE; brats $7-8; lunch & dinner;
This former hole-in-the-wall has doubled in size, which serves as a warning to all who overindulge in Schultzy's meaty goodness. Its claim to fame is straightforward and simple: bratwurst, burgers and beer. There are also veggie dogs, but come on, seriously – you can eat vegan food practically everywhere else in the U District.

RUBY Map p83   Eclectic $
☎ 206-675-1770; 4241 University Way NE; sandwiches $6; breakfast, lunch & dinner to 2am
This attractive space next to Flowers had just been remodeled when we visited, but it still has a Casablanca feel, and the core of the menu is built around fragrant jasmine rice bowls ($8 to $12) in just about any combination you can imagine. The bar is hopping at night, and drinks are large and well crafted.

ORANGE KING Map p83   Burgers $
☎ 206-632-1331; 1411 NE 42nd St; burgers $2-5; lunch & dinner, closed Sun
At this tiny, old-fashioned greasy spoon just off the Ave, miraculously, you can still get a burger and fries for less than $5. It's not gourmet, but it's fast, cheap and, in its own way, charming.

LATE-NIGHT EATS

Seattle is the kind of city that rolls up the streets and turns out the lights at 2am, and it doesn't matter how long it's been since dinner. But there are a handful of places where you can still get a snack – or even a proper, decent meal – late at night.

Experienced bar-hoppers know that a 3am breakfast is a pretty reliable way to stave off a mean hangover. Beth's (p134) is open all night long and serves hearty food in portions big enough to soak up whatever liquid damage you've inflicted upon yourself. People who might've been standing next to you at the dive-bar jukebox serve dauntingly huge omelets all hours of the night.

Several locals have raved about the black-bean crab at the Sea Garden (Map p60; ☎ 206-623-2100; 509 7th Ave S; to 2am Sun-Thu, to 3am Fri & Sat). Also in the International District, the Purple Dot (p124) sees a lively late-night dinner crowd after the bars close.

Though it doesn't quite qualify as after-hours, Belltown's Palace Kitchen (p128) offers a so-called 'late-night breakfast' after 10pm. But there's really nothing better for a post-bar-crawl snack than cheap Mexican food consumed in a parking lot, which is why Rancho Bravo (opposite) gets our vote for number-one choice in late-night dining.

FREMONT & WALLINGFORD

Fun-loving Fremont is changing fast, but it's still known for its lively mix of old hippies, young professionals and gregarious students who fill the neighborhood's pubs, restaurants and coffeehouses every evening.

TILTH Map p91 — Organic $$$

☎ 206-633-0801; 1411 N 45th St; small plates $7-21, large plates $13-30, brunch plates $5-15; ⊙ brunch Sat & Sun, dinner daily

The only ingredients on chef Maria Hines's menu that aren't organic are those found in the wild – like mushrooms and seafood. Everything else, from asparagus to cheese, is carefully selected to meet certified-organic standards and prepared in a manner that preserves its essence. Try the mini duck burgers, made with the first organically raised ducks in Washington. Servers in the small restaurant are unpretentious and friendly, and will gamely answer any questions about the food or wine. Reservations are recommended; there's also a small bar in the corner.

BIZZARRO Map p91 — Italian $$

☎ 206-545-7327; 1307 N 46th St; starters $8-12, mains $14-20; ⊙ dinner

With a name like Bizzarro you'd never guess that this Wallingford hotbed is an excellent neighborhood Italian cafe. When you learn that it's actually someone's garage crammed with kitschy art and weird antiques, the name makes sense. Deliciously buttery pasta dishes, a good wine list and frequent live music add to the experience.

KABUL Map p91 — Afghani $

☎ 206-545-9000; 2301 N 45th St; starters $4-7, mains $10-20; ⊙ dinner; Ⓥ

You won't find the cuisine of Afghanistan on every street corner – if you'd like to give it a try (it's like a blend of Pakistani and Middle Eastern cooking, with lots of yogurt and stewed eggplant, grilled lamb kebabs and korma, a mild and creamy curry), head to Kabul. Vegetarians have plenty of great options here.

PASEO Map p87 — Cuban $

☎ 206-545-7440; 4225 Fremont Ave N; sandwiches $6-9, mains $12-13; ⊙ 11am-9pm Tue-Sat

Paseo has achieved legendary status throughout Seattle for its Cuban sandwiches, particularly the roasted pork shoulder, and its Caribbean rice bowls. Most likely you'll have to wait in line; the secret is to call ahead and place an order to go. (If the weather's nice, take your loot down to Gasworks Park and enjoy the view while you eat.)

BAGUETTE BOX Map p87 — Sandwiches $

☎ 206-632-1511; 626 N 34th St; sandwiches $5-8; ⊙ 11am-8pm

Handy when you just want to grab a quick lunch on the way to the Fremont Troll but don't want corporate fast food, this sub shop makes a dozen sandwiches on fresh baguettes. The choices range from the decadent drunken chicken or leg of lamb to heart-healthy options like squash and eggplant or crispy tofu.

RANCHO BRAVO Map p91 — Mexican $

211 NE 45th St; mains $2-6; ⊙ Sun-Thu hours vary, to 2:30am Fri & Sat

A taco stand in the parking lot of Winchell's Donuts, Rancho Bravo serves cheap, filling tacos and burritos that are pretty good anytime and *awesome* at 2am.

DICK'S DRIVE-IN Map p91 — Burgers $

☎ 206-632-5125; 111 NE 45th St; meals $2-5; ⊙ breakfast, lunch & dinner; ⊛

Sometimes you don't want gourmet. Sometimes you just want a big, greasy burger at 2am, with fries and a shake, and you want it all for less than $5. At Dick's, you can have it – plus a bonus sideshow of parking-lot hi-jinks right after the bars close. It's not just fast food; it's an institution. There are other locations around town; their bright orange signs are hard to miss. The most theatrically rewarding, of course, is in Capitol Hill (Map p79; ☎ 206-323-1300; 115 Broadway E).

BOULANGERIE Map p91 — Bakery $

☎ 206-634-2211; 2200 N 45th St; pastries $2-5; ⊙ 7am-2:30pm

One of Seattle's best neighborhood bakeries, Boulangerie whips up French-style pastries and bread loaves delivered with a smile.

GREEN LAKE & PHINNEY RIDGE

This area has an everybody-knows-each-other neighborhood feel to it, and the cafes and restaurants consequently tend to be welcoming and casual.

NELL'S Map p93 — Continental $$

☎ 206-524-4044; 6804 E Green Lake Way N; mains $19-29, tasting menu $48; 🕑 dinner

For fine dining near Green Lake, Nell's serves up classic European dishes with Northwestern flair. It inhabits the space formerly occupied by Saleh al Lago, and it actually maintains one of that beloved eatery's dishes – the calamari with aioli – to widespread critical acclaim. Opt for seafood dishes, and don't skip dessert.

TANGLETOWN PUB Map p93 — Northwest $

☎ 206-547-5929; 2106 N 55th St; mains $7-12; 🕑 breakfast Sat & Sun, lunch & dinner daily

This outpost of the Elysian Brewing Company quickly made friends in the neighborhood, despite having taken over the space that was once the worshipped Honey Bear Bakery. It's a more child-friendly space than Capitol Hill's Elysian brewery, and the building itself is gorgeous: when afternoon sunlight comes streaming into the leaded-glass windows and hits those burgundy walls, look out! Glorified pub food (chicken wings, an eggplant panini) and Elysian beer carry the day.

BETH'S CAFÉ Map p93 — Breakfast

☎ 206-782-5588; 7311 Aurora Ave N; omelets $6-12; 🕑 24hr

The best – or at least biggest – hangover breakfast in the world is at Beth's, and you can get it all day long. Key words: all-you-can-eat hash browns. You can't smoke in here anymore, which, depending on your view, either ruins everything or makes it possible to enjoy Beth's infamous 12-egg omelet while breathing. Feel free to contribute a piece of scribbled artwork to the wall, preferably one that's strongly pro- or anti-pirate.

PETE'S EGG NEST Map p93 — Breakfast $

☎ 206-784-5348; 7717 Greenwood Ave N; breakfast $8-10; 🕑 7am-3pm

This Greek-leaning breakfast joint is famous for humongous portions of the satisfying standards – omelets, biscuits and gravy, and mountainous hash browns. Seasonal specials are recommended.

MAE'S PHINNEY RIDGE CAFÉ

Map p93 — American $

☎ 206-782-1222; 6412 Phinney Ave N; mains $5-12, cinnamon rolls $3.50; 🕑 breakfast daily, lunch Mon-Fri; 👶

Breakfast is heavenly, and the tasty milkshakes make it a worthwhile trip anytime. Not that there's anything wrong with having a milkshake for breakfast, mind you. Mae's famous cinnamon rolls are now available in stores, but they're inevitably best here in the homey little cafe.

NOT SO FAST!

It sounds downright un-American, this idea of sitting still and patiently waiting for who knows how long, while someone prepares your sustainably farmed, hand-selected, all-organic food from scratch. There's a reason every intersection in the US has a fast-food outlet and every fast-food outlet has a drive-through window. This is not a patient nation. When we order a burger and fries, we'd like them *now*, please.

But what many Americans are just starting to think about is how our food managed to get so fast in the first place. Those French fries weren't born stick-shaped at the bottom of a deep fryer. Along with the popularity of Eric Schlosser's best-selling book *Fast Food Nation* and similar high-profile examinations of the fast-food industry has come greater attention for the handful of folks who have, for years, been going against the fast-food grain: the Slow Food movement.

Begun in Italy in 1986, the Slow Food idea has gradually spread to other countries and expanded its mission. The Pacific Northwest is home to several Slow Food chapters, including six in western Washington.

One of the Seattle area's biggest priorities in terms of Slow Food is, no surprise, seafood. Increasing demand and better means of transportation mean that, for example, those fresh oysters you're slurping up might not be local at all. And some of them may be locally grown representatives of non-native species. Consequently, urging people to take the time to find out what they can about the origins of what they're eating is a key part of the Slow Food movement – in Seattle and elsewhere.

To find out more about the Slow Food movement and how you can help, visit www.slowfoodseattle.org.

RED MILL BURGERS Map p93 Burgers $

☎ 206-783-6362; 312 N 67th St; burgers $4-10;
☺ lunch & dinner

This place is constantly collecting accolades
for grilling up the best burger in town, and
it also fries up the fattest, yummiest onion
rings. There's usually a line out the door
but it moves along quickly. Cash only.

BALLARD & DISCOVERY PARK

An old Scandinavian fishing town that's
transformed itself into a dining and nightlife
destination, Ballard offers a number of rep-
utable places to eat and drink. It's an ever-
changing scene, so don't hesitate to ask
around and check local papers for the latest
recommended places.

RAY'S BOATHOUSE Map p96 Seafood $$$

☎ 206-789-3770; 6049 Seaview Ave NW; mains
$24-39, kids' menu $5-10; ☺ dinner until 9pm; ♿

OK, so it's a cliché, but Ray's offers views
over the Olympics, nautical decor and an
exhaustive fresh-fish menu. It offers tourists
everything they imagine when they think
about a nice dinner out in Seattle. Reservations are required; if you can't get in for
dinner, at least come for a drink on the sun-
deck: the bar's open until midnight. Ray's is
about a mile northwest of the Ballard Locks.

CHINOOK'S AT SALMON BAY
Map p96 Seafood $$$

☎ 206-283-4665; 1900 W Nickerson St; mains
$6-30; ☺ breakfast Sat & Sun, lunch Mon-Sat,
dinner daily

Across the Ballard Bridge in the Fisherman's
Terminal, Chinook's is where fish practically
leap out of the water and into the kitchen.
You can't get it much fresher than this, and
the selection of fish and range of prepara-
tions is vast. Another plus is watching the
fishing fleet coming in or fishers mending
their nets from the massive restaurant
windows or the sundeck in summer.

LA ISLA Map p96 Puerto Rican $$

☎ 206-789-0516; 2320 NW Market St; starters
from $4, mains $12-17; ☺ 11:30am-2am

What started as a food stand at Fremont
Sunday Market has become this always-
packed little cafe, offering possibly the

only Puerto Rican cuisine in the area. As
a starter, try the empanadillas ($4), little
fried dough pockets filled with your choice
of shrimp, pulled pork, garlicky potatoes,
cheese, tofu, chicken or beef. Better yet, go
for the appetizer platter ($9.99), which lets
you also sample the salted cod fritters and
the *alcapurria*, made with plantains and
green bananas. The enormous *pernil* (pulled
pork) platter ($15) has a huge pile of juicy
meat alongside saucy rice, beans, avocados
and cheese, plus a couple of piquant
sauces. It's hard to beat – you'll be eating it
for hours and still be sad when it's gone.

MADAME K'S Map p96 Italian $$

☎ 206-783-9710; 5327 Ballard Ave NW; starters
$5-8, pasta $13, pizza $16-24; ☺ dinner daily, from
2pm Sat & Sun

An elegant red-and-black pizza parlor with
an old bordello feel (the building was once
a brothel), this small, chic place is packed
out for dinner. It's also a popular place for
drinks and desserts. There's a really nice
patio out back, or you can let history repeat
itself in the upstairs dessert room with a
decadent 'Chocolate Chip Orgasm' ($7.50).

LA CARTA DE OAXACA Map p96 Mexican $

☎ 206-782-8722; www.lacartadeoaxaca.com; 5431
Ballard Ave NW; mains $7-12; ☺ lunch Tue-Sat,
dinner Mon-Sat

This lively place serves the cuisine of Oaxaca, particularly black *mole* sauce – try the
mole negro Oaxaqueno, the house specialty.
You can sample the same stuff on tamales
or go for a combination of various small
plates. Seating is mostly picnic-style, and
there's a full bar – handy considering
there's usually a wait for a table.

CENTRAL DISTRICT, MADRONA & MADISON PARK

This area has everything from some of the city's
best barbecue joints to upscale French cuisine
and a long-standing vegetarian restaurant.

ROVER'S Map p101 French $$$

☎ 206-325-7442; 2808 E Madison St; starters $6-
20, mains $16-22, set menus $55-135; ☺ lunch Fri,
dinner daily; ♥

Many locals consider this Seattle's best restaurant. Chef Thierry Rautureau ('the Chef in the Hat') offers three prix-fixe menus a day (one vegetarian), as well as á la carte items. The food is upscale French with a Northwest twist – Oregon quail, for example, or Copper River salmon with morels. The cozy space is one of the few in Seattle where you'll want to dress up, and reservations are definitely advised.

MADISON PARK CAFÉ Map p101   American $$
☎ 206-324-2626; 1807 42nd Ave E; brunch $8-12, starters $6-8, mains $20-28; ☽ dinner Tue-Sat, brunch Sat & Sun

Down in Madison Park, in a converted house at the end of Madison St just before you hit Lake Washington, the Madison Park Café is a favorite breakfast and lunch spot. It's a cute little space with blue-and-white checked tablecloths, an extremely cheery feel and welcoming owners. The menu is half old-school (filet mignon, duck confit) and half new-school (foie gras, baby octopus confit) – no need to decide, really; just try some of each.

CAFÉ FLORA Map p101   Vegetarian $$
☎ 206-325-9100; 2901 E Madison St; starters & sandwiches $4-12, mains $13-18; ☽ brunch Sat & Sun, breakfast & lunch Mon-Fri, dinner daily; **V**

A longtime favorite for vegan and vegetarian food, Flora has a gardenlike feel and a creative menu, with dinner treats like seitan spring rolls and breaded coconut tofu dipped in chili sauce, a portobello French dip, caprese pizza and black-bean burgers. Or go for the hoppin' john fritters or tomato asparagus scrambles at brunch.

CACTUS Map p101   Tapas/Mexican $$
☎ 206-324-4140; 4220 E Madison St; lunch $7-10, dinner $10-18; ☽ lunch & dinner

Instantly cheery, this Mexican-Southwest restaurant – with branches in Kirkland and Alki Beach – is a fun place to go and pretend you're on a sunny vacation even if it's pouring rain. A margarita and a king salmon torta or butternut squash enchilada will scare off the grayest clouds, and the jaunty staff and fun music do the rest.

R & L HOME OF GOOD BAR-B-QUE
Map p101   Southern $
☎ 206-322-0271; 1816 E Yesler Way; sandwiches $8, mains $10-15; ☽ lunch & dinner Tue-Sat

You can't get within a block of this little neighborhood joint without drooling from the smell of barbecue. The storefront looks a little unpromising, but inside there's a wood-paneled cafeteria with curtained windows, a few tables and a counter for takeout orders.

HI SPOT CAFÉ Map p101   Breakfast $
☎ 206-325-7905; 1410 34th Ave; cinnamon rolls $3.25, breakfast scrambles $9-10, mains $10-14; ☽ breakfast & lunch daily, brunch Sat & Sun

The cinnamon rolls here are bigger than your head, and that's no exaggeration. It's a comfy little space on multiple levels, where you can either get a sit-down meal or a quick espresso and pastry on the go.

CATFISH CORNER Map p101   Southern $
☎ 206-323-4330; 2726 E Cherry St; catfish dinners $6-12, gumbo $10.50; ☽ lunch & dinner

For traditional, inexpensive Southern-style fare, head to this no-frills corner hangout. Catfish strips are the specialty, and you can accessorize them with all the trimmings, including collard greens or red beans and rice, while meeting the neighbors and catching up on all the local gossip.

ATTIC ALEHOUSE & EATERY
Map p101   American $
☎ 206-323-3131; 4226 E Madison St; burgers $7-9; ☽ breakfast, lunch & dinner daily, to 1am Fri & Sat

Decades ago, according to legend, the Attic was a shooting gallery–bowling alley combo. It first became a restaurant in the mid-'30s, then became a tavern in the '50s. The current building dates from 1967 – it's a friendly neighborhood pub and a good spot to watch a game of footy while you have a beer and a hand-made burger.

top picks

DINING ROOMS WITH A VIEW

- Chez Shea (p126)
- Ivar's Acres of Clams (p126)
- Chandler's Crab House (p129)
- Ray's Boathouse (p135)
- Salty's on Alki (opposite)

EZELL'S FRIED CHICKEN

Map p101 Southern $

☎ 206-324-4141; 501 23rd Ave; meals $6-10; ☺ lunch & dinner

There's fast food and then there's fast food. This is the good kind. Ezell's dishes out crispy, spicy chicken and equally scrumptious side dishes like coleslaw and sweet-potato pie. This place experienced a boom after Oprah Winfrey hyped the fried chicken here as some of the best in the country.

WEST SEATTLE

Most of the action in West Seattle is found along a short strip across from Alki Beach or along California Ave SW.

SALTY'S ON ALKI

Map p103 Steak & Seafood $$$

☎ 206-937-1600; 1936 Harbor Ave SW; starters $7-9, mains from $15; ☺ dinner daily, lunch Mon-Fri, brunch Sat & Sun

While many restaurants afford views onto Alki Beach and its strutting revelers, most people drive to West Seattle for the view at Salty's on Alki. This steak and seafood house looks across Elliott Bay onto downtown Seattle; at sunset, the spectacle of lights, shining towers and the rising moon is amazing. The food is secondary, but still good.

PHOENICIA AT ALKI

Map p103 Mediterranean $$

☎ 206-935-6550; 2716 Alki Ave SW; mains $12-22; ☺ lunch Sat & Sun, dinner Wed-Mon

Mediterranean and Middle Eastern food, and particularly artisan pizza, is the focus at Phoenicia. The owner is Lebanese, but the flavors are pulled from as far afield as Italy and Morocco and combined with a bounty of fresh local seafood.

ALKI CAFÉ Map p103 Northwest $

☎ 206-935-0616; 2726 Alki Ave SW; mains $8-12; ☺ 8am-3pm; V

One of Seattle's favorite spots for breakfast and brunch, the Alki serves fresh baked goods, seafood or vegetable-filled omelets and hotcakes. The menu features a couple of vegetarian scrambles and a heart-healthy 'special diet' option.

ALKI BAKERY Map p103 Bakery $

☎ 206-935-1352; 2738 Alki Ave SW; sandwiches $6-8, breakfasts $4-6; ☺ 7am-5pm Mon-Thu, 7am-8pm Fri & Sat, 7am-7pm Sun

This is a great place to grab a coffee and pastry, then sit down at a window seat to partake of the bakery's free wi-fi connection while digging your beach-front view. Cinnamon rolls and cookies reign supreme, but you can also get takeout sandwiches and salads to eat on the beach.

SPUD FISH & CHIPS Map p103 Seafood $

☎ 206-938-0606; 2666 Alki Ave SW; fish & chips $5-9; ☺ 11am-9pm; ♿

The competition is fierce over which Alki institution has the best fish and chips, here or Sunfish (below). (Why not try both?) Spud gets the tourist vote, with its crisp, beachy interior, friendly staff and large portions of fried fish, clam strips and oysters.

SUNFISH Map p103 Seafood $

☎ 206-938-4112; 2800 Alki Ave SW; fish & chips $5-9; ☺ lunch & dinner; ♿

Locals swear by this fish and chips institution. Options include cod, halibut or salmon and chips, fried oysters and clam strips – or combinations thereof. Sit at one of the outdoor tables and enjoy the boardwalk feel.

top picks

- **Brouwer's** (p147)
- **Mecca Café** (p143)
- **Smarty Pants** (p149)
- **Shorty's** (p142)
- **Zeitgeist** (p141)

DRINKING

It's hard to complain too much about Seattle's crappy weather when the two best forms of rainy day solace – coffee and beer – are available in such abundance. No doubt about it, Seattle's a inviting place to get a buzz on, caffeine or otherwise. Hearty, European-style craft-brewed beer are one of the city's trademarks, and you can try them in burly brick ale houses or sleek cocktail lounges, whichever you prefer. And as for coffee, well, this is the birthplace of Starbucks, and the espresso epidemic hasn't let up since then.

Most coffee shops are open from 7am until 6pm. Bars usually serve from lunchtime until 2am (when state liquor laws demand they stop selling booze), although some don't open until 5pm and others start as early as 7am. Variations from the norm are noted in the individual reviews below In general, pints cost $3 to $5 – and often less for domestics or during happy hours. Cocktails a an ordinary bar will run you $4 to $6, and closer to $10 for something really special.

DOWNTOWN & FIRST HILL

Hotel bars are your best bet for drinking here, as there aren't too many watering holes in the downtown commercial core. Oliver's Lounge in the Mayflower Park Hotel, p176, is a nice little oasis. Coffee shops abound, but those with character are scarce.

NITELITE LOUNGE Map p50   Bar

☎ 206-443-0899; 1926 2nd Ave; ☾ noon–2am
This little place attached to the Moore Hotel (p176) has an outsize charm, thanks mostly to the seen-it-all-and-liked-most-of-it bartenders and regulars. Some of its classic patina has been lost in a recent facelift, and there's a whole new section with its own look and feel, but the reasons to stop in are the same: it's never crowded and the drinks are strong and cheap. When you go in the door, turn right for the old-school regular crowd or left to see what the youngsters are up to.

PIONEER SQUARE

Though it lends itself more to frenzied clubbing than casual pint-sipping, Pioneer Square is home to some of the city's oldest and most atmospheric bars. If you prefer a saloon to a salon, this historical part of town is your best bet. See the Nightlife chapter (p151) for more ambitious forms of entertainment here.

PYRAMID ALE HOUSE Map p56   Brewpub

☎ 206-682-3377; 1201 1st Ave S; pints $4-5;
☾ 11am–10pm Mon-Thu, 11am–11pm Fri & Sat, 11am–9pm Sun

South of Pioneer Square by Safeco Field, this brewpub has the cleaned-up-industrial feel – all bricks and brass and designer lighting – that defines the Pacific Northwest brewpub. It's a nice and mainstream (but still appreciably Seattle-ish) place to take your parents or tenderfoot visitors. But don't even try on a game day, unless you want to squeeze into the standing-room-only beer tent outdoors.

MARCUS' MARTINI HEAVEN
Map p56   Cocktail Lounge

☎ 206-624-3323; 88 Yesler Way; martinis $6-9;
☾ 11am–2am, closed Sun
A shadowy, black-and-red dungeon (albeit a pleasant, friendly dungeon) situated beneath a *pho* restaurant, Marcus' is renowned for its excellent happy hour (3pm to 6pm), during which you can wrap a fist around one of its 30-plus martinis for as little as $4. The room feels atmospheric yet modern, free of the 'Olde Pioneere' kitsch that afflicts many other bars in the area.

CHERRY STREET COFFEE HOUSE
Map p56   Coffee Shop

☎ 206-621-9372; 103 Cherry St; bagels $2-4, breakfast wraps $5, sandwiches $6.95; ☾ 6:30am–5pm Mon-Fri, 8am–5pm Sat, closed Sun
The cutest branch of a small chain of coffee shops, this comfy den is furnished with attractively worn, rickety chairs and a homey vibe. Espresso is artfully pulled and poured, and there's a large underground seating area. The huge chicken-salad sandwich can make two meals; there's also a good vegan menu.

ZEITGEIST Map p56   Coffee Shop
☎ 206-583-0497; 171 S Jackson St; sandwiches $6-8, salads $5-6; ☾ 6am-7pm Mon-Fri, 8am-7pm Sat & Sun

One of the prettiest coffee shops around, this converted warehouse space serves coffee, pastries and sandwiches that have locals lined up all the way out the door in the morning and lunchtime rushes. But its blond-wood tables, picture windows, brick walls and wrought-iron accents make it an aesthetically pleasing place to work or read when it's quiet. It's also very handy to the Amtrak station.

CENTRAL SALOON Map p56   Pub
☎ 206-622-0209; 207 1st Ave S; happy hour pints from $2; ☾ 11:30am-2am, happy hour 4-7pm Mon-Fri

It may be two years younger than the official Oldest Bar in Seattle, the nearby Merchant, but the Central isn't exactly new and shiny. More of a locals' hangout than an object of historical interest, this long, narrow joint makes grody bathrooms and blah food seem charming, by virtue of cheap suds, friendly barkeeps and a comfortable, unfussy vibe. Live music most nights means that anyone who disapproves of metal should get in and out fairly early.

INTERNATIONAL DISTRICT

The lounges inside many of the restaurants in the ID are good haunts for hiding away with a cocktail any time of day; many of them have afternoon happy-hour food specials, too. The ID is also the place to come for things like bubble tea and unusual herbal tea concoctions. Hipster cachet roams the area freely, so explore on your own to find the current coolest spot.

PANAMA HOTEL TEA & COFFEE HOUSE Map p60   Tea House
☎ 206-515-4000; 607 S Main St; bean-paste sweets $3.25, cup/pot of tea $3/8; ☾ 8:30am-11pm Mon-Sat, 9am-9pm Sun

Housed in a historical 1910 building that contains the only remaining Japanese bathhouse in the US (tours are available), this beautifully restored space doubles as a memorial to the neighborhood's Japanese residents who were forced into internment camps during WWII. The owners found trunks full of left-behind belongings in the basement of the old hotel and have put them on display. Historical photos line the walls, and a glass window in the floor offers a peek at the building's secrets.

PIKE PLACE MARKET & WATERFRONT

There are some extremely romantic and very cozy drinking spots tucked away among the warrenlike market buildings in this area, and many of them have incredible views across the water. Also here is the atmospheric Irish pub, Kells (p154).

ATHENIAN INN Map p63   Bar
☎ 206-624-7166; 1517 Pike Place Market; happy hour well drinks $3; ☾ 11am-8pm Mon-Sat, 9am-4pm Sun, happy hour 4-8pm

There's nothing fancy about the Athenian, but it's a landmark and a bastion of unpretentious, frontier-era Seattle, a holdover from the days before Starbucks and Grand Central Bakery (way before – it opened in 1909). It's been a bakery and a lunch counter, and now seems to have settled in as a diner-bar combination where, especially in the off hours, you can snuggle into a window booth and gaze over Elliott Bay with a plate of fried fish and a frosty mug of Manny's Pale Ale.

PIKE PUB & BREWERY Map p63   Brewpub
☎ 206-622-6044; 1415 1st Ave; pints from $4, growlers $6; ☾ 11:30am-2am

The '80s-industrial decor and abundance of nooks and crannies make this market-side brewpub feel like a Chuck E Cheese for grown-ups. Mammoth burgers ($8 to $10), inventive vegetarian specials and Pike's signature beers (try the Kilt Lifter) add function to the fun.

ALIBI ROOM Map p63   Cocktail Lounge
☎ 206-623-3180; 85 Pike Pl; cocktails from $7; ☾ 3pm-2am Mon-Thu, noon-2am Fri-Sun, happy hour 3-6pm Mon-Thu, noon-6pm Fri-Sun

The perfect place to hide from the perfect crime, the Alibi provides entertainment as well as a hideout, with regular DJ nights, art installations, stand-up performances and experimental-film screenings. Good eats, too, and the happy hour menu includes $5 food items, $4 well drinks and $3 beers.

ZIG ZAG CAFÉ Map p63   Cocktail Lounge
☎ 206-625-1146; 1501 Western Ave; cocktails from $8; ☯ 5pm-2am, happy hour 5-7pm Mon-Fri
For serious cocktails, this is the unmissable destination in town. Classic and inventive drinks are made with precision by handsome and nattily attired alchemists – including Murray Stenson, widely acknowledged as the best bartender in Seattle, and the charming Erik, who vaguely resembles *Twin Peaks'* Agent Dale Cooper. These fellows know how to sling a bottle of chartreuse; sitting at the bar on a quiet night and watching them command the stage is a treat. You'll see all manner of potions behind the bar, most of which you've probably never heard of (and if you're nice, you might be offered a taste). Drinks start from $5 during happy hour.

VIRGINIA INN TAVERN Map p63   Pub
☎ 206-728-1937; 1937 1st Ave; cocktails/beers $8.50/5; ☯ 11:30am-11pm Mon-Thu & Sun, 11:30am-2am Fri & Sat
Near Pike Place Market is one of Seattle's most likable bars. Lots of draft beers, a nice brick interior and friendly staff make this a good rendezvous point for forays elsewhere.

WHITE HORSE TRADING COMPANY
Map p63   Pub
☎ 206-441-7767; 1908 Post Alley; ☯ 4pm-midnight Mon-Thu, 4pm-2am Fri & Sat, closed Sun
This small, intimate pub is full of books and known for its Pimms cup. The beer list is deliberately small, and the couches and easy chairs dangerously soft.

BELLTOWN

For many folks, this is the pinnacle of Seattle nightlife. Others say it's been completely ruined by an influx of hipsters who then departed, leaving frat boys in their wake. Whichever view you hold, Belltown is definitely not the sketchy grungeville it once was, but it still has the advantage of numerous bars lined up in tidy rows that lend themselves to all-night bar-hopping.

FIVE POINT CAFÉ Map p68   Bar
☎ 206-448-9993; 415 Cedar St; ☯ 24hr, bar 6am-2am

Not 'retro,' just old and endearingly grim, the Five Point Café in Tillicum Square has been around since 1929, and so have many of its patrons. Half diner, half bar and too worn-in to be mistaken for hip, it's where seasoned barflies and young punks go to get wasted, any time of day. Check out the men's bathroom – 'allegedly' the urinal offers a periscope view of the Space Needle.

FRONTIER ROOM Map p68   Bar
☎ 206-441-3377; 2203 1st Ave; ☯ to 2am Tue-Sat, private parties only Sun-Mon
Once an old-school holdover from Belltown's gritty whiskey-drinkin' days, the Frontier Room went through a phase of being colonized by frat boys and par-tay-ers – sort of a microcosm of Belltown as a whole. It now seems to have calmed down some and is focused on serving pretty good barbecue to the late-night crowd.

SHORTY'S Map p68   Bar
☎ 206-441-5449; 2222A 2nd Ave; alco-slushies $5.50; ☯ noon-2am
If you hate what's happened to Belltown, you'll love Shorty's: a lowbrow, punk-rock holdout amid rows of sleek and chic lounges. This game-themed dive has cheap beer and hot dogs, alcoholic slushies, and a whole back room of pinball heaven.

LAVA LOUNGE Map p68   Cocktail Lounge
☎ 206-441-5660; 2226 2nd Ave; ☯ 3pm-2am
This tiki-themed dive has games of all kinds and over-the-top art on the walls (you can't miss the Mt St Helens mural). High-backed booths encourage all-night lingering.

ROB ROY Map p68   Cocktail Lounge
☎ 206-956-8423; 2332 2nd Ave; cocktails $9, glass of wine from $6; ☯ 4pm-2am
A proper cocktail lounge, Rob Roy (formerly the Viceroy) is dignified yet comfortable – there's a long, dark bar and sophisticated touches like cologne in the restroom, but there's also puffy wallpaper, squishy leather couches and a boar's head and antlers on the wall.

TWO BELLS TAVERN Map p68   Pub
☎ 206-441-3050; 2313 4th Ave; pints $4.25, glass of wine from $6; ☯ 11am-late Mon-Fri, 1pm-late Sat, 11:30am-late Sun

Flee the white belt/skinny jeans crowd and seek refuge in the Two Bells, a neighborhood pub with the friendliest barkeeps in town and a familiar crew of regulars whose intense discussions of the previous night's adventures are portable enough to be taken out back to the patio for a smoke. The house special is a meaty burger stacked thigh-high ($9). Show up Sundays at 1pm for help with the *Times* crossword.

SEATTLE CENTER & QUEEN ANNE

When it comes to drinking, this neighborhood is all over the map. There are some music-focused options in Seattle Center, and then there's pleasantly sleepy Queen Anne, with everything from traditional beer halls and dives to swank jazz bars.

REVOLUTION BAR & GRILL

Map p72   Cocktail Lounge

☎ 206-770-2777; Experience Music Project, 325 5th Ave N; happy hour drinks $3-5; ☽ 10am-7pm
The bar inside the Experience Music Project (p72) makes for a good excuse to check out the EMP building without forking out the cash for a ticket, if you're feeling cheapish. There's good music playing, a good happy hour (5:30pm to 8pm), and 50 beers on tap!

UPTOWN ESPRESSO BAR

Map p75   Coffee Shop

☎ 206-285-3757; 525 Queen Anne Ave N; ☽ 5am-10pm Mon-Thu, 5am-11pm Fri, 6am-11pm Sat, 6am-10pm Sun
This is the place to meet in Lower Queen Anne; it's always crowded with filmgoers from Seattle Center and Uptown Cinemas (☎ 206-285-1022; 511 Queen Anne Ave N), but still has an intimate neighborhood feel.

MECCA CAFÉ Map p75   Dive

☎ 206-285-9728; 526 Queen Anne Ave N; burgers $8/75; ☽ 7am-2am
The Mecca has been called – by folks who know – the best bar in Seattle. Half of the long, skinny room is a diner, but all the fun happens on the other side, where decades' worth of scribbles on beer mats line the walls, the jukebox still works the way a jukebox should, the bartenders know the songs on it better than you do, and you can get waffles with your beer until 3pm or so.

HILLTOP ALE HOUSE Map p75   Pub

☎ 206-285-3877; 2129 Queen Anne Ave N; ☽ 11:30am-11pm Sun-Thu, 11:30am-midnight Fri & Sat
Hilltop is a comfy neighborhood hang-out on Queen Anne Hill, sister to the 74th Street Ale House (p147). It has a friendly vibe and a large selection of microbrews served in proper 20oz pints, and the menu is well above your standard pub fare.

CAPITOL HILL & VOLUNTEER PARK

Capitol Hill is *the* place to go out for drinks, whether you want a fancy cocktail, a cappuccino or a beer. It's also where most of the city's gay bars are located.

HIGH LINE Map p79   Bar

☎ 206-328-7837; 210 Broadway E; ☽ 11am-2am Mon-Fri, 9am-2am Sat & Sun; V
From the folks who ran the late and much-lamented Squid & Ink vegan cafe in Georgetown comes this bar-restaurant hybrid (mostly a bar, but with the distinct advantage of serving hearty food until 1am). As the door guy put it, 'We have lots of games, cheap booze and a full vegan menu' – he strongly recommends the biscuits and gravy for brunch. Also live music.

ELYSIAN BREWING COMPANY

Map p79   Brewpub

☎ 206-860-1920; 1221 E Pike St; ☽ 11:30am-2am Mon-Fri, noon-2am Sat & Sun
The Elysian should be cooler than it is. Its beers sound totally metal, with names like Loki Lager and Dragon's Tooth Stout, but the place itself leans more toward a soccer-mom-sports-bar vibe. Pros: it's large enough to accommodate big groups, it has giant windows that make for good people-watching, it serves a good veggie burger, and let's not forget the Immortal IPA.

BARÇA Map p79   Cocktail Lounge

☎ 206-325-8263; 1510 11th Ave; ☽ 5pm-2am
Velvet couches, filmy curtains, plush booths, a serpentine bar – this is one sexy, decadent lounge. Settle in among the other pretty people for seduction or quiet conversation.

COFFEE CULTURE

When the first Starbucks opened in Pike Place Market in 1971, Seattle was suddenly the center of the coffee universe. It still is, although these days Starbucks is loved and loathed in equal measure.

In addition to creating a new class of high-brow caffeine addicts, the city's coffee fanaticism has also served to revitalize the coffee shop as a social meeting place. And it's great for officeless working types, too – coffee and wi-fi go hand in hand, and it's not unusual for a packed coffee shop to be dead silent except for the quiet clattering of laptop keys and occasional screams from the espresso machine.

Still, ordering coffee in one of these places can be a daunting enterprise – particularly if you haven't had your coffee yet. Standing in line gives you a front-row seat in the theater of the absurd. It takes the average customer longer to place an order than it takes the frantic baristas to whip up the concoction. Makes you wonder – someone who's capable of walking up to a counter first thing in the morning and ordering a double-tall extra-hot skinny soy caramel latte on the dry side – well, does that person really *need* coffee?

Here are some tips to help you navigate the surprisingly complicated world of the Northwest coffee-shop menu:

- There's no such thing as small, medium and large. This is America; the tiniest available size is enormous. At Starbucks, a 'small' is a Tall (12oz), a 'medium' is a Grande (16oz) and a 'large' is a Venti (20oz). If you want an 8oz drink, ask for a 'short.'
- Ordering a cappuccino 'dry' means you want more foam than liquid; 'wet' means the opposite.
- 'Skinny' means you want nonfat milk.
- When the server looks at you and says 'Room?' it's not a come-on; they're asking if you want them to leave space for cream in the cup.

TAVERN LAW Map p79 Cocktail Lounge
☎ 206-322-9734; 1406 12th Ave; cocktails $9, dishes $9-15; ☺ 5pm-2am

Named for the 1832 law that legalized drinking in public bars and saloons and sparked the golden age of cocktails, Tavern Law is a mandatory stop for those making the rounds of the best drinks in Seattle. Drinks are crafted by star local bartender David Nelson. The food menu consists of whatever's written on the chalkboard that day; if you're lucky, it will say 'provolone pork belly cheeseburger.'

B&O ESPRESSO Map p79 Coffee Shop
☎ 206-322-5028; 204 Belmont Ave E; ☺ 7am-midnight Mon-Thu, 8am-1am Fri, 7am-2am Sat, 8am-midnight Sun

This casually elegant spot has loads of atmosphere and is a nice place to take a date for a leisurely dessert. Meals are nothing special, but the dessert case is like a window at Tiffany's. You can get Turkish coffee here, as well as all kinds of tea, beer, wine and cocktails.

BAUHAUS Map p79 Coffee Shop
☎ 206-625-1600; 301 E Pine St; ☺ 6am-1am

Bauhaus looks like the most beatnik library in the world, with floor-to-ceiling bookshelves and stylish-looking people of all stripes sitting around reading. Big windows make it a good spot for Capitol Hill people-watching.

CAFFÉ VITA Map p79 Coffee Shop
☎ 206-709-4440; 1005 E Pike St; ☺ 6am-11pm

Vita is known for small-batch roasts and expertly poured shots. The cafe also hosts seminars and other educational events, many to do with teaching people about sustainable coffee-growing practices.

ESPRESSO VIVACE ROASTERIA
Map p79 Coffee Shop
☎ 206-860-2722; 532 Broadway E; ☺ 6am-11pm

Asked what's the best coffee in Seattle, most people will mention Vivace. The main location is vast and open with Vivace's trademark curved bar. There's also a tiny walkup window on Broadway (321 Broadway E) where you can get an espresso on the run or stand around and watch the overcaffeinated street theater.

ONLINE COFFEE COMPANY
Map p79 Coffee Shop
☎ 206-328-3731; www.onlinecoffeeco.com; 1720 E Olive Way; ☺ 7:30am-midnight

Just because there's wi-fi in every corner of every scraggly soup-kitchen bathroom these days doesn't necessarily mean you brought your laptop with you to Capitol Hill. If you need a quiet place to check your email over a latte, this coffee shop in a renovated house is a good bet. Internet use is free for the first half-hour with the purchase of a drink. There's free wi-fi too, of course. The branch on E Pine Street (☎ 20 -323-7798; 1404 E Pine St) is larger and more office-like.

STUMPTOWN ON 12TH

Map p79   Coffee Shop
☎ 206-323-1544; 1115 12th Ave; ⏲ 6am-11pm Mon-Fri, 7am-10pm Sat & Sun

Serious bean freaks will be pleased to know that the small but internationally acclaimed coffee-roasting company Stumptown Coffee Roasters, based in Portland, Oregon and known for its fair-trade practices, now has two branches in Seattle. The cafe on 12th Ave is home to the company's Seattle roasting head-quarters. Coffee tastings are open to the public at 3pm daily. The tiny, adorable Pine St Cafe (☎ 206-329-0115; 616 E Pine St; ⏲ 7am-9pm) is also perfect for a quick caffeine hit.

COMET Map p79   Dive
☎ 206-323-9853; 922 E Pike St; ⏲ noon-2am
The diviest dive on Capitol Hill, the Comet's a blessed refuge for anyone allergic to the surrounding plethora of basil-infused cocktails and shimmery clothing. This is the domain of cheap pool tables, tattooed barkeeps and loud rock and roll. Live bands play most nights.

LINDA'S Map p79   Dive
☎ 206-325-1220; 707 E Pine St; happy hour microbrews $3; ⏲ 4pm-2am Mon-Fri, 10am-2am Sat & Sun, happy hour 7-9pm
The back patio here is an excellent place to observe the nocturnal habits of *Hipsterus Northwesticus*. Linda's is also one of the few joints in town where you can recover from your hangover with an Emergen-C cocktail and a vegetarian brunch while taxidermied moose heads stare at you from the walls.

CC ATTLE'S Map p79   Gay Bar
☎ 206-726-0565; 1501 E Madison St; ⏲ noon-2am Mon-Fri, 11am-2am Sat & Sun
A self-proclaimed 'drinkin' bar,' CC Attle's is a little cheesy, but it's a longstanding favorite hangout for gay men. The drinks are famously stiff and cheap, and the crowd is pretty well mixed as well as welcoming. A large outdoor deck adds to the fun in summer.

R PLACE Map p79   Gay Bar
☎ 206-322-8828; 619 E Pine St; ⏲ 4pm-2am Mon-Fri, 2pm-2am Sat & Sun
Weekend cabaret performances, amateur strip shows, go-go boys and DJs – there's something entertaining going on every night of the week at this welcoming gay bar. Relax with a beer on the deck or dance your ass off. Three floors of dancing to hip-hop and R&B DJs and plenty of sweaty body contact make this club a blast for pretty much everyone who isn't terribly uptight. If you're feeling brave, take a shot at winning a hundred bucks in the all-male wet-undies contest.

WILDROSE Map p79   Lesbian Bar
☎ 206-324-9210; 1021 E Pike St; ⏲ 5pm-midnight Mon, 3pm-1am Tue-Thu, 3pm-2am Fri & Sat, 3pm-midnight Sun
This small, comfortable lesbian bar has theme nights (dykes on bikes, drag-king shows) as well as a light menu, pool, karaoke and DJs. On weekends it gets packed, so figure on a bit of a wait to get in.

CANTERBURY ALE & EATS Map p79   Pub
☎ 206-322-3130; 534 15th Ave E; ⏲ 10am-2am Sat & Sun, 11am-2am Mon-Fri
If you can get past the suit of armor guarding the door, you'll find that every-thing else about this Old English–style pub in a pretty, black-and-white building makes for a cozy hangout, from the snugs and the tapestried booths to the fireplace and friendly service.

U DISTRICT

Explore 'the Ave' (University Way) and sur-rounding streets for some of the city's most mellow coffee shops, a literary landmark and some lively watering holes.

CAFÉ RACER Map p83   Bar
☎ 206-523-5282; 5828 Roosevelt Way NE; ⏲ 9am-1am, closed Wed
Conspicuously friendly to two-wheeled transport, this tiny bar-cafe has a rec room upstairs where you can lounge on couches and watch movies from the bar library on the bar TV. Downstairs there's a counter, a few tables and a microscopic open kitchen, and decor includes the occasional taxider-mied gazelle poised above a MotoGuzzi

gas tank. And um, there's a hair salon inside. Live music most nights.

BIG TIME MICROBREW & MUSIC
Map p83   Brewpub

☎ 206-545-4509; 4133 University Way NE; four 4oz samples $5, pints $4-5, daily special $3; ☽ 11:30am-2am

A fun hangout in the U District, this expansive brewpub is quiet and casual in the daytime, but gets hopping at night. During the school year, it can be crowded with students still testing out their alcohol limits.

CAFÉ ALLEGRO Map p83   Coffee Shop

☎ 206-633-3030; 4214 University Way NE; drinks from $2; ☽ to 11pm

This exposed-brick cafe, tucked in the alley between NE 42nd and NE 43rd Sts, east of University Way, helped launch the Seattle coffee scene. It's full of students scribbling over papers or mooning over professors.

UGLY MUG Map p83   Coffee Shop

☎ 206-547-3219; 1309 NE 43rd St; egg muffin $4, bagels $1.50-3; ☽ 8am-11pm Mon-Fri, 10am-10pm Sat

Good soups, sandwiches and the atmosphere of a cozy living room make this coffee shop just off the Ave worth a peek. It also serves excellent coffee, as is standard for any Seattle coffee shop.

BLUE MOON TAVERN Map p83   Pub

☎ 206-633-626; 712 NE 45th St; pints $2-4

This legendary home of literary drunks, both famous and infamous, is almost exactly a mile from campus, thanks to an early zoning law. Going in sober can be a harsh awakening. Everyone in the place has a limp and an unlikely story to tell. Hang onto your beer with both hands and be prepared for impromptu recitations of poetry, jaw-harp performances, formless rants and/or halfhearted groping – relax, you'll have made new friends by night's end. If things get too weird, try hiding behind one of the books that line the worn-in wooden booths.

FREMONT & WALLINGFORD

These low-key residential neighborhoods are home to a nice variety of bars, taverns and brewpubs.

DAD WATSON'S RESTAURANT & BREWERY Map p87   Brewpub

☎ 206-632-6505; 3601 Fremont Ave N; pints $4.50, cocktails $6-9; ☽ 11:30am-1am Mon-Thu, 11:30am-2am Fri & Sat, 11:30am-midnight Sun

Fremont's representative of the McMenamins brewpub chain, head-quartered in Portland, has worn wooden booths and a big open dining room with a long, crescent-shaped bar; despite its spaciousness, the place feels warm and cozy. Signature burgers like the Captain Neon ($8.95) complement McMenamins microbrews – try the Hammerhead.

HALE'S BREWERY & PUB Map p87   Brewpub

☎ 206-782-0737; 4301 Leary Way NW; ☽ 11am-10pm Mon-Thu, 11am-11pm Fri, 9am-11pm Sat, 9am-10pm Sun

Nestled between Fremont and Ballard, Hale's makes some fantastic beer, most

MACRO AMOUNTS OF MICROBREWS

The microbrew explosion rocked the Northwest around the same time as the gourmet coffee craze – not coincidentally, Seattle's Redhook brewery was cofounded in 1981 by Gordon Bowker, one of the guys who founded Starbucks. Redhook is no longer brewed in Seattle itself, but in two other breweries – one in Woodinville, 20 miles east of Seattle, and the other in New Hampshire.

Most local microbreweries started out as tiny craft breweries that produced European-style ales. Many of these small producers initially lacked the capital to offer their brews for sale anywhere but in the brewery building itself, hence the term brewpub – an informal pub with its own on-site brewery.

Though you can find microbrews at practically every bar in town, brewpubs often feature signature beers and ales not available anywhere else. It's worth asking about specialty brews or seasonal beers on tap. Most of the brewpubs listed in this chapter offer a taster's selection of the house brews. Pints range in price from $4 to $6, so a sampler can be good value if you're not sure what you like.

otably its ambrosial Cream Ale. But its flagship brewpub feels a bit like a corporate hotel lobby. It's worth a quick stop, though; ask the friendly staff about the personalized mugs hanging above the bar. There's a miniature self-guided tour in the entryway.

BROUWER'S Map p87   Pub
☎ 206-267-2437; 400 N 35th St; ☺ 11am-2am
Shaped like a giant industrial oubliette, this dark cathedral of beer has rough-hewn rock walls and a black metal grate on the ceiling, plus two curved metal balconies, a bunch of cozy, black-leather couches, snug booths and an epic bar behind which are tantalizing glimpses into a massive, expertly stocked beer fridge. A replica *Mannequin Pis* statue at the door and the Belgian crest everywhere clue you in to the place's specialty: yes, you can have framboise. With 47 beers on tap, you can probably have anything you want.

TEAHOUSE KUAN YIN Map p91   Tea House
☎ 206-632-2055; 1911 N 45th St; cup/pot of tea $2/8; ☺ 9am-10pm Sun-Thu, 9am-11pm Fri & Sat
For a switch from the coffee shop routine, the Teahouse Kuan Yin has an impressive selection of black, oolong, green and herbal teas, as well as all the paraphernalia you need to enjoy a pot of same. It's open later than most coffee shops and has wi-fi and good desserts.

GREEN LAKE & PHINNEY RIDGE

This area is all aflutter with new bars and restaurants. Below are some highlights, but make sure to wander further afield if you have time.

EL CHUPACABRA Map p93   Bar
☎ 206-706-4889; 6711 Greenwood Ave N; ☺ 11am-2am Mon-Fri, 2pm-2am Sat & Sun
The patio is where it's at for sipping margaritas at this kitschy neighborhood hangout. Be warned, service can be slow when the place is crowded.

74TH STREET ALE HOUSE Map p93   Pub
☎ 206-784-2955; 7401 Greenwood Ave N; pints $4-5, gumbo $5, dinner specials $12-14;

top picks

DRINKS WITH A VIEW

- **Alibi Room** (p141) For those who want to see rather than be seen.
- **Five Point Café** (p142) A peek at the Space Needle from an odd standpoint.
- **Revolution Bar & Grill** (p143) A stunning view of the interior of the Experience Music Project building.
- **Linda's** (p145) A look at hipsters in their natural habitat.
- **Bauhaus** (p144) Big windows for watching the world go by.

☺ 11:30am-11pm Sun-Thu, 11:30am-midnight Fri & Sat
A sibling to the Hilltop Ale House (p143) in Queen Anne, this is the kind of place that, if you lived nearby, you'd find yourself in several times a week. It's immediately comfortable, to the point that you feel like an instant regular – plus there are dozens of outstanding beers on tap, and the food is miles above usual pub standards. The goat cheese salad ($9) is rightly famous.

PROST! Map p93   Pub
☎ 206-706-5430; 7311 Greenwood Ave N; ☺ 3pm-2am
You can order German beer in liters at this tavern, whose name means 'Cheers!' There are free pretzels on the bar and bratwurst on the menu ($3 to $6). It's a small, usually crowded place with black-and-white photos, deep-red walls, darts in the back, and a sticker behind the bar that says 'My bartender can kick your psychiatrist's ass.'

BALLARD & DISCOVERY PARK

Ballard is probably the city's most buzzing neighborhood to hang out in these days. Some people like that and others mourn the fact – but, if nothing else, this type of buzz certainly makes for a diverting nightlife.

COPPER GATE Map p96   Bar
☎ 206-706-3292; 6301 24th Ave NW; ☺ 5pm-midnight

Formerly one of Seattle's worst dives, the Copper Gate has been converted into a bizarre upscale bar-restaurant focused on meatballs and naked ladies. A Viking longship forms the bar, with a peepshow pastiche for a sail and an assortment of helmets and gramophones as cargo. Barstools arranged two-deep encourage conversation. Food and drinks are Scandi-themed. Try an aquavit or an exotic bottled beer: the Sinebrychoff Porter from Finland pours like motor oil.

HATTIE'S HAT Map p96　　　　　　Bar
☎ 206-784-0175; 5231 Ballard Ave NW; ☉ 11am-2am Mon-Fri, 9am-2am Sat & Sun
A classic old divey bar that's been revived with new blood without losing its charm, Hattie's Hat is a perfect storm of stiff drinks, fun-loving staff and cheap greasy-spoon food. This might be the best place in town to make that ever-so-delicate transition from weekend breakfast to dinner and drinks – you can get coffee with eggs and toast all day long, and nobody will find it odd when you switch to beer, even if it's not quite noon yet.

KING'S HARDWARE Map p96　　　　Bar
☎ 206-782-0027; 5225 Ballard Ave NW; ☉ 4pm-2am Mon-Fri, noon-2am Sat & Sun
Owned by the Linda of Linda's (p145), King's Hardware has a hunting-lodge-meets-Old-West-game-room feel. There's pinball and skeeball towards the rear wooden booths, and taxidermied jackalopes propped between bottles of liquor behind the bar. The spacious hangout also has a good jukebox and, in case you're feeling shaggy, easy access to Rudy's Barbershop (it's attached).

NOBLE FIR Map p96　　　　　　　　Bar
☎ 206-420-7425; www.thenoblefir.com; 5316 Ballard Ave NW; pints $5, wine by the glass $6-15; ☉ 4-11pm Mon-Wed, 4pm-1am Thu-Sat, noon-11pm Sun
Possibly the first bar devoted to the theme of wilderness hiking, the Noble Fir is a bright, shiny new Ballard spot with an epic beer list that might just make you abandon all your plans for outdoor adventure. Should your resolve begin to flag, head to the back corner, where there's a library of activity guides and maps that will re-inspire you. Bonus: Magners Irish cider on tap!

JOLLY ROGER TAPROOM
Map p96　　　　　　　　　　　　Brewpub
☎ 206-782-6181; 1514 NW Leary Way; pitchers $13.50, pints $4-4.50; ☉ closed Sun
A secret treasure tucked away off busy Leary Way, Maritime Pacific Brewing's Jolly Roger Taproom is a tiny, pirate-themed bar with a nautical chart painted onto the floor. Though lately it's gone less scurvy-barnacle and more placid-yachtsman, the beer's still tops – and served in 20oz pints. The food's not bad either; try a chef's special ($4 to $8.50) or a mess of clams and mussels ($8.95). There are about 15 taps, all serving Maritime Pacific brews. The strong winter ale, Jolly Roger, is highly recommended.

CONOR BYRNE Map p96　　　　　　Pub
☎ 206-784-3640; 5140 Ballard Ave NW; Guinness $4; ☉ 4-7pm
A friendly pub notable primarily for its gorgeous, original mahogany bar, it has live music most nights, leaning mostly toward old-timey and blues, plus trivia and comedy events.

OLD TOWN ALE HOUSE Map p96　　Pub
☎ 206-782-8323; 5233 Ballard Ave NW; sandwiches $10.75, pints $4.75, schooners $3.75
This cavernous, warmly lit, red-brick pub specializes in beers from Washington and Belgium. It's also known for its giant sandwich 'wedges' (try the rustic eggplant) and stacks of delicious fries. Ask about daily drink specials (like $3 pints of IPA on Mondays – a fine idea).

WEST SEATTLE

Though it feels isolated from the rest of the city, West Seattle has the beachy charm of a vacation community and a few good watering holes to explore. It also has a great record store (p117) where you can drink a beer while you browse.

ELLIOTT BAY BREWERY & PUB
Map p103　　　　　　　　　　　Brewpub
☎ 206-932-8695; 4720 California Ave SW; ☉ 11am-midnight Mon-Sat, to 11pm Sun
Long and narrow, with a loft at the back of the room and a beer garden outdoors, this comfortable brewpub makes a nice retreat after a day at Alki Beach. Pub food emphasizes organic, locally sourced ingredients

and includes monthly specials. There are always two cask-conditioned beers available.

WEST 5 Map p103 Cocktail Lounge
☎ 206-935-1966; 4539 California Ave SW
A long, skinny space lined with tall, white leather wingback chairs and crowned with neon at the far end, West 5 is an oasis of cool on California Ave.

GEORGETOWN
Head to Georgetown to find the preferred drinking holes of those in the know.

JULES MAES SALOON Map p106 Bar
☎ 206-957-7766; 5919 Airport Way S
Built in the late 1800s, this traditional saloon now benefits from punk rock and tattoos, pinball and other vintage games, and no need to hide its booze from the authorities (the place operated as a speakeasy during Prohibition).

NINE POUND HAMMER Map p106 Bar
☎ 206-762-3373; 6009 Airport Way S; ⏰ 5pm-2am
You can bring your dog to this darkened beer hall. The place is generous with the pours and the peanuts, and the mixed crowd of workers, hipsters, punks and bikers vacillates between energetic and rowdy.

SMARTY PANTS Map p106 Bar
☎ 206-762-4777; 6017 Airport Way; sandwiches $7.50-8.50; ⏰ 11am-2am Mon-Fri, 10am-2am Sat, 10am-3pm Sun; Ⓥ
This giant industrial hangout for scooterists and sportbike riders has vintage motorcycles propped up in the windows, a hearty sandwich menu (plus a weekend brunch) and an obvious fondness for two-wheeled mischief of all types. Wednesdays are Bike Nights, when fans watch the week's recorded MotoGP, SuperMoto and superbike races. The kitchen is open until midnight Monday to Saturday.

ALL CITY COFFEE Map p106 Coffee Shop
☎ 206-767-7146; 1205 S Vale St
This coffee shop, opened by a designer who'd discovered there was nowhere to get a decent latte in the area, looks fantastic and pulls a perfect espresso shot. Plan to linger.

NIGHTLIFE

top picks

What's your recommendation? www.lonelyplanet.com/seattle

NIGHTLIFE

This chapter covers live music, clubbing and other nightlife events that don't fall under the general Arts heading (eg theater, comedy, film, classical music and dance). See p157 for the Arts chapter and p139 for listings of bars, cocktail lounges, pubs and coffee shops.

LIVE MUSIC

Most visitors will tend to associate Seattle with a particular era and style of music, depending on their age and interest – whether it's Jimi Hendrix, Nirvana or the Presidents of the United States of America. These days, grunge is little more than a mummified corpse taking up a hefty chunk of the Experience Music Project, and most Seattleites would prefer to forget about the national music media's brief love affair with their city. Nevertheless, grunge's influence was tremendously important to Seattle's live music scene, and many of the clubs it spawned are still around in some form or another, helping local bands to get established and providing some medium-sized venues for touring indie-rock bands. Beyond punk and indie rock, there's also a healthy jazz and blues scene, a strong and growing hip-hop scene, and plenty of places where you can hear techno and electronica.

Seattle's status in the live-music world means most touring bands will make a stop here. On any given night, there's a wide array of shows and concerts to choose from. As anywhere, the club scene here can be capricious. Name changes and small-venue closures happen frequently, so before you head out, check music listings and ads in the Stranger (www.thestranger.com) or the Seattle Weekly (www.seattleweekly.com) for the most up-to-date information.

The free papers also have club directories that list phone numbers and addresses for local venues, and they're good places to find out about up-and-coming new bands, all-ages shows, house parties and one-off performances in galleries or warehouses – often the best way to get an insider's view of the local music scene.

Look for posters stapled to telephone poles, too, and flyers stacked up around the entrances to most coffee shops and record stores. And, of course, every band and every venue in the modern era keeps a regularly updated calendar on its MySpace or Facebook page.

Typically, live music starts between 9pm and 10pm and goes until 1am or 2am. For most of the venues below, you can pay admission at the door; for a small to medium-size venue, the cover charge can be anywhere from $5 to $15. Larger venues sell advance tickets at their box offices or through TicketsWest (☎ 800-992-8499), TicketMaster (☎ 800-745-3000), Tickets.com or Etix.com, usually tacking on a service fee.

FESTIVALS

Children, hipsters and hippies alike enjoy the Northwest Folklife Festival (p17). Held at Seattle Center in May on the Memorial Day long weekend, this is a fun event with music, dance, food and crafts.

The absolutely best way to kiss the sweetness of Northwest summer goodbye is at Bumbershoot (p18). Held in September on the Labor Day long weekend, Bumbershoot brings hundreds of musicians to 25 stages throughout Seattle Center, as well as readings, artwork and other performances.

INDIE ROCK, PUNK, METAL & HIP-HOP

CHOP SUEY Map p79
☎ 206-860-5155; www.chopsuey.com; 1325 E Madison St; cover

top picks

LIVE MUSIC VENUES

- Crocodile Café (opposite) A landmark of the grunge era, still going strong.
- Neumo's (opposite) A classic punk and indie-rock venue.
- Sunset Tavern (p154) Hipster haunt with garage-rock bands and cult movies.
- Chop Suey (above) A well-established venue for touring and local rock bands.
- Tractor Tavern (p154) Classy, amber-lit acoustic theater.

With its slightly facetious Asian theme achieved via a giant pagoda-like stage prop and a few Chinese lanterns over the bar, this wide-open, uncluttered space hosts national and local rock bands, DJs and karaoke nights. The crowd and the atmosphere depend on who's playing.

CROCODILE CAFÉ Map p68
☎ 206-441-5611; http://thecrocodile.com; 2200 2nd Ave; cover $5-15
One of the best rock clubs in the country and a Seattle institution, this Belltown space helped launch the grunge and alt-rock scenes. It has showcased virtually every important Seattle band during the grunge years and since (including, of course, Nirvana). It closed in 2007, but has been rescued and is now once again home to some of the city's best indie-rock shows, whether local or touring bands. The attached cafe also serves a decent greasy-spoon breakfast, lunch and dinner.

EL CORAZON Map p77
☎ 206-381-3094; www.elcorazonseattle.com; 109 Eastlake Ave E; cover
Formerly the Off-Ramp, then Graceland, El Corazon has lots of history echoing around its walls – and lots of sweaty, beer-drenched bodies bouncing off them. Save your clean shirt for another night, and don't expect perfect sound quality at every show, but it does draw some really good bands. It's also one of the few bars that often has all-ages shows.

FUNHOUSE Map p72
☎ 206-374-8400; www.thefunhouseseattle.com; 206 5th Ave N; free or cover
A great, grubby punk venue near Seattle Center, the Funhouse is a very Seattle-ish tattoos-and-black-T-shirts watering hole where you go to drink cheap beer, check out bands like the Trashies and maybe hook up with a Rat City roller derby girl. Try not to slip on beer and fall down, or you'll stick to the checkered floor.

MONKEY PUB Map p83
☎ 206-523-6457; www.myspace.com/monkeypub; 5305 Roosevelt Way NE; free or cover
This U-District dive is one of the few places in town where you can slug pitchers of cheap beer, shoot pool and catch a live punk show on a weekend night without

having to do any planning whatsoever. If the band sucks, it'll be over soon and did we mention the beer's cheap? Slices from the pizza shop next door are available, or you can pop over to eat and play video games between sets.

MOORE THEATER Map p50
☎ 206-443-1744; www.stgpresents.org/moore; 1932 2nd Ave; cover
Bands love playing this 1500-seat borderline-Belltown venue for its classy style and great acoustics. Attached to a stately old hotel, it exudes battered grace and sophistication whether the act is a singer-songwriter, a jazz phenomenon or a rock band.

NECTAR Map p87
☎ 206-632-2020; www.nectarlounge.com; 412 N 36th St; cover
A small and comfortable rock venue in Fremont that has grown out of its humble beginnings to become a well-established, scenester-approved club, Nectar hosts everything from reggae and dub to funk to Americana, as well as DJ nights.

NEUMO'S Map p79
☎ 206-709-9467; www.neumos.com; 925 E Pike St; cover
Your classic Northwest midsized rock club, Neumo's has a small stage, a balcony and a new separate bar in the back, Moe's Bar. It books some of the best rock shows in town.

RENDEZVOUS Map p68
☎ 206-441-5823; www.rendezvousseattle.com; 2320 2nd Ave; cover
This classy place has a curved bar upfront and a small theater in the back room. Emblematic of the chic makeover of Belltown, the Jewel Box Theater was once a slightly grubby venue for punk bands but now sparkles enough to live up to its name. It hosts a variety of music, film and theatrical performances.

SHOWBOX Map p63
☎ 206-628-3151; www.showboxonline.com /market; 1426 1st Ave; cover
This cavernous showroom – which hosts mostly national touring acts, ranging from indie rock to hip-hop – reinvents itself

every few years. Between sets, hop over to the attached Green Room, the venue's smaller bar and restaurant.

STUDIO SEVEN off Map p106
☎ 206-286-1312; www.studioseven.us; 110 S Horton St; free or cover
This all-ages club is south of Safeco Field, in what is called SODO, just off 1st Ave S one block N of Spokane St. It books local and touring punk and metal shows; recent headliners include Sick of It All, TSOL and the Vibrators. Bring your ID to get in to the bar (pretty much always a good idea).

SUNSET TAVERN Map p96
☎ 206-784-4880; www.sunsettavern.com; 5433 Ballard Ave NW; cover
The Sunset is a Ballard bar that books great dirty-rock shows of local and touring bands, and frequently has free movie nights, including a series of B-grade kung-fu films most weeks.

TRACTOR TAVERN Map p96
☎ 206-789-3599; www.tractortavern.com; 5213 Ballard Ave NW; cover
The premier venue for folk and acoustic music, the elegant Tractor Tavern also books local songwriters and regional bands such as Richmond Fontaine, plus touring acts like John Doe and Wayne Hancock. It's a gorgeous room, usually with top sound quality.

TRIPLE DOOR Map p50
☎ 206-838-4333; www.thetripledoor.net; 216 Union St; cover
This club downstairs from Wild Ginger (p122) has a liberal booking policy that includes country and rock as well as jazz, gospel, R&B, world music and burlesque performances. There's a full menu and valet parking; the club is all-ages before 9:30pm.

VERA PROJECT Map p72
☎ 206-956-8372; www.theveraproject.org; cnr Republican & Warren N Aves; free or cover
An excellent nonprofit community center run by and for teenagers, the Vera Project books exclusively all-ages shows in a smoke-free and alcohol-free environment. It's also dedicated to giving youth a place to learn skills, make art and get involved in the community.

ELECTRONICA

BALTIC ROOM Map p79
☎ 206-625-4444; www.thebalticroom.net; 1207 Pine St; free or cover
Classy and high ceilinged, with wood-paneled walls, paper lanterns and an elegant balcony, this Capitol Hill club hosts an excellent mix of local and touring DJs in a range of genres, from reggae and house to drum-and-bass.

CONTOUR Map p56
☎ 206-447-7704; www.clubcontour.com; 807 1st Ave
This plush venue is open late and has a more extensive food menu than you might expect of a club whose top priority is clearly to keep your booty shaking until dawn. Contour hosts local and visiting DJs, with after-hours dance nights until 4:30am Thursdays through Saturdays.

CELTIC & COUNTRY

KELLS Map p63
☎ 206-728-1916; www.kellsirish.com/seattle; 1916 Post Alley
Part of a small West Coast chain of Irish pubs, this location is the most atmospheric and authentic, with its exposed-brick walls, multiple nooks and crannies, and rosy-cheeked crowd. The perfectly poured Imperial pints of Guinness are divine and there's live Irish (or Irish-inspired) music nightly (no cover charge).

LITTLE RED HEN Map p93
☎ 206-522-1168; www.littleredhen.com; 7115 Woodlawn Ave NE; free or cover
This is Seattle's primary (or only) venue for authentic, live country music. Nightly entertainment includes country karaoke and good-time honky-tonk bands – or you can make like Billy Ray Cyrus with weekly line-dancing lessons.

OWL & THISTLE Map p56
☎ 206-621-7777; www.owlnthistle.com; 808 Post Ave; free or cover
The schedule here varies, but most nights it books Celtic folk bands or acoustic singer-songwriters. It's also just a comfortable pub to stop in for a pint if you don't feel like committing to an evening of music.

JAZZ & BLUES

As well as the places listed below, check out the New Orleans Creole Restaurant (p123) for Dixieland, blues and zydeco.

DIMITRIOU'S JAZZ ALLEY Map p68

☎ 206-441-9729; 2033 6th Ave; cover
Hidden in an unlikely spot behind a boring-looking office building is Seattle's most sophisticated and prestigious jazz club. Dimitriou's hosts the best of the locals and many national acts passing through.

TULA'S Map p68

☎ 206-443-4221; www.tulas.com; 2214 2nd Ave; cover
Tula's has live jazz seven nights a week, from big bands and Latin jazz to up-and-coming names on tour. It's a non-indie-rock oasis in the booze alley that is Belltown.

DANCE CLUBS

The dance clubs listed below are places you go to shake your booty, not so much to hear the latest experiments in electronica by nationally known techno DJs. However, flexibility reigns in Seattle's clubs; many of the city's live-music venues also have DJ nights that transform them into dance clubs. Check the local weeklies to see what's going on at a given place on a given night.

The best and most fun dance scenes are found in gay discos and nobody much cares if you like boys or girls or both as long as you're out to have a good time. Most of these clubs charge a cover ($5 to $15) Thursday through Saturday nights. See also R Place (p145) in the Drinking chapter.

CENTURY BALLROOM Map p79

☎ 206-324-7263; www.centuryballroom.com; 915 E Pine St
Dance lessons followed by an everyone-out-on-the-floor dance free-for-all makes a night at the Century the perfect combination of spectating and participating.

PIONEER SQUARE JOINT COVER

Designed with the bar-hopper in mind, this deal (which vanished for a while, but was back in effect at the time of research) gets you into five Pioneer Square (Map p56) nightspots for one flat fee on Friday and Saturday nights. A joint cover fee of $10 buys you in-and-out privileges at the following clubs: the friendly, no-frills, rock and metal Central Saloon (p141); DJ dance tracks at the Last Supper Club (☎ 206-748-9975; http://lastsupperclub.com; 124 S Washington St); the faux-Polynesian meat market at Tiki Bob's Cantina (☎ 206-382-8454; http://tikibobsseattle.com; 166 S King St); the rough and tumble J&M Café (☎ 206-292-0663; www.thejmcafe.com; 201 1st Ave S); and the sports bar-dance club Fuel (☎ 206-405-3835; www.fuelseattle.com; 164 S Washington St). It's a better deal for men than women, as ladies frequently get in free anyway. But if you're looking to make the rounds, the joint cover deal might be good value. Pay the cover at the first club you visit.

Dance nights include everything from the lindy hop to salsa. Check the website for a schedule of events.

NEIGHBOURS Map p79

☎ 206-324-5358; www.neighboursnightclub.com; 1509 Broadway E
Referred to on one occasion as a 'big, soulless, cha cha palace,' Neighbours is ostensibly a gay disco but attracts a varied crowd – even newbie suburbanites come in for its weekly '80s night (Thursdays, at press time).

RE-BAR Map p50

☎ 206-233-9873; www.rebarseattle.com; 1114 Howell St
The Re-Bar hosts everything ranging from hip-hop DJs to drag shows and attracts a lively crowd that comes to boogie on various theme nights. Whether you're gay, lesbian, bi, straight or undecided, you'll have a fun night out at the classic weekly Queer Disco.

top picks

- Seattle International Film Festival (p160)
- Richard Hugo House (p158)
- Annex Theater (p159)
- Intiman Theater Company (p159)
- Northwest Film Forum (p160)

THE ARTS

There's a good range of cultural diversions available in Seattle at any given moment. Author readings, dance, opera, ballet, theater and film are all going strong here. Ranked the most literate city in the nation in 2005, Seattle is a book-loving town. It's home to a number of big-name writers, and the plethora of bookstores and coffee shops here help to fuel its book culture. There's a literary event of one kind or another happening practically every night of the week.

Film is also big news in Seattle these days. The Seattle International Film Festival (p160) is among the most influential festivals in the country, and a thriving independent film scene has sprung up in a handful of underground venues, including the Alibi Room (p141).

Live theater runs the gamut from big productions, such as Ibsen at the Intiman Theater (opposite), to staged readings of obscure texts in cobbled-together venues or coffee shops.

The Seattle Symphony (p161) has become nationally known and widely respected, primarily through its excellent recordings.

Some of the city's more interesting cultural events, whether film, music, theater or a combination, occur in makeshift venues, galleries, warehouses and the like. To find a current listing, check the Stranger (www.thestranger.com) or Seattle Weekly (www.seattleweekly.com).

TICKETS & RESERVATIONS

Tickets for big events are available through TicketMaster (☎ 206-628-0888, 206-292-2787; www.ticketmaster.com) online, by phone or at ticket centers located around Seattle; check online for locations. (At research time, Fred Meyer grocery stores were a good bet.) Ticket centers are open 8am to 9pm Monday to Saturday and 10am to 6pm Sunday. But if you can buy tickets at the door and there's no risk of the show being sold out, do so: it'll save you the service fee TicketMaster tacks on (usually $6 to $10).

TicketsWest (☎ 800-992-8499, 800-632-8499; www.ticketswest.rdln.com) is a regional ticketing service, with outlets at Rudy's Barbershops and QFC grocery stores.

Brown Paper Tickets (☎ 800-838-3006; www.brownpapertickets.com) handles sales for a number of smaller and quirkier venues, from theater to live music. The company keeps service fees low, donates a percentage of sales to charities, and runs an environmentally friendly office.

READINGS

Maybe it's because of the rain, or maybe it's all that good coffee, but Seattleites read voraciously – whether it's the latest literary novel, an underground comic or a home-stapled zine. A lot of authors live here and there are some important literary landmarks worth checking out. Not the least of them is Blue Moon Tavern (p146), which was the retreat of choice for the great poet Theodore Roethke,

who taught at the nearby University of Washington. It may not feel entirely literary these days, but don't let the subtle scent of pee and cheap beer distract you from appreciating its bookish past.

The Elliott Bay Book Company (p113) is a mandatory stop on any major author's book tour. Several other bookstores host readings on a regular basis; see the Shopping chapter (p107).

For detailed event schedules and to find offbeat happenings at nonmajor venues, check listings in the *Stranger* or the *Seattle Weekly* or look for events calendars posted in bookstores around town. Most readings and open-mic events are free.

BORDERS BOOKS & MUSIC Map p50
☎ 206-622-4599; 1501 4th Ave
Borders stages readings by touring authors, plus occasional live music and children's events, mostly during the day.

RICHARD HUGO HOUSE Map p79
☎ 206-322-7030; www.hugohouse.org; 1634 11th Ave; ☺ house noon-6pm Mon-Fri & noon-5pm Sat, zine archive 4-8pm Wed, 1-5pm Thu & Sat
Established in honor of famed Northwest poet Richard Hugo (see the box opposite), and the nexus of Seattle's literary community, the Hugo House hosts readings, classes and workshops, as well as offering various events around town. Writers-in-residence keep office hours at this 1902 house (a former mortuary), during which

RICHARD HUGO

Who was Richard Hugo, and why is the literary center of Seattle named after him? Like his mentor and fellow Seattle writer Theodore Roethke, Hugo (1923–82) was a poet and a great teacher of poetry.

Born in White City, a suburb of Seattle, he was raised by his grandparents after his father left the family. In 1943 he volunteered for the Army Air Corps, serving as a bombardier on 35 missions. Afterwards, on the GI Bill, he majored in English at the University of Washington, where he enrolled in Roethke's first two workshops. He earned a bachelor of arts degree from U Dub in 1948. From 1951 until 1963 Hugo worked for Boeing. In 1965 he left Seattle to teach at the University of Montana.

Hugo was a hard-working, hard-drinking (for most of his life), perpetually self-questioning man. The 1930s Seattle of his childhood was a place he described as having a Scandinavian character, with a reputation for the second-highest number of suicides for a city (after Berlin). He explained this as being due to the fact that people who wanted to run away from either themselves or their life would arrive in Seattle and discover there was nowhere left to run.

He died of leukemia in Seattle on October 22, 1982. *The Real West Marginal Way – A Poet's Autobiography* is a collection of Hugo's essays describing his childhood in Seattle as well as his later teaching career. It's worth seeking out for the picture it paints of a city in flux. *The Triggering Town* (1979) is an affecting and heartening book about writing. Perhaps his best-known poem is the oft-anthologized *Degrees of Gray in Philipsburg* – the importance of place and detail define his work. Many of his best-known poems are collected in the anthology *Making Certain It Goes On* (1991).

they're available for free consultations about writing projects. The extensive zine library invites all-day lingering, and there's also a library, conference room, theater and cafe with a small stage.

THEATER & COMEDY

Seattle has one of the most vibrant theater scenes on the West Coast, from weird experimental troupes to elaborate productions of Shakespearean classics. Check the local newspapers for openings and reviews.

5TH AVENUE THEATER Map p50

☎ 206-625-1900; 1308 5th Ave; ☷ box office 9:30am-5:30pm Mon-Fri
Built in 1926 with an opulent Asian motif, the 5th Avenue opened as a vaudeville house; it was later turned into a movie theater and closed in 1979. An influx of funding and a heritage award saved it in 1980, and now it's Seattle's premier theater for Broadway musical revivals. It's worth going just for a look at the architecture. Tickets are available by phone or at the box office at the theater.

A CONTEMPORARY THEATER (ACT) Map p50

☎ 206-292-7676; 700 Union St; ☷ box office noon-7pm Tue-Sun
One of the three big companies in the city, ACT fills its $30-million home at Kreielsheimer Place with excellent performances featuring Seattle's best thes-

pians, and occasionally big-name actors, too. Tickets are available by phone or at the box office.

ANNEX THEATER

☎ 206-728-0933; 1100 E Pike St; tickets ☎ 800-838-3006, www.brownpapertickets.com
Seattle's main experimental-fringe theater group is the Annex. It has its offices inside the Capitol Hill Arts Center (Map p79; ☎ 800-838-3006; www.capitolhillsarts.com; 1621 12th Ave) and produces shows and a monthly cabaret at various locations, including the adorable, swanked-up Jewel Box Theater, which can be found at the Rendezvous (p153) in Belltown.

COMEDY UNDERGROUND Map p56

☎ 206-628-0303; 222 S Main St
As its good deed, this gritty club hosts a weekly nonprofit comedy show, currently on Tuesdays – go and have a laugh for a good cause. For details and a complete schedule, visit nonprofitcomedy.com. Buy tickets through TicketWeb (www.ticketweb.com).

INTIMAN THEATER COMPANY Map p72

☎ 206-269-1900; www.intiman.org; 201 Mercer St, Seattle Center; ☷ ticket office noon-5pm Tue-Sun
Intiman Theater is Seattle's mainstay for classic dramas and heavy-hitting, serious theater (by Henrik Ibsen and Langston Hughes, for example). The emeritus artistic director Bartlett Sher, who joined Intiman in 2000, amped up the edginess of the company's schedule to include striking new

work before handing the reins to current artistic director Kate Whoriskey in 2010.

MARKET THEATER Map p63

☎ 206-781-9273; www.unexpectedproductions
.org; 1428 Post Alley
The Market Theater hosts improvisational comedy, called Theatersports, on Friday and Saturday night at 10:30pm. Weekday shows are varied and usually start around 8:30pm. Buy tickets at www.brownpaper tickets.com or call ☎ 800-838-3006.

SEATTLE REPERTORY THEATER
Map p72

☎ 206-443-2222; www.seattlerep.org; 155 Mercer St, Seattle Center; ☺ box office 10am-6pm Tue-Fri
The Seattle Repertory Theater (the Rep) won a Tony Award in 1990 for Outstand-ing Regional Theater. The largest nonprofit resident theater outfit in the Pacific North-west, it's known for elaborate productions of big-name dramas and second-run Broadway hits.

FILM

Although colossal multiscreen cinema com-plexes are plentiful in Seattle, there is still a number of small independent theaters that go out of their way to feature the unusual and obscure. Some of the first-run houses, including those listed below, also show foreign and smaller independent films alongside mainstream smash hits. To really delve into Seattle's film culture, though, you have to seek out the tiny independent festivals and screenings.

The biggest event of the year for cinephiles is the Seattle International Film Festival (SIFF; ☎ 206-464-5830; www.siff.net; tickets $8-11, packages $57-180). Film geeks wait all year for this annual three-week extravaganza of international art films, experi-mental works and newly unearthed classics. The festival operates at a half-dozen venues around town and usually starts in mid-May.

SIFF Cinema, the festival headquarters, also shows films at Bumbershoot (p18) and throughout the year at its own dedicated cinema in Seattle Center's McCaw Hall (☎ information 206-633-7151).

The Seattle Lesbian & Gay Film Festival (☎ 206-323-4274; http://threedollarbillcinema.org/programs/SLGFF; tickets $10), a popular festival in October, shows new gay-themed films from directors worldwide.

Check film listings in the weekly papers, or ask around at the cinemas listed here

top picks

MOVIE THEATERS

- Cinerama (Map p68; ☎ 206-441-3653; www
  .cinerama.com; 2100 4th Ave) One of the very few Cineramas left in the world, it has a fun, sci-fi feel.
- Grand Illusion Cinema (Map p83; ☎ 206-523-3935; www.grandillusioncinema.org; 1403 NE 50th St) Antique theater in the U District known for director retrospectives and other cool, under-the-radar series.
- Harvard Exit (Map p79; ☎ 206-781-5755; www.
  landmarktheatres.com/market/seattle/harvar-dexittheatre.htm; 807 E Roy at Harvard) Seattle's first independent theater, built in 1925, it's run by Landmark and now shows mainstream and arthouse films.
- Northwest Film Forum (Map p79; ☎ 206-329-2629; www.nwfilmforum.org; 1515 12th Ave) Impeccable programming, from restored classics to cutting-edge independent and international films. The forum also holds classes and workshops.
- Jewel Box Theater (p153) A restored jewel-box theater tucked away behind the sleek Rendezvous cocktail bar, with live music and independent theater events.
- Varsity Theater (Map p83; ☎ 206-632-3131; www.landmarktheatres.com/market/seattle/varsity theatre.htm; 4329 University Way NE) Independent and international arthouse films, usually in one-week runs.

(see the box above). For a full list of theaters, times and locations, check the *Stranger*, the *SeattleWeekly* or the arts sections of the daily papers.

OPERA, CLASSICAL MUSIC & DANCE

Seattle is a sophisticated city with a well-regarded symphony, an ever-strengthening opera and a vibrant dance scene. It's hard to go wrong with any of the following options. Keep an eye out for the University of Washington's annual World Series (☎ 206-543-4880, 800-859-5342; www.uwworldseries.org; Meany Hall, University of Washington; tickets $39-55) of international music, performance and dance scheduled at various times throughout the year.

MEGAVENUES

Tickets for these major concert and event venues can generally be purchased from TicketMaster (for a fee) or through the box office of the venue at the number listed.

Benaroya Concert Hall (Map p50; ☎ 206-215-4747; 200 University St) The Seattle Symphony's home venue.

Gorge Amphitheater (754 Silica Rd NW, George, WA) A 20,000-person venue for huge concerts (Sting, Aerosmith) and festivals (Sasquatch, the Warped Tour); it's about 150 miles from Seattle.

McCaw Hall (Map p72; ☎ 206-684-7200; 321 Mercer St) Home of the Seattle Opera.

Meany Hall (Map p83; ☎ 206-543-4880; University of Washington) A large performance space on the U Dub campus.

WaMu Theater (Map p56; ☎ 206-628-0888; 800 Occidental Ave S) The new venue for music and live entertainment at Qwest Field seats up to 7000 people.

White River Amphitheater (☎ 360-825-6200; 40601 Auburn Enumclaw Rd, Auburn, WA) This giant outdoor arena opened in June 2003 and serves the entire Seattle-Tacoma region; it's about 30 miles from Seattle.

PACIFIC NORTHWEST BALLET Map p72

☎ 206-441-9411; www.pnb.org; McCaw Hall, Seattle Center

This is the foremost dance company in the Northwest. The ballet does more than 100 performances a season from September through June.

SEATTLE MEN'S CHORUS

☎ 206-323-2992; www.seattlemenschorus.org

The largest community chorus in the USA and the largest gay men's chorus in the world, the Seattle Men's Chorus has nearly three dozen engagements throughout the year. Its annual Christmas concert is a popular event.

SEATTLE OPERA Map p72

☎ 206-389-7676; www.seattleopera.org; McCaw Hall, Seattle Center

The Seattle opera features a program of four or five full-scale operas every season, including Wagner's *Ring* cycle, which draws sellout crowds in summer. It offers a number of tickets to every performance at the bargain price of $25 each, available from the ticket office (1020 John St; 9am-5pm Mon-Fri & noon-4pm Sat when there's a performance) or by phone.

SEATTLE SYMPHONY Map p50

☎ 206-215-4747; www.seattlesymphony.org; Benaroya Concert Hall, 200 University St; tickets from $48

Under maestro Gerard Schwartz, the symphony earned its reputation as the heart of the Seattle classical music scene. At the time of research, Schwartz was in the midst of his final season with the symphony, to be replaced by French conductor Ludovic Morlot. Since Schwartz's arrival in 1983 the symphony has presented several successful series and released a number of recordings to critical acclaim, in addition to building a spectacular concert hall and stellar reputation. Worth noting is the symphony's Discover Music! series – concerts designed to introduce children to various aspects of classical music.

THE ARTS OPERA, CLASSICAL MUSIC & DANCE

SPORTS & ACTIVITIES

top picks

What's your recommendation? www.lonelyplanet.com/seattle

Never mind the rain – that's why Gore-Tex was invented. When you live this close to the mountains, not to mention all that water and a stunning range of parks, it's just criminal no to get outdoors, come rain, hail or shine.

Getting out there is easy, too: the Olympic and North Cascade mountains, Mt Rainier National Park and the fingers of Puget Sound are right outside the door. But Seattle is rare for a large city in that many forms of outdoor recreation (hiking, kayaking, cycling and windsurfing) are available within the city itself. If you'd rather watch other people sweat, there's plenty to do in the way of spectator sports, too.

Sure, they had to put a retractable roof on the stadium to avoid perpetual rainouts, but Seat-tleites love their sports. It's an active city, for starters. There's a reason people like to preserve their environment here, and it's not so they can sit back and look at it. Numerous urban parks and trails, combined with an eminently walkable downtown core, have helped make Seattle one of the easiest-to-walk big cities in the US. It's also near the top of the list for cycling. And all that water doesn't go to waste, either: locals put it to use for canoeing, kayaking and windsurfing. In the winter, skiing and snowboarding are popular activities close to town.

When they're not out there doing sports themselves, Seattleites love to watch a good game of baseball. The Mariners got a double bonus when the old Kingdome was replaced by fancy new Safeco Field (in 1999) and an outfielder from Japan named Ichiro Suzuki joined the team (in 2001). Starting in 2002, fans turned out in record numbers, with Safeco Field setting Major League records for attendance.

Seattle's National Basketball Association (NBA) team, the SuperSonics, won its sixth division title in the 2004–05 season before depressing everyone by being relocated to Oklahoma and becoming the Oklahoma City Thunder. (If you want to make a sports fan grumpy, be sure to ask about the relocation.)

In 2004 the Women's NBA team, the Seattle Storm, won the city its first professional sports championship since 1979. Storm games are hugely popular family events that draw enthusiastic crowd participation.

The Seattle Seahawks made it to the Super Bowl in 2006 and, as underdogs, beat the Pittsburgh Steelers for the National Football League (NFL) championship.

The University of Washington, of course, has the full range of college sports going. And with the Seattle Sounders, even soccer is represented. See p166 for details on how to catch a game or a match.

When it comes to finding out where to go, what to do or where to rent equipment, a couple of places deserve special notice. Recreational Equipment Inc, better known as REI (p76), is a Seattle native and one of the largest sporting and recreational gear and equipment outfitters in the nation. Gearheads go giddy at this flagship store, a wild paean to the outdoor spirit, with a mock mountain-bike trail, a rock gym, a simulated hiking trail (to test boots), and more tents, canoes and rucksacks than you've probably ever seen in one place. The eager staff are very knowledgeable about local recreation, and there are several bulletin boards with information on talks, gatherings, outings, clubs and courses. REI's good selection of books and maps on regional recreation is helpful, especially the topographic maps of nearby mountains. The rental department can rent you most kinds of equipment or tell you where to go to do so. REI Adventures (☎ 800-622-2236) organizes trips.

Upstairs at REI, the Forest Service/National Park Service (Map p77; ☎ 206-470-4060) runs an Outdoor Recreation Center, and its staff can tell you anything you need to know about nearby national parks.

Another Seattle-based travel resource, the Mountaineers (☎ 206-284-6310; www.mountaineers.org; 7700 Sand Point Way NE) in Magnuson Park, specializes in Northwest recreation. It offers courses in hiking, mountaineering, kayaking, every type of snow sport and other outdoor skills, such as first aid and backcountry travel. Events such as film and slide shows are enough to tickle anyone's adventurous spirit, and the bookstore boasts an unbeatable collection of books, maps and videos about the outdoors, many of which are available for loan through the Mountaineers library.

SPECTATOR SPORTS

With state-of-the-art stadiums and teams that flirt with glory, Seattle is a great town to watch the pros play. College games, too, are hugely popular with locals and a fun way to spend an afternoon.

You can buy tickets for the teams listed here through TicketMaster (☎ 206-628-0888; www.ticketmaster.com) or on the individual team's website. We've listed price ranges for single-game tickets, but if you're able to attend four or more games you'll usually get a better deal.

BASEBALL
SEATTLE MARINERS
☎ 206-628-3555; www.mariners.org; single game tickets $7-60

There was a time when Seattle's professional baseball team was nothing but an annoying itch on the upper right shoulder of the USA, but not anymore. The Mariners won a division title in 1995 and promptly moved into the shiny new $417 million open-air Safeco Field (p58). In 2000 the Ms (as they are fondly referred to) missed a World Series berth by a hair, but snagged even more love from their devoted fans. The season runs April to August (October if they make the playoffs), and games usually start at 7:05pm, or 1:05pm on Sundays. There are also occasional midday games during the week; check the website for a full schedule.

BASKETBALL
SEATTLE STORM
☎ 206-217-9622; www.wnba.com/storm; single game tickets $20-200

With the demise of the SuperSonics, local basketball fans have turned to Seattle's female team, the WNBA championship–winning Storm. Boasting several star US and international players, they've consistently made the play-offs in recent years, taking the title in 2004 and 2010. They play at Key Arena (Map p72) in Seattle Center from May to September.

FOOTBALL
SEATTLE SEAHAWKS
☎ 425-827-9777; www.seahawks.com; single game tickets $52-110

The Northwest's only National Football League (NFL) franchise, the Seattle Seahawks have enjoyed both roaring success and dismal slumps, one of which prompted its former owners to put the team on the selling block, which left Seattleites fearing its relocation. In 1997 Microsoft cofounder Paul Allen saved the day by purchasing the Seahawks franchise, with the stipulation that the Hawks get a new stadium. So the Hawks' former home, the Kingdome, was spectacularly imploded and replaced in 2002 by the new 72,000-seat Qwest Field (Seahawks Stadium; p58).

UNIVERSITY OF WASHINGTON HUSKIES
☎ 206-543-2200; www.gohuskies.com; single game tickets $38-72

The University of Washington Huskies football and basketball teams are another Seattle obsession. The Huskies football team plays at Husky Stadium (Map p83) and you'll find the men's and women's basketball teams at the Edmundson Pavilion (Map p83), both of which are on campus. The women's basketball team draws massive crowds.

HOCKEY
SEATTLE THUNDERBIRDS
☎ 206-448-7825; www.seattlethunderbirds.com; single game tickets $15-25

The Seattle Thunderbirds rip around the ice in the Western Hockey League (WHL) from September to March. The games are lively and well attended, and tickets are reasonably priced, but most home games these days take place at ShoWare Center in Kent, around 20 miles south of Seattle.

ROLLER DERBY
RAT CITY ROLLERGIRLS
www.ratcityrollergirls.com; tickets $14-27, Key Arena box office

The Rat City Rollergirls are Seattle's roller derby league, and if you've never seen a roller derby bout, you shouldn't miss it. The league includes four teams, all female, competing in flat-track roller-skate races that can end up getting more violent than hockey matches. These girls are intense, and it's a ton of fun to watch. Home games are at Key Arena (Map p72), with after-parties at the Funhouse (p153).

SOCCER

SEATTLE SOUNDERS Map p56

☎ 206-622-3415; www.seattlesounders.net; single game tickets $25-95

Soccer's no stranger in Seattle either. The MLS (Major League Soccer) Seattle Sounders play at Qwest Field (Seahawks Stadium; p58), admittedly looking a little lost in the gigantic facility; soccer has yet to become huge in the USA, but those who love it, *really* love it. The soccer season runs May to mid-September.

ACTIVITIES

On the water, on wheels, or on your own two feet – there's plenty of variety in the kind of fun to be had outdoors in and around Seattle. Equipment rental is widely available, too, so here's your chance to try something you've always wanted to do, whether it's golf, rock climbing, rollerblading or paddling a canoe.

ON THE WATER

Rumor has it that one in three people who live in Seattle owns a boat of some sort. It could be a rubber dinghy, a crusty kayak or a salty sailboat, but regardless, the locals here love to play in the water. Whether you learn to windsurf on Green Lake, kayak past the houseboats on Lake Union or hoist the sails on Lake Washington, there are plenty of organizations here that are geared toward having fun on the water.

Sea kayaking can soothe your soul or wake up your adventurous spirit, and it's one of the easiest sports for beginners to pick up. Seattle's many waterways are ideal for kayak exploration, and it doesn't take long before controlling your paddle is as natural as waving your arm. White-water kayaking on regional rivers is also popular, though a little more challenging to pick up. But have no fear, many organizations offer excellent lessons or tours led by able instructor-guides.

Despite the flood of water in Seattle, summer sailing isn't that great; in fact, you're lucky if the calm days cough up enough of a breeze to keep you moving. In the spring, fall and winter, however, a soft wind exhales over the Sound and sailing becomes a spectacular way to spend time outside. Even on days when you have to keep the motor running, sailing offers views and perspectives you can only get from the water. More adventurous sailors head out on Puget Sound and along its inland waterways, or all the way up the coast to British Columbia.

Windsurfing is a big sport in Seattle. It's part of that quintessential Seattle mix of being in a band, having a job at an espresso stand and putting your sail up on the lake. As such, windsurfing draws more locals than tourists. Lake Washington is the most popular place to sail – it's big enough to accommodate traffic and out-of-control newbies. The warm waters of Green Lake are good for beginners, but it can get pretty congested in summer. Between the sailboats, floatplanes and motorboat traffic, Lake Union is not good for anyone but expert windsurfers with full control. Usual launch spots are Magnuson and Mount Baker parks. In summer, the calm waters of Puget Sound are good for experienced windsurfers. Try setting out from Alki Beach (p104) in West Seattle or from Golden Gardens Park (p98) northwest of Ballard.

Some people shy away from plunging into the chilly waters surrounding Seattle, but local divers will tell you that the marine biodiversity in the Northwest rivals any tropical clime. Sure, you're not likely to see colorful tropical fish, but dive sites in Puget Sound and along the Northwest coast offer year-round diving and regular sightings of octopus, huge ling cod, cabezon, cathedral-like white anemones and giant sea stars.

Most of the area's best dive sites are outside of Seattle, in sheltered coves and bays up and down the coast. Popular spots include Alki Cove, on the east side of Alki Point; Saltwater State Park, south of Seattle in Des Moines; and Edmonds Underwater Park near the Edmonds Ferry Dock, north of Seattle. Other popular spots include Port Angeles, Keystone and the San Juan Islands. For more information on area dive sites, look for *Northwest Shore Dives* by Stephen Fischnaller, considered the dive-site bible. It's usually available at most diving shops.

MOSS BAY ROWING & KAYAK CENTER Map p77

☎ 206-682-2031; www.mossbay.net; 1001 Fairview Ave N; kayak/sailboat rental per hr $13/35; ⏰ 8am-8pm summer, 10am-5pm Thu-Mon winter
Moss Bay offers rentals, extensive lessons and tours on Lake Union.

NORTHWEST OUTDOOR CENTER Map p77

☎ 206-281-9694; www.nwoc.com; 2100 Westlake Ave N; s/d kayak rental per hr $13/19

The center offers a vast selection of rentals, guided tours and instruction in sea and white-water kayaking.

UNDERWATER SPORTS off Map p93
☎ 206-362-3310; www.underwatersports.com; 10545 Aurora Ave
This is the best place to go for gear repair; it also offers courses in its on-site pool.

WASHINGTON KAYAK CLUB
www.washingtonkayakclub.org
The Kayak Club doesn't have a physical location, but its website acts as a clearing house for both white-water and sea kayaking courses. It's also in the business of educating paddlers about conservation and safety.

Gear Rental
In addition to the above, water-sport equipment rentals are available at the following establishments, as well as the Center for Wooden Boats (p76).

AGUA VERDE PADDLE CLUB Map p83
☎ 206-545-8570; 1303 NE Boat St; s/d kayak per hr $15/18; ⊗ 10am-dusk Mon-Sat & 10am-6pm Sun Mar-Oct
On Portage Bay, near the university, you can rent kayaks from this friendly place right at the edge of the water. When you get back from your paddle, be sure to visit the café (p000) upstairs to eat fish tacos on the covered deck.

GREEN LAKE SMALL CRAFT CENTER
Map p93
☎ 206-684-4074; 7351 W Green Lake Dr
Green Lake's still waters help keep beginner kayakers calm, though the crowds might also keep you waiting. Run by Seattle Parks & Recreation (☎ 206-684-4075; www.cityofseattle.net/parks), the center runs classes in rowing, sailing, canoeing and kayaking. It doesn't rent boats, but you can rent kayaks, canoes, rowboats and paddleboats from March to October from Green Lake Boat Rental (☎ 206-527-0171; rentals per hr $15-20; ⊗ 11am-dusk Apr-Sep) on the eastern shore of the lake.

SAILING IN SEATTLE Map p77
☎ 206-289-0094; www.sailing-in-seattle.com; 2046 Westlake Ave N, Slip 28; lessons per hr $100
On Friday evenings Sailing in Seattle holds races on Lakes Washington and Union.

Anyone can come join a racing crew and, though you should be somewhat fit, no experience is necessary; they'll show you what to do. For information on hiring Sailing in Seattle's 33ft *Whoodat*, see p207.

UW WATERFRONT ACTIVITIES CENTER Map p83
☎ 206-543-9433; canoe & rowboat per hr weekday/weekend $8.50/10; ⊗ approx 10am-7pm, closed Nov-Jan
Another good way to explore the waters surrounding the Arboretum is to rent a canoe or rowboat from the University of Washington's facility. You need a current driver's license or passport. The center is in the southeast corner of the Husky Stadium parking lot.

BICYCLING
Despite frequent rain and hilly terrain, cycling is still a major form of both transportation and recreation in the Seattle area. Both bicycle touring and mountain biking are widespread, so whether you're a clipless mudhound or a casual cruiser, you'll find plenty of places to ride.

In the city, commuter bike lanes are painted on many streets; city trails are well maintained; and the friendly and enthusiastic cycling community is happy to share the road. The wildly popular 16.5-mile Burke-Gilman Trail winds from Ballard to Log Boom Park in Kenmore on Seattle's Eastside. There, it connects with the 11-mile long Sammamish River Trail, which winds past the Chateau Ste Michelle winery in Woodinville before terminating at Redmond's Marymoor Park. Marymoor Park boasts the only velodrome (☎ 206-957-4555; admission $5) in the Pacific Northwest. You'll need to be a trained velodrome rider before you can get on the track, but the untrained can watch the exciting races, which are held Monday, Wednesday and Friday mid-May to September. Admission to the amateur races is free Monday and Wednesday; when the pros hit the track on Friday, admission costs $3.

More cyclists than you can imagine pedal the loop around Green Lake, making it downright congested on sunny days. Closer to downtown, the scenic 2.5-mile Elliott Bay Trail runs along the waterfront through Myrtle Edwards and Elliott Bay Parks. The 8-mile Alki Trail in West Seattle makes a pretty ride as it follows Alki Beach before connecting to the

11-mile Duwamish Trail that heads south along W Marginal Way SW.

Though they are not specified trails, the tree-lined roads winding through the Washington Park Arboretum and along Lake Washington Blvd make for lovely road rides. The bike trail around Seward Park gives cyclists the sensation of looping a forested island. The 14-mile Mercer Island Loop is another residential ride along E and W Mercer Way around the perimeter of the island.

Bainbridge and Vashon Islands are popular with cyclists and are just a ferry ride away, offering near-rural isolation on rolling country back roads. Bike stores and the folk who work there are usually gushing fountains of good information. Most shops stock cycling publications and can point you in the right direction for public rides, trails and places to avoid. Anyone planning on cycling in Seattle should pick up a copy of the *Seattle Bicycling Guide Map*, published by the City of Seattle's Transportation Bicycle and Pedestrian Program (☎ 206-684-7583) and available at bike shops. Alternatively you can order the map free of charge over the phone or online at www.cityofseattle.net/transportation /bikemaps.htm.

Cycling Clubs

Seattle's active cycling community thrives in part because of organized clubs.

BACKCOUNTRY BICYCLE TRAILS CLUB
☎ 206-524-2900; www.bbtc.org

Fat-tire riders will want to contact this club, which organizes rides on mountain-biking trails and offers bike repair and technical-riding courses.

CASCADE BICYCLE CLUB
☎ 206-522-3222; www.cascade.org

With more than 5500 members, this is the largest cycling club in the USA. It holds organized rides daily as well as various special events, such as races and long-distance rides. It also publishes the *Cascade Corner,* a newsletter that describes what's happening in the cycling world.

HIKING

In Seattle, it's possible to hike wilderness trails without ever leaving the city. Seward Park, east of Georgetown, offers several miles of trails in a remnant of the area's old-growth forest, and an even more extensive network of trails is available in 534-acre Discovery Park (Map p96), northwest of downtown. At the northern edge of Washington Park Arboretum, Foster Island (Map p101) offers a 20-minute wetlands trail winding through marshlands created upon the opening of the Lake Washington Ship Canal. This is also a great place for bird-watching, fishing and swimming. The trail begins at the bottom of the Museum of History & Industry (p101) parking lot.

Several parks now offer family-friendly hiking activity packs for sale or loan, complete with field guides, binoculars, games and so on. Washington Park Arboretum has one pack for $8 for two hours; they are also available at Discovery, Carkeek and Magnuson Parks.

Outside the city, hiking opportunities are practically endless in the Olympic Range, the north, central and south Cascades and in the Issaquah Alps. For specific trail information, contact REI (p76), the Mountaineers (p164) or the following groups.

CRITICAL CONDITION

If you've ever been stuck behind them, or looking out the window when they roll past, most of them in wildly colorful costumes, you've probably wondered just what Critical Mass cyclists are all about.

Critical Mass' *raison d'être* could be boiled down to something like this: cycling, fun and provocation, with a purpose. The main agenda is to assert cyclists' right to the road and to promote bicycling as a better alternative to cars (in terms of health, the environment and traffic congestion) – it's hard to argue with that, especially when you're stuck in Seattle gridlock or searching for a parking space.

It's a communal, antiauthoritarian group, so there's no official leadership or bylaws or website – anyone can start a Critical Mass wherever they live, simply by setting a time and a meeting place for the rides and spreading the word. It's easy to find information, goals and manifestos about Critical Mass on the internet.

Seattle's Critical Mass (www.seattlecriticalmass.org) goes on a group ride the last Friday of each month, rain or shine, leaving at 5:30pm from Westlake Center.

BIKE RENTALS

The following places are recommended for bicycle rentals and repairs:

Recycled Cycles (Map p83; ☎ 206-547-4491; 1007 NE Boat St; bike rental per half/full day $20/40; ⏱ 10am-8pm Mon-Fri, 10am-6pm Sat & Sun) In the U District, toward the water at the lower end of the 'Ave,' this place has a friendly, unpretentious vibe – unlike at some other bike shops in town, you'll never get the feeling you're underdressed.

Counterbalance Bicycles (Map p83; ☎ 206-922-3555; www.counterbalancebicycles.com; 2943 NE Blakeley St; bike rental per hr/day $10/30; ⏱ 7:30am-7pm Mon-Fri, 10am-6pm Sat & Sun) Having closed its longstanding Queen Anne location, this shop is now concentrated in the U District, where the Burke-Gilman Trail runs right past its front door. Rentals include Breezer three-speed commuter bikes.

Bob's Bike n Board (Map p83; ☎ 206-524-2642; 3605 NE 45th St; bike rental per hr/day $7/35; ⏱ 11am-7pm Mon & Wed-Fri, 10am-6pm Sat, noon-4pm Sun, closed Tue) This old-school sports shop rents skis, boards and bicycles and all the accompanying accessories.

SIERRA CLUB Map p75

☎ 206-378-0114; cascade.sierraclub.org; 180 Nickerson St, Ste 202

The Cascade chapter of the Sierra Club is a busy and active group. Its extremely diverse offerings range from beachcombing and botany walks at Alki to weekend day-hiking and car-camping trips along the Pacific Crest Trail. Call for a recorded message of future events. Most day trips are free; longer trips may have fees.

WASHINGTON TRAILS ASSOCIATION

☎ 206-625-1367; www.wta.org

This nonprofit group organizes hiking trips, conservation efforts and trail-building jaunts into local mountains.

RUNNING

With its many parks, Seattle provides a number of good trails for runners. If you're in the downtown area, the trails along Myrtle Edwards Park – just north of the Waterfront along Elliott Bay – make for a nice run, affording views over the sound and of the downtown skyline. Green Lake includes two paths, the 2.75-mile paved path immediately surrounding the lake and a less crowded, unpaved path going around the perimeter of the park. The Washington Park Arboretum is another good choice for running, as the trails lead through some beautiful trees and flower gardens. The trails in the arboretum connect to the Lake Washington Blvd trail system, which extends all the way south to Seward Park, just in case you happen to be training for a marathon. Most of the bicycling routes listed earlier also make good routes for running.

Running Clubs

Runners looking to hook up with running mates can contact a number of Seattle's running clubs, most of which offer organized runs that usually turn into social events. Active clubs include the Seattle Frontrunners (☎ 206-322-7769; www.seattlefrontrunners.org) and the West Seattle Runners (☎ 206-938-2416; www.westseattlerunners.org). Also, check sports stores for *Northwest Runners,* a monthly publication which is a good resource for running-related information.

IN-LINE SKATING

Call 'em in-line skaters, rollerbladers or just kickbacks from the disco era, skaters are everywhere in Seattle, wearing everything from Nike's latest trends to groovy pink legwarmers. Seattle's paved paths are perfect except when it rains, which is why you should beware the skating storm on sunny days. Popular skating spots include the Burke-Gilman Trail, around Green Lake, Alki Point, Lake Washington Blvd and the Sammamish River Trail on the Eastside.

ROCK CLIMBING

There's plenty of climbing and mountaineering to be had in the Olympics and the Cascades, but even if your travel plans don't allow time for an excursion to the mountains, you can keep in shape by clambering up the faces at Seattle-area rock walls. If the weather is good, head to Marymoor Park in Redmond (on the Eastside), where there's a 45ft outdoor climbing structure for all levels of climbers.

Otherwise, head for the REI megastore, where a 65ft artificial wall awaits (see p76).

STONE GARDENS: THE CLIMBERS GYM Map p96
☎ 206-781-9828; 2839 NW Market St
This is a full climbing gym with 14,000 sq ft of climbing surface on more than 100 routes. The gym also has weights, lockers and showers. Courses, from beginner climber to anchoring, are also offered. The drop-in rate is $16 ($11 for children).

ULTIMATE FRISBEE
Ultimate Frisbee is popular in the Northwest, and many mixed leagues offer games for players of every level. The Potlatch tournament, held annually in Redmond in July, attracts the West Coast's top players.

DISC NORTHWEST
☎ 206-781-5840; www.discnw.org
Disc Northwest runs summer and winter leagues and is the primary resource for ultimate Frisbee in the Seattle area. Check out the website for a detailed schedule of regular pick-up games, as well as where they're held and how to get there.

TENNIS
Many of Seattle's public parks have tennis courts, and you don't have to wait long to play. Seattle Parks & Recreation (☎ 206-684-4075; www.cityofseattle.net/parks) maintains a number of courts in parks throughout the city; most operate on a first-come, first-served basis. You can play tennis on any of the four courts in Volunteer Park on Capitol Hill; the 10 courts in lower Woodland Park, adjacent to Green Lake; or the four courts in Magnolia Playfield on 34th Ave W and W Smith St. For a full listing of public tennis courts, contact Seattle Parks & Recreation.

AMY YEE TENNIS CENTER off Map p101
☎ 206-684-4764; 2000 Martin Luther King Jr Way; games s/d $25/30
The giant Amy Yee Tennis Center in the Central District has 10 courts indoors and four outside.

GOLF
Seattle Parks & Recreation (☎ 206-684-4075; www.cityofseattle.net/parks) operates three public golf courses in Seattle, along with a short (nine-hole) pitch-and-putt course located at Green Lake (Map p93; ☎ 206-632-2280; 5701 W Green Lake Way N),

a fun spot to go if you're just learning or lack the patience or experience to go a full round. Green fees for city courses are $32 per person on weekdays and $37 on weekends. When they are not booked, the courses also offer reduced rates in the evenings.

JACKSON PARK GOLF COURSE
☎ 206-363-4747; 1000 NE 135th St
The most popular municipal course, Jackson Park is on the far northern edge of Seattle. This 18-hole course is best on weekdays, when there are fewer lines at the first tee.

JEFFERSON PARK GOLF COURSE
Map p106
☎ 206-762-4513; 4101 Beacon Ave S
Another convenient tee-off spot, Jefferson Park is an 18-hole course with short fairways and lots of lovely mature (but sometimes troublesome) trees and bushes.

WEST SEATTLE MUNICIPAL GOLF COURSE Map p103
☎ 206-935-5187; 4470 35th Ave SW
With 18 holes and superior views across Elliott Bay, this is one of the area's best public courses.

SWIMMING
When summer temperatures rise, there's no more popular place to be than on one of Seattle's beaches. One of the most popular is Alki Beach (p104) in West Seattle, a real scene with beach volleyball, acres of flesh and teenagers cruising in their cars. Green Lake Park (p93) has two lakefront swimming and sunbathing beaches, as do several parks along the western shores of Lake Washington, including Madison Park (Map p101), Madrona Park (p102), Seward Park, Magnuson Park and Mt Baker Park. Lifeguards are on duty at public beaches between 11am and 8pm mid-June to Labor Day (beginning of September).

Swimming is a great way to keep in shape. Many pools host swim clubs or masters programs. The following are public pools that offer a variety of open swim sessions, lessons and lap swimming. Drop-in fees are about $3. For information on other pools, contact Seattle Parks & Recreation (☎ 206-684-4075; www.cityofseattle.net/parks).

Evans Pool at Green Lake (Map p93; ☎ 206-684-4961; 7201 E Green Lake Drive N)

Medgar Evers Aquatic Center (Map p101; ☎ 206-684-4766; 500 23rd Ave)

Queen Anne Pool (Map p75; ☎ 206-386-4282; 1920 1st Ave W)

HEALTH & FITNESS

Most of Seattle's large hotels have workout facilities available to guests. But if you're looking for more expansive facilities, including group classes and personal trainers, try one of the gyms listed below. Seattle also has plenty of yoga studios, several of which are included here. And for a real treat, try one of the city's posh day spas.

GYMS

24-HOUR FITNESS Map p50
☎ 206-624-0651; 1827 Yale Ave; initial fee about $150, monthly dues $35; ⏰ 24hr
Downtown, it has an indoor pool, spa, sauna and steam room, child care, classes and

tanning, plus the usual weights and cardio equipment. Ask about specials or check online before you go; free 10-day passes are often available, and you can usually get around the initiation fee if you time it right.

DOWNTOWN SEATTLE YMCA Map p50
☎ 206-382-5010; 909 4th Ave; day pass $10-15; ⏰ 5am-9pm Mon-Fri, 7am-6:30pm Sat, 11am-6:30pm Sun
The Y is notably traveler-friendly, and this location has clean, classy, updated equipment including a pool, free weights, cardio equipment and child care.

GOLD'S GYM Map p50
☎ 206-583-0640; 825 Pike St; day pass $10-15; ⏰ 5:30am-10pm Mon-Fri, 8am-8pm Sat & Sun
The downtown Seattle branch of this chain has first-rate facilities for cardio and

---

SKI SEATTLE

The variety of terrain in Washington ski areas is such that just about any level of skier or snowboarder can find a good fit. As a plus, most of the resorts here aren't all that 'resorty'. Several of them are in parklands, meaning development can't get out of control, so they have an understated feel – the opposite of Hollywood-friendly places like Aspen, for example. Washington resorts are also notably friendly toward snowboarders and – at the opposite end of the spectrum – backcountry Nordic skiers.

Daily adult lift-ticket prices range from about $45 to $60 or more. Hours of operation and ticket prices vary according to the point in the season and snow and weather conditions; check the appropriate websites or call for updated information.

Crystal (☎ 360-663-2265; www.skicrystal.com; 33914 Crystal Mountain Blvd, Hwy 410) Just off the eastern flank of Mt Rainier National Park, this majestic ski area offers unparalleled views of Mt Rainier, Washington's highest mountain, and some of the best skiing on the West Coast. Located 80 miles from Seattle, Crystal is the largest of the ski areas with the most accessible peak skiing, a solid variety of terrain and a reputation for powder. It is consistently rated by ski magazines as a top North American ski destination.

Mt Baker (☎ 360-734-6771; www.mtbaker.us; east of Bellingham on Hwy 542) Not technically on its namesake, Baker is located on the adjacent Shuksan Arm. It blows the mind with an average annual snowfall of 647in and holds the unofficial world record for seasonal snowfall at an established ski area (1140in during the 1998–99 season). Rightly famous for powder, expert runs and backcountry, Baker is also home to the Legendary Banked Slalom every February. The Slalom started in 1985 and was the first organized snowboarding competition in the world. Baker is about three hours' drive from Seattle, but is worth the longer trip.

Stevens Pass (☎ 206-812-4510; www.stevenspass.com; Summit Stevens Pass, US Hwy 2) Stevens Pass is some 80 miles east, and slightly north, of Seattle. It is known for its surprising variety of terrain with everything on offer from glades to bowls to bumps to an elaborate terrain park. Throw in a huge lift-accessible 'backside' area that gives a backcountry experience without the danger or extra effort and you can't go wrong. Stevens is also good for families and groups that vary in skill level but want something more challenging than the Summit West or Central.

The Summit at Snoqualmie (☎ 425-434-7669; www.summitatsnoqualmie.com; 1001 State Route 906, Snoqualmie Pass) The Summit is a network of four ski areas that lie 50 minutes due east of downtown Seattle on Interstate 90. Alpental is a smaller mountain best for advanced and expert skiers; it is known for its steeps, extensive backcountry and limited but challenging tree skiing. Summit West is the main area of the Summit; it's for beginners and families and has gear rentals and the most developed lodge and dining facilities. It is possible to ski from Summit West over to Summit Central, which is for beginners and intermediates and is home to the Summit's largest terrain park. Summit East is the smallest of the areas and is good for intermediates. It's the location of the Nordic ski center.

SPORTS & ACTIVITIES HEALTH & FITNESS

strength training, plus classes in aerobics, yoga, Pilates, dance, kickboxing and karate. Massage, personal training, a sauna and a women-only section are also available.

SOUND MIND & BODY Map p87

☎ 206-547-3470; 437 N 34th St; ⏱ 5:30am-10pm Mon-Thu, to 9pm Fri, 8am-7pm Sat, 9am-7pm Sun

You'll find this Fremont gym vast but quiet. It has close to 40,000 sq ft of weight training and cardio equipment, plus basketball and volleyball courts, a sauna and a steam room. There are also group classes in yoga, Pilates and kickboxing, as well as a ski-conditioning class. Most unusual is that there's hardly a blaring TV or stereo to be found (viewers must wear headphones while working out).

YOGA

8 LIMBS YOGA CENTER Map p79

☎ 206-523-9722; 500 E Pike St; classes $8-15; ⏱ 6:30am-8:30pm

This Capitol Hill yoga studio emphasizes a supportive, noncompetitive environment and integrating yoga with the rest of life.

YOGA TREE Map p87

☎ 206-545-0316; www.yogatree.com; 4250 Fremont Ave N; 2hr intro class $25

This calm yoga studio in Fremont comes highly recommended. A set of four

introductory classes ($60) is specifically geared toward beginners, but all levels of classes are available. Check the website for the latest schedule.

DAY SPAS

SPA BLIX Map p77

☎ 206-274-5681; 213 Yale Ave N, Alley 24; ⏱ 9am-7pm Mon-Sat, 10am-7pm Sun

Get pampered with a manicure, pedicure, seaweed face wrap, haircut and a full-body exfoliation at this South Lake Union day spa. Feel good that charities receive 10% of its monthly profits.

SPA DEL LAGO Map p101

☎ 206-322-5246; 1929 43rd Ave E, Ste 100; ⏱ 11am-5pm Mon, 9am-8pm Tue-Thu, 9am-6pm Fri, 9am-4pm Sat, 10am-5pm Sun

A salon up front with private rooms in the back for facials and massages, this cute place is right by the water in Madison Park.

SPA NOIR Map p68

☎ 206-448-7600; 2231 2nd Ave; ⏱ 10am-10pm Tue, Thu & Fri, noon-10pm Wed, 10am-8:30pm Sat, noon-5pm Sun

Looking more like a chic cocktail lounge than a spa, with its deep red walls and heavy velvet curtains, this place caters to the funkier Belltown set. The last Tuesday of the month is bargain day.

lonely planet Hotels & Hostels

Want more sleeping recommendations than we could ever pack into this little ol' book? Craving more detail – including extended reviews and photographs? Want to read reviews by other travellers and be able to post your own? Just make your way over to **lonelyplanet.com/hotels** and check out our thorough list of independent reviews, then reserve your room simply and securely.

SLEEPING

top picks

- **Moore Hotel** (p176)
- **College Inn** (p182)
- **Edgewater** (p177)
- **Ace Hotel** (p179)
- **Sorrento Hotel** (p175)

As in many large cities, sleeping options are plentiful and varied in Seattle. Want to drive up to a motor inn and park your beater where you can see it through the window from your mauve-and-blue synthetic-covered bed? You can do that. Rather slink up in a limo and look down your nose as a bellhop lugs your bags to the penthouse suite? You can do that too, as well as pretty much everything in between.

The rates listed in the price guide below are what you can expect to pay in peak season – generally May through August. Be aware, though, that prices can vary wildly depending on day of the week and whether there are festivals or events going on in town. Seattle hotel rooms are also subject to a room tax of 15.6% (less for most B&Bs and historical properties) that will be tacked on to the final bill. The rates listed here don't include tax.

Essentially all downtown hotels charge extra for parking, if they have it. It's been said half the population of Portland, Oregon, consists of people who couldn't find a place to park in Seattle and, searching in ever-widening circles, eventually wound up in Portland, where they stayed. Many hotels downtown don't offer parking but can direct you to paid lots nearby. Our reviews note whether parking is available; usual rates start around $20 a night. If there's no Ⓟ icon in the review, you're on your own. Look for street meters and paid parking garages downtown, or off-street parking elsewhere.

Many hotels charge extra for high-speed wireless internet service, usually $9 to $15 a day, but most also have a computer available in the lobby for guests to use free of charge.

Booking ahead is wise at any time of year but essential during summer (June to August) and around the more popular festival times (see Festivals, p16).

Check-out times vary but are usually 11am or noon, and check-in usually starts between 2pm and 4pm. Most places are flexible if notified ahead of time; definitely call ahead if you're going to arrive late.

Washington state has passed a law banning smoking in public buildings, but hotels are exempt from this; therefore, in the reviews below, the nonsmoking icon (Ⓧ) means a hotel is 100% nonsmoking. Every hotel listed offers at least some nonsmoking rooms.

Many downtown hotels participate in Seattle Super Saver Packages (☎ 800-535-7071; www.seattlesupersaver.com), a program run by the Convention & Visitors Bureau. Room prices are generally 50% off the rack rates from November through March, with substantial discounts all year, and they come with a coupon book that offers savings on dining, shopping and attractions.

The Seattle B&B Association (☎ 206-547-1020, 800-348-5630; www.lodginginseattle.com) has a searchable list of affiliated B&Bs. You can also visit Lonely Planet Hotels & Hostels (hotels.lonelyplanet.com) to book Lonely Planet author-reviewed rooms.

Unless otherwise indicated, prices in this chapter are for a double room, not including tax or extra fees such as parking, breakfast or internet access. Reviews are divided by neighborhood and listed in order of price, from highest to lowest, based on the cheapest room normally available in high season (May to August).

DOWNTOWN & FIRST HILL

Some of the city's coolest, most characterful hotels are downtown, and getting from here to any other part of the city on foot or by public transport is a cinch. If you have a car, things get more complicated: driving the nest of hilly one-way streets is maddening, and you'll need to factor parking fees in to the cost of accommodations. Most of the following hotels offer some kind of parking program with in-and-out privileges, usually starting at $20 a day.

FAIRMONT OLYMPIC HOTEL
Map p50   Hotel $$$
☎ 206-621-1700; www.fairmont.com/seattle; 411 University St; r from $349; Ⓟ Ⓧ 🖥 💻 🍽 ♿ 🛗
Built in 1924, the Fairmont Olympic is listed with the National Register of Historic Places, so it's not too surprising that it feels like a museum of old money. Over the years, remodels to the bathrooms and the

PRICE GUIDE

Prices indicated are for a standard double room in high season.

$$$	more than $200 a night
$$	$101-200 a night
$	under $100 a night

main lobby have kept the place functional without destroying the period glamour of its architecture. With 450 rooms and every imaginable service, this place is certainly a splurge, but it's worth exploring even if you don't stay here – have an oyster at Shuckers, the oak-paneled hotel bar. The palpable decadence of the place has been balanced out lately by earth-friendly policies such as free parking for hybrid cars.

SEATTLE RENAISSANCE HOTEL

Map p50   Hotel $$$

☎ 206-583-0300, 800-468-3571; 515 Madison St; r from $330; **P ✕ ⋈ 🖵 🖵**

With a calming green-and-brown color scheme, this gigantic, 553-room tower (part of the Marriott chain) is one of the city's nicest hotels. Rooms are large, all have views and windows that open, and pets are welcome (nominal fee). Other features include an indoor pool, two restaurants, a bar-lounge, a beauty shop and a spa.

SORRENTO HOTEL Map p50   Hotel $$$

☎ 206-622-6400, 800-426-1265; www.hotel sorrento.com; 900 Madison St; d from $269; **P ✕ ⋈ 🖵**

William Howard Taft, 27th US president, was the first registered guest at the Sorrento, an imposing Italianate hotel known since its birth in 1909 as the jewel of Seattle. The combination of luxurious appointments, over-the-top service and a pervasive sense of class add up to a perfect blend of decadence and restraint. The hotel's award-winning restaurant, the Hunt Club, is worth a stop whether you're staying here or not. Continental breakfast ($11) and a shuttle to the airport ($65) are among the extras on offer.

HOTEL MONACO SEATTLE

Map p50   Hotel $$$

☎ 206-621-1770, 800-945-2240; www.monaco -seattle.com; 1101 4th Ave; r from $259; **P ✕ ⋈ 🖵 🖵**

The hip, gay-friendly Hotel Monaco is housed in the old Seattle Phone Building, which sat vacant before the Kimpton group from San Francisco took it over and converted it. The suite-style rooms have stripy wallpaper and heavy curtains; a friend described it as 'like sleeping inside of a clown.' Leopard-print bathrobes are part of the deal. If you're lonely for your pet, you can borrow a goldfish for the length of your stay. The hotel's restaurant, Sazerac, is a popular New Orleans-style joint with a following of its own. It's certified to the Green Seal Environmental Standard on energy efficiency and waste and water minimization.

HOTEL VINTAGE PARK Map p50   Hotel $$$

☎ 206-624-8000, 800-624-4433; www.hotel vintagepark.com; 1100 5th Ave; r from $259; **P ✕ ⋈ 🖵 🖵**

The rooms at this award-winning, gay-friendly hotel are a little smaller than at some other downtown hotels and they get a bit of street noise, but it's a pleasant place to stay, especially if you get a west-facing room. The theme is wine: rooms are named after Washington vineyards and wineries, and there's wine tasting in the lobby every afternoon.

WESTIN HOTEL SEATTLE

Map p50   Hotel $$$

☎ 206-728-1000, 800-228-3000; 1900 5th Ave; r from $229; **P ✕ ⋈ 🖵 🖵 🖵**

This impossible-to-miss, two-cylinder luxury business hotel has almost 900 rooms, some of which contain Jacuzzis, CD players or a range of workout equipment. There's a heated pool, an exercise room, a gift shop, internet access (free in the lobby, for a fee in guest rooms) and a business center – not to mention great views and a popular restaurant.

HOTEL MAX Map p50   Hotel $$

☎ 206-441-4200, 800-426-0670; www.hotelmax seattle.com; 620 Stewart St; r from $189; **P ⋈ 🖵**

There's something mildly obnoxious about a place (or a person) that describes *itself* as hip and artistic, but in the case of Hotel Max, the description fits. Original artworks by local and national artists hang in the (small but cool) guest rooms and public areas of the hotel, and it's tough to get any hipper than the place's supersaturated color scheme – not to mention locally relevant package deals like the Grunge Special or the Gaycation. Rooms include not only a pillow menu, but also one for spirituality. Best of all: for $50,000 or so, you can buy your entire hotel room and have it delivered to your home.

PARAMOUNT HOTEL Map p50 Hotel $$
☎ 206-292-9500, 800-426-0670; www.paramount hotelseattle.com; 724 Pine St; r from $179, ste from $450; P X X L
The Paramount has 146 large rooms that, like the lobby areas, are furnished with heavy antiques perhaps meant to give the relatively new hotel an old-world feel. The downstairs restaurant-bar, Dragonfish, has a 'sushi happy hour' and is a convenient place to meet for a drink before hitting the town.

MAYFLOWER PARK HOTEL
Map p50 Hotel $$
☎ 206-623-8700, 800-426-5100; www.mayflower park.com; 405 Olive Way; r from $179; P X X L
If you're coming to Seattle to shop, this is the hotel for you. Attached by indoor walkway to the Westlake Center, it's also handy for taking the monorail out to Seattle Center for an event. The lobby bar is a nice hideaway for a drink. High-speed internet access is free throughout the hotel.

EXECUTIVE HOTEL PACIFIC
Map p50 Hotel $$
☎ 206-623-3900, 800-426-1165; www.pacificplaza hotel.com; 400 Spring St; r from $159; P X X L
This reliable but not flashy hotel, located next-door to the Seattle public library, is starting to show some wear, but the location makes it a good deal nonetheless. Rooms are fairly small but functional, with free high-speed internet, voice mail and data ports, in-room coffee and tea, and windows that open. Small dogs are welcome.

INN AT VIRGINIA MASON
Map p50 Hotel $$
☎ 206-583-6453, 800-283-6453; www.innat virginiamason.com; 1006 Spring St, First Hill; r from $111; P X
On First Hill, just above the downtown area near a complex of hospitals, this nicely

top picks
PET-FRIENDLY HOTELS
- **Sorrento Hotel** (p175) Your pet gets the same classy treatment you do.
- **Alexis Hotel** (opposite) They'll offer to walk your dog for you.
- **Hotel Monaco Seattle** (p175) If you bring a dog, she gets to wear a monogrammed dog jacket; if you don't, you can borrow a goldfish from the front desk.
- **Hotel Vintage Park** (p175) Pooch gets his own dog tags, plus doggie treats during afternoon wine tastings.

maintained older hotel caters to families needing to stay near the medical facilities. It also offers a number of basic rooms for other visitors and has a nice rooftop garden with a view from First Hill overlooking the rest of the city. There are discounts if you are staying at the hotel for family medical reasons.

MOORE HOTEL Map p50 Hotel $
☎ 206-448-4851, 800-421-5508; 1926 2nd Ave; s/d $59/71, with private bathroom s/d $74/86, ste from $117; X L
An excellent value for its location, the once grand Moore Hotel offers 120 rooms of varying sizes and configurations, including some suites set up for business travelers and families. The building is no longer fancy but has been refurbished with an understated elegance. The early-20th-century lobby, with its molded ceiling and marble accoutrements, speaks of the Moore's long history, which is echoed in the better rooms (ask for one with a view of the Sound). Wireless internet service is free but unreliable; it works best in the lobby. Children under age 10 stay free.

PIONEER SQUARE
There aren't tons of sleeping options in this neighborhood, but we've found a couple of good choices that put you right in the heart of the action, be it sports, nightlife or old-Seattle history.

HOTEL 1000 Map p56 Hotel $$$
☎ 206-957-1000; www.hotel1000seattle.com; 1000 1st Ave; r from $289, water view from $350; P X X L

If you love the clean lines and simple elegance of IKEA, but you happen to have just won the lottery, you might design a hotel like this. Leather-clad egg chairs cuddle around a concrete-and-steel tube fireplace in the lounge; rooms have bedside tables made of chrome and wood; bathrooms have granite counters and freestanding tubs that fill from the ceiling; beds are curtained off in luxurious earth-toned textiles. Each room has art reflecting guests' taste (you tell them what kind of art you like when you book or check in and they adjust the art in the room) and a 40in HDTV with surround sound. Some have a private bar, and some are pet-friendly. There is also virtual golf.

SILVER CLOUD HOTEL Map p56   Hotel $$$
☎ 206-204-9800; 1046 1st Ave S; r from $249;
🅿 ⊠ 🕸 🖵 🖳 ♿

Sports fans are in luck – this relatively new hotel is smack in the middle of the action, across the street from Safeco Field and next to Qwest Field. Rooms are spacious and modern, with a refrigerator and microwave in the room, an iPod dock on the alarm clock, and Aveda bath products. A free shuttle service takes guests practically anywhere within two miles. And in warm weather you can splash around in the rooftop pool.

ALEXIS HOTEL Map p56   Hotel $$$
☎ 206-624-4844, 888-850-1155; www.alexishotel.com; 1007 1st Ave; r/ste from $249/284;
🅿 ⊠ 🕸 🖵 ♿

Each of the 109 rooms in this gay-friendly Kimpton hotel is decorated with original artwork. Some suites include fireplaces and jetted tubs. Ask about the 'Miles Davis Suite,' which contains art, biographies and CDs by the jazz legend. There's wine tasting in the lobby each evening. Even your dog gets distilled water in its bowl on arrival, along with a complimentary doggie bed and the canine equivalent of a pillow mint. The attached Library Bistro and Bookstore Bar are cozy nooks. You can also get room-service facials from the nearby Aveda spa.

BEST WESTERN PIONEER SQUARE HOTEL Map p56   Hotel $$
☎ 206-340-1234, 800-800-5514; 77 Yesler Way; r from $159; 🅿 ⊠ 🖵 ♿

Rooms and common areas at this historical hotel feature period decor and a comfortable atmosphere. The only hotel in the historical heart of Seattle, it can't be beaten for location – as long as you don't mind some of the saltier characters who populate the square in the off hours. Nightlife, restaurants and shopping are just steps from the door.

PIKE PLACE MARKET & WATERFRONT

The Waterfront and Pike Place Market areas are prime real estate, and hotels here consequently tend to be on the expensive side, but you can't beat the location – or the views. And a popular hostel provides a good budget option.

EDGEWATER Map p63   Hotel $$$
☎ 206-728-7000, 800-624-0670; www.edgewaterhotel.com; 2411 Alaskan Way, Pier 67; r with city/water views from $289/349; 🅿 ⊠ 🕸 🖵 ♿

Perched over the water in Elliott Bay, the Edgewater is one of the few places that lives up to its storied past. The timber-lodge theme, with its rock fireplaces and rough-hewn pine furniture, is pure Pacific Northwest, but a seriously classed-up version thereof. Half of the 223 rooms have bay views and the rest overlook the Seattle skyline; many contain gas fireplaces. OK, so you can't fish out of the windows anymore, but that's probably just about the only wish this place won't fulfill.

INN AT THE MARKET Map p63   Hotel $$$
☎ 206-443-3600, 800-446-4484; www.innatthemarket.com; 86 Pine St; r without/with water views from $255/370; 🅿 ⊠ 🕸 🖵

Right in the thick of things, the Inn at the Market is an elegant and architecturally interesting hotel and the only lodging in the venerable Pike Place Market. This 70-room boutique hotel has large rooms, many of which enjoy grand views onto market activity and Puget Sound. Its two restaurants, Campagne (p125) and Café Campagne (p126), are renowned for their excellent French cuisine.

PENSIONE NICHOLS Map p63   B&B $$
☎ 206-441-7125; www.pensionenichols.com; 1923 1st Ave; s/d/ste $110/140/255; 🖵

In a town with few cheap hotels and hardly any B&Bs right downtown, Pensione Nichols is a treat. Right in the urban thick of things between Pike Place Market and Belltown, this charmingly remodeled European-style pensione has 10 rooms that share four retro-cool bathrooms, two large suites and a spacious common area that overlooks the market. Rooms come with a complete and tasty breakfast. Parking is in a nearby garage.

GREEN TORTOISE HOSTEL
Map p63   Hostel $
☎ 206-340-1222; www.greentortoise.net; 105 Pike St; 8-/6-/4-bed dm $28/30/32; 🖳
This hostel is one of the few budget options in the city and has an unbeatable location right across the street from Pike Place Market. Once pretty crusty, the place has moved to the Elliot Hotel Building and now offers 30 bunk rooms and 16 European-style rooms (shared bath and shower). Free breakfast includes waffles and eggs. The hostel offers a free dinner three nights a week and there are weekly events such as open-mic nights.

BELLTOWN

Some of the city's best budget- and hipster-friendly accommodations can be found in Belltown, which is handy when you're finished with your pub crawl and need to make your way back to your room for the night. This area is also an easy walk from downtown, Pike Place Market and the Seattle Center. It can get a little loud at night, though, so light sleepers beware.

HOTEL ÄNDRA Map p68   Hotel $$$
☎ 206-448-8600, 877-448-8600; hotelandra .com; 2000 4th Ave; r/ste from $229/279; P X X 🖳 &
Wild fabric patterns and vivid colors combine with sleek Scandinavian-influenced design to give this hotel (formerly the Claremont) a calming yet sharply modern feel. Its 119 rooms have a sense of luxury without being claustrophobically overfurnished with the usual trappings of decadence. The trappings here, in fact, are quite unusual: alpaca headboards, anyone? There are blue-glass wall sconces, brushed-steel fixtures, gigantic walnut work desks – even the fitness room has spartan prints and

flat-screen TVs on the walls. Some of the suites have plasma-screen TVs. Bathroom toiletries come from Face Stockholm. The hotel is attached to chef Tom Douglas' Greek-via-Northwest restaurant, Lola.

INN AT EL GAUCHO Map p68   Hotel $$
☎ 206-728-1133, 866-354-2824; inn.elgaucho .com; 2505 1st Ave; ste from $153; P X X 🖳
In 18 suites decorated '50s-style, above the type of anachronistic steakhouse that harks back to the good ol' days when vegetarians were eaten by the wealthy as snacks between meals, the Inn at El Gaucho offers a particularly outsized, swaggering American luxury. Plasma-screen TVs, Bose stereo systems, 'Rain System' showers and buttery leather couches grace all the suites. And if it's too much to leave for even a moment, El Gaucho restaurant will serve you steak in bed.

LOYAL INN BEST WESTERN
Map p68   Hotel $$
☎ 206-682-0200; www.bestwestern.com/prop _48062; 2301 8th Ave; r from $149; P X X 🖳
More plush than other similarly priced options in the area, this chain hotel is in a convenient location for both Seattle Center and Belltown, and has a Jacuzzi and sauna, a small exercise room and free continental breakfast. Beds are enormous and rooms are relatively spacious; some include mini-refrigerators and microwaves. Self-parking is a reasonable $10 a night.

RAMADA INN DOWNTOWN
Map p68   Hotel $$
☎ 206-441-9785, 800-272-6232; 2200 5th Ave; r from $149; P X X 🖳 &
This conveniently located hotel is close to Belltown, downtown and Seattle Center, and parking is comparatively cheap ($12). It's also within the Ride Free Area for buses, although most of this area is within easy walking distance. Some of the rooms have views of the Space Needle or downtown, and all have the basic amenities such as in-room coffee and cable TV.

SIXTH AVENUE INN Map p68   Motel $$
☎ 206-441-8300, 800-627-8290; www.sixth avenueinn.com; 2000 6th Ave; r from $129; P X X 🖳
Situated just a five-minute walk north of the downtown shopping frenzy, this motor

inn possesses an old-fashioned glamour, mostly thanks to its clubby, low-lit bar and lounge area, full of big comfy chairs and a fireplace. Spacious rooms feature vehemently '80s-style brass beds and square lamps – if unironic retro is your thing, you're in luck. There's room service and a fitness room, and free wi-fi is available in the lobby and the lounge.

ACE HOTEL Map p68 Hotel $

☎ 206-448-4721; www.acehotel.com; 2423 1st Ave; r without/with bathroom $99/195; P 💻
Each of the Ace's 28 hospital-tidy rooms is unique and so stylish you quickly get the feeling you're the star of an art film. Ranging from European style with shared bathrooms to deluxe versions with private bathrooms, CD players and enough mirrors to make you paranoid, the rooms are stocked with condoms and (where your average Mid-western motor inn would place the Gideon Bible) a copy of the *Kama Sutra*. Obviously this isn't the place for the uptight – it's also bad for light sleepers, as the always-hopping Cyclops bar and restaurant is just downstairs. Barflies and night owls have it made.

CITY HOSTEL SEATTLE Map p68 Hostel $

☎ 206-706-3255, 1-877-846-7835; www.cityhostel seattle.com; 2327 2nd Ave; dm $35-38, r without/with bathroom $79/99 incl tax; 💻
This fun, friendly hostel is a great budget option right in the midst of Belltown. It's an 'art hostel,' which means work by local and regional artists decorates every available surface in dorm rooms and common areas, and the hostel is part of the Belltown 2nd Friday Art Walk. The owners' welcome speech conveys their irrepressible enthusiasm for what they do. The place is spotless, down to the tile floors in the large bathrooms. There are three guest kitchens, a nice outdoor garden, a fastidiously maintained hot tub and a 20-seat theater where guests can watch free DVDs. Breakfast and bedding are included in the nightly rate.

SEATTLE CENTER & QUEEN ANNE

Staying around Seattle Center makes sense for a number of reasons: it's only five minutes from downtown on the monorail or bus (and just slightly more to walk), and room prices are often lower than those downtown (except when big concerts or festivals are on). Parking fees at most hotels are usually much lower here than downtown, and that's no small matter – it'll save you the cost of a nice dinner out.

Most of the hotels around here are fairly anonymous, motor-court type lodgings from the 1960s, and many of them cater to business travelers – so they're efficient and have all the amenities you might need, if not a lot of character.

Immediately to the west of Seattle Center is Lower Queen Anne. It's a five-minute walk from here to the opera house or Key Arena and a 10-minute walk to reach the Space Needle.

MARQUEEN HOTEL Map p75 Hotel $$

☎ 206-282-7407, 888-445-3076; 600 Queen Anne Ave N; r from $175; P 🞨 🞨 💻
A classic old-school apartment building (built in 1918), the MarQueen has hardwood floors throughout and a variety of rooms, all with kitchenettes leftover from their days as apartments. The neighborhood is an under-visited gem, handy to various attractions. If hill walking isn't your thing, there is a courtesy van to take you to nearby sights. Children 17 and under stay free with a parent. Note that there are no elevators in this three-story building.

HAMPTON INN Map p75 Hotel $$

☎ 206-282-7700; 700 5th Ave N; r from $159; P 🞨 💻 ♿ 🞨
A couple of blocks north of Seattle Center, the Hampton Inn has 198 rooms, most of which have balconies. There's a wide variety of rooms, from standards to two-bedroom suites with fireplaces, and a cooked breakfast is included.

BEST WESTERN EXECUTIVE INN
Map p72 Hotel $$

☎ 206-448-9444, 800-351-9444; 200 Taylor Ave N; r from $144; P 🞨 🞨 💻
In the shadow of the Space Needle, the Executive Inn has a terrifying, almost brutalist facade, but is perfectly decent inside. Pillow-top beds, in-room coffee and tea, microwaves and refrigerators, room service, a fitness room and a sports lounge are available, and there's a complimentary shuttle to downtown.

TRAVELODGE BY THE SPACE NEEDLE
Map p72   Hotel $$

☎ 206-441-7878, 800-578-7878; 200 6th Ave N; r from $140; P ⊠ ⊠ ▣ ▣

It looks a bit grim from the outside, but rooms in this motor lodge are larger and nicer than you'd find in some of the pricier downtown hotels, and equally convenient. There's a seasonal, outdoor pool and a year-round Jacuzzi, exercise room, in-room coffee or tea and a free continental breakfast.

INN AT QUEEN ANNE Map p75   Hotel $$

☎ 206-282-7357, 800-952-5043; www.innatqueen anne.com; 505 1st Ave N; r from $109; P ⊠ ⊠ ▣

The Inn at Queen Anne is a 1929 apartment building-turned-hotel in a cool neighborhood. Its 68 rooms come with kitchenettes, complimentary internet access and a free continental breakfast. Weekly and monthly rates are available. Note there are no elevators in this three-story building.

LAKE UNION

The shores of Lake Union hold several convenient, business-oriented hotels with easy driving access to the rest of the city and some killer views across the water.

MARRIOTT RESIDENCE INN
Map p77   Hotel $$$

☎ 206-624-6000, 800-331-3131; 800 Fairview Ave N; ste from $229; P ⊠ ⊠ ▣ ▣

A convenient place to settle in for a lengthier stay, the Residence Inn has work-friendly studio suites and family-size two-room suites, all with kitchens. There's a lap pool, exercise room and spa, free breakfast

and evening desserts in the lobby. Rooms on the west side of the hotel have good views of Lake Union – rates vary depending on whether you get a view or not.

COURTYARD MARRIOTT Map p77   Hotel $$

☎ 206-213-0100, 800-321-2211; 925 Westlake Ave N; r from $189; P ⊠ ⊠ ▣ ▣ ▣

Over on the southwest side of Lake Union, the Courtyard Marriott has all the big hotel amenities you'd expect, including an indoor pool and a restaurant. It's set up to suit the business traveler, but is comfy enough to justify not getting any work done. There's a small convenience store on-site for impromptu snacks.

SILVER CLOUD INN LAKE UNION
Map p77   Hotel $$

☎ 206-447-9500, 800-330-5812; 1150 Fairview Ave N; r/ste from $188/243; P ⊠ ⊠ ▣ ▣ ▣

This hotel has 184 rooms, some of which have stunning views of Lake Union. There's also a gym, indoor and outdoor pools, laundry facilities and complimentary breakfast, plus a free shuttle service to downtown and free parking – both very handy in this area. On Tuesday evenings the hotel hosts a regional beer and wine tasting.

CAPITOL HILL & VOLUNTEER PARK

Beyond its nightlife-oriented main drags, Capitol Hill is full of beautiful, well-maintained homes on quiet, tree-lined residential streets. Luckily for the traveler, many of them have been converted into plush B&Bs. These are friendly, welcoming places where you can

---

GREEN HOTELS

Nearly all hotels these days have little notes placed on the bed and in the bathroom advising guests that, in an effort to conserve water and energy, sheets and towels will not be washed every day unless requested. But some hotels in Seattle go beyond these basics. The city's three Kimpton hotels – the Alexis Hotel (p177), the Hotel Monaco Seattle (p175) and the Hotel Vintage Park (p175) – all benefit from the chain's EarthCare program, which emphasizes sustainable, ecofriendly practices without sacrificing luxury. These include recycling, using soy ink and recycled paper, serving organic or fair-trade coffee in the lobby, and using environmentally friendly cleaning products. The luxurious Fairmont Olympic (p174) has added ecofriendly policies as well, such as free parking for hybrid cars, compact fluorescent light bulbs, recycling containers in rooms, and composting facilities. The Edgewater (p177) has received a 2 Green Eco-Leaf Rating (or 'good') from the organization iStayGreen.org, for things like water-saving shower fixtures, composting and compact-fluorescent bulbs. The Courtyard Marriott (above) in Lake Union participates in the Energy Star for Hospitality program, which rewards hotels for reducing energy use and greenhouse gas emissions.

start your day with a giant breakfast, hear a local's advice on what to see and usually park free of charge on the street. (Note, however, that parking becomes much more difficult on weekend evenings as you approach Broadway and the Pike–Pine Corridor.)

SALISBURY HOUSE B&B Map p79 B&B $$
☎ 206-328-8682; www.salisburyhouse.com; 750 16th Ave E; r $125-195; ✗ ▣
Salisbury House, in a quiet, tree-lined neighborhood near Volunteer Park, is a 1904 home with four elegant corner rooms and one suite, all equipped with private bathrooms, phone with voice mail, and wireless internet access. It's comfortably modern, not the floral overload of a typical B&B. The full breakfast is vegetarian and served family-style. Downstairs there's a library with a fireplace. Children over 12 are welcome.

HILL HOUSE B&B Map p79 B&B $
☎ 206-720-7161, 800-720-7161; www.seattlehill house.com; 1113 E John St; r $99-199; ℗ ✗ ▣
Close to the hub of Capitol Hill, the guestrooms in this pair of 1903 homes feature queen beds, down comforters, fluffy robes and a range of moods from over-the-top lacy to English gentleman – the eclectic decorating style might not suit everyone's taste, but the place is certainly homey. Some rooms have private bathrooms, and two are large suites with garden and patio access.

BACON MANSION B&B Map p79 B&B $
☎ 206-329-1864, 800-240-1864; www.bacon mansion.com; 959 Broadway E; r $99-179, Capitol Suite $159-234; ☒ ▣
A 1909 Tudor mansion whose imposing exterior belies the quirky charm of its friendly hosts, this four-level B&B on a quiet residential street just past the Capitol Hill action has a grand piano in the main room that guests are invited to play. The 11 rooms come in a variety of configurations, including a carriage house that's wheelchair-accessible, and include TV and voice mail. One large suite has a view of the Space Needle, one has a fireplace, and another has an Italian fountain as a backdrop.

GASLIGHT INN B&B Map p79 B&B $$
☎ 206-325-3654; www.gaslight-inn.com; 1727 15th Ave; s $98-128, d $118-168; ✗ ▣ ▣

lonelyplanet.com

AIRPORT HOTELS

If you're flying in to Sea-Tac late at night or out early in the morning, you might want to stay near the airport for the sake of convenience. The following hotels all offer complimentary airport shuttles and do a good job of getting you to and from the airport on time.

Days Inn at Sea-Tac Airport (☎ 206-244-3600, 800-325-2525; 19015 International Blvd S; r from $90; ℗ ▣ ☒) Some of the 86 rooms at this hotel have Jacuzzis and some have kitchenettes. There's also a small gym, free continental breakfast and a 24-hour airport shuttle.

Radisson Hotel Gateway Seattle-Tacoma Airport (☎ 206-244-6000, 800-333-3333; 17001 Pacific Hwy S; r from $119; ℗ ☒ ▣ ☒) One of the fancier options around here, the Radisson has 204 rooms, a restaurant, lounge, pool, gym and sauna. The free 24-hour airport shuttle will also take you to nearby restaurants or car-rental agencies.

In two neighboring homes, the Gaslight Inn has 15 rooms available, 12 of which have private bathrooms. In summer, it's refreshing to dive into the outdoor pool or just hang out on the sun deck. No pets: the B&B already has a cat and a dog.

U DISTRICT

This area is another good place to find good-value rates at hotels and B&Bs. Accommodations here are also more likely to include free parking, as real estate is less limited than it is downtown.

WATERTOWN Map p83 Hotel $$
☎ 206-826-4242, 866-944-4242; www.watertown seattle.com; 4242 Roosevelt Way NE; r/ste from $189/209; ℗ ✗ ▣
Easy to miss because it looks like one of those crisp new modern apartment buildings, the Watertown has more of an arty-industrial feel than its sister hotel, the University Inn (p182). Bare concrete and high ceilings in the lobby make it seem stark and museum-like, but that translates to spacious and warmly furnished rooms with giant beds, swivel TVs and huge windows. Thematic 'Ala Carts' (eg a Relaxation Cart, a Seattle Cart or a Game Cart) are delivered free to your room. Guests can borrow bicycles or use the hotel's free shuttle to explore the area.

HOTEL DECA Map p83   Hotel $$

☎ 206-634-2000, 800-899-0251; www.hoteldeca
.com; 4507 Brooklyn Ave NE; s/d from $148/189;
P ✕ ✕ ▢

The same architect who designed the Old
Faithful Lodge in Yellowstone National Park
built this hotel in 1931. Formerly the Meany
Tower Hotel, the Deca has since had a $2
million renovation. Its 16 stories offer rooms
with either a Cascade view or a downtown
view. Rooms also feature flat-screen TVs
with DVD players and iPod docks. There's a
workout room, a bar and a restaurant, plus a
Tully's coffee shop in the building.

SILVER CLOUD INN Map p83   Hotel $$

☎ 206-526-5200, 800-205-6940; 5036 25th Ave NE;
r from $177; P ✕ ✕ ▢ ☒

Just a little nicer and a little friendlier
than it has to be, the Silver Cloud is ideal
for business travelers or those staying
long enough to want to make use of the
kitchenettes in each suite. In-room coffee
and tea, flat-screen TVs, soft couches and
huge beds add to the comfort, and the
free breakfast, guest laundry, indoor pool,
spa and fitness room don't hurt, either.
The Burke-Gilman Trail abuts the parking
lot, and a free hotel shuttle will drop you
anywhere in town within 3 miles.

CHAMBERED NAUTILUS B&B INN
Map p83   B&B $$

☎ 206-522-2536, 800-545-8459; www.chambered
nautilus.com; 5005 22nd Ave NE; d $139-164;
✕ ✕ ▢

The 1915 Georgian-style Chambered
Nautilus has six guest rooms that are
decorated with authentic British antiques,
as well as an annex with one- and two-
bedroom suites. All B&B rooms here come
with private bathrooms, down comforters,
handmade soaps and a teddy bear. The
communal living room has a welcoming

fireplace, and the full gourmet breakfast is
reason enough to stay. It's found in a handy
but quiet location, tucked into the forested
hillside that lies between the university and
Ravenna Park.

UNIVERSITY INN Map p83   Hotel $$

☎ 206-632-5055, 800-733-3855; www.university
innseattle.com; 4140 Roosevelt Way NE; r from
$120; P ✕ ✕ ▢ ☒ ♿

What pushes this spotless, modern, well-
located place over the edge into great-
ness is, believe it or not, the waffles served
at the complimentary breakfast. They're
amazing. The hotel is three blocks from
campus, and its 102 rooms come in three
levels of plushness. All of them offer such
basics as a coffee maker, hair dryer and
wi-fi; some have balconies, sofas and CD
players. There's a Jacuzzi, an outdoor pool,
laundry facilities and a guest computer in
the lobby. Attached to the hotel is the
recommended Portage Bay Cafe, and
there's also a free shuttle to various
sightseeing areas.

COLLEGE INN Map p83   Hostel/B&B $

☎ 206-633-4441; www.collegeinnseattle.com;
4000 University Way NE; s/d from $60/80; ✕ ▢

The College Inn is a great budget option.
Built for the 1909 Alaska-Yukon Exposition, the building has 27 European-style
guestrooms with shared bathrooms down
the hall. There's no TV, but there's a ton
of atmosphere, and some of the rooms
have a view of the Space Needle through
big bay windows. South-facing rooms get
the most light. Rates include a continental
breakfast served in the communal lounge.
Downstairs there's a coffee shop that serves
full meals, a convenience store and a lively
pub. Note that the building lacks elevators,
and the 'front desk' is four flights up a
narrow stairway.

EXCURSIONS

EXCURSIONS

Seattle's location makes it ideal for getting out of the city and exploring the natural beauty of its surroundings. With very little effort, you can trade that caffeinated urban buzz for a tranquil island retreat, an orchard-strewn valley or a rugged mountain peak – even all three.

Puget Sound, the sparkling jewel that surrounds Seattle, is dotted with tiny islands once dismissed as agricultural backwaters but now among the most popular tourist destinations in the area. Visiting the islands does take some planning in the summer months, when everybody else wants to be there too, but you'll understand why as soon as you start paddling your rented kayak out on the water. The sparse population of many of the islands also makes them great places for bicycle fiends. Or, if you prefer, you can always sit at a dockside pub and sip a microbrew while you watch active people do their thing. Most of the hotels, B&Bs and restaurants in island towns are open all year, so if you'd like to avoid the crowds, plan on an off-season visit. For the purposes of ferry schedules and seasonal business hours, 'summer' refers to mid-June through September.

Those looking to take their minds off city life with a serious physical challenge also have a couple of options. The most tempting is Mt Rainier, mostly because its pointy peak beckons from the horizon almost everywhere you go in Seattle. Reaching the summit is no picnic, but the whole Mt Rainier National Park area has an abundance of hikes at all skill levels and distances. Climbing the summit of Mt St Helens is another alternative for serious hikers. Or, for peace and quiet, enjoy your lunch along the shores of Coldwater Lake at the base of the dramatically scarred mountain.

Drive a bit further and feel infinitely more distant from urban chaos by visiting the Olympic Peninsula. This remote area feels steeped in mystery – partly because of its thick, misty, moss-laden forests and partly because there is only one major road going through it. Combine the wild nature of the Hoh River Rain Forest with the charm of Victorian-era Port Townsend and you might just accidentally forget to catch that flight home.

For those with less time and energy, the Snoqualmie Valley makes a quick and easy escape from the city. Its pastoral landscape, dotted with orchards and imbued with an eerie feel, is a lovely place for a leisurely drive.

Just a short ferry ride away is Victoria, the Olde English-style capital of Canada's province of British Columbia. Its high teas, B&Bs and famed botanical garden make it a pleasantly quiet retreat.

ISLANDS

It's almost criminal to be in Seattle and not get out on the water. Puget Sound (p187) has some of the most gorgeous islands in the country, and it's a great area to explore by ferry. An outing on the sound makes a relaxing day trip, whether you're going by car or bike or just on foot.

Bainbridge Island (p188) makes an easy day or half-day trip from downtown Seattle. Explore the island's main town, Winslow, with a stop at the local winery. Rent bicycles to pedal around the easily accessible island.

If you have time for a longer island-hop, start with Lopez Island (p191), the closest and most agricultural, and full of pastoral charm. Then press on toward Shaw Island (p193), where the traffic-free roads are a cyclist's paradise. And don't miss San Juan Island (p190) with its fetching Friday Harbor that's hard not to love. This is a fairly substantial town, so there are plenty of options for dining and sleeping, while the picturesque farmlands just outside the town are close enough to reach on foot.

NATURE

Seattle has the advantage of being one of the few major cities in the US with easy access to wilderness right outside its back door. Nature wild enough to get lost in is as close as Discovery Park (see p98), but it's even easier to get lost on the Olympic Peninsula, where misty trails meander through the regal forests of the Hoh River Rain Forest (p198). At the end of your hike, play on the rugged beach – but be on the lookout for vampires and werewolves (see the box, p38).

To see what happens when nature has a bad day, visit the Mt St Helens Visitors Center (p196). The site does an amazing job of displaying the terrifying power of a volcano.

SEATTLE AREA FERRY ROUTES

lonelyplanet.com

0 — 20 km
0 — 12 miles

British Columbia

CANADA
USA

Sidney

Sucia Island

Straight of Georgia

Waldron Island

Eastsound

Bellingham

Lake Whatcom

Orcas Island

Rosario

Orcas

Cypress Island

Guemes Island

San Juan Island

Shaw Island

Blakey Island

Friday Harbor

Lopez Island

Anacortes

Rosario Strait

Vancouver Island

Haro Strait

Mt Vernon

Skagit River

VICTORIA

La Conner

Washington

Skagit Bay

Strait of Juan de Fuca

Whidbey Island

Oak Harbor

Dungeness Spit

Port Angeles

Port Townsend

Keystone

Whidbey Island

Langley

Freeland

Clinton

Everett

48°00'N

48°00'N

Olympic National Park

Mukilteo

Puget Sound

Edmonds

Quilcene

Port Gamble

Kingston

Olympic Mountains

Bangor

Poulsbo

Keyport

Suquamish

Silverdale

Bainbridge Island

SEATTLE

Bellevue

Seabeck

Lake Sammamish

Bremerton

Blake Island

Fauntleroy

Belfair

Southworth

Renton

Lake Cushman

Hood Canal

Kitsap Peninsula

Vashon Island

Tahuya

Tahlequah

Point Defiance

Shelton

Tacoma

Auburn

Enumclaw

OUTDOOR ACTIVITIES

It's hard to resist a visit to majestic Mt Rainier (p193); after all, you've probably been gazing wistfully at it through restaurant and hotel windows throughout your stay in Seattle. Tackle the summit and linger in Paradise (p193) to mingle with the wildlife.

There's also great hiking around the infamously volcanic Mt St Helens (p195). For adventures on a flatter scale, the islands of Puget Sound (right), as well as the San Juan Islands (p189), have leisurely but spectacular cycling routes. The islands are also great for water sports such as canoeing and sea kayaking. For downhill skiing and snowboarding, haul your gear over to Snoqualmie Valley (p194). See p166 for more about outdoor activities.

TIME TRAVEL

The well-preserved historical buildings lining the streets of Port Townsend (p197), many of them housing shops filled with antiques and Victorian knick-knacks, make it easy to believe you've taken the ferry to another era. Fort Worden State Park (p197), where the movies *The Ring* and *An Officer and a Gentleman* were filmed, enhances the illusion.

Destination	Operator	Departs
Bainbridge Island	Washington State Ferries	Pier 52
Blake Island	Washington State Ferries	Pier 55
Lopez Island	Washington State Ferries	Anacortes
Orcas Island	Washington State Ferries	Anacortes
San Juan Island	Washington State Ferries	Anacortes
	Victoria Clipper	Pier 69
Shaw Island	Washington State Ferries	Anacortes
Vashon Island	Washington State Ferries	Fauntleroy
Victoria, BC	Victoria Clipper	Pier 69
	Victoria Express	San Juan Island
	Victoria Express	Port Angeles
Victoria, BC (Sidney)	Washington State Ferries	Anacortes

PUGET SOUND

The islands of Puget Sound make a fantastic escape from the city. Aside from their scenic beauty – which is very different from the natural landscapes you'll find in and around Seattle, despite their proximity – two activities draw people here: rest and relaxation. These come in many forms, from berry picking or leisurely cycling to wine sampling or lolling on beaches. Reset your internal clock to 'slow' while you take in the gorgeous views of the

MAKING SENSE OF SEATTLE FERRIES

Ferries are by far the most fun means of travel in the Seattle area, and a handy way to get to the surrounding islands, but it's not always easy to figure out how to use the system. Schedules are pretty chaotic at first glance – not every ferry goes to every island every day – and the payment system can be confusing, too.

There are three operators: Washington State Ferries, Victoria Express and Victoria Clipper. Their services are summarized in the table above, but see each island's listing for more details.

Most of the destinations we cover in this chapter are served by Washington State Ferries (☎ 206-464-6400, in Washington 800-808-7977, automated information 800-843-3779, ferry traffic info 551; www.wsdot.wa.gov/ferries). See the website for online or downloadable schedules for all possible routes. There are also notes about delays or service interruptions. A complicated code, explained in the page's margins, tells you the name of the boat that will be making each run, as well as whether it has disabled access, and specifies that certain routes are only on weekends or only on weekdays.

Then there's a link to the fare information. Fares depend on the length of the route and the size of your vehicle, if you have one. Also, each route seems to have a different way of collecting the fares: some collect on departure, some mid-trip and some when you arrive. These are specified on the website's trip planner.

Note that services to Vashon Island leave from Fauntleroy in West Seattle, while services to the San Juan Islands leave from the Anacortes Ferry Terminal, 85 miles north of Seattle (follow the I-5 north for 65 miles to exit 230, then drive 20 miles west on Hwy 20 to the terminal). There's no charge for journeys back toward Anacortes from Friday Harbor (San Juan Island); the full round-trip fare will have been collected on your way out. Between the San Juan islands, transportation is by inter-island ferries, which travel a circular route exclusively between the four main islands. There is a fee for vehicles (by length) and drivers traveling west-bound only; there is no charge for walk-ons or bicycles.

Victoria Clipper (☎ 800-888-2535, 360-448-5000, 206-443-2560; www.clippervacations.com) operates services from Seattle to Victoria, BC, and from Seattle to Friday Harbor (San Juan Island).

Victoria Express (☎ 360-452-8088; www.victoriaexpress.com) operates services to Victoria, BC, from both Port Angeles and Friday Harbor (San Juan Island).

city and mountains during the ferry ride there, and you'll make the most of a vacation from your vacation.

BAINBRIDGE ISLAND

When it comes to visiting Bainbridge Island, getting there really is half the fun. It's a popular destination with locals and visitors alike, largely because it's the quickest and easiest way to get out on the water from Seattle. It's also one of the loveliest. The ferry ride alone provides enough stunning views of Seattle and the Sound to make the trip worthwhile. Once you get to the island, prepare to stroll around lazily, tour some waterfront cafes, taste unique wines at the Bainbridge Island Winery, maybe rent a bike and cycle around the invitingly flat countryside, and generally relax until it's time to ferry back.

The family-owned Bainbridge Island Winery (☎ 206-842-9463; ☯ tastings 11am-5pm Fri-Sun) near Winslow is a good destination for cyclists, or for wine-lovers who don't mind a walk – the winery has moved to a place at the edge of its vineyards, about 4 miles north of town on Hwy 305. On Sundays at 2pm there's a winegrower's tour around the vineyards.

Information

Chamber of Commerce (☎ 206-842-3700; www .bainbridgechamber.com; 590 Winslow Way E)

Classic Cycle (☎ 206-842-9191; 310 Winslow Way NE; rentals per 2hr/2 days/1 week $25/60/150; ☯ 10am-5pm) This bike shop, part vintage-cycle museum, also rents out bicycles.

TRANSPORTATION: BAINBRIDGE ISLAND

Distance from Seattle 9 miles

Direction West

Travel time 35 minutes

Ferry Washington State Ferries to Bainbridge Island board at Pier 52. Ferries run from 5:30am until about 1:30am, hourly in summer and several times a day in winter. Round-trip fares for an adult are $6.90, and for a car and driver it's $14.85. Cyclists pay an extra $1. Passenger and vehicle fares are collected at Seattle Pier 52, while vehicle-only fares are collected at Bainbridge Island. No reservations accepted.

Eating

Café Nola (☎ 206-842-3822; 101 Winslow Way; lunch mains $12-16, dinner mains $16-25; ☯ brunch, lunch & dinner) One highlight of a visit to Bainbridge is a meal at this popular bistro, serving a classy blend of Mediterranean and Northwest cooking.

Harbour Public House (☎ 206-842-0969; 231 Parfitt Way; starters $6-12, mains $10-20; ☯ 11am-midnight) After your bike ride, sit back and quaff microbrews at this public house. Seafood dishes, including the Asian salmon bowl ($14.95) and a calamari appetizer ($9.95), are recommended.

Mora Iced Creamery (☎ 206-855-1112; www.mora icedcreamery.com; 139 Madrone Lane; ♿) Luscious ice creams and sorbets made locally on Bainbridge Island come in cones, cups or pints – and, as a bonus, it's all low-fat.

VASHON ISLAND

More rural and countercultural than Bainbridge Island to the north, Vashon Island has resisted suburbanization – a rare accomplishment in Puget Sound. Much of the island is covered with farms and gardens, and its little towns double as commercial hubs and artists' enclaves. Vashon Island also provides unencumbered vistas of the Cascades mountain range, with views from Mt Rainier in the south to Mt Baker in the north. Vashon is a good island to explore by bicycle or car, stopping here and there to pick berries or fruit at a 'u-pick' garden or orchard along the way. Plan a hike in one of the county parks.

Note that the ferry from Seattle deposits you in the north of the island, some distance from the centers of Vashon commerce and culture, so you'll need to bring a bike or car, or have a lift arranged.

Eating & Sleeping

Monkey Tree Cafe (☎ 206-463-4635; 17817 Vashon Hwy SW; mains $6-12; ☯ 8am-3pm, closed Tue-Wed in winter; Ⓥ) This fun vegetarian place is a local fave; try the awesome pastries (croissant French toast!), pizzas or one of the many carefully executed sandwiches. Cash only.

Vashon Tea Shop (☎ 206-463-5202; 17608 Vashon Hwy; snacks $2-6; ☯ 9am-6pm Mon-Sat, noon-5pm Sun) A cute little tea shop that also serves gluten-free snacks, brunches and light meals.

HI Seattle/Vashon AYH Ranch (☎ 206-463-2592; www .vashonhostel.com; 12119 SW Cove St; tent/dm/r $13/23/65; ☯ May-Sep) Budget travelers will be glad of this great hostel with bunk beds, teepees, covered wagons, private rooms and camping available

TRANSPORTATION: VASHON ISLAND

Distance from Seattle About 8 miles

Direction Southwest

Travel time 20 minutes

Ferry Washington State Ferries has daily departures from Fauntleroy in West Seattle. Passenger and vehicle fares (adult/car and driver $4.45/19) are collected at Fauntleroy; no fares are collected at Vashon Island.

in the summer; during the winter (November to April) it operates as a lodge with private rooms in cabins ($65 to $300). It also has bicycles for rent ($6 per hour).

BLAKE ISLAND

Blake Island is a state park and can be approached only by boat. This made it a safe place to host the 1993 APEC conference, where former President Bill Clinton met with 14 Asia-Pacific leaders. Most people, however, go to the island to visit Tillicum Village, which features the Northwest Coast Indian Cultural Center & Restaurant. A popular tour package (p207) includes a traditional Indian salmon bake, dancing and a film about Northwest Native Americans. After the meal, there's time for a short hike or a bit of shopping. You can also get there on your own boat and explore without the formal tour, or opt to watch the performances and skip dinner (or vice versa).

SAN JUAN ISLANDS

The San Juan archipelago contains 457 islands sprawled across 750 sq miles of Pacific waters in the area where Puget Sound and the straits

TRANSPORTATION: BLAKE ISLAND

Distance from Seattle About 8 miles

Direction Southwest

Travel time Four hours (entire tour)

Ferry Washington State Ferries has departures from Pier 55 in Seattle daily in summer, weekends only from October to March. Fares are adult/child/senior $79.95/72.95/30.

of Juan de Fuca and Georgia meet. About 200 of the islands are named and only a few are inhabited. Washington State Ferries (see the box, p187) provides service to the four largest islands – San Juan, Orcas, Shaw and Lopez – while others are accessible only by private boat or plane.

San Juan itself is also known as the Pig War Island. The so-called Pig War of 1859 was sparked when an American settler in San Juan shot and killed a hog belonging to Bellevue Farm, which supported the Hudson's Bay Company's controversial fur-trapping operations. The settler, Lyman Cutler, said he killed the hog because it kept invading his garden. British troops then tried to arrest Cutler, and, because the boundary between Canada and the US at the time was hazy, US troops went in to confront the British. All of this, absurdly enough, nearly led to a battle; British warships popped up off the coast of San Juan, and things grew tense. But reason won out: the two governments agreed to a joint occupation of the San Juans until the boundary dispute could be settled. The joint agreement lasted 12 years until, in 1872, Kaiser Wilhelm of Germany settled the dispute in favor of the United States. That decision ended the last territorial conflict between the US and Great Britain and made San Juan Island the last piece of American soil occupied by Great Britain.

Until about 30 years ago the islands were considered inaccessible and backward. Their patchwork fields, forests, lakes, sheep pastures and fishing boats setting sail from tiny rock-lined harbors were ignored by all but the fishers and farmers inhabiting them. Today, however, tourism is the mainstay of local economies: the islands are a major holiday destination without enough lodging to handle the crowds during the summer high season. And yet, despite the inevitable adulteration that 'discovery' brings, the islands retain their bucolic charm and make for a restful retreat.

Although many people come to the San Juan Islands for rest and recuperation, the outdoor activities are another reason to visit. The islands are small, largely flat and laced with deserted roads, making this a great getaway for cyclists. Sea kayaking is another favorite sport: the rocky coast and relatively protected waters make for a perfect environment to explore by kayak. Wildlife along the coastline – seabirds, seals and sea lions, otters and even orcas – is also abundant. Most marinas have sailboats for rent. Whale-watching trips are also popular excursions. Tours go all year, but the most sightings of orcas happen from May to September.

Keep in mind that many of the islands' beaches are privately owned, so your best bet for lying on the beach might be at a resort that owns some sandy oceanfront.

Lodging frequently fills up during the summer; don't even think about heading out without reservations during July and August or you may end up having to take the last ferry back to the mainland. Most reservations are made months ahead, and the most attractive places to stay are often booked even further in advance – but if your heart's set on a place, it's worth calling to ask if there have been cancellations. Accommodations are not inexpensive: you'll be hard pressed to find rooms for less than $100 a night during the summer. Maps of the islands are available at the San Juan Islands Visitor Information Center.

Information

Friday Harbor Tourist Information (☎ 360-378-6977)

Island Air (☎ 888-378-2376; www.sanjuan-islandair.com) Provides charter services from SeaTac or Boeing Field/King County Airport.

Island Airporter (☎ 360-378-7438; www.islandairporter.com) Daily, non-stop services from SeaTac to San Juan Island (Friday Harbor and Roche Harbor.)

Kenmore Air (☎ 800-543-9595; www.kenmoreair.com) Land and seaplanes fly direct daily from Lake Union, Lake Washington and Boeing Field/King County Airport to San Juan Island, with free shuttle service between SeaTac and the terminals.

San Juan Islands Visitor Information Center (☎ 360-468-3663; www.guidetosanjuans.com; PO Box 65, Lopez, WA 98261) Great website with all sorts of useful info.

SAN JUAN ISLAND

Most visitors find that San Juan, of all the islands, offers the most hospitable blend of sophisticated amenities, rural landscapes and bustling harbors. It's the most developed and most visited of the four main San Juan islands. A large part of the island's draw is Friday Harbor – with a population of about 2000, it's the only real town in all the San Juan Islands. Even so, it's small enough to navigate on foot. Legend has it that when the early European explorers first arrived, one of them said, 'What bay is this?' and was misheard as asking 'What day is this?' But the harbor is, in fact, less colorfully

TRANSPORTATION: SAN JUAN ISLAND

Distance from Seattle 104 miles

Direction North

Travel time 70 minutes (from Anacortes)

Ferry Washington State Ferries runs daily from Anacortes to Friday Harbor for $13.45/52.55 per adult/car and driver. Victoria Clipper has seasonal daily departures from downtown's Pier 69 to Friday Harbor for adult/child $80/40 (round trip).

named for an early settler from the 1800s called Joe Friday.

Most of the hotels and restaurants are either on or just off the main drag, Spring St, which runs uphill half a block over from the ferry landing. But follow any of the streets out of Friday Harbor and you're soon on a central plateau where small farms, dairies and lakes fill the verdant landscape.

The only other community of any size is Roche Harbor, on a beautiful bay to the northwest. It was originally a company town built to support the Tacoma and Roche Harbor Lime Company, set up in 1886. The surrounding structures included lime kilns, a grand hotel, a private estate, workers' cottages, a small railway, a company store, a chapel and a shipping wharf. The lime factory closed in the 1950s and the extensive buildings are now part of the Roche Harbor Resort. There's also a huge, busy marina here, thanks to the strategically sheltered nature of the harbor.

Eating

Friday Harbor House (☎ 360-378-8455; 130 West St; starters $8-12, mains $19-25) This small, modern, comfortable hotel-restaurant overlooks the harbor. The intimate dining room has a fireplace and great views. The menu is brief but tempting, with seasonal Northwest cuisine.

Front St Ale House & San Juan Brewing Company (☎ 360-378-2337; 1 Front St; shared plates $8-15, mains $5-10) The island's only brewery serves up British-style beers in a real pub atmosphere. The food's good, too. Traditional British favorites like steak-and-kidney pie and bangers and mash keep good company with standbys such as chili, chowder and hamburgers.

Backdoor Kitchen (☎ 360-378-9540; 411 A St; starters $6-14, mains $24-34; ☾ dinner Wed-Mon) This lovely garden cafe serves up gourmet dishes built around snapping-fresh local vegetables and seafood – try the seared scallops.

Sleeping

Blair House B&B (☎ 360-378-5907; blairhouse@rockisland .com; 345 Blair Ave; r incl breakfast from $165) This woodsy, 1909 home has four rooms and a cottage.

Friday Harbor House (☎ 360-378-8455; www.friday harborhouse.com; 130 West St; r incl breakfast from $279/180 summer/winter) The most exclusive and whimsically elegant lodging in Friday Harbor, it's a modern boutique hotel with great views over the harbor. All rooms have a fireplace, Jacuzzi tub and other upscale niceties.

Lakedale Campground (☎ 360-378-2350; 2627 Roche Harbor Rd; campsites $32-45, canvas cabins from $149; ☼ May-Sep) This enormous campground is tucked into 50 acres of wilderness dotted with trout-stocked lakes (no license is required to fish; you just pay a fee at the campground). Canoe, paddle-boat and kayak rentals are available. In addition to campsites and log cabins, there are some yurt-like canvas cabins available; there's also a resort attached if you're really not into roughing it.

Roche Harbor Resort (☎ 360-378-2155, 800-451-8910; www.rocheharbor.com; r with shared bathroom from $79-139, cabin or ste $199-399; ☒) Just about the nicest place to stay in all the San Juans, the Roche Harbor Resort incorporates some of the relics of the original lime-company settlement. You can still spend the night at the imposing old Hotel de Haro on the resort's grounds, which has wide, ivy-covered verandas and formal gardens. Refurbished workers' cottages, just a few yards from the swimming pool and playground, fill a grassy meadow above the harbor. Modern condominiums are discreetly tucked behind a stand of trees. In addition to the lodgings, there's a marina with boat rentals, restaurant, lounge and – on the dock – an old general store. You can even land your private jet on the airstrip.

LOPEZ ISLAND

Lopez is the most agricultural of the San Juan Islands and the closest to the mainland. It has resisted the commercialization of its farmland better than the other islands. Here, pastures are for grazing sheep or hay-making – not merely the aesthetic backdrop for quaint country inns and B&Bs. The island has a vineyard and some nice pebbly beaches. If you want quiet, pastoral charm and don't need organized fun, Lopez is hard to beat.

lonelyplanet.com

TRANSPORTATION: LOPEZ ISLAND

Distance from Seattle 99 miles

Direction North

Ferry Washington State Ferries runs daily from Anacortes to Lopez Island for $13.45/36.80 per adult/car and driver.

Fields and pastures stretch across the island's central plateau, and the island gets rockier toward the south; near MacKaye Harbor, the stony fields and cliff-lined bay look for all the world like the Hebrides.

Don't be surprised if people wave as you drive along – it's a longstanding tradition in this friendly farming community and people do it now out of habit whether they recognize the person they're waving to or not. Take care not to get too distracted as the roads are winding. A bicycle might be a wiser option: the terrain is relatively flat and uncommonly scenic, making Lopez a top choice for cyclists.

Eating

Nearly all the places to eat on Lopez are in Lopez Village; in fact, they practically constitute the village.

Bay Café (☎ 360-468-3700; 9 Old Post Rd; mains from $12; ☼ dinner) The most noted restaurant on Lopez occupies an old storefront. Inventive ethnic seafood dishes and locally raised grass-fed beef headline the menu.

Love Dog Café (☎ 360-468-2150; 1 Village Centre; sandwiches from $6; ☼ 8am-8pm Mon-Fri, 8am-9pm Sat & Sun) Sit on the veranda below the grape arbor and watch the boats in the harbor while munching on a hot deli sandwich.

Sleeping

Edenwild Inn (☎ 360-468-3238; www.edenwildinn .com; r incl breakfast $170-195) Built to resemble a Victorian mansion, this eight-room inn is the most eye-catching building on the island, with lovely formal gardens, a wide porch and gables.

Lopez Islander Resort (☎ 360-468-2233, 800-736-3434; www.lopezislander.com; 2864 Fisherman Bay Rd; tent/RV site $25/35, r $75-100, studio incl kitchen $145) South of Lopez Village, this is as close to a bona fide motel as you'll find in the San Juans. Across from the units is a bar and restaurant that gives onto a marina. All rooms have a deck, and there are a lot of nice campsites overlooking the water.

MacKaye Harbor Inn (☎ 360-468-2253; www.mackaye harborinn.com; 949 MacKaye Harbor Rd; r $175-195, ste $235) Standing stalwart and white at the edge of a shallow bay near the south end of the island, this inn – a sea captain's home in the 1920s – provides bicycles, rowboats and kayaks for its guests.

Spencer Spit State Park (☎ 360-468-2251, reservations 800-452-5687; www.stateparks.com/spencer_spit.html; campsites from $28) Five miles southeast of the ferry landing on Baker View Rd is this quiet campsite near the water.

ORCAS ISLAND

Orcas is the largest of the San Juan Islands and, in terms of rugged physical beauty, it is probably the most fetching. At 2407ft, Mt Constitution is the highest point in the San Juans, but it is only one of several forested peaks around which the rest of the island folds in steep valleys. Along the rocky coast, narrow cliff-lined inlets serve as harbors for small pleasure boats.

In some ways Orcas Island is the most exclusive of the San Juans: the rocky promontories and isolated harbors look good in real-estate brochures, so retirement homes, resort communities and weekend manses have taken the place of agriculture.

Orcas Island's main tourist attraction is Moran State Park, the San Juans' largest and a favorite of hikers. Its namesake, Robert Moran, was a shipbuilder who owned what is now Rosario Resort at Cascade Bay; he owned thousands of acres on the island and donated a large chunk of it to the state for the park. There are now 30 miles of hiking and mountain-bike trails here, as well as 150 campsites. If you're not up for a hike, and are traveling by car, it's a 6-mile drive to

TRANSPORTATION: ORCAS ISLAND

Distance from Seattle 112 miles

Travel time: 70 minutes

Direction North

Travel time 70 minutes (from Anacortes)

Ferry Washington State Ferries runs daily from Anacortes to Orcas Island for $13.45/44.15 per adult/car and driver.

DOWN ON ORCAS

Eddie Bauer, he of the sporting-goods empire, was born on Orcas Island in 1899. As a young man working in an outdoors store he earned a reputation for stringing tennis rackets, even winning a tournament for speed. On a fishing trip on the Olympic Peninsula in 1934, Bauer nearly died of exposure when he took off his wet woolen jacket. Two years later, in Seattle, he invented the down parka. The Skyliner, the quilted down jacket he patented in 1936, became a popular item in the Eddie Bauer store.

the summit of Mt Constitution and a short climb to the top of the stone watchtower for a panoramic view of the whole San Juan Archipelago.

There isn't really a town on Orcas Island – the charming Eastsound is just a collection of businesses at a crossroads. Life revolves around the resorts, which are scattered around the island. One indication of the pace of life you'll find here: the only traffic light in the county, which hung for years in Eastsound, now sits in the Orcas Island Historical Museum.

Eating & Sleeping

Lulu's Pasta Rustica (☎ 360-376-2335; 325 Prune Alley; mains $12-20) A reliable option for Italian food on the island, Lulu's is recommended especially for its seafood pasta. There's also a good beer and wine selection.

Doe Bay Resort & Retreat (☎ 360-376-2291; www.doe bay.com; dm $35-55, yurts $75-120, cabins $70-275) About 18 miles east of Eastsound off the Horseshoe Hwy on Pt Lawrence Rd, this crunchy, mellow vacation spot is by far the cheapest option around. It has a distinctly 'alternative' vibe and a clothing-optional hot tub, so the uptight might prefer someplace else.

Moran State Park campgrounds (☎ 888-226-7688; campsites $14-28) A huge park with views of the Olympic mountains, plus 30 miles of trails and several lakes. Campsites range from full utilities to primitive.

Rosario Resort & Spa (☎ 800-562-8820; www.rosario resort.com; r from $220; 🔊) The Rosario mansion, built in the early 20th century, is the centerpiece of this resort complex about 4 miles south of Eastsound off the Horseshoe Hwy. There are some 130 modern rooms, tennis courts, swimming pools, elaborate tiled spa facilities in the basement, two fine restaurants and a marina.

TRANSPORTATION: SHAW ISLAND

Distance from Seattle 95 miles

Direction North

Travel time 70 minutes (from Anacortes)

Ferry Washington State Ferries runs daily from Anacortes to Shaw Island for $13.45/44.15 per adult/car and driver.

SHAW ISLAND

The smallest of the San Juan Islands with a ferry service, Shaw Island has the fewest facilities for travelers – which is to say, practically none. There are about 200 people on the island at most, and only one small shop and a handful of primitive campsites. But this lack of development is itself a good reason to disembark at Shaw, especially if you're on two wheels: it means the island's roads are mostly free of traffic. The rolling hills are covered with sheep, whose wool plays a large part in Shaw's cottage industries – spinning and knitting. If it's peace and quiet and uninterrupted time outdoors you're looking for, this is the place. Comb the beach, ride around, take long walks, camp out – a few mornings in a row of waking up to a quiet sunrise on a pristine beach and you'll happily forget the meaning of words like 'mall' and 'skyscraper.'

For years the ferry landing at Shaw was operated by Franciscan nuns with fluorescent safety vests over their habits; they also ran the small general store and the gas station at the tiny marina near the ferry landing. Though the nuns all retired in 2004 and the facilities are now run by a local couple, many visitors to the island still ask about the Franciscans. There are still nuns on Shaw Island, however: eight Benedictine nuns (who wear black-and-white habits rather than the brown ones of the Franciscans) live in Our Lady of the Rock Monastery, founded on the island in 1977. The Benedictines raise cattle, sheep, llamas, poultry, vegetables, herbs and flowers.

Sleeping

South Beach Park (☎ 360-378-1842; www.sanjuanco.com /parks; campsites $14-18) Run by San Juan County, this is basically the only place to stay on the island, with a dozen primitive campsites, some by the waterside ($18) and others in the woods ($14). Sites fill up months in advance for summer, so reservations are strongly recommended; online reservations are preferred.

MT RAINIER NATIONAL PARK

At 14,410ft, Mt Rainier is the highest peak in the Cascades. The main entrance road, Hwy 706 (also known as the Nisqually–Longmire Rd), comes in through the town of Ashford, near the park's southwest corner, and follows the Nisqually River into the park. This route leads up to the Paradise Viewpoint and to the Paradise Inn (p194). Paradise is especially known for its alpine wildflower meadows, which are laced with hiking trails. Follow the Skyline Trail on foot for a good view of the Nisqually Glacier. All other roads to the park close down in the winter, but this route is plowed as far as Paradise, which then becomes the setting-off point for cross-country skiers and snowshoers.

Some of the best views of Mt Rainier – with Emmons Glacier sliding down its face, Little Tahoma Peak in the foreground and the craggy Goat Rocks Wilderness Area off to the southeast – are from Sunrise. Sunrise's open meadows are scattered with trees and linked by hiking trails. Since it's on the mountain's east side, the Sunrise area benefits from Mt Rainier's rain shadow and receives less precipitation than the damp west side.

It doesn't take long for hikers to become enraptured with Sunrise, which usually means you have to deal with crowds. Try to hike on a weekday and hit the trail early in the morning. Park naturalists lead a 1.5-mile hike each Sunday afternoon on a Sunrise Goat Watch from the Sourdough Ridge to explore the mountain goat's habitat. Get to Sunrise by following Hwy 410 east from Enumclaw.

TRANSPORTATION: MT RAINIER

Distance from Seattle 95 miles

Direction Southeast

Travel time About three hours

Car The park has four entrances: Nisqually, on Hwy 706 via Ashford, near the park's southwest corner; Ohanapecosh, via Hwy 123; White River, off Hwy 410; and Carbon River, the most remote entrance, at the northwest corner. Only the Nisqually entrance is open in winter, when it's used by cross-country skiers.

For overnight trips, get a wilderness camping permit (free) from ranger stations or visitors centers. The six campgrounds in the park have running water and toilets, but no RV (recreational vehicle) hookups.

Park admission is $15/5/free (car/pedestrian/pedestrian under 17).

Information

Carbon River ranger station (☎ 360-829-9639)

Gray Line (☎ 206-624-5077; www.graylineseattle.com) Runs a 10-hour tour from Seattle for $65.

Jackson Visitors Center (☎ 360-569-2211, ext 2328; Paradise; ☒ May-Oct)

Longmire Hiker Information Center (☎ 360-569-2211, ext 3317; ☒ summer) Trail information and backcountry permits.

Packwood ranger station (☎ 360-494-0600)

Rainier Mountaineering (☎ 253-627-6242, in summer 360-569-2227; www.rmiguides.com; 4-day climb $926) Guided summit climbs.

Road conditions (☎ 800-695-7623)

Superintendent's office (☎ 360-569-2211, ext 3314; www.nps.gov/mora) Entry passes.

Sleeping

Plenty of accommodations can be found at Ashford, Packwood and Enumclaw. There are also two campgrounds near Longmire at the southwest corner of the park; for information on all of the area's campgrounds, call ☎ 360-569-2211 (ext 2304). Reservations (☎ 800-365-2267; www.recreation.gov; reserved campsites on-/off-season $15/12) are strongly advised during summer months and can be made up to two months in advance by phone or online.

Hotel Packwood (☎ 360-494-5431; 104 Main St; r $35-49) A historical landmark, this neat old wooden building has nine clean, charming rooms and a mountain-view veranda.

Paradise Inn (☎ 360-569-2275; www.mtrainierguestservices.com; r with bathroom $154-190, without bath $104-140; ☒ May-Oct) Recently renovated, the grand Paradise Inn has been designated one of the 'Great Lodges of the West.' It's a fantastic old log lodge on the mountain's south flank. Huge fireplaces anchor each end of the lobby, massive timbers hold up the ceiling and comfortable leather sofas and chairs face windows with views of the peak. Meanwhile, the National Park Inn (same contact information; rooms $110 to $184) is open year-round.

top picks

SCENIC DRIVES

- 101 Loop The lonesome highway loops around the Olympic Peninsula from Olympia through Hoquiam, Forks and Sequim, then back down toward Olympia.
- Mt St Helens (opposite) The 52-mile Spirit Lake Memorial Hwy (Hwy 504) up the back of the mountain to Windy Ridge is legendary.
- I-90 Scenic Drive A 100-mile byway that starts at Seattle's waterfront and heads east over the Cascade Mountains to end up on the plains of eastern Washington.
- Mt Rainier National Park (p193) Yes, you can drive to Paradise – and then, at least in summer, continue north to form a loop that goes over Chinook Pass and back to Enumclaw.

SNOQUALMIE VALLEY

East of Seattle's Eastside, the Snoqualmie Valley has long been a quiet backwater of dairy farms, orchards and produce gardens. Although suburbs are quickly taking over the valley, there's still enough of a rural, small-town ambience to make for a pleasant drive or bike ride.

North Bend, on Hwy 202 just off I-90, is *Twin Peaks* country, the setting for David Lynch's surreal TV series from the early 1990s. The former Mar T's Café, now called Twede's (☎ 425-831-5511; 137 W North Bend Way; pie $4.50; ☒ 6:30am-8pm Mon-Thu, 6:30am-9pm Fri & Sat, 6:30am-7pm Sun), was the diner with the famous cherry pie and cups of joe; a fire gutted it in 2000, but it has been rebuilt and is still a good place for lunch or a slice á la mode.

Continue along Hwy 202 to the little town of Snoqualmie, where you'll find antique shops and a store devoted to Northwest wines. Just north of town, Salish Lodge and Spa (☎ 425-888-2556, 800-826-6124; www.salishlodge.com; 6501 Railroad Ave; d from $229 plus tax) is a beautiful resort that sits atop 268ft Snoqualmie Falls. *Twin Peaks* fans know the hotel as the Great Northern; the exterior of the lodge appeared in the opening credits, and an observation point near the parking lot offers the same view. Visitors can also see the falls from the lodge's dining room or hike to them along a winding trail.

Hwy 203 branches off from 202 at Fall City; follow it north to Carnation, where the

TRANSPORTATION:
SNOQUALMIE VALLEY

Distance from Seattle 31 miles

Direction East

Travel time 30 to 40 minutes

Car Follow I-90 east from Seattle. Exit at North Bend (31 miles) and get onto Hwy 202, which follows the Snoqualmie River north.

Snoqualmie and Tolt Rivers meet at John McDonald Park. This is a great place for a riverside picnic, swim or hike. Carnation was once the center of the valley's dairy industry, and several farms here sell fruit and vegetables at roadside stands.

Duvall, about 25 miles north of North Bend along Hwys 202 and 203, has a rural small-town atmosphere despite its recent growth spurt. Wander Main St and check out the shops and nurseries. From here, head west on Woodinville–Duvall Rd for about 10 miles to reach Woodinville, home of several good wineries and the legendary Herbfarm (☎ 425-485-5300; www.theherbfarm.com; 14590 NE 145th St; dinner $179-195; ☺ 7pm Thu-Sat, 4:30pm Sun), where nine-course dinners are drawn from the gardens and farm itself, as well as small local growers, and matched with locally produced wines. There's a trail along the Sammamish River, if you fancy walking it off. From here it's a quick drive along I-405 back to Seattle.

MT ST HELENS

Thanks to a 1980 eruption that set off an explosion bigger than the combined power of 21,000 atomic bombs, Washington's 87th-tallest mountain needs little introduction. What it lacks in height Mt St Helens makes up for in fiery infamy; 57 people perished on the mountain on that fateful day in May 1980 when an earthquake of 5.1 on the Richter scale sparked the biggest landslide in recorded history and buried 230 sq miles of forest under millions of tons of volcanic rock and ash.

More recently, in October 2004 magma bubbled up to reach the surface of the volcano, resulting in a new lava dome on the existing dome's south side. This new dome continued to grow throughout 2005 and into 2006, accompanied by (so far) harmless spewings and sputterings. In March 2005 a 36,000ft plume of steam and ash big enough to be seen from Seattle came up; though exciting, the eruption was relatively minor, and was considered a pressure-release typical of volcanic dome building. The release was accompanied by a magnitude 2.5 earthquake. Steam-releasing activity and small eruptions continue around the dome. To view a webcam from the Johnston Ridge observatory, visit www.spiritoftruth.org/mtstheleswatch.htm.

Still recovering from the devastation of the 1980 eruption, the 171 sq miles of volcano-wracked wilderness can be visited as a day trip. Although driving from Seattle makes for a long day, the sights here are unique; for anyone interested in geology and natural history, this trip is well worth the expenditure of time. The whole experience is even more dramatic for the contrast between the scarred mountainside and the gorgeous, shimmering Coldwater Lake at its foot – an ideal place to picnic.

If you're looking to go hiking on Mt St Helens, you'll need to get a $15 permit ($22 including all fees; free November to March), which you must buy online in advance at www.mshinstitute.org. The climb takes about four hours up and two hours down, though the difficulty of the climb changes, depending on the weather. Be sure to check on conditions before heading up, and be prepared for dramatic changes in temperature.

Information

Coldwater Ridge Visitors Center (☎ 360-274-2131; ☺ 9am-5pm summer, 9am-4pm winter)

Johnston Ridge Visitors Center (☎ 360-274-2131; pass adult/child $8/free; ☺ 10am-6pm) At the end of Hwy 504, in the heart of the blast zone, this center provides views directly into the mouth of Mt St Helens' north-facing crater.

Monument Headquarters (☎ 360-247-3900) Issues hiking permits.

TRANSPORTATION:
MT ST HELENS

Distance from Seattle 120 miles (to Mt St Helens Visitors Center)

Direction South

Travel time Three hours

Car Take I-5 south to Castle Rock; the Mt St Helens Visitors Center is 5 miles east along Hwy 504. It's a further 45 miles to the mountain itself.

Mt St Helens Visitors Center (☎ 360-274-2100; ☽ 9am-5pm) Presents an overview of the site's history and geology. A dramatically situated observation point puts you practically inside the crater that was blown out of the side of the mountain more than 20 years ago. The adventurous (and fit) can hike up to the crater's edge, though you'll need to book in advance. The center is just off I-5, exit 49 near Castle Rock.

VICTORIA, BRITISH COLUMBIA

The nearest you can get to hopping across the pond, Victoria is a pretty (if a little grand-motherly) town famous for afternoon teas, botanical gardens and little old houses. It's the capital of British Columbia, Canada, and just a short ferry ride across the Strait of Juan de Fuca from Seattle. With a picturesque crescent-shaped downtown that faces onto the busy Inner Harbour, it makes for a lovely day trip or weekend escape.

Some sights worth a look are the Art Gallery of Greater Victoria (☎ 250-384-4101; www.aggv.bc.ca; 1040 Moss St; adult/senior/child $13/11/2.50; ☽ 10am-5pm, to 9pm Thu), the Butchart Gardens (☎ 250-652-5256, 866-652-4422; www.butchartgardens.com; 800 Benvenuto Ave; adult/youth/child 5-12 mid-Jun–Sep $28/14/3, reduced rest of year; ☽ 9am-10:30pm mid-Jun–Aug, to dusk rest of year), Craigdarroch Castle (☎ 250-592-5323; 1050 Joan Cres; adult/child $13.75/5; ☽ 9am-7pm mid-Jun–early Sep, 10am-4:30pm rest of year) and the Royal British Columbia Museum (☎ 250-356-7226, 888-447-7977; www.royalbc museum.bc.ca; 675 Belleville St; adult/child incl IMAX film $23/14; ☽ 9am-6pm Sun-Thu, 9am-10pm Fri & Sat in summer, 9am-5pm rest of year). Also based here is SpringTide Whale Watching Tours (☎ 250-386-6016;

TRANSPORTATION: VICTORIA, BRITISH COLUMBIA

Distance from Seattle 153 miles

Direction Northwest

Travel time One to three hours

Ferry Victoria Clipper runs a daily service from Seattle to Victoria ($85, 2¾ hours). Victoria Express runs a passenger-only ferry service between Port Angeles and Victoria ($10, one hour), plus a service between Friday Harbor (San Juan Island) and Victoria ($42.50, 2½ to three hours). Washington State Ferries shuttle between Anacortes and Sidney, just north of Victoria ($16.40, 1½ to 2½ hours).

---

www.springtidecharters.com; 950 Wharf St; tours adult/chi $100/80; ☽ 9am-6pm Apr-Oct), which takes peopl out to spot orcas.

Keep in mind that the prices listed in thi section are in Canadian dollars.

Information

Cycling Victoria (www.cyclingvictoria.com)

Tourism Victoria Visitor Information Centre (☎ 250-953-2033, 800-663-3883; www.tourismvictoria.com; 812 Wharf St; ☽ 8:30am-6:30pm mid-Jun–Sep, 9am-5pm Oct–mid-Jun) Activity and accommodation booking services.

Eating

Fairmont Empress Hotel (☎ 250-384-8111, 866-540-4229, www.fairmont.com/empress; 721 Government St) Victoria's 1908 grand dame has a regal, bygone-era opulence that knows no bounds. It's where honeymooners stay and tour groups take high tea.

Pagliacci's (☎ 250-386-1662; 1011 Broad St; lunch $7-12, dinner $12-25; ☽ 11:30am-3pm & 5:30-10pm, to 11pm Fri & Sat) At Pagliacci's, unlimited baskets of fresh focaccia bread are delivered to the marble-topped tables. Generous pasta servings from the cinema-themed menu almost defy devouring; try the Hemingway Short Story (beef-stuffed tortellini).

Reef (☎ 250-388-5375; 533 Yates St; mains $9-17.50; ☽ 11am-midnight Sun-Wed, 11am-1am Thu-Sat) Delectable Caribbean dishes are served here.

Sam's Deli (☎ 250-382-8424; 805 Government St; sand-wiches $7-12; ☽ 7:30am-7pm) Opposite the info centre, Sam's is the perfect spot for a coffee or bottle of beer and a sandwich big enough to feed two.

Strathcona Hotel (☎ 250-383-7137; 919 Douglas St) This multivenue complex includes the rooftop volleyball courts of Sticky Wicket Pub; the hillbilly, peanut-shell-on-the-ground haven of Big Bad John's; and touring musical acts at Legends.

Sleeping

Chateau Victoria (☎ 250-382-4221, 800-663-5891; www .chateauvictoria.com; 740 Burdett Ave; r from $149) The hotel's 177 rooms are not particularly remark-able, but they offer excellent value given all of their business-traveler amenities. The Vista 18 (18th floor) lounge unfurls the city's best views.

HI Victoria Hostel (☎ 250-385-4511, 888-883-0099; www.hihostels.ca; 516 Yates St; dm $27.50) This hostel is found in a great location, located just up from the Inner Harbour and close to all of the sights. Although it has room for more than 100 people in barrack-style dorms, it's wildly popular with travelers of all ages, so book ahead.

James Bay Inn (☎ 250-384-7151, 800-836-2649; www .jamesbayinn.com; 270 Government St; r $104-184) This old-time, dark-wood inn offers well-kept rooms with bay windows; some rooms have kitchens. It's in a quiet location, yet not far from the action.

Ocean Island Backpackers Inn (☎ 250-385-1788, 888-888-4180; www.oceanisland.com; 791 Pandora Ave; 4–6-bed dm $19-28, r $28-84) Catering more to a younger crowd, this fun, colorful hostel has a licensed lounge as well as helpful staff who are able to plan cheap day trips and group outings in the evenings.

OLYMPIC PENINSULA

The Olympic Peninsula is a rugged, isolated area characterized by wild coastlines, deep old-growth forests and craggy mountains. The Makah, a tribe of seafaring Native Americans who recently stirred up mild controversy by reinstituting their right to hunt whales, have lived here for thousands of years. Only one road, US 101, rings the peninsula, and at its outer stretches it can feel very remote indeed. Although the highway is in excellent condition, the distances are great, and visitors often find it takes a lot longer than expected to get where they're going. From Seattle, the fastest access to the peninsula is by ferry and bus via Bainbridge Island or on Washington State Ferries from Keystone, Whidbey Island.

PORT TOWNSEND

Ferrying in at dusk to Port Townsend, one of the best-preserved Victorian-era seaports in the USA, is like sailing into a sepia-toned old photograph. The city experienced a building boom in 1890 followed by an immediate bust, leaving its architectural splendor largely intact. Beyond just strolling the main street and admiring the handsome town, one highlight is historical Fort Worden State Park (☎ 360-385-4730), which contains the Coast Artillery Museum (admission $2; ☼ 11am-4pm daily Jun-Aug, Sat & Sun Mar-May & Sep-Oct) and the Commanding Officer's Quarters (admission $1; ☼ 10am-5pm daily Jun-Aug, 1-4pm Sat & Sun Mar-May & Sep-Oct). To get to Fort Worden, go west from the ferry dock until you reach Walker St, take a right, and head north as Walker St becomes

TRANSPORTATION: PORT TOWNSEND

Distance from Seattle 56 miles

Direction Northwest

Travel time Two hours

Ferry To reach Port Townsend, take the ferry from downtown Seattle to Bainbridge Island ($6.90). At the ferry dock catch bus 90 to Poulsbo ($1, 20 minutes), then pick up bus 7 to Port Townsend ($1, one hour). Alternatively, take the Washington State Ferries service from Keystone (Coupeville) on Whidbey Island to Port Townsend ($3, 30 minutes).

Cherry St, which takes you into the park (about two miles from the ferry landing).

Information

Peninsula Taxi (☎ 360-385-1872)

Port Townsend Visitors Center (☎ 360-385-2722; 2437 E Sims Way; ☼ 9am-5pm Mon-Fri, 9am-4pm Sat & Sun)

Eating

Fountain Cafe (☎ 360-385-1364; 920 Washington St; starters & sandwiches $9-11, mains $12-14; ☼ breakfast, lunch & dinner) A small cafe that's a favorite with locals, the Fountain serves up home-cooked meals in large portions.

Public House Grill (☎ 360-385-9708; 1038 Water St; starters $6-10, burgers $10, mains $14-24; ☼ lunch & dinner) This pretty pub on the main drag has the perfect blend of comfort and elegance – it's both fancy and convivial, with its dark-wood tables, lace curtains, big windows and massive wooden bar. The menu favors the white-tablecloth side of the place more than the beer-hall side.

Sleeping

HI Olympic Hostel (☎ 360-385-0655; olyhost@olympus.net; 272 Battery Way; dm/r $29/68) Within Fort Worden State Park in Port Townsend, this hostel has impeccable if spartan quarters in a former barracks; it's up the hill behind the Park Office. Dorms are a good deal, but private rooms are less so.

Manresa Castle (☎ 360-385-5750, 800-732-1281; www .manresacastle.com; cnr 7th & Sheridan Sts; r $109-229) The turreted Prussian-style Manresa Castle, built in 1892, was later expanded to house Jesuit priests. The smallish rooms are decorated in a pretty, old-fashioned style that suits the town. Even if you don't stay here, it's worth taking the self-guided tour; check out the former chapel, truncated to form a breakfast room and a banquet room. The rates depend on size of room, views, number of occupants, and whether or not it's in a tower.

Waterstreet Hotel (☎ 360-385-5467, 800-735-9810; www.waterstreethotelporttownsend.com; 635 Water St; r with shared/private bathroom from $50/75) This hotel in the center of town has loads of old-world charm at reasonable rates. The suite has a deck over the water and a kitchen. There's a brewpub on the 1st floor (so light sleepers should beware potential noise) and an art gallery surrounding the front desk. There are all kinds of different rooms and suites; the prices vary by room.

HOH RIVER RAIN FOREST

Isolated by distance and inclement weather, and facing the Olympic Coast National Marine Sanctuary, the Pacific side of the Olympics remains its wildest. Only US 101 offers access to its spectacular rain forests and wild coastline. The Hoh River Rain Forest can get 12ft to 14ft of annual precipitation. And, as remote as it feels, it's relatively easy to get to. Walking trails from the visitors center and campground, at the end of 19-mile Hoh River Rd, plunge immediately into thick clusters of old-growth trees wearing furry green sweaters of moss.

Recently the town of Forks and the beaches of LaPush have seen a huge influx of tourists, thanks to the tween-friendly book and

TRANSPORTATION: HOH RIVER RAIN FOREST

Distance from Seattle 140 miles (to Forks)
Direction West
Travel time About four hours (to Forks)
Car Hwy 101 circles the Peninsula.

movie series *Twilight*, which sets its vampire-and-werewolf love-triangle story here. The visitor center (inside the Forks Chamber of Commerce) will happily answer questions about visiting sites from the movie or taking an organized *Twilight* tour. For more, see the box, p38.

Information

Forks Visitor Information Center (☎ 360-374-2531, 800-443-6757; 1411 S Forks Ave; �y 10am-4pm) Suggested itineraries and seasonal information, plus *Twilight* tours.

Hoh Forest Visitors Center (☎ 360-374-6925; �y 9am-4:30pm Sep-Jun, 9am-6pm Jul & Aug)

Sleeping

Forks Motel (☎ 360-374-6243; www.forksmotel.com; 351 S Forks Ave; d from $89) This is a basic roadside motel with friendly service, clean rooms and a handy location, and it has so far resisted the temptation to inflate its prices by adding *Twilight* 'themes' to its rooms.

TRANSPORTATION

Flights, tours and rail tickets can be booked online at www.lonelyplanet.com/travel_services.

AIR
Airlines

For toll-free numbers of airlines in the US, call ☎ 800-555-1212 or check the websites of individual airlines. Airlines serving Sea-Tac include Air Canada, Alaska, America West, American, Asiana, British Airways, China Airlines, Continental, Delta, EVA Air, Frontier, Hawaiian, Horizon Air, Jet Blue, Korean Air, Northwest, SAS, SkyWest, Southwest, Sun Country, United, United Express and US Airways.

Buying tickets online in advance has become the norm. Try the following links to find the best deals on airfares into Seattle:

Cheap Tickets (www.cheaptickets.com)

Expedia (www.expedia.com)

Hotwire (www.hotwire.com)

Orbitz (www.orbitz.com)

Priceline (www.priceline.com)

STA Travel (www.statravel.com)

Travelocity (www.travelocity.com)

Airports

Seattle is served by the Seattle-Tacoma International Airport (Sea-Tac; ☎ 206-431-4444, www.portseattle.org/seatac), located 13 miles south of downtown Seattle. The Port of Seattle spent $126 million on a makeover of the airport's central terminal, adding an extensive food-and-shops hub called Pacific Marketplace and large windows that provide a sweet view of the runway. There's also a cell-phone parking lot where the poor souls assigned to fetch new arrivals can wait until they're called to the baggage-claim curb. There are baggage storage facilities (http://kensbaggage.com; suitcases, duffels & backpacks per day $6-10) in the airport as well as currency-exchange services (see Changing Money, p205). Car-rental agencies are located in the baggage-claim area. For a map of the airport's ground-transport options, go to www.portseattle.org/about/maps/ground.shtml.

THINGS CHANGE...

The information in this chapter is particularly vulnerable to change. Check directly with the airline or a travel agent to make sure you understand how a fare (and ticket you may buy) works and be aware of the security requirements for international travel. Shop carefully. The details given in this chapter should be regarded as pointers and are not a substitute for your own careful, up-to-date research.

BICYCLE

Bicycling is still a major form of both transportation and recreation in the Seattle area, despite the mad traffic and hilly terrain. Many streets downtown have commuter bike lanes. Pick up a copy of the *Seattle Bicycling Guide Map,* published by the City of Seattle's Transportation Bicycle and Pedestrian Program (☎ 206-684-7583) and available at bike shops. Alternatively you can order the map free of charge over the phone or online at www.cityofseattle.net/transportation/bikemaps.htm.

Bike fans might want to check out Marymoor Park, which boasts the only velodrome (see p167) in the Pacific Northwest.

Seattle and all of King County require that bicyclists wear helmets. If you're caught without one, you can be fined $30 to $80 on the spot. Most places that rent bikes will rent helmets to go with them, sometimes for a small extra fee. It's also important to make sure your bike has sufficient lights and reflectors attached. See the box, p169, for recommended bicycle rental and repair places.

BOAT

Seattle's a watery place, and boats are a well-used mode of transport, both for fun and for getting around. But figuring out how to make them take you where you want to go can be a challenge. Planning ahead is key. Arrive at your ferry dock about 90 minutes ahead of departure time, particularly on weekends or for popular routes. Note that no reservations are taken for the San Juan Islands routes: they're strictly first come, first served.

For a full discussion of Seattle's ferry services, see the box, p187.

CLIMATE CHANGE & TRAVEL

Climate change is a serious threat to the ecosystems that humans rely upon, and air travel is the fastest-growing contributor to the problem. Lonely Planet regards travel, overall, as a global benefit, but believes we all have a responsibility to limit our personal impact on global warming.

Flying & Climate Change

Pretty much every form of motor transport generates carbon dioxide (the main cause of human-induced climate change) but planes are far and away the worst offenders, not just because of the sheer distances they allow us to travel but because they release greenhouse gases high into the atmosphere. The statistics are frightening: two people taking a return flight between Europe and the US will contribute as much to climate change as an average household's gas and electricity consumption over a whole year.

Carbon Offset Schemes

Climatecare.org and other websites use 'carbon calculators' that allow travellers to offset the greenhouse gases they are responsible for with contributions to energy-saving projects and other climate-friendly initiatives in the developing world – including projects in India, Honduras, Kazakhstan and Uganda.

Lonely Planet, together with Rough Guides and other concerned partners in the travel industry, supports the carbon offset scheme run by climatecare.org. Lonely Planet offsets all of its staff and author travel.

For more information check out our website: www.lonelyplanet.com.

BUS

Greyhound (Map p50; ☎ 800-231-2222, 206-628-5561, baggage 206-628-5555; www.greyhound.com; 811 Stewart St; ⊙ 6am-midnight) connects Seattle with cities all over the country, including Chicago ($203 one way, two days, two daily), Spokane ($39, eight hours, three daily), San Francisco ($116, 20 hours, three daily) and Vancouver, BC ($32, four hours, five daily).

In town, public buses are the main form of public transportation; they are operated by Metro Transit (☎ schedule info 206-553-3000, customer service 206-553-3060; http://metro.kingcounty.gov; fares $2-2.75), part of the King County Department of Transportation.

Sound Transit (☎ 800-201-4900, 206-398-5000; www .soundtransit.org) also operates Express buses to regional destinations, including Tacoma, although these are designed for commuters and not as likely to be used by travelers.

Most of the time you pay or show your transfer when you board. For trips on Metro Transit and Sound Transit Express buses that originate in downtown Seattle between 6am and 7pm, you pay when you leave the bus instead. Exceptions to this are Metro Transit routes 116, 118 and 119. For these routes, pay upon boarding when leaving downtown Seattle and traveling south. Pay when you leave when traveling to downtown Seattle. It sounds complicated, but if you follow the lead of the people around you it'll become clear.

Be aware that very few buses operate between 1:30am and 5am, so if you're a long way from home when the bars close, plan on calling a cab instead. Metro has discontinued its $5 Visitor Pass, so unless you'll be in town for a month or more, your best bet is still to buy single tickets as you need them.

CAR & MOTORCYCLE
Driving

Seattle traffic is disproportionately heavy and chaotic for a city of its size, and parking is scarce and expensive. Add to that the city's bizarrely cobbled-together mishmash of skewed grids, the hilly terrain and the preponderance of one-way streets and it's easy to see why driving downtown is best avoided if at all possible. If you are traveling with a car, consider stashing it at your hotel and using public transportation to get around within the city center.

Rental

As much of a hassle as it can be in the city, having your own set of wheels can be handy for reaching neighborhoods that are further afield, such as Ballard or Georgetown, and for exploring areas outside of Seattle proper. To rent a car, you need a valid driver's license and a major credit card.

There are rental agencies in Sea-Tac airport, located in the baggage-claim area, with pickup and drop-off service from the 1st floor of the garage. Car-rental agencies within Seattle include the following:

Avis (☎ 800-331-1212; www.avis.com)

Budget (☎ 800-527-0700; www.budget.com)

Dollar (☎ 800-800-3665; www.dollar.com)

Enterprise (☎ 800-261-7331; www.enterprise.com)

Hertz (☎ 800-654-3131; www.hertz.com)

Another good option for those who need only limited use of a vehicle is FlexCar (☎ 206-332-0330; www.flexcar.com; membership per year $50, rates per hr/day $7/69). Membership (there's a one-time $25 application fee) gives you access to a number of car-sharing vehicles distributed throughout the city. Members can make reservations online or by phone for as long as they need the car, then return it to the parking place where they picked it up when they're done. Rules for gas and mileage charges vary depending on which plan you choose.

TAXI

You can hail a cab from the street, but it's a safer bet to call and order one. All Seattle taxi cabs operate at the same rate, set by King County. At the time of research the rate was $2.50 at meter drop, then $2.50 per mile. There may be an extra charge for extra passengers and baggage.

Any of the following offer reliable taxi services:

Graytop Cabs (☎ 206-282-8222)

Orange Cab Co (☎ 206-522-8800)

STITA Taxi (☎ 206-246-9999)

Yellow Cab (☎ 206-622-6500)

TRAIN

Sound Transit (☎ 800-201-4900, 206-398-5000; www.soundtransit.org) operates trains connecting Seattle to outlying communities to the north and south. It's set up more for commuters than travelers, but if you happen to want to visit, for example, Everett ($2.50, 40 minutes, several daily), Woodinville ($2.50, one hour, several daily) or, more realistically, Tacoma ($3 to $4.75, one hour, several daily), the trains are new and clean and schedules run smoothly. Sound Transit also runs the light rail service to Sea-Tac airport (see the box below).

Although it doesn't exactly count as a train, the Monorail (☎ 206-905-2600; www.seattlemonorail.com; adult/senior/child $4/2/1.50; ☼ 9am-11pm) was originally intended as public transportation. It only goes one mile, from Westlake Center (p51) straight to Seattle Center and back every

---

GETTING INTO TOWN

The options for making the 13-mile trek from the airport to downtown Seattle have improved drastically with the completion of the airport light-rail line. It's fast, cheap and takes you directly to the heart of downtown, as well as a handful of other stops along the way.

Sound Transit (☎ 206-398-5000; www.soundtransit.org) runs the light rail service to the airport. Trains go every 15 minutes or better between 5am and just after midnight. Stops in town include Westlake Center, Pioneer Square, the International District and SODO. The ride between the two farthest points, Westlake and Sea-Tac, takes 37 minutes and costs $2.50/2 per adult/child.

Shuttle Express (☎ 800-487-7433; www.shuttleexpress.com; $10-55) has a pickup and drop-off point on the 3rd floor of the airport garage; ask about the $10 Sea-Tac airport special, which applies to certain locations within their drop-off area. Gray Line's Airport Express (☎ 206-626-6088; graylineseattle.com; adult/child one way $15/11) fetches passengers in the parking lot outside door 00 at the south end of the baggage-claim level (check the website for a diagram).

Taxis and limousines (respectively about $35 and $40) are available at the parking garage on the 3rd floor.

Metro buses ($2 to $4 one way) stop outside door six by baggage carousel five, on the baggage-claim level, although the light rail makes them practically obsolete for getting into town from Sea-Tac. Buses 194 Express and 174 go downtown. From there, the free bus 99 goes to the Waterfront, Pioneer Square and the International District, or use Metro Transit's online trip planner (http://tripplanner.kingcounty.gov).

Rental-car counters are located in the baggage-claim area. Some provide pickup and drop-off service from the 1st floor of the garage, while others provide a shuttle to the airport. Ask when you book your car.

Driving into Seattle from the airport is fairly straightforward – just take Interstate 5 north. It helps to find out whether your downtown exit is a left-hand or right-hand one, as it can be tricky to cross several lanes of traffic at the last minute during rush hour.

You can dial ☎ 55 from any of the traveler information boards at the base of the baggage-claim escalators for on-the-spot transport information. There's also an information booth on the 3rd floor of the parking garage. For further details on ground transport to and from the airport, check the Sea-Tac website (www.portseattle.org/seatac/ground).

10 minutes, but it's a fun if kitschy way to get there.

Amtrak (☎ 800-872-7245; www.amtrak.com) serves Seattle's King Street Station (303 S Jackson St; ⏱ 6am-10:30pm, ticket counter 6:15am-8pm). Three main routes run through town: the Amtrak Cascades (connecting Vancouver, BC, Seattle, Portland and Eugene), the extremely scenic Coast Starlight (connecting Seattle, Oakland and Los Angeles) and the Empire Builder (connecting Seattle, Spokane, Fargo and Chicago).

Examples of one-way ticket prices from Seattle:

Destination	Cost ($)	Duration (hr)	Frequency
Chicago	341	40	1 daily
Los Angeles	200	30	1 daily
Oakland	188	22	1 daily
Portland	37-42	3-4	5 daily
Spokane	39	6½	2 daily
Vancouver, BC	37.50	3-4	5 daily

DIRECTORY

BUSINESS HOURS

Banks are typically open from 9am or 10am until 5pm or 6pm weekdays. Some banks are also open from 10am to 2pm or so on Saturdays. Most businesses generally operate from 9am until 5pm or 6pm from Monday to Friday. Some are also open 10am to 5pm Saturdays. Shops are usually open from 9am or 10am to 5pm or 6pm (or until 9pm in shopping malls) Monday to Friday, as well as noon to 5pm or so (later in malls) on weekends. Some places, like record stores and bookstores, may keep later hours, such as from noon to 8pm or 9pm.

Restaurants tend to serve breakfast between 7am and 11am, brunch from 7am to 3pm, lunch from 11:30am to 2:30pm and dinner from 5:30pm to 10pm. Meals served and exceptions to the normal opening times are noted in specific listings (see p119).

CHILDREN

Like any major city, Seattle has some especially kid-friendly things to do. Aside from the obvious attractions (see the box, p71), there are several other sights and activities in Seattle that are particularly welcoming and entertaining for the younger set. Many of them are parks, where parents can let the little ones run free and expend some of that excess energy.

Try the following suggestions, collected from several parents in the Seattle area:

5 Spot (p129) A kid-friendly diner in Queen Anne.

Discovery Park (p98) The visitors center offers parking passes so you can drive to the beach and avoid the long hike down.

Ella Bailey Park (off Map p96; 2601 West Smith St) A park with beautiful views of the city and Mt Rainier, a nice paved loop trail and fun things to play on.

Fremont Troll (p88) Seattle's most endearingly creepy public art.

Hiram M Chittenden Locks (p95) & the Ballard Fish Ladder (p97) Watch salmon make their way home to spawn. As exciting as it sounds!

Pier 69 pool Park (Map p68) There's a small wading pool at the end of Pier 69 on the waterfront. If there isn't a cruise ship there, you have an obstructed view. If there is, you get to watch the cranes loading up the ship with all the supplies. For a list of shoreline public-access points, visit www.portseattle.org/community/resources/public access.shtml.

Shilshole Bay Marina (p98) Another fun beach and park area to explore near the marina.

Lonely Planet's *Travel with Children* by Cathy Lanigan offers a wealth of tips and tricks for keeping kids happy and occupied while on vacation.

CLIMATE

It does rain a lot in Seattle, but the temperature stays mild most of the year. For more information see Getting Started (p16).

CUSTOMS REGULATIONS

US customs allows each person over the age of 21 to bring 1L of liquor and 200 cigarettes duty-free into the USA. US citizens are allowed to import, duty-free, up to $800 worth of gifts from abroad, while non-US citizens are allowed to import $100 worth. If you're carrying more than $10,000 in US and foreign cash, traveler's checks, money orders etc, you need to declare the excess amount. There is no legal restriction on the amount that may be imported, but undeclared sums in excess of $10,000 will probably be subject to investigation. If you're bringing prescription drugs, make sure they're in clearly marked containers. For updates, check www .customs.gov.

DISCOUNT CARDS

For details on the CityPass and Go Seattle card, see the box, p92.

ELECTRICITY

The US electric current is 110v to 115v, 60Hz AC. Outlets are made for flat two-prong or three-prong plugs. If your appliance is made for another electrical system, you'll need a US converter, which can be bought from hardware stores and drugstores.

EMBASSIES

If your country does not have a consulate in Seattle, call directory information (☎ 202-555-1212) in Washington, DC, for the number of your national embassy.

Australian Consulate (☎ 206-575-7446; 401 Andover Park E)

Austrian Consulate (☎ 360-466-1100; 1111 3rd Ave)

Belgian Consulate (☎ 206-728-5145; 2200 Alaskan Way)

Bolivian Consulate (☎ 206-244-6696; Ste 100, 15215 52nd Ave S)

Canadian Consulate General (☎ 206-443-1777; Ste 600, 1501 4th Ave)

Cypriot Consulate (☎ 425-827-1700; Ste 200, 5555 Lakeview Dr)

Danish Consulate (☎ 206-230-0888; 6204 E Mercer Way)

Ethiopian Honorary Consulate (☎ 206-364-6401; 12612 Blakely Pl NW)

Finnish Consulate (☎ 425-451-3983; 17102 NE 37th Pl, Bellevue)

French Consulate (☎ 206-256-6184; Ste 490, 2200 Alaskan Way)

Hungarian Consulate (☎ 425-739-0631; 703 4th Ave, Kirkland)

Japanese Consulate General (☎ 206-682-9107; Ste 500, 601 Union Street)

Korean Consulate General (☎ 206-441-1011; Ste 1125, 2033 6th Ave)

Mexican Consulate (☎ 206-448-3526; 2132 3rd Ave)

Netherlands Consulate (☎ 425-637-3050; 40 Lake Bellevue Dr, Bellevue)

Norwegian Consulate (☎ 206-623-3957; 7301 5th Ave NE)

Russian Consulate General (☎ 206-728-1910; Ste 2323, 2001 6th Ave)

EMERGENCY

Community Information Line (☎ 206-461-3200) Information on emergency services, housing, legal advice etc.

Police, Fire and Ambulance (☎ 911)

Seattle Police (☎ 206-625-5011)

Washington State Patrol (☎ 425-649-4370)

GAY & LESBIAN TRAVELERS

Seattle is a progressive, left-leaning city with thriving gay and lesbian communities; census data shows that approximately 12.9% of the city's population identifies itself as gay or lesbian, and there doesn't tend to be much sexual orientation-based hostility among the rest of the population.

At research time, the Seattle LGBT Community Center had been forced to move out of its current location and was looking for a new home.

Some other resources and events to look for:

Seattle Gay News (www.sgn.org) A weekly newspaper focusing on gay issues.

Seattle Lesbian & Gay Film Festival (p18) Usually held in the third week of October.

Seattle Pride (p18) Seattle's popular gay-pride parade occurs in June. Seattle Out and Proud, the organization that runs the gay-pride festivities, also serves as an information center (call ☎ 206-322-9561).

HOLIDAYS

National public holidays are celebrated throughout the USA. On public holidays, banks, schools and government offices (including post offices) are closed and public transportation follows a Sunday schedule. Plan ahead if you're traveling during many public holidays. Flights are full, highways are jammed and on Christmas and Thanksgiving, many grocery stores and restaurants close for the day.

New Year's Day January 1

Martin Luther King Jr Day Third Monday in January

Presidents' Day Third Monday in February

Easter Sunday March or April

Memorial Day Last Monday in May

Independence Day (Fourth of July) July 4

Labor Day First Monday in September

Columbus Day Second Monday in October

Veterans' Day November 11

Thanksgiving Day Fourth Thursday in November

Christmas Day December 25

INTERNET ACCESS

Seattle seems to be one big wi-fi hotspot. It's free nearly everywhere, in most hotels, many bars and all but a handful of coffee shops. Some of the main free public wi-fi hotspots include Occidental Park (p57) in Pioneer Square, Seattle Public Library (p49), some Metro buses and Sound Transit buses, the University District (p82), Victor Steinbrueck Park (p66) and some Washington State Ferries.

For laptop-free travelers, there are several good internet cafes (most of which offer 30 minutes free if you buy a coffee or snack), including the Online Coffee Company p144).

LEGAL MATTERS

If you're arrested, you have the right to remain silent. There is no legal reason to speak to a police officer if you don't wish to – especially since anything you say 'can and will be used against you' – but never walk away from an officer until given permission. All persons who are arrested have the legal right to make one phone call. If you don't have a lawyer or a family member to help you, call your consulate. The police will give you the number upon request.

MAPS

There are basic, free online maps available via the Seattle's Convention and Visitors Bureau (see Tourist Information, p208) and at www.see-seattle.com/map.htm, among other places, but for an extended stay it's best to have something more detailed. Good options can be found at any decent bookstore, or ask the experts at Metsker Maps (p111) or Wide World Books & Maps (p116).

MEDICAL SERVICES

Health care is a major problem in this country, as health insurance is still extremely costly for most Americans. People living below the poverty line are eligible for Medicaid, which covers many costs, and seniors can apply for Medicare, which works in a similar way. As a visitor, know that all hospital emergency rooms are obliged to receive sick or injured patients whether they can pay or not.

Clinics

If you're sick or injured, but not badly enough for a trip to the emergency room, try one of the following options:

45th St Community Clinic (Map p91; ☎ 206-633-3350; 1629 N 45th St, Wallingford) Medical and dental services.

Harborview Medical Center (Map p50; ☎ 206-731-3000; 325 9th Ave) Full medical care, with emergency room.

Health South (Map p68; ☎ 206-682-7418; 1151 Denny Way) Walk-in clinic for nonemergencies.

MONEY

The US dollar is divided into 100 cents. US coins come in denominations of one cent (penny), five cents (nickel), 10 cents (dime), 25 cents (quarter), the practically extinct 50 cents (half-dollar) and the not-often-seen golden dollar coin, which was introduced in 2000. The latter features a picture of Sacagawea, the Native American guide who famously led the explorers Meriwether Lewis and William Clark on their expedition through the western US. The new coins are often dispensed as change from ticket machines and stamp machines.

Notes come in $1, $2, $5, $10, $20, $50 and $100 denominations.

To check the exchange rate, though it changes daily, see the Quick Reference guide inside this book's front cover.

ATMs

ATMs are easy to find in Seattle. There's practically one per block in the busier commercial areas, as well as one outside every bank. Many bars, restaurants and grocery stores also have the machines, although the service fees for these can be steep ($2 to $4, plus your own bank's fees). Getting money this way saves you a step – no need to change money from your own currency – and is a safer way to travel, as you only take out what you need as you go.

Changing Money

Banks and moneychangers will give you US currency based on the current exchange rate. See Business Hours (p203) for bank opening hours.

American Express (Map p50; ☎ 206-441-8622; 600 Stewart St; ⏰ 8:30am-5:30pm Mon-Fri)

Travelex-Thomas Cook Currency Services Sea-Tac Airport (☎ 206-248-6960; ⏰ 6am-8pm); Westlake Center (Map p50; ☎ 206-682-4525; Level 3, 400 Pine St; ⏰ 9:30am-6pm Mon-Sat, 11am-5pm Sun) The booth at the main airport terminal is behind the Delta Airlines counter.

Credit & Debit Cards

Major credit cards are accepted at most hotels, restaurants and shops throughout Seattle, although visitors will find that many smaller cafes and restaurants will tack on an extra 30c or 50c amount for paying with plastic. Places that accept Visa and MasterCard generally also accept (and will often prefer) debit cards, which deduct payments directly from your check or savings account. Be sure to confirm with your bank before you leave that your debit card will be accepted in other states or countries. Debit cards from large commercial banks can often be used worldwide.

If your cards are lost or stolen, contact the issuing company immediately. Toll-free numbers for the main credit card companies:

American Express (☎ 800-528-4800)

Diners Club (☎ 800-999-9093)

Discover (☎ 800-347-2683)

MasterCard (☎ 800-627-8372)

Visa (☎ 800-847-2911)

Traveler's Checks

This old-school option offers the traveler protection from theft or loss. Checks issued by American Express and Thomas Cook are widely accepted, and both offer efficient replacement policies. Keeping a record of the check numbers and the checks you've used is vital when it comes to replacing lost checks. Keep this record in a separate place from the checks themselves.

Bring most of the checks in large denominations. Toward the end of a trip you may want to change a small check to make sure you aren't left with too much local currency. Of course, traveler's checks are losing their popularity due to the proliferation of ATMs and you may opt not to carry any at all.

NEWSPAPERS & MAGAZINES

Seattle's newspapers and magazines include the following. For more information, see p40.

Northwest Asian Weekly (www.nwasianweekly.com)

Puget Sound Business Journal (www.bizjournals.com /seattle) Daily.

RealChange (www.realchangenews.org) Weekly paper focused on the city's homeless community.

Seattle Daily Journal of Commerce (www.djc.com) Focuses on the region's business world.

Seattle Gay News (www.sgn.org) Weekly.

Seattle Magazine (www.seattlemag.com) A slick monthly lifestyle magazine.

Seattle Post-Intelligencer (www.seattlepi.com) The former morning daily, now online only.

Seattle Times (www.seattletimes.com) The state's largest daily paper.

Seattle Weekly (www.seattleweekly.com) Free weekly with news and entertainment listings.

Stranger (www.thestranger.com) Irreverent and intelligent free weekly, edited by Dan Savage of 'Savage Love' fame.

ORGANIZED TOURS

ARGOSY CRUISES Map p63

☎ 206-623-1445, 800-642-7816; www.argosy cruises.com; Harbor Tour adult/child $22/9.75
One of the major operators, Argosy has a number of different tours departing daily from Pier 55 year-round. Its popular Seattle Harbor Tour is a one-hour narrated tour of Elliott Bay, the Waterfront and the Port of Seattle. This tour is covered by the CityPass (p92). Argosy also offers tours of the Hiram M Chittenden locks, speedboat cruises and a fine-dining cruise.

BILL SPEIDEL'S UNDERGROUND TOUR Map p56

☎ 206-682-4646; www.undergroundtour.com; 608 1st Ave; adult/senior/child $15/12/7;
⊙ departs every 30min 11am-4pm Oct-Mar, 11am-6pm Apr-Sep
Speidel was a local historian (he wrote the book *Sons of the Profits*) who relished stories of Seattle's sordid past: the good old days of hard-drinking politicians and hard-working 'seamstresses,' as the bordello girls were called. This famous 'underground' tour, which takes you through the tunnels and sidewalks hidden beneath the streets of Pioneer Square, might get a little corny at times, but it delivers the goods on historic Seattle as a rough and rowdy industrial town (see the box, p26). The tour starts at Doc Maynard's Public House, named after one of the city's founding fathers and quite a character. An Ohio native, Maynard was divorced when he arrived in the city and was out for a good time; he was vivacious and generous and he liked his liquor. This combination led him to give away cash or land to almost anyone with a promising idea, and he died essentially landless and broke. (The rather revealing epitaph on his second wife, Catherine's, tombstone reads, 'She did what she could.') The tour is massively popular,

especially in prime tourist season. No reservations are accepted, so try to arrive half an hour early if you want to be sure you get in.

CHINATOWN DISCOVERY TOURS

☎ 425-885-3085; www.seattlechinatowntour.com; 90min tour adult/child $17.95/12.95; ☯ departs 10:15am & 2pm Tue-Fri, 10:15am, 1 & 3pm Sat
This tour group leads travelers through the International District with stops at historical sites, a fortune-cookie factory and various shops. Options include a daytime tour with a dim-sum lunch and an afternoon tour, as well as student-group tours. Reservations are required: call ahead or buy advance tickets at the Wing Luke Asian Museum (p59).

GRAY LINE OF SEATTLE Map p50

☎ 206-626-5208, 800-426-7532; www.grayline ofseattle.com; 800 Convention Place; tour $35; ☯ departs 8:30am
Gray Line has a whole catalog of Seattle-area bus tours, but its three hour-plus City Sights Tour is recommended as a quick-hit rundown of the city's highlights in a 20-passenger coach. Gray Line also offers multiday package tours to the San Juan Islands and Victoria, BC. All trips depart from the Gray Line ticket desk at the convention center at 800 Convention Place.

SAILING IN SEATTLE Map p77

☎ 206-289-0094; www.sailing-in-seattle.com; 2046 Westlake Ave N; up to 6 people $250
Sailing in Seattle offers 2½-hour sunset sails around Lake Union on the 33ft *Whoodat* every evening. There's also a Puget Sound Day Cruise that includes a trip through the Hiram M Chittenden Locks and lasts from eight to 10 hours. Trips meet on Lake Union at Sailing in Seattle's dock behind the China Harbor Restaurant on Westlake Ave.

SEE SEATTLE WALKING TOURS
Map p50

☎ 425-226-7641; www.see-seattle.com; per person $20; ☯ 10am Mon-Sat
See Seattle runs a variety of theme tours, from public-art walks to scavenger hunts. While reservations aren't required for the walking tour that starts at the Westlake Center, they are recommended. A Sunday tour will run if at least six people have signed up.

GHOSTBUSTERS

Should things go really awry while you are staying in Seattle and you begin to hear bumps in the night, or glimpse vague and filmy shapes loitering around by the foot of your bed, well, who *are* you gonna call?

Allow us to suggest Aghost, the Advanced Ghost Hunters of Seattle-Tacoma (☎ 253-203-4383; www.aghost.us). Experts in paranormal activity, the ghost hunters use surveillance equipment like motion detectors and recording devices to check for monsters under your bed, skeletons in the closet and so forth.

They can also tell you all about resident phantoms in Seattle, like the ghosts who lurk in the city's underground or the undead Irishman who sits at the back of the College Inn Pub after closing time.

TILLICUM VILLAGE Map p63

☎ 206-933-8600, 800-426-1205; www.tillicum village.com; adult/senior/child $79.95/72.95/30; ☯ Mar-Dec
From Pier 55, take a trip to Blake Island, the birthplace of Seattle's namesake Chief Sealth. The four-hour trip includes a salmon bake, a native dance and a movie at an old Duwamish Indian village.

POST

Rates for sending mail go up every few years. At time of research, rates for 1st-class mail within the US are 44c for letters up to 1oz and 28c for postcards. For package and international-letter rates, which vary, check with the local post office or with the online postal-rate calculator (http://ircalc.usps.gov). For other postal service questions, call ☎ 800-275-8777 or visit the US Post Office website (www.usps.com).

Seattle's most convenient post office locations are the main branch (Map p50; ☎ 206-748-5417; 301 Union St), University Station (Map p83; ☎ 206-675-8114; 4244 University Way NE, U District), Broadway Station (Map p79; ☎ 206-324-5474; 101 Broadway E) and Queen Anne (Map p75; 415 1st Ave N).

RADIO

KEXP 90.3 FM (stream at http://kexp.org) Legendary independent music and community station.

KHKS 106.1 FM (www.1061kissfm.com) Top 40.

KJR 95.7 FM (www.957kjrfm.com) Classic rock.

KJR 950 AM (www.kjram.com) Sports.

KPLU 88.5 FM (www.kplu.org) Public radio (NPR) and jazz.

DIRECTORY POST

KUOW 94.9 FM (www.kuow.org) NPR news from the University of Washington.

TELEPHONE

Phone numbers within the USA consist of a three-digit area code followed by a seven-digit local number. If you're calling long distance, dial ☎ 1 + the three-digit area code + the seven-digit number. To call internationally, first dial ☎ 011 then the country code and phone number.

Phone numbers in Seattle have a 206 area code. Even local calls made to the same area code require you to dial the full 10-digit number (no need to dial 1 first, though).

Toll-free numbers are prefixed with an 800, 877, 866 or 888 area code. Some toll-free numbers for local businesses or government offices only work within the state or the Seattle region, but most can be dialed from abroad. Just be aware that you'll be connected at regular long-distance rates, which could become a costly option if the line you're dialing regularly parks customers on hold.

TELEVISION

KCPQ Channel 13 (Fox)

KCTS Channel 9 (public broadcasting station)

KING Channel 5 (NBC)

KIRO Channel 7 (CBS)

KMYQ Channel 22 (MyNetwork TV)

KOMO Channel 4 (ABC)

KSTW Channel 11 (CW Network)

TIME

Seattle is in the Pacific Standard Time Zone. Seattle time is two hours ahead of Hawaii (Hawaii-Aleutian Standard Time), one hour ahead of Alaska (Alaska Standard Time), one hour behind Colorado (Mountain Standard Time), two hours behind Alabama (Central Standard Time) and three hours behind New York (Atlantic Standard Time). In spring and summer, as in most of the time zones in the US, Pacific Standard Time becomes Pacific Daylight Time. Clocks are reset an hour forward in early spring, and reset an hour back in early fall.

TIPPING

Bartenders and wait staff should be tipped 15% to 25% if the service was good. Hotel porters expect $1 to $3 per bag. Tip taxi drivers around 10% to 15%.

TOURIST INFORMATION

The main Seattle visitors center, Seattle's Convention and Visitors Bureau (Map p50; ☎ 206-461-5888; www.visitseattle.org; 701 Pike St; ✆ 9am-5pm) is inside the Washington State Convention and Trade Center. It also operates the useful Citywide Concierge service.

TRAVELERS WITH DISABILITIES

All public buildings (including all hotels, restaurants, theaters and museums) are required by law to provide wheelchair access and to have appropriate restroom facilities available. Telephone companies provide relay operators for the hearing impaired. Many banks provide ATM instructions in Braille. Dropped curbs are standard at intersections throughout the city.

Around 80% of Metro's buses are equipped with wheelchair lifts. Timetables marked with an 'L' indicate wheelchair accessibility. Be sure to let the driver know if you need your stop to be called and, if possible, pull the cord when you hear the call. Seeing-eye dogs are allowed on Metro buses. Passengers with disabilities qualify for a reduced fare but first need to contact Metro Transit (☎ 206-553-3060, TTY 206-684-2029) for a permit.

Most large private and chain hotels have suites for guests with disabilities. Many car-rental agencies offer hand-controlled models at no extra charge. Make sure you give at least two days' notice. All major airlines, Greyhound buses and Amtrak trains allow guide dogs to accompany passengers and often sell two-for-one packages when attendants of passengers with serious disabilities are required. Airlines will also provide assistance for connecting, boarding and disembarking the flight. Ask for assistance when making your reservation.

The following organizations and tour providers specialize in the needs of travelers with disabilities:

Access-Able Travel Service (www.access-able.com) Packed full of information, with tips on scooter rental, wheelchair travel, accessible transportation and more.

Easter Seals of Washington (☎ 206-281-5700; http://wa.easterseals.com) Provides technology assistance, workplace services and camps, among other things.

MossRehab Hospital's Travel Information Service
(☎ 215-456-9900, TTY 215-456-9602; www.mossresource net.org; 1200 W Tabor Rd, Philadelphia, PA 19141-3099)

Society for Accessible Travel & Hospitality (☎ 212-447-7284; www.sath.org; No 610, 347 Fifth Ave, New York, NY 10016)

VISAS

Foreigners needing visas to travel to the US should plan ahead. There is a reciprocal visa-waiver program in which citizens of certain countries may enter the USA for stays of 90 days or less with a passport but without first obtaining a visa. Currently these countries include Australia, Austria, Denmark, France, Germany, Italy, Japan, the Netherlands, New Zealand, Spain, Sweden, Switzerland and the UK. Under this program you must have a round-trip ticket that is nonrefundable in the USA, and you will not be allowed to extend your stay beyond 90 days.

As of January 2009, citizens of the 27 countries in the US Visa Waiver Program will need to register with the government online (https://esta.cbp.dhs.gov) three days before their visit. The registration is valid for two years.

Other travelers will need to obtain a visa from a US consulate or embassy. In most countries, the process can be done by mail. Visa applicants may be required to 'demonstrate binding obligations' that will ensure their return home. Because of this requirement, those planning to travel through other countries before arriving in the USA are generally better off applying for their US visa while they are still in their home country, rather than after they're already on the road.

The Non-Immigrant Visitors Visa is the most common visa. It is available in two forms: the B1 for business purposes and the B2 for tourism or visiting friends and relatives. The validity period for US visitor visas depends on which country you're from. The length of time you'll be allowed to stay in the USA is ultimately determined by US immigration authorities at the port of entry. Non-US citizens with HIV should know that they can be excluded from entry to the USA.

For updates on visas and other security issues, you can visit the US government's visa page (www.unitedstatesvisas.us), the US Department of State (www.travel.state.gov) and the Travel Security Administration (www.tsa.gov).

VOLUNTEERING

If Seattle's progressive leanings become contagious during your trip and you decide to devote part of your travel time to doing volunteer work, the following resources can help:

Seattle Community Network (www.scn.org/volunteers) Maintains an online list of all kinds of local organizations that are looking for volunteers.

Service Board (☎ 206-324-7771; theserviceboard.org) Teaches skill-building and confidence to Seattle-area high-school kids through an active mentorship program.

Seattle Parks and Recreation (☎ 206-684-8028; www.seattle.gov/parks/volunteers/workparty.htm) Frequently organizes work parties in which volunteers gather to help build park equipment, water and weed plants, and clean up public areas.

WOMEN TRAVELERS

Seattle is a generally safe place for women travelers as long as some common-sense practices are observed. Avoid walking alone at night through sketchy-looking or unlit areas. If you're out late bar-hopping, spring for a cab home instead of walking or waiting around for public transit. If you're ever assaulted, call the police (☎ 911).

WORK

To work legally in the USA you generally need both a work permit and working visa. To apply for the correct visa at the US embassy you are usually first required to obtain a work permit from the Immigration and Naturalization Service (INS).

A prospective employer must file a petition with the INS for permission for you to work, so you will first need to find a company that wants to hire you and will file all the necessary paperwork. More detailed information is available at the website of the US Department of State (www.travel.state.gov).

BEHIND THE SCENES

THIS BOOK

This 5th edition of Seattle was researched and written by Becky Ohlsen. The previous two editions were also written by Becky Ohlsen. This guidebook was commissioned in Lonely Planet's Oakland office, laid out by Cambridge Publishing Management, UK and produced by the following:

Commissioning Editors Catherine Craddock, Suki Gear

Coordinating Editors Catherine Burch, Pete Cruttenden, Kate Taylor

Coordinating Cartographer Jennifer Johnston

Coordinating Layout Designer Paul Queripel

Senior Editor Katie Lynch

Managing Editor Melanie Dankel

Managing Cartographers Shahara Ahmed, Alison Lyall

Managing Layout Designer Celia Wood

Assisting Editors Scarlett O'Hara, Jackie Staddon

Cover Research Pepi Bluck, lonelyplanetimages.com

Internal Image Research Sabrina Dalbesio, lonelyplanetimages.com

Color Designer Paul Queripel

Indexer Marie Lorimer

Thanks to Helen Christinis, Heather Dickson, Michelle Glynn, Nora Gregory, Carol Jackson, Craig Kilburn, Yvonne Kirk, Lisa Knights

Cover photographs Coffee cup neon sign, Nick Gunderson (top); cityscape at night, Mark & Audrey Gibson (botttom)

Internal photographs All images are copyright of the photographer unless otherwise indicated. Many of the images in this guide are available for licensing from Lonely Planet Images: www.lonelyplanetimages.com.

THANKS

Becky would like to thank John Graham, Abby Margulies, Richard Rose, Maureen O'Hagan, Jason Simms, AP Kryza, Janice Logan, Heidi Messer, Deb Raftus, Matthew Stearns and Tom Burnett for their help in providing inspiration and local intel during the research of this book.

OUR READERS

Many thanks to the travelers who used the last edition and wrote to us with helpful hints, useful advice and interesting anecdotes:

Olivier Beyssac, Tara Cashman, Chetan Chandrashekhar, Amanda Depaul, Arleen Fields, James Gibson, Jacob Hyman, Michael Lee, Evelina Makarova, James Mann, Susan Mathew, Carrie Nichols, Spence Patterson, Erin Prosser, Stephanie Senescall, Christopher Sonne, Emily Wilcox, Brigitte Zbiek

THE LONELY PLANET STORY

Fresh from an epic journey across Europe, Asia and Australia in 1972, Tony and Maureen Wheeler sat at their kitchen table stapling together notes. The first Lonely Planet guidebook, *Across Asia on the Cheap*, was born.

Travelers snapped up the guides. Inspired by their success, the Wheelers began publishing books to Southeast Asia, India and beyond. Demand was prodigious, and the Wheelers expanded the business rapidly to keep up. Over the years, Lonely Planet extended its coverage to every country and into the virtual world via lonelyplanet.com and the Thorn Tree message board.

As Lonely Planet became a globally loved brand, Tony and Maureen received several offers for the company. But it wasn't until 2007 that they found a partner whom they trusted to remain true to the company's principles of traveling widely, treading lightly and giving sustainably. In October of that year, BBC Worldwide acquired a 75% share in the company, pledging to uphold Lonely Planet's commitment to independent travel, trustworthy advice and editorial independence.

Today, Lonely Planet has offices in Melbourne, London and Oakland, with over 500 staff members and 300 authors. Tony and Maureen are still actively involved with Lonely Planet. They're traveling more often than ever, and they're devoting their spare time to charitable projects. And the company is still driven by the philosophy of *Across Asia on the Cheap*: 'All you've got to do is decide to go and the hardest part is over. So go!'

SEND US YOUR FEEDBACK

We love to hear from travelers — your comments keep us on our toes and help make our books better. Our well-traveled team reads every word on what you loved or loathed about this book. Although we cannot reply individually to postal submissions, we always guarantee that your feedback goes straight to the appropriate authors, in time for the next edition. Each person who sends us information is thanked in the next edition and the most useful submissions are rewarded with a free book.

To send us your updates — and find out about Lonely Planet events, newsletters and travel news — visit our award-winning website: lonelyplanet.com/contact.

Note: We may edit, reproduce and incorporate your comments in Lonely Planet products such as guidebooks, websites and digital products, so let us know if you don't want your comments reproduced or your name acknowledged. For a copy of our privacy policy visit lonelyplanet.com/privacy.

Notes

Notes

Notes

Notes

INDEX

A

accommodations 173-82, *see also individual neighborhoods*, Sleeping *subindex*
 airport hotels 181
 costs 19
 couch surfing 20
 green hotels 180
 pet-friendly hotels 176
 room tax 174
 sustainable 20
activities 163-72, *see also individual activities*, Sports & Activities *subindex*
air travel
 airlines 199
 airports 199
 environmental issues 200
 to/from airport 201
airport hotels 181
Alaskan Way Viaduct 29, 65, 66
Alexie, Sherman 33, 34, 37
Alki Point 103
Allen, Paul 3, 30, 72, 76
ambulance service 204
antiques, *see* Shopping *subindex*
architecture 38-9
 walking tours 52-4, **53**
area codes, *see inside front cover*
art galleries, *see* Sights *subindex*

arts 30-8, 158, *see also individual arts*, Arts, Shopping *subindexes*
 tickets & reservations 158
arts festivals 16, 17, 18
Asian Americans, *see also* International District
 anti-Chinese riots (1886) 25-6
 festivals 16, 17
 Seattle Asian Art Museum 80
 Wing Luke Museum of the Asian Pacific American Experience 59-60, **5**
ATMs 205

B

Bainbridge Island 184, 188
Ballard 95-9, **96**, **11**
 drinking 147-8
 food 135
 shopping 117
 walking tours 98-9, **99**
ballet 38, 161
banks 203
Barry, Lynda 35
bars 140, *see also* Drinking *subindex*
baseball 58, 164, 165
basketball 164, 165
Bauer, Eddie 192
beaches, *see* Sights *subindex*
beer 105, *see also* Drinking *subindex*
 microbreweries 146
Belltown 67-70, **68**, **7**
 accommodations 178-9
 drinking 142-3
 food 127-9
 shopping 112-13
 walking tours 69-70, **69**
bicycling 167-8, 199, *see also* Sports & Activities *subindex*
 Alki Trail 167-8
 bike rentals 169
 Burke-Gilman Trail 82, 92, 167
 helmets 199

 Mercer Island Loop 168
 Sammamish River Trail 167
 velodrome 167
Binns, Archie 32-3
Bite of Seattle 18
Blake Island 189
blogs 17, 19-20
blues 31-2, 155
boat travel 76, 199, 206, 207, *see also* ferries
Boeing 28-9
Boeing, William 28
books, *see also* literature, Shopping *subindex*
 history 24
 libraries 49, 84
 readings 33, 158-9
brewpubs 146, *see also* Drinking *subindex*
buildings & structures, *see* Sights *subindex*
Bumbershoot 18
bus travel 200
 tours 207
business hours 203, *see also inside front cover*

C

cameras, *see* Shopping *subindex*
Capitol Hill 78-81, **79**, **9**
 accommodations 180-1
 drinking 143-5
 food 130-1
 shopping 113-14
car travel 200-1
 car rental 20, 200-1
 car-sharing programs 20
 scenic drives 194
carbon offset schemes 200
Carnation 194-5
cartoonists 35
Carver, Raymond 33-4
Celtic music 154
Central District 100-2, **101**
 food 135-7
Central Plaza 84
Charles, Ray 32, 72
Cherry Blossom & Japanese Cultural Festival 17
Chief Sealth (Seattle) 22-3

children, travel with 203, *see also* Shopping, Sights *subindexes*
 Seattle International Children's Festival 17
Chinatown, *see* International District
Chinese New Year 16
Cinco de Mayo 17
cinema 36-7, 38, 160, *see also* Arts *subindex*
 film festivals 17, 18, 160
 Twilight 38, 198
CityPass 17, 92
climate 16, 203
climate change 200
climbing walls 76, 169
clinics 205
clothing, *see* fashion, Shopping *subindex*
clubs, *see* Nightlife *subindex*
Cobain, Kurt 32, 72, 102
cocktail lounges, *see* Drinking *subindex*
coffee 144
coffee shops 140, 144, *see also* Drinking *subindex*
comedy 159-60, *see also* Arts *subindex*
comic book artists 35
community associations 86
consulates 204
costs 19
 accommodations 19
 drinking 140
 food 19, 120
country music 154
credit cards 205-6
culture 3
customs regulations 203
cycling, *see* bicycling

D

dance 38, 160-1, *see also* Arts *subindex*
dance clubs 155
day spas 172
debit cards 205-6
Denny, Arthur 24, 32, 78, 80
Denny, David 24

INDEX

INDEX

GREENDEX

GOING GREEN

Lonely Planet defines sustainable tourism in three key areas: environmental (eg organic foodstores or hotels with energy-saving policies), social/cultural (eg organizations that support local cultural traditions) and economic (eg businesses whose profits benefit the local community). Providing our readers with a guide to sustainable content is a continuous process, and we'd love it if readers would tell us how we're doing. Send us your feedback at www.lonely planet.com/feedback. For more information on sustainable travel, visit www.lonelyplanet.com/responsibletravel.

MAP LEGEND

ROUTES

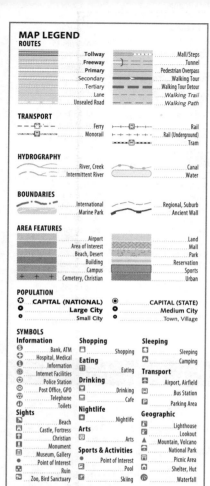

- Tollway
- Freeway
- Primary
- Secondary
- Tertiary
- Lane
- Unsealed Road
- Mall/Steps
- Tunnel
- Pedestrian Overpass
- Walking Tour
- Walking Tour Detour
- Walking Trail
- Walking Path

TRANSPORT

- Ferry
- Monorail
- Rail
- Rail (Underground)
- Tram

HYDROGRAPHY

- River, Creek
- Intermittent River
- Canal
- Water

BOUNDARIES

- International
- Marine Park
- Regional, Suburb
- Ancient Wall

AREA FEATURES

- Airport
- Area of Interest
- Beach, Desert
- Building
- Campus
- Cemetery, Christian
- Land
- Mall
- Park
- Reservation
- Sports
- Urban

POPULATION

- ⊙ CAPITAL (NATIONAL)
- ● Large City
- ● Small City
- ◉ CAPITAL (STATE)
- ● Medium City
- ● Town, Village

SYMBOLS

Information
- Bank, ATM
- Hospital, Medical
- Information
- Internet Facilities
- Police Station
- Post Office, GPO
- Telephone
- Toilets

Sights
- Beach
- Castle, Fortress
- Christian
- Monument
- Museum, Gallery
- Point of Interest
- Ruin
- Zoo, Bird Sanctuary

Shopping
- Shopping

Eating
- Eating

Drinking
- Drinking
- Cafe

Nightlife
- Nightlife

Arts
- Arts

Sports & Activities
- Point of Interest
- Pool
- Skiing

Sleeping
- Sleeping
- Camping

Transport
- Airport, Airfield
- Bus Station
- Parking Area

Geographic
- Lighthouse
- Lookout
- Mountain, Volcano
- National Park
- Picnic Area
- Shelter, Hut
- Waterfall

Published by Lonely Planet Publications Pty Ltd
ABN 36 005 607 983

Australia (Head Office)
Locked Bag 1, Footscray, Victoria 3011,
☎03 8379 8000, fax 03 8379 8111,
talk2us@lonelyplanet.com.au

USA 150 Linden St, Oakland, CA 94607,
☎510 250 6400, toll free 800 275 8555,
fax 510 893 8572, info@lonelyplanet.com

UK 2nd fl, 186 City Rd, London, EC1V 2NT,
☎020 7106 2100, fax 020 7106 2101,
go@lonelyplanet.co.uk

© Lonely Planet 2011
Photographs © as indicated 2011

All rights reserved. No part of this
publication may be copied, stored in a
retrieval system, or transmitted in any
form by any means, electronic, mechanical,
recording or otherwise, except brief
extracts for the purpose of review, and
no part of this publication may be sold or
hired, without the written permission of
the publisher.

Printed by Fabulous Printers Pte Ltd,
Printed in Singapore.

Lonely Planet and the Lonely Planet logo
are trademarks of Lonely Planet and are
registered in the US Patent and Trademark
Office and in other countries.

Lonely Planet does not allow its name or
logo to be appropriated by commercial
establishments, such as retailers,
restaurants or hotels. Please let us know of
any misuses: lonelyplanet.com/ip.

Although the authors and Lonely Planet have taken
all reasonable care in preparing this book, we make
no warranty about the accuracy or completeness of
its content and, to the maximum extent permitted,
disclaim all liability arising from its use.

MIX
Paper from
responsible sources
FSC™ C021741
www.fsc.org